Dollar Politics

Congressional Quarterly Inc.

Congressional Quarterly Inc., an editorial research service and publishing company, serves clients in the fields of news, education, business and government. It combines specific coverage of Congress, government and politics by Congressional Quarterly with the more general subject range of an affiliated service, Editorial Research Reports.

Congressional Quarterly was founded in 1945 by Henrietta and Nelson Poynter. Its basic periodical publication was and still is the CQ *Weekly Report,* mailed to clients every Saturday. A cumulative index is published quarterly.

CQ also publishes a variety of books. The CQ *Almanac,* a compendium of legislation for one session of Congress, is published every spring. *Congress and the Nation* is published every four years as a record of government for one presidential term. *Politics in America,* a CQ reference book published every two years, evaluates the performance of each member of Congress. Other books include paperbacks on public affairs and textbooks for college political science classes.

The public affairs books are designed as timely reports to keep journalists, scholars and the public abreast of developing issues, events and trends.

They include such recent titles as *Environment and Health, Budgeting for America* and the fifth edition of *The Middle East.* College textbooks, prepared by outside scholars and published under the CQ Press imprint, include such recent titles as *Congress and Its Members; Understanding Congressional Leadership;* and *A Tide of Discontent, the 1980 Elections and their Meaning.*

In addition, CQ publishes *The Congressional Monitor,* a daily report on present and future activities of congressional committees. This service is supplemented by *The Congressional Record Scanner,* an abstract of each day's *Congressional Record,* and *Congress in Print,* a weekly listing of committee publications.

CQ Direct Research is a consulting service that performs contract research and maintains a reference library and query desk for clients.

Editorial Research Reports covers subjects beyond the specialized scope of Congressional Quarterly. It publishes reference material on foreign affairs, business, education, cultural affairs, national security, science and other topics of news interest. Service to clients includes a 6,000-word report four times a month, bound and indexed semi-annually. Editorial Research Reports publishes paperback books in its fields of coverage. Founded in 1923, the service merged with Congressional Quarterly in 1956.

Library of Congress Cataloging in Publication Data

Main entry under title:

Dollar Politics.

Bibliography: p.
Includes index.
1. Campaign Funds — United States. I. Congressional Quarterly, inc.
JK1991.D64 1982   324.7'8'0973   81-19572
ISBN 0-87187-220-X   AACR2

Editor: Nancy Lammers
Supervisory Editor: John L. Moore
Major Contributor: Rhodes Cook
Contributors: Irwin Arieff, Edna Frazier-Cromwell, Jeremy Gaunt, Charles W. Hucker, Bill Keller, Larry Light, William Korns, Nancy Stier
Indexer: Claire L. Tury
Design: Mary McNeil
Cover: Robert O. Redding
Graphics: Richard A. Pottern, Robert O. Redding, Cheryl B. Rowe

Book Department

Congressional Quarterly Inc.

Contents

Editor's Note. *Dollar Politics, Third Edition,* traces the history of
campaign finance regulation from colonial efforts through the 1971
Federal Election Campaign Act and the amendments Congress adopted
in 1974, 1976 and 1979. The impact of the law is examined as it applied
to Ronald Reagan's electoral triumph in 1980 and to the Republican
takeover of the Senate for the first time in 26 years. Another chapter
looks at the Federal Election Commission and the criticisms it has faced
in its short but turbulent lifetime. The phenomenal growth of political
action committees (PACs) as a source of campaign money is covered in
detail, along with the changing role of the political parties. Other
chapters examine the use of independent expenditures for or against
candidates, the search for loopholes, the work of Washington fund-
raisers and the general operation of the campaign finance system,
including a summary of each state's restrictions. An appendix contains
excerpts from the landmark *Buckley v. Valeo* decision, major provisions
of the election laws and campaign receipts and expenditures of individual House and Senate candidates in 1976 and 1978. A bibliography and
an index are included. *Dollar Politics, Third Edition,* is one of CQ's
public affairs books designed as timely reports to keep journalists,
scholars and the public abreast of issues, events and trends.

Dollar Politics

THIRD EDITION

CONGRESSIONAL QUARTERLY INC.
1414 22nd STREET, N.W.
WASHINGTON, D.C. 20037

Controls on Political Spending

Money and politics in America have mixed about as smoothly over the years as oil and water. While many European democracies have adopted tightly regulated systems of campaign finance, politicians in the United States still are struggling to define the relationship between money and their craft.

Prior to the 1970s, campaign finance, American style, was freewheeling. It was a shadowy area with virtually toothless legislation covering the disclosure of campaign contributions and expenditures.

But in the early 1970s the pendulum began to swing sharply in the other direction. Spiraling media costs provided the first impetus for reform. The Watergate scandal accelerated the movement. By the middle of the decade, three major pieces of campaign finance legislation had been passed, transforming the practically unregulated "industry" into one with strict controls.

By the late 1970s, however, the reform tide clearly was ebbing. Criticism was growing that the law was an overreaction to Watergate that stifled contributors, candidates and political parties alike. As America entered the 1980s, the pendulum was swinging back.

Lack of Consensus

One of the major difficulties politicians have faced in molding campaign finance legislation has been an absence of consensus.

There is no national system of campaign finance that covers all political races. The legislation of the 1970s dramatically overhauled presidential elections, establishing a system of partial public financing for the nominating process and virtually complete federal funding for the general election. But Congress never extended public financing to its own contests, which remain privately financed. Races at the state and local levels are a mixture of the two systems.

The lack of a national system of campaign finance reflects disagreement on what constitutes an appropriate level of campaign spending. For every person who believes that too much money is being spent on political campaigns, there is another who feels the amount is too low.

Reformers wanting tight federal controls on spending point to the escalating costs of U.S. elections since the technological boom after World War II. Campaign expenditures quadrupled from $200 million in 1964 to about $900 million in 1980, an increase nearly double the rate of inflation as measured by the Consumer Price Index. *(Total political spending in presidential election years, box, p. 9)*

And, reformers warn, as the costs of campaigns increase, candidates are more apt to be "bought" by special interest groups and wealthy contributors and less likely to serve the people who elected them.

But critics of lower spending maintain that charges of influence-buying are rarely substantiated, and that the costs of all political campaigns in 1980 were still less than the price tag of one nuclear-powered, missile-launching Trident submarine.

Critics also can point to the conclusions of a 1979 study of federal campaign finance legislation by the Harvard University Institute of Politics.

"The most competitive elections," the report pointed out, "where the voters have the most information about candidates, are those in which the most money is spent. Election contests in which spending is comparatively high are also those in which voter participation tends to be highest."

Incumbency, Money and Victory

Reformers and critics would agree that campaigns are growing more and more expensive. With the escalating costs of the staples of political campaigns — such as candidate staff and travel, media advertising and public opinion polling — it is expensive for a candidate even to run a competitive race.

And unless a candidate is an incumbent, a wealthy challenger or a contender in a closely contested open-seat race, fund raising can be difficult. For every House or Senate candidate whose expenses run in six or seven figures, there are dozens of "mom and pop" campaigns that cannot afford any professional help.

The extent to which an election can be won by outspending the opposition is debated during and after almost every political contest. Generally, there has always been a strong link between incumbency, money and electoral success.

The stringent controls of the new campaign finance system do not appear to have broken that link in House races. In 1978 House contests, for example, a Congressional Quarterly study found that 95 percent of all incumbents won re-election and 87 percent of incumbents outspent their challengers. In races for open seats, where there were no incumbents, the winners also tended to be the big spenders. *(Congressional spending, Chapter 7, p. 102)*

But in Senate and presidential races, the new system may be having a different impact. The number of incumbent senators winning re-election has declined from 77 percent in 1970 to 55 percent in 1980. And in both publicly financed presidential elections (1976 and 1980) administered under the new system, the incumbents lost.

Legislative Goals

Campaign finance reformers over the years have sought to curb campaign spending by limiting and regulating campaign expenditures and donations made to candidates as well as by informing voters of the amounts and sources of the donations, and the amounts, purposes and payees of the expenditures. Disclosure was intended to reveal which candidates, if any, were unduly indebted to interest groups, in time to forewarn the voters. But more than a century of legislative attempts to regulate campaign financing resulted in much controversy and minimal control.

Until the 1970s, the basic federal law regulating campaign spending and requiring public disclosure was the Corrupt Practices Act of 1925, described by some as "more loophole than law." The act set a statutory maximum of $25,000 in expenditures for a Senate campaign and $10,000 for a House race. But it was not enforced.

Watergate, though, changed all that. The scandal became the code word in the 1970s for government corruption. Although there were many aspects to the scandal, money in politics was at its roots.

Included in Watergate's catalog of misdeeds were specific violations of campaign spending laws, violations of other criminal laws facilitated by the availability of virtually unlimited campaign contributions and still other instances where campaign funds were used in a manner that strongly suggested influence peddling.

Faced with escalating media costs, Congress had begun to move on campaign finance legislation even before the June 1972 break-in at the Democratic national headquarters. In 1971 it passed legislation requiring disclosure of campaign contributions and placing a limit on the amount of money candidates could spend on media advertising. (The media spending limits were repealed by the 1974 campaign finance act.)

But Watergate focused public attention on campaign spending at all levels of government and produced a mood in Congress that even the most reluctant legislators found difficult to resist. In the aftermath of the scandal came the most significant overhaul in campaign finance legislation in the nation's history. Major legislation passed in 1974 and 1976, coming on the heels of the 1971 legislation, radically altered the system of financing federal elections.

From complete private financing of campaigns — the situation in 1972 — Congress in the next four years set up partial public financing of candidates in the presidential primaries, a flat grant for major party candidates in the presidential election and virtually complete public financing of major party national nominating conventions.

Departing from the loose, largely unenforceable controls on campaign money at the beginning of the decade,

the legislation passed in the 1970s established stringent controls. An independent election commission was created to monitor campaign contributions and expenditures in federal elections and to review the detailed disclosure reports required by law.

Unexpected Repercussions

The reform measures of the 1970s, which originally imposed strict limits on campaign contributions and expenditures and provided for the public financing of presidential campaigns, were supposed to curtail drastically the role of money in campaigns. Candidates were expected to devote less effort to wooing contributors. Overall campaign spending was expected to be reduced. Challengers and incumbents were supposed to be placed on a more equal footing than in previous campaigns, because big money at last had been de-emphasized and the spending and fund-raising advantages of incumbents had been curbed.

But it didn't work out that way. While the reforms drew high marks for disclosure provisions that for the first time tracked the flow of money in federal elections, other aspects of the legislation drew criticism. Many candidates complained that to comply with the strict new disclosure requirements they had to hire an accountant or a lawyer before picking their campaign manager. Campaign funds had to be diverted from communicating with the voters into complying with the law.

Challengers complained that the law was a boon to incumbents and was responsible for longer and longer campaigns. Challengers could no longer offset the established fund-raising sources of incumbents by tapping several wealthy supporters. They had to begin their campaigns earlier to raise money in the small chunks available under the law, with expensive direct-mail drives emerging for many as the prime source of funds.

And there were complaints that, rather than accenting the small individual giver, the law was encouraging the growth of a new force in American politics — political action committees (PACs). PACs are the political arms of labor unions, corporations and trade associations, in particular, although they are also a vehicle for groups espousing a particular cause or viewpoint to become financially involved in political campaigns. PACs blossomed, particularly in the corporate world, after the 1974 legislation and have proliferated at a rapid pace ever since. They have become somewhat slimmer replacements of the large individual givers in the old system, known as "fat cats." *(PACs, Chapter 3, p. 41)*

Part of the problem with the new campaign finance system was that the Supreme Court extensively revised the statute in January 1976 before the sweeping 1974 law received its first real test. The court upheld public financing of presidential campaigns, limits on the size of campaign contributions and spending limits in presidential campaigns if candidates accepted public campaign funds.

However, the court struck down most of the measure's attempts to limit campaign expenditures. It did that by eliminating spending ceilings for congressional campaigns. In addition, the court held that an individual could spend an unlimited amount of his own money to support a candidate, so long as he did not coordinate the expenditures with the candidate or his campaign organization.

These two loopholes placed a new premium on wealthy candidates and opened the door for individuals and PACs to make millions of dollars in independent expenditures, a tactic generally derided by candidates and party leaders as unwelcome "loose cannons" in the political process. *(Independent expenditures, Chapter 6, p. 79)*

Throughout the late 1970s, reformers sought to curb campaign spending by pressing for the extension of public financing to congressional races. But the post-Watergate mood in Congress was less amenable to major campaign finance reforms. Legislative drives in 1977, 1978 and 1979 all failed. In late 1979 — with public financing buried — Congress approved some non-controversial changes in the law that encouraged more grass-roots and political party activity in federal campaigns.

The revisions enabled the nation's campaign finance system to operate a little more smoothly. But there was no certainty in the early 1980s as to whether the years ahead would see more minor tinkering or a massive overhaul.

FINANCING CAMPAIGNS IN AMERICA'S EARLY YEARS

Money has been a major issue in American politics since colonial times. In his race for the House of Burgesses in Virginia in 1757, George Washington was accused of campaign irregularities. He was charged with dispensing during his campaign 28 gallons of rum, 50 gallons of rum punch, 34 gallons of wine, 46 gallons of beer and two gallons of cider royal. "Even in those days," noted George Thayer, a historian of American campaign financing, "this was considered a large campaign expenditure, because there were only 391 voters in his district, for an average outlay of more than a quart and a half per person."

Campaign spending first emerged as a central issue in a presidential campaign in 1832, the race in which President Andrew Jackson and Henry Clay, his Whig opponent, fought over the fate of the Bank of the United States. During the campaign, the U.S.-chartered but semi-autonomous bank spent heavily to support the Whip challenger. Clay pressed for congressional action on a bill to renew the bank's charter, believing that if Jackson vetoed the bill, he would lose Pennsylvania — the bank was located in Philadelphia — and other Eastern states in the election. The strategy backfired. Jackson met the challenge with a strong veto message describing the bank as a "money monster." He campaigned against it effectively and won the election easily.

The first provision of federal law on campaign financing was incorporated into an act of March 2, 1867, making naval appropriations for the fiscal year 1868. The final section of the act read: "And be it further enacted, That no officer or employee of the government shall require or request any workingman in any navy yard to contribute or pay any money for political purposes, nor shall any workingman be removed or discharged for political opinion; and any officer or employee of the government who shall offend against the provisions of this section shall be dismissed from the service of the United States."

Reports circulated in the following year that at least 75 percent of the money raised by the Republican Congressional Committee came from federal officeholders. Continuing agitation on this and other aspects of the spoils system in federal employment led to adoption of the Civil Service Reform Act of Jan. 16, 1883. This bill authorized establishment of Civil Service rules, one of which stated "That no person in the public service is for that reason under any obligation to contribute to any political fund . . . and that he will not be removed or otherwise prejudiced for refusing to do so." The law made it a crime for any federal employee to solicit campaign funds from another federal employee.

But shrewd campaign managers found money elsewhere. In the legendary 1896 campaign between Republican William McKinley and Democrat-Populist William Jennings Bryan, McKinley's successful effort was managed by wealthy financier Marcus A. Hanna. His genius as a fund-raiser has been described by historian Eugene H. Roseboom: "For banks the [campaign finance] assessment was fixed at one quarter of one percent of their capital. Life insurance companies contributed liberally, as did nearly all the great corporations. The Standard Oil Company gave $250,000 to Hanna's war chest. The audited accounts of the national committee revealed collections of about $3,500,000."

The Muckrakers

Reacting to the increasing lavish corporate involvement in political campaigns, the hearty band of reformers known as the muckrakers pressed for the nation's first extensive campaign finance legislation. During the first decade of the 20th century, they worked to expose the influence on government that was exerted by big business through unrestrained spending on behalf of favored candidates.

After the 1904 election, a move for federal legislation took shape in the National Publicity Law Association headed by former Rep. Perry Belmont, D-N.Y. (1881-88). They succeeded in gaining national attention. President

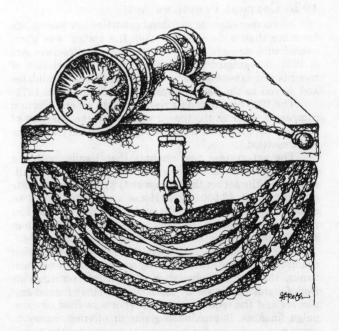

Theodore Roosevelt, in his annual message to Congress on Dec. 5, 1905, proposed that: "All contributions by corporations to any political committee or for any political purpose should be forbidden by law." Roosevelt repeated the proposal in his message of Dec. 3, 1906, suggesting that it be the first item of congressional business.

In response to the president's urging, Congress on Jan. 26, 1907, passed the Tillman Act, which made it unlawful for a corporation or a national bank to make "a money contribution in connection with any election" of candidates for federal office.

The first Federal Corrupt Practices Act was passed in 1910, and it established disclosure requirements for U.S. House candidates. Specifically, the law required every political committee "which shall in two or more states influence the result or attempt to influence the result of an election at which Representatives in Congress are to be elected" to file with the clerk of the House of Representatives, within 30 days after the election, the name and address of each contributor of $100 or more, the name and address of each recipient of $10 or more from the committee, and the total amounts that the committee received and disbursed. Individuals who engaged in similar activities outside the framework of committees were also required to submit such reports.

The following year, legislation was passed extending the filing requirements to committees influencing senatorial elections and to require filing of financial reports by candidates for the office of either senator or representative. In addition, it required statements to be filed both before and after an election. The most important innovation of the 1911 act was the limitation on the amount that a candidate could spend toward his nomination and election: a candidate for the Senate, no more than $10,000 or, if less, the maximum amount permitted in his state; for the House, no more than $5,000 or, if less, the maximum amount permitted in his state.

1925 Corrupt Practices Act

No further changes in federal campaign law were made for more than a decade. But then the system was overhauled with passage of the Federal Corrupt Practices Act of 1925. It regulated campaign spending and disclosure of receipts and expenditures by House and Senate candidates and served as the basic campaign finance law until 1971.

The 1925 act limited its restrictions to general election campaigns, since at the time it was passed the question of whether Congress had power to regulate primary elections was unsettled.

The act revised the amounts that legally could be spent by candidates. Unless a state law prescribed a smaller amount, the act set the ceilings at 1) $10,000 for a Senate candidate and $2,500 for a House candidate; or 2) an amount equal to 3 cents for each vote cast in the last preceding election for the office sought, but not more than $25,000 for the Senate and $5,000 for the House.

The 1925 act incorporated the existing prohibition against campaign contributions by corporations or national banks, the ban on solicitation of political contributions from federal employees by candidates or other federal employees and the requirement that reports be filed on campaign finances. It prohibited giving or offering money to anyone in exchange for his vote. In amending the provisions of the 1907 act on contributions, the new law substituted for the word "money" the expression "a gift, subscription, loan, advance, or deposit of money, or anything of value."

The Corrupt Practices Act, however, was riddled with loopholes, making reported amounts merely indicative and by no means complete. For example, the act did not require reports of contributions or expenditures in congressional primary or presidential campaigns. Nor did it require reports by political committees so long as they confined their activities to a single state and were not actual subsidiaries of a national political committee. Frequently, congressional candidates reported they had received and spent nothing on their campaigns, maintaining that the campaign committees established to elect them to office had been working without their "knowledge and consent."

Candidates were able to evade the spending limitations by channeling most of their campaign expenditures through separate committees that were not required to report federally, thus making the federal ceilings, from a practical standpoint, meaningless.

No candidate for the House or the Senate ever was prosecuted under the 1925 act although it was widely known that most candidates spent above the limits set in the act and did not report the full extent of their spending. Only two persons elected to Congress — two senators-elect in 1927 — were ever excluded for spending in excess of the act's limits. One of them, William S. Vare, R-Pa., was barred after reports indicated that his campaign had cost $785,000. The Senate also refused to seat Frank L. Smith, R-Ill., who had received more than 80 percent of his campaign fund from three men who had a direct interest in a decision of the Illinois Commerce Commission, of which Smith continued to be a member throughout the campaign.

In 1934 a case reached the Supreme Court that required the court to rule, among other things, on the constitutionality of the 1925 act's requirement that the amounts of campaign contributions and expenditures be filed publicly. The case, *Burroughs and Cannon v. United States,* involved primarily the applicability of the act to the election of presidential electors. Justice George Sutherland on Jan. 8, 1934, delivered the court's opinion. Applicability of the act to presidential campaigns was upheld. The decision included the following statement on disclosure: "Congress reached the conclusion that public disclosure of political contributions, together with the names of contributors and other details, would tend to prevent the corrupt use of money to affect elections. The verity of this conclusion reasonably cannot be denied."

'Clean Politics' and Other Laws

Between the early efforts to regulate spending and the broad reforms of the 1970s, some legislation related to campaign financing had less direct effects than the corrupt practices laws.

An act of Aug. 2, 1939, commonly called the Hatch Act but also known as the Clean Politics Act, affected campaign financing in only a secondary way. It barred federal employees from active participation in national politics and prohibited collection of political contributions from persons receiving relief funds provided by the federal government.

But an amendment to the Hatch Act, approved July 19, 1940, made three significant additions to campaign finance law. It forbade individuals or business concerns doing work for the federal government under contract to

Major Campaign Finance Legislation

1867 — First provision on campaign financing at the federal level appears in a naval appropriations bill. It makes it illegal for a naval officer or government employee to request political contributions from workmen in navy yards.

1883 — Civil Service Reform Act protects federal workers from any obligation to contribute to any political fund and makes it illegal for any federal employee to solicit campaign funds from another federal employee.

1907 — Tillman Act makes it unlawful for a corporation or a national bank to make a monetary contribution to federal candidates.

1910 — Legislation establishes first disclosure requirements for House candidates.

1911 — Legislation extends disclosure requirements to Senate candidates and sets first expenditure limits for House and Senate candidates.

1925 — Federal Corrupt Practices Act establishes new limits for campaign expenditures and new regulations for the disclosure of receipts and expenditures by House and Senate candidates in general elections. It serves as the basic federal campaign finance law until 1971.

1940 — Hatch Act amendments extend federal regulations on campaign contributions to primary elections, set a $5,000 individual contribution limit per federal candidate for each election, and forbid individual or business concerns doing work for the federal government to contribute to any political committee or candidate.

1943 — War Disputes Act extends prohibition on political contributions by national banks and corporations to include certain financial activities of labor unions.

1947 — Taft-Hartley Act extends ban on contributions by corporations, banks and labor organizations to cover primaries as well as general elections.

1971 — Two landmark pieces of legislation overhaul campaign finance field. The Federal Election Campaign Act (FECA) sets a ceiling on the amount federal candidates can spend on media advertising and requires full disclosure of campaign contributions and expenditures. Income tax checkoff bill allows taxpayers to contribute to a general public campaign fund for eligible presidential candidates.

1974 — Most comprehensive campaign finance law in the nation's history enacted in the wake of Watergate scandal. The legislation introduces the first use of public money in federal campaigns, by providing for full public financing in presidential general election campaigns and a matching grant system in the primaries. It also establishes the first spending limits for candidates in the presidential primary and general elections and in primary campaigns for the House and Senate. Spending ceilings in House and Senate general election campaigns are revised to replace limits in the 1925 act that never were effectively enforced and were repealed in 1971. Contribution limits are tightened.

1976 — Supreme Court in *Buckley v. Valeo* decision strikes down spending limits in 1974 law and questions constitutionality of the Federal Election Commission (FEC). Legislation reconstitutes the FEC and revises some contribution limits.

1979 — Legislation makes non-controversial adjustments in FECA, reducing paperwork burden for candidates and political committees, and encouraging more volunteer as well as grass-roots party activity.

contribute to any political committee or candidate. The legislation also asserted Congress' right to regulate primary elections for the nomination of candidates for federal office and made it unlawful for anyone to contribute more than $5,000 to a federal candidate or political committee in a single year. Specifically exempted from this limitation were "contributions made to or by a state or local committee."

The 1940 amendment also placed a ceiling of $3 million in a calendar year on expenditures by a political committee operating in two or more states. In practice, however, the parties evaded this stipulation by forming new committees under various names, each of which was then free to spend up to $3 million.

Three years later Congress passed the War Labor Disputes Act, extending the 1907 prohibition on political contributions by national banks and corporations to include labor unions. This prohibition was made permanent by the Taft-Hartley Labor-Management Relations Act of 1947.

Primaries

Legislative and judicial decisions in the first half of the 20th century constantly redefined the relationship of campaign finance laws to primary elections. The 1911 act limiting campaign expenditures in congressional elections covered primaries as well as general elections. However, the Supreme Court in the 1921 *Newberry v. United States* decision struck down the law's application to primaries on the ground that the power the Constitution gave Congress to regulate the "manner of holding election" did not extend to party primaries and conventions. The Federal Corrupt Practices Act of 1925 exempted primaries from its operation.

The Hatch Act amendments of 1940 made primaries again subject to federal restrictions on campaign contributions despite the *Newberry* decision. This legislation was upheld in 1941, when the Supreme Court handed down its decision in *United States v. Classic et al.*, which reversed the *Newberry* decision. The *Classic* decision was confirmed by the Supreme Court in 1944 in *Smith v. Allwright*. When the Taft-Hartley Act was adopted in 1947, its prohibition of political contributions by corporations, national banks and labor organizations was phrased to cover primaries as well as general elections.

POSTWAR ERA: 'MORE LOOPHOLE THAN LAW'

Even with the revisions of the 1930s and 1940s, America's postwar campaign finance system was regarded widely as riddled with loopholes.

Rep. Jim Wright, D-Texas, testifying July 21, 1966, before the Subcommittee on Elections of the House Administration Committee, said that legislation on campaign financing was "intentionally evaded by almost every candidate." He added: "I dare say there is not a member of Congress, myself included, who has not knowingly evaded its purpose in one way or another." President Johnson echoed Wright's admission in a message he sent to Congress May 25, 1967, proposing election reforms. The message said of the Federal Corrupt Practices Act and the Hatch Act: "Inadequate in their scope when enacted, they are now obsolete. More loophole than law, they invite evasion and circumvention."

Contributors' Loopholes

The Federal Corrupt Practices Act required the treasurer of a political committee active in two or more states to report at specified times the name and address of every donor of $100 or more to a campaign. To evade such recording, a donor could give less than $100 to each of numerous committees supporting the candidate of his choice. A Senate subcommittee in 1956 checked the contributions of sums between $50 and $99.99 to one committee. It found that, of 97 contributions in that range, 88 were over $99, including 57 that were exactly $99.99.

Technically, an individual could not contribute more than $5,000 to any national committee or federal candidate. However, he could contribute unlimited funds to state, county and local groups that passed along the money in the organization's name.

Members of the same family could legally contribute up to $5,000 each. But a wealthy donor wanting to give more than $5,000 to a candidate or a political committee could privately subsidize gifts by his relatives. Each such subsidized gift could amount to $5,000. In this way, the donor could arrange for his brothers, sisters, uncles, aunts, wife and children to make $5,000 gifts.

According to data from the Survey Research Center at the University of Michigan, only about 8 percent of the population contributed in 1968. Both parties relied on big contributors. In every presidential election in the 1950s and 1960s, with one exception, the Democratic National Committee (DNC) relied on contributors of more than $500 for more than 60 percent of its funds. For the same period, again with the exception of one election year, the Republican National Committee (RNC) received more than 50 percent of its contributions from donations of over $500.

There were certain wealthy contributors who could be counted on regularly by each party. Among the Republicans were the Mellons, Rockefellers and Whitneys. Among the Democrats were the Laskers, Kennedys and Harrimans.

Contributions also came from foreigners. A. Onassis contributed $2,000 to the RNC in 1969 and 1970. A spokesman for the RNC said "it is probably safe to assume this is Aristotle Onassis," the Greek shipping magnate. Another Greek shipowner, Constantine Diamantis of Piraeus, contributed $10,000 to the Republican Party effort in 1970.

Corporations could skirt the prohibition of contributions to a political campaign by giving bonuses or salary increases to executives in the expectation that as individuals they would make corresponding political contributions to candidates favored by the corporation.

Political campaign managers learned to watch for contribution checks drawn directly on corporate funds and to return them to avoid direct violation of the law. Often this money made its way back to the political managers in some other form.

Corporations were allowed to place advertisements in political journals, even though there was no apparent benefit to the corporations from the ads, and they could lend billboards, office furniture, equipment, mailing lists and airplanes to candidates or political committees. If a loan of this kind was deemed a violation of the letter of the law, the corporation could rent these items to a candidate or committee, instead of lending them, and then write off the rental fee as uncollectible.

Labor unions could contribute to a candidate or political committee funds collected from members apart from dues. Money could be taken directly from union treasuries and used for technically "non-partisan" purposes, such as promoting voter registration, encouraging members to vote, or printing voting records of members of Congress or state legislatures.

Organized labor's registration and get-out-the-vote drives overwhelmingly supported Democratic candidates, being keyed to areas where regular Democratic efforts were considered deficient or where an overwhelming Democratic vote was traditionally necessary to overcome a Republican plurality in some other section of the district, state or country.

Public service activities, such as union newspapers or radio programs, could be financed directly from regular union treasuries. As with corporate newspapers and radio programs, a sharply partisan viewpoint could be and often was expressed.

Candidates' Loopholes

Federal or state limitations on the amount of money a candidate might knowingly receive or spend were easily evaded. Former President Eisenhower, in a 1968 *Reader's Digest* article, wrote:

Another gaping loophole in the 1925 law results from the phrase referring to the candidates' 'knowledge or consent.' A congressional candidate simply makes sure that he 'knows nothing' about the activities created by his backers. One committee, for example, may pay for the use of 100 billboards, but the candidate — and this must be quite a feat — never 'sees' them as he campaigns through his district.

The loophole opened by the law enabled numerous candidates to report that they received and spent not one cent on their campaigns because any financial activity was conducted without their "knowledge and consent." In 1964 four senators reported that their campaign books showed zero receipts and zero expenditures — Vance Hartke, D-Ind., Roman L. Hruska, R-Neb., Edmund S. Muskie, D-Maine, and John C. Stennis, D-Miss.

Four years later, when Sen. George McGovern, D-S.D., reported no receipts or expenditures, his executive assistant, George V. Cunningham, said: "We are very careful to make sure that Sen. McGovern never sees the campaign receipts." Two senators elected in 1968 — William B. Saxbe, R-Ohio, and Richard S. Schweiker, R-Pa. — reported general election expenditures of $769,614 and $664,614, respectively, to their state authorities but expenditures of only $20,962 and $5,736, respectively, to the Secretary of the Senate.

Another measure of the recorded figures' incompleteness was the contrast between the reported total political spending in 1960 — $28,326,322 — and the $175,000,000 actual total spending estimate by political experts. In 1962, $18,404,115 was reportedly spent in congressional races, but Congressional Quarterly estimated that almost $100 million was actually spent.

The credibility gap fostered by the "knowledge or consent" loophole was widened further because the Federal Corrupt Practices Act applied only to political committees operating in two or more states. If a committee operated in one state only and was not a subdivision of a national committee, the law did not apply. If a committee operated in the District of Columbia only, receiving funds there and mailing checks to candidates in a single state, the law did not cover it.

Limits on the expenditures that a political committee might make were evaded by establishing more than one committee and apportioning receipts and expenditures among them so that no one committee exceeded the limit. Because the law limited annual spending by a political committee operating in two or more states to $3 million annually, the major parties formed committees under various names, each of which was free to spend up to $3 million.

Although criminal penalties were provided for failure to report or false reporting under the Corrupt Practices Act, they had been ignored even though newsmen repeatedly uncovered violations. Attorney General Herbert Brownell in 1954 had stated the Justice Department's position that the initiative in such cases rested with the Secretary of the Senate and the Clerk of the House, and that policy was continued.

Secretaries of the Senate and Clerks of the House for many years winked at violations of the legal requirement that candidates and supporting committees periodically file with them detailed statements of contributions received and disbursements made. The situation changed in 1967 when former Rep. W. Pat Jennings, D-Va. (1955-67), was elected Clerk of the House. He began sending lists of violations to the Justice Department for prosecution, but then the department refused to act.

Initial Failures

Attempts to rewrite the 1925 act had been made regularly during the late 1950s and 1960s with little success. In 1960 the Senate passed a bill increasing the limits on campaign spending but tightening provisions for disclosure. It died in the House, as did a similar Senate-passed measure the following year.

In April 1962 the President's Commission on Campaign Costs issued a report recommending proposals to encourage greater citizen participation in financing presidential campaigns. The commission had been named in October 1961 by President John F. Kennedy. The chairman was Alexander Heard, then dean of the University of North Carolina Graduate School. Among the commission's recommendations were that:

● Individuals be given a credit against their federal income tax of 50 percent of political contributions, up to a maximum of $10 per year or, as an alternative, a deduction from taxable income for contributions up to $1,000 a year.

● The existing $3 million annual limit on expenditures of interstate political committees and the $5,000 limit on contributions by individuals to those committees be repealed, leaving no limit.

● All candidates for president and vice president and committees spending at least $2,500 a year be required to report expenditures made in both primary and general election campaigns.

● A Registry of Election Finance be established to help enforce political financing regulations.

● The government pay the "reasonable and necessary costs" of a president-elect's facilities and staff during the "transition" period between election and inauguration.

In May 1962 President Kennedy submitted five draft bills to Congress encompassing proposals identical or similar to the commission's. But the only bill reported was one to finance transition costs, and it died on the House floor.

Congress did not act again in the area of campaign finance until the mid-1960s, when it passed a tax checkoff plan to provide government subsidies to presidential election campaigns. An act approved in 1966 authorized any individual paying federal income tax to direct that $1 of the tax due in any year be paid into a Presidential Election Campaign Fund. The fund, to be set up in the U.S. Treasury, was to disburse its receipts proportionately among political parties whose presidential candidates had received 5 million or more votes in the preceding presidential election. However, Congress failed to adopt the required guidelines for distribution of the funds, so the 1966 act was in effect voided in 1967.

But the mood in Washington was beginning to change. In addition to growing irritation with the toothlessness of the disclosure laws, uneasiness was increasing over rising campaign costs. The 1968 and 1970 federal election campaigns saw spending skyrocket by both major parties, and a profusion of affluent candidates made political spending a major campaign issue in itself.

Against this backdrop, the administration of Richard M. Nixon tightened enforcement of the Federal Corrupt Practices Act, successfully pressing charges in 1969 against corporations (mostly in California) that had contributed money in 1968.

Media Costs

Rising campaign costs were evident soon after World War II. "Radio and television broadcasting eat up millions," wrote Heard in 1960. "Thousands go to pay for rent, electricity, telephone, telegraph, auto hire, airplanes, airplane tickets, registration drives, hillbilly bands, public relations counsel, the Social Security tax on payrolls.

Money pays for writers and for printing what they write, for advertising in many blatant forms, and for the boodle in many subtle guises. All these expenditures are interlarded with outlays for the hire of donkeys and elephants, for comic books, poll taxes and sample ballots, for gifts to the United Negro College Fund and the Police Relief Association, for a $5.25 traffic ticket in Maryland and $66.30 worth of 'convention liquor' in St. Louis...."

Electronic campaigning — radio and television — came to occupy a greater and greater portion of campaign budgets. In the presidential election year 1956, overall campaign spending in all political campaigns in the United States was estimated at $155 million, according to the Citizens Research Foundation. Of this, only $9.8 million was used for radio and television broadcasts.

Over the next decade, however, broadcasting emerged as the dominant political medium. While overall campaign spending was doubling by 1968 to $300 million, broadcasting outlays increased nearly sixfold to $58.9 million.

Congressional incumbents feared that without some curb on the costs of media candidates would simply be unable to finance their campaigns in the future, becoming increasingly dependent on wealthy contributors and powerful lobbying groups for the money to seek re-election.

Two other factors entered into the media and TV limits. Many Democrats saw the limit on TV outlays as a way of overcoming what they viewed as a lopsided advantage enjoyed by the Republicans — particularly in the 1972 presidential race — in the ability to raise money. Without any limit, the GOP with its funding advantage, the argument ran, would increasingly be able to blanket the airwaves and make it impossible for Democratic candidates to be heard. In addition, at the time of passage of the 1971 legislation, a grave fear had arisen that rich challengers could use TV "blitzes" to overpower incumbents.

Although in retrospect this fear may seem exaggerated, incumbent Republicans and Democrats shared it at the time, and the perception was fanned by two primary races in 1970. In New York, Rep. Richard L. Ottinger, barely known statewide at the start of the Democratic primary campaign for the U.S. Senate, spent nearly $1 million for TV advertising and ran off with the nomination from several better-known opponents, although he eventually lost. In Ohio, parking-lot magnate Howard M. Metzenbaum, known to only 10 percent of the population compared with a 95 percent recognition figure for astronaut John Glenn, spent about $500,000 on a television campaign and bested Glenn for the Democratic Senate nomination. He too lost the general election that year.

For all these reasons, TV, viewed as the political supermedium of the future, was seen ripe for spending limitations, lest the voters turn into political robots manipulated by media people and advertising agencies.

THE 1970s:
DECADE OF REFORM

All sides acknowledged the need for new campaign finance legislation when the 92nd Congress convened in 1971. Within five years, Congress passed four major laws

that changed the ways political campaigns for national office were financed and conducted. Stunned by the campaign abuses that came to light during the Watergate scandal, state governments and the courts also moved to alter the methods of campaign financing.

Two 1971 Laws

Congress worked hard on campaign finance in 1971 and passed two separate pieces of legislation: 1) the Federal Election Campaign Act (FECA) of 1971, which for the first time set a ceiling on the amount federal candidates could spend on media advertising and required full disclosure of campaign contributions and expenditures, and 2) the Revenue Act of 1971, a tax checkoff bill to allow taxpayers to contribute to a general public campaign fund for eligible presidential and vice presidential candidates.

The FECA: Limits and Disclosure

The FECA of 1971 was the first major piece of campaign finance legislation passed since 1925. It combined two sharply different approaches to reform. One section clamped limits on how much a federal candidate could spend on all forms of communications media. The second part provided, for the first time, for relatively complete and timely public reports by candidates on who was financing their campaigns and how much they were spending. Meaningful disclosure would reduce the likelihood of corruption and unfair advantage, it was theorized.

The bill went into effect April 7, 1972, 60 days after it was signed by the president. The heart of the new law was the section placing ceilings on media costs, which were applicable separately to the primary campaign and to the general election. For a House candidate, the limit was set at $50,000 or 10 cents for each voting-age person in the congressional district, whichever was greater. For a Senate candidate, the limit was $50,000 or 10 cents for each voting-age person in the state.

The ceiling, which was to rise automatically with the cost of living, applied to spending for newspaper, radio, TV, magazine, billboard and television advertising. The centerpiece of this section was the restriction that no more than 60 percent of the overall media total could go for radio and television advertising. In practice, this meant in the 1972 elections that a candidate for the House could spend no more than $52,150 for *all* media outlays in his primary campaign and no more than $52,150 in his general election campaign. (The cost-of-living factor had raised these figures from the initial $50,000.) In each case, only $31,290 of the overall media total could go for radio and television.

Because of population differences between states, the figures for Senate races ranged from an overall media limit of $52,150 in thinly populated states such as Alaska and Montana (of which only $31,290 could be for radio and TV) to as much as $1.4 million in California (of which about $850,000 could be for radio and TV).

Presidential limits also were computed on the basis of 10 cents per eligible voter. For each presidential candidate, the overall media limit was $14.3 million of which no more than $8.5 million could be used for radio and TV.

In the disclosure area, the FECA required that any candidate or political committee in a federal campaign file quarterly spending and receipts reports, listing contributors or recipients of $100 or more by name, place of busi-

The Rising Costs of Campaign Spending

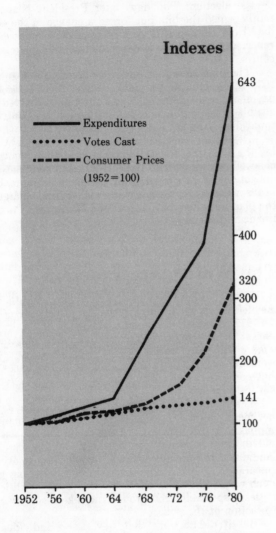

Indexes

—— Expenditures
•••••• Votes Cast
------ Consumer Prices
(1952 = 100)

643

400

320
300

200

141
100

1952 '56 '60 '64 '68 '72 '76 '80

These two graphs considered together show the relationship between the total number of votes cast and the total political spending in presidential election years from 1952 through 1980. Even when the inflationary impact of the rising Consumer Price Index is considered, the increase in political spending far exceeds the increase in the number of voters.

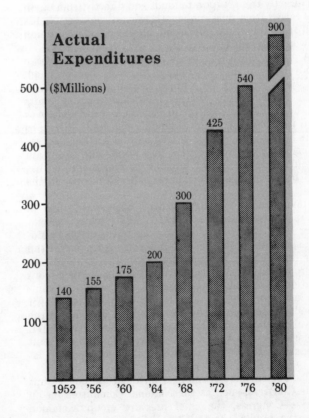

Actual Expenditures

($Millions)

1952	140
'56	155
'60	175
'64	200
'68	300
'72	425
'76	540
'80	900

500

400

300

200

100

Source: Expenditures, Herbert E. Alexander; Consumer Price Index, U.S. Bureau of the Census; votes for president, America Votes series.

ness and address. During election years, added reports were required to be filed 15 and five days before an election, and any contribution of $5,000 or more had to be reported within 48 hours of receipt.

Closing up numerous loopholes in previous law, the statute applied the reporting requirements to primaries, conventions and runoffs as well as the general election. Any political committee, even if it operated in only one state, provided it spent or received $1,000 or more a year, had to report. This meant, in effect, that the loophole of avoiding reports by having separate campaign fund groups in each state was closed for presidential candidates and that members of Congress with campaign fund groups operating only in their home states would henceforth have to report its receipts and expenditures.

The reports were to be filed with the House Clerk for House candidates, Secretary of the Senate for Senate candidates, and General Accounting Office (GAO) for presidential candidates. These would be made available for public inspection within 48 hours of being received and periodically published; reports also were required to be filed with the secretary of state of each state and made available for public inspection by the end of the day on which received.

On the theory that disclosure alone would eliminate corruption, all the ineffective spending and contribution limits were repealed, except provisions barring contributions directly from corporate funds and directly from union funds raised from dues money. (However, *voluntary* funds raised from union members and administered by a union unit were permitted.)

A purely political factor in passage of the FECA was a commitment in 1970 by Senate Minority Leader Hugh Scott, R-Pa., to work for a broad campaign reform bill. In 1970 a bill containing sharper television spending limits than the FECA, but no broad disclosure provisions, was vetoed by President Nixon as unduly restrictive. Scott, as Senate Republican leader, worked hard to sustain the veto and pledged to senators that if they would vote to sustain he would help sponsor a broader reform measure that would be acceptable to Nixon as well as Congress in the next session.

Having made this commitment, Scott was bound to support a broad measure in 1971. With Senate Majority Leader Mike Mansfield, D-Mont., one of the major Democratic sponsors in the Senate, this provided a bipartisan leadership push for passage of a bill in 1971.

Proponents of reform, cognizant of the partisan considerations that could have threatened any revision of campaign laws, worked to avoid writing a law that would favor any political party or candidate. Republicans, aware of the relatively healthy financial condition of their party in 1971, were eager to protect their coffers; Democrats did not want to jeopardize their large contributions from organized labor.

The reform movement also included various groups outside Congress, such as the National Committee for an Effective Congress, the chief pressure group; Common Cause, the public affairs lobby; labor unions and some media organizations.

Eight months after enactment of the new law, legislation to modify one of its provisions — prohibiting corporations and labor unions having federal government contracts from making direct political contributions — was passed by the House. But the Senate refused to act and the bill died at the end of the 92nd Congress.

Income Tax Checkoff

Congress passed the income tax checkoff bill, called the Revenue Act of 1971, on Dec. 8, 1971, after a bitter partisan debate dominated by the approaching 1972 presidential election. Two days later President Nixon reluctantly signed the bill, but forced a change in the effective date from 1972 to 1976 as a price of his acquiescence. He reportedly planned to leave challenges to Congress or the courts.

The plan gave each taxpayer the option beginning in 1973 of designating $1 of his annual federal income tax payment for a general campaign fund to be divided among eligible presidential candidates. Those filing joint returns could designate $2.

Democrats, whose party was $9 million in debt following the 1968 presidential election, said the voluntary tax checkoff was needed to free presidential candidates from obligations to their wealthy campaign contributors. Republicans, whose party treasury was well stocked, charged that the plan was a device to rescue the Democratic Party from financial difficulty.

The Watergate Election

Both 1971 laws were campaign finance milestones, but they left intact the existing system of private financing for the 1972 presidential campaign. While the FECA drew high marks for improving campaign disclosure and received some credit for reducing media costs, its successes were overshadowed by the massive misuse of campaign funds that comprised Watergate, one of the nation's foremost political scandals.

The predominant theory at the time of passage was that merely by writing a good, tight campaign finance law emphasizing disclosure, Congress could reduce excessive contributions from any one source to any one candidate. Candidates, the theory continued, would want to avoid the appearance of being dominated by a single "big giver," which would allow the public to identify the political activities of special interest groups and take necessary corrective action at the polls.

But it didn't work that way. Large individual and corporate donations were near the center of the Watergate scandal as largely unreported private contributions financed the activities of the 1972 Nixon re-election campaign. Of the $62 million collected by the Nixon camp, nearly $20 million was raised before the FECA disclosure rules took effect on April 7, 1972. About $1.5 million of the early donations were in cash.

The Finance Committee for the Re-election of the President kept its pre-April 7 lists confidential until a Common Cause lawsuit forced them into the open in 1973. Such reticence was partly explained by the existence of questionable contributions: the $200,000 in Robert Vesco's attaché case, the $100,000 secret donation to the Nixon campaign from Howard Hughes that Nixon confidant Bebe Rebozo purportedly kept locked in a safe deposit box, and the $2 million pledged to Nixon by the dairy industry.

The existence of a substantial number of illegal corporate donations also motivated secrecy. In a report issued in July 1974, the Senate Select Committee on Presidential Campaign Activities charged that "during the 1972 presidential campaign, it appears that at least 13 corporations made contributions totaling over $780,000 in corporate funds. . . . Of these, 12 gave approximately $749,000 to the president's re-election campaign, which constituted the bulk of the illegal corporate contributions."

The primary sources of such corporate money, according to the Senate committee, were "foreign subsidiaries." Other sources included corporate reserves and expense accounts. The committee added that "although the bulk of the contributions preceded April 7, 1972, there was no disclosure of any of the contributions until July 6, 1973 — or 15 months after almost all of them were made."

Presidential lawyer Herbert Kalmbach, who headed the corporate gifts campaign, in June 1974 was sentenced to six to 18 months in jail and fined $10,000 after pleading guilty to illegal campaign operations. Kalmbach collected more than $10 million from U.S. corporations, the bulk of it prior to April 7, 1972.

According to staff reports of the Senate Select Watergate Committee, Kalmbach and other fund-raisers sought donations on an industry-by-industry basis, using an influential corporate executive to raise money among other executives in his industry.

The leading individual giver in the 1972 campaign was Chicago insurance executive W. Clement Stone, chairman of the Combined Insurance Company of America. In the April 7-Dec. 31, 1972, reporting period monitored by the GAO, Stone was listed as giving $73,054 to re-elect Nixon. But even before the revelations forced by Common Cause, Stone had admitted to pre-April giving of $2 million. The second highest giver was Richard Scaife, heir to the Mellon banking and oil fortune, who contributed $1 million to Nixon's re-election before April 7.

John Gardner, head of Common Cause, said in April 1973: "Watergate is not primarily a story of political espionage, nor even of White House intrigue. It is a particularly malodorous chapter in the annals of campaign financing. The money paid to the Watergate conspirators before the break-in — and money passed to them later — was money from campaign gifts."

Gardner's charge was dramatically acknowledged by former President Nixon on Aug. 5, 1974, when he released a June 23, 1972, tape recording of conversations between himself and H. R. Haldeman, then Nixon's chief of staff. The recording revealed that Nixon was told at that time of the use of campaign funds in the June 17, 1972, Watergate break-in and agreed to help cover up that fact. Nixon's resignation Aug. 9, 1974, followed the Aug. 5 disclosure.

Disclosure Provisions

The campaign disclosure provisions of the 1971 law, though, did prove extremely useful, enabling scholars and the relevant committees of Congress to get a clear picture for the first time of patterns of spending. Enormous contributions by the milk industry, formerly concealed large contributions by individuals, and even information playing a key role in the Watergate scandal, relating to "laundered money" and corporate contributions, emerged from the reports.

Although there were thousands of late and faulty reports, the disclosure law on the whole probably met with fair compliance.

Nevertheless, a great many problems with the disclosure law remained. The reports, especially those made in the last few days before the election, were extremely difficult for a reporter or a rival political camp to collate and decipher. Multiple contributions by a wealthy individual made to one candidate through a system of dummy organizations with cryptic names were difficult to track rapidly. Investigating an industrywide campaign of financial support to a candidate or a group of candidates proved to be an extremely tedious task.

The state finance committees and other committees — with titles such as Democrats for Nixon or Writers for McGovern — were created to prevent big contributors from being inhibited by high gift taxes. An individual could give up to $3,000, tax-free, to an independent campaign committee. Records show that the Nixon campaign benefited from 220 of these finance committees. McGovern had 785 such committees, according to his national campaign treasurer, Marian Pearlman, "created for Stewart Mott." Mott, an investor who donated a net of about $350,000, even declared himself a campaign committee.

The Internal Revenue Service interpreted campaign committees as being independent if one out of three officers was different from officers for other committees, if the candidates supported by the committees were different or if the committee's purposes were different. As a result, campaign finance committees proliferated in 1972, and contributors were hardly deterred from giving large sums to one candidate.

More important, the crucial element in effectiveness of the law was enforcement. The Justice Department was given sole power to prosecute violations, despite its 46-year record of somnolence in enforcing previous regulations. It was traditionally understood that Justice Department bureaucrats feared to undertake vigorous enforcement lest they endanger the party in power and be fired.

The question became: Would the department make a powerful, massive effort not only to round up serious violators but to require that reports be on time and complete? Without such action from the department the practice of filing slovenly, incomplete reports, or even misleading reports, and filing them late, would clearly vitiate much of the effect of the law and render it null in practice.

Although thousands of violations — some serious but most technical (late or incomplete) — were referred to the Justice Department in 1972 and 1973 by the House and Senate and GAO, there were only a handful of prosecutions. During the 1972 campaign the department had only one full-time attorney supervising enforcement of the act, according to reports.

Enforcement was impeded further by another provision in the law requiring periodic reporting of contributions and expenditures. According to many members of Congress, the frequent filing of these reports during election campaigns by all political committees of candidates — required for both primary and general elections — created monumental bookkeeping chores for the candidates. Correspondingly, the mammoth number of reports filed with the House Clerk, the Senate Secretary and the comptroller general made closer scrutiny practically impossible.

To remedy the problem of getting reports to the public and to reporters quickly with the information well-organized, Common Cause, at a cost of more than $250,000 and thousands of hours from volunteer workers, organized teams of people in 1972 to collect and collate information on reports, which it then distributed to the press in time for use before Election Day.

Fred Wertheimer, then legislative director of Common Cause, said the aim was to make the law work and to give it a good start. But it was clear that depending on private organizations alone probably would be inadequate. Unless some permanent way were found, perhaps at government expense, to speed up collation and distribution of the materials — particularly late in the campaign — the objectives of disclosure would be undermined.

Media Costs Drop

The 1972 election was more expensive than any that preceded it. About $425 million was spent in all races, with the Senate Watergate Committee estimating that President Nixon's and Sen. George McGovern's presidential campaigns together cost $100 million. The figure more than doubled the $44.2 million spent in the 1968 presidential election. During the 1972 campaign, Senate and presidential outlays for radio and television campaign advertising dropped sharply as compared with 1968 and 1970 but it was unclear whether this resulted from the TV spending limits.

The Federal Communications Commission (FCC) reported that presidential candidates spent $14.3 million on radio, television and cable TV advertising in 1972, compared with $28.5 million in the previous presidential election. Senatorial candidates spent $6.4 million in 1972, compared with $16 million in 1970 and $10.4 million in 1968. Broadcast spending in House races increased, however, from $6.1 million in 1970, when the FCC first computed it, to $7.4 million in 1972.

In the presidential race, part of the drop was due to the strength of the incumbent, who had loads of free air time available to him when he chose to address the nation in "non-political" speeches as president, instead of seeking paid time as merely a candidate. Nixon was in a position to spend far less than he did.

The drop in Senate spending was less easily explained, but many senators said one factor was the realization that electronic media, while enormously effective, did not provide the quantum leap in campaigning techniques that had been expected. The notion that television could "do it all," which was virtually an article of faith in the late 1960s and in 1970, had begun to fade, and more resources were put into other forms of advertising and into traditional organizational and legwork efforts. Broadcast spending totals also were reduced by the requirement in the 1971 law that TV stations charge politicians the lowest unit rate for any time slot.

Also, many senators learned in 1972 that TV station coverage was not well designed for campaign purposes in many areas. In some large states, for example Kentucky, it was impossible to cover the whole state with stations broadcasting only within that state. To cover border areas, it was necessary to buy time on stations located in other states, only a portion of whose viewers were in Kentucky. This meant that to send a message to one corner of the state, a candidate had to pay for coverage outside the state as well, a wasteful and costly practice.

The same was true in some large central metropolitan areas located between two or three states. For northern New Jersey, a candidate had to pay rates for New York too, since many of the stations in that area broadcast simultaneously to New York City, Connecticut and northern New Jersey.

Some senators found it cheaper under these conditions to use other ways of reaching the voters. The great television boom, if not ended, was at least slowed. FCC reports showed that while a handful of senators went slightly over their campaign limits, the TV limits as a whole were observed.

Because of the TV "targeting" problems, many in Congress began to argue that a flat spending limit for TV was too inflexible. They said an overall spending limit for all campaign costs — similar to that repealed in 1971, but with real scope and enforcement teeth — would be better. Such a proposal, they argued, would still limit any massive use of TV because a candidate would not be able to exceed his total campaign spending limit. But it would allow greater flexibility as to which portion of overall costs went to TV and which to other items.

The 1974 Law

Almost two and a half years after it passed the FECA of 1971 — a factor in breaking open the Watergate scandal — Congress, reacting to presidential campaign abuses, enacted another landmark campaign reform bill that substantially overhauled the existing system of financing election campaigns. Technically the 1974 law was a set of amendments to the 1971 legislation, but in fact it was the most comprehensive ever passed.

The new measure, which President Ford signed into law Oct. 15, established the first spending limits ever for candidates in presidential primary and general elections and in primary campaigns for the House and Senate. It set new expenditure ceilings for general election campaigns for Congress to replace the limits established by the 1925 Federal Corrupt Practices Act that were never effectively enforced and were repealed in the 1971 law.

The 1974 law also introduced the first use of public money to pay for political campaign costs by providing for optional public financing in presidential general election campaigns and establishing federal matching grants to cover up to one-half of the costs of presidential primary campaigns. The final bill did not contain Senate-passed provisions for partial public financing of congressional campaigns.

The pressure that led to the passage of campaign finance reform legislation in 1974 directly resulted from the Watergate scandal. The disclosures of widespread campaign contribution and spending abuses made by the Senate Watergate Committee fueled a searching debate on campaign financing and how it could be reformed.

Calls for reform had multiplied since the Senate Watergate committee in 1973 began exposing abuses in the collection and spending of huge sums of money in the 1972 Nixon re-election campaign. The Gallup Poll in September 1973 found that 65 percent of those surveyed favored public financing and a ban on private contributions, a significant increase over previous years. Many members of Congress also took up the cry for reform, particularly in the wake of a January 1974 Harris Survey that showed Congress ranking even lower than the president in public esteem (21 percent, compared with Nixon's poll rating of around 27 percent).

Public Financing: A New Approach

While no one could be sure just what the effects of public financing would be, it was apparent they would be profound: on candidates, both challengers and incumbents alike; on individuals and groups accustomed to giving money and other assistance to candidates; on the political parties, both major and minor; on the taxpayers; and perhaps most of all, on the process of government itself.

Highlights of 1974 Campaign Law

Following is a summary of the 1974 Federal Election Campaign Act, as signed into law. Some provisions were later declared unconstitutional in the 1976 *Buckley v. Valeo* decision, or were superseded by amendments. *(For additional provisions, see p. 135)*

Contribution Limits

$1,000 per individual for each primary, runoff and general election, and an aggregate contribution of $25,000 for all federal candidates annually; $5,000 per organization, political committee and state party organization for each election.

Candidate's and his family's contributions: $50,000 for president; $35,000 for Senate, $25,000 for House.

Individual unsolicited expenditures on behalf of a candidate limited to $1,000 a year.

Cash contributions of more than $100 and foreign contributions barred.

Spending Limits*

Presidential primaries — $10 million total per candidate for all primaries.

Presidential general election — $20 million.

Presidential nominating conventions — $2 million for each major political party, lesser amounts for minor parties.

Senate primaries — $100,000 or eight cents per eligible voter, whichever was greater.

Senate general elections — $150,000 or 12 cents per eligible voter, whichever was greater.

House primaries — $70,000.

House general elections — $70,000.

Senate limits apply to House candidates who represent a whole state.

Repealed the media spending limitations in the Federal Election Campaign Act of 1971.

Party Spending*

National parties permitted to spend independently $10,000 per candidate in House general elections; $20,000 or two cents per eligible voter, whichever was greater, for each candidate in Senate general elections; and two cents per eligible voter in presidential general elections. The expenditure would be above the candidate's individual spending limit.

Exemptions

Exempted from contribution and spending limits: expenditures of up to $500 for food and beverages, invitations, use of personal property and spending on "slate cards" and sample ballots.

Fund-raising costs of up to 20 percent of the candidate spending limit exempted from spending limits.

Public Financing

Full optional public funding for presidential general elections; public funding of national party nominating conventions voluntary; matching public funds in presidential primaries of up to $5 million per candidate* after meeting fund-raising requirement of $100,000 raised in amounts of at least $5,000 in each of 20 states or more and through individual contributions of $250 or less. All federal money for public funding of campaigns would come from the Presidential Election Campaign Fund. Proportional funding for minor party candidates.

Congressional campaigns not publicly financed.

Disclosure and Reporting Dates

Candidates required to establish a central campaign committee; bank loans treated as contributions; government contractors, unions and corporations permitted to maintain separate segregated political funds. Dislosure filing dates: 10 days before an election (postmarked no later than 12 days before the election), 30 days after an election and quarterly, unless the committee received or spent less than $1,000.

Enforcement

An eight-member bipartisan, full-time supervisory board controlled by six voting public members. Two of the public members appointed by the House Speaker, two by the president of the Senate and two by the president, all of whom would be confirmed by Congress. The House Clerk and the Secretary of the Senate would be ex-officio members.

The Federal Election Commission would have civil enforcement powers and would be able to seek court injunctions. Criminal cases would be referred to the Justice Department for prosecution. The House and Senate had veto power over regulations issued by the board.

Other Provisions

Increased fines for violations to a maximum of $50,000. Provided that a candidate for federal office who failed to file reports could be prohibited from running again for the term of that office plus one year.

Permitted use of excess campaign funds to defray expenses of holding federal office or for other lawful purposes.

Subject to annual cost-of-living adjustment.

Debate tended to center on the need to end specific Watergate-type abuses, on various formulas for setting up public financing and on its effect on individuals and groups. Some observers, on both sides of the issue, believed that the system itself — so reliant upon the close relationship, more than 100 years old, between big money and the American government — would feel the greatest long-term effects.

Aside from a warning in March 1974 by President Nixon that he would veto any public financing bill, the White House kept its distance from the major campaign reform issue in the second year of Watergate. So did most groups such as the U.S. Chamber of Commerce that opposed public financing legislation.

Public financing is one of the few issues that directly involves the self-interest of members of Congress. Thus, in the 1974 debate much action was centered in the Capitol itself, and the legislation did not generate typical lobbying patterns. Legislators and outside lobby groups supporting major changes in the way political campaigns were financed dominated the debate. And that created a deceptive picture of how Congress handled the legislation. It might best have been described as an iceberg issue: Open opposition to the bill was difficult, when most of its detractors, both in and out of Congress, were hidden from direct view.

"Public financing today is like the motherhood issue," said John Gabusi, an aide to Rep. Morris K. Udall, D-Ariz., who cosponsored a public financing bill in the House. "Voting against it is like voting for the evils of Watergate, yet there are many guys who would do that if their votes were not made public."

Congressional Action

The Senate passed campaign financing legislation in July and November 1973. The first measure would have limited campaign contributions and expenditures and repealed the "equal time" provision of the Federal Communications Act. The November measure was more radical. It would have made federal financing of presidential general elections mandatory, set up matching grants for candidates in presidential primaries and provided public money in congressional election contests.

The latter provision was approved 52-40, with the support of 42 of the 54 Democrats who voted and 10 of the 38 Republicans. But the House refused to accept either bill.

Soon after Congress reconvened in January 1974, the Senate Rules and Administration Committee, chaired by Howard W. Cannon, D-Nev., began work anew on a comprehensive public financing bill.

The bill was designed to provide complete disclosure of campaign contributions and expenditures, both public and private, in elections for federal office. Proponents claimed that it would reduce the influence of wealthy campaign contributors and give citizens without access to such sources equal opportunity to run for public office.

After 13 days of debate, the Senate April 11 passed the bill on a 53-32 vote two days after the Senate voted April 9 to shut off a filibuster of Southern Democrats and conservative Republicans, led by James B. Allen, D-Ala., against the public financing provisions.

Throughout the debate, Allen charged that the bill was a "raid" on the public Treasury for the benefit of politicians. Other opponents, such as Lowell P. Weicker Jr., R-Conn., opposed public financing because they said it did not attempt to control campaign costs. According to Weicker, the bill did not deal with this problem, one of the prime lessons of Watergate.

Supporters, such as Edward M. Kennedy, D-Mass., maintained that the public financing bill would remove the influence of big money in politics and would return integrity to campaign financing. Senate supporters fended off attempts to significantly weaken the public financing provisions in the measure.

The measure reported by the House Administration Committee was much more limited in scope than the version passed by the Senate, with major differences in public financing and enforcement. It did not include congressional public financing. On the House floor, committee Chairman Wayne L. Hays, D-Ohio, dominated debate and fended off all major challenges to his committee's bill. Reps. John B. Anderson, R-Ill., and Udall tried unsuccessfully to win approval of an amendment that would publicly fund congressional races through a system of matching federal grants.

"Surely today," said Udall, "the American people are ready to put up a dollar or two a year to have a clean, decent, brand new system of House and Senate elections. . . ." Countered Hays: "I think it is a scheme to break down the two-party system." Public financing should be tried only in presidential campaigns, he added, "where all the people have gone to jail."

By a vote of 187-228, the House on Aug. 8, 1974, defeated the Anderson-Udall amendment. Republicans rejected it by a 73-110 vote, while Democrats broke nearly even, 114-118 against. Southern Democrats, however, overwhelmingly disapproved of congressional public financing, voting against the amendment, 18-60.

Later that day, a few hours before President Nixon announced that he intended to resign as a consequence of his involvement in the Watergate cover-up, the House approved the bill by a 355-48 vote.

But House and Senate conferees were slow to solve their differences. They were deadlocked for three weeks before agreeing Oct. 1 on the basic provisions of a new campaign finance law.

The legislation had been stymied in conference because of a bitter dispute over public financing of congressional races. Senate conferees, especially Dick Clark, D-Iowa, and Kennedy, had pressed for some form of public financing for House and Senate races. They were staunchly opposed by the House conferees, led by Hays. Clark and Kennedy did not give up their fight until the evening of Sept. 30 when they met with Cannon and worked out the compromise package that was accepted Oct. 1.

During the Sept. 30 meeting, Kennedy offered several fallback alternatives to full congressional public financing such as public financing for Senate campaigns only and partial public financing of House and Senate races. But all were decisively defeated.

In return for dropping congressional public financing from the bill, Senate public financing backers got increased spending limits for House and Senate campaigns and a stronger independent election commission to enforce the law.

The compromise measure was closer to the House-passed bill because it included the House version of presidential public financing and the independent election commission, with four of its six voting members appointed by the House Speaker and president of the Senate and the other two by the president. And it omitted congressional public financing.

The final campaign spending limits were closer to those in the Senate version. The Senate conferees also pushed successfully for permitting the national parties to independently spend money on candidates above the candidates' own spending limit. *(Major provisions of 1974 law, box, p. 13)*

Once established, the Federal Election Commission (FEC) found it impossible to get the House and Senate to accept its regulations to implement the 1974 law. The FEC's first two regulations, on congressional office accounts and on where disclosure reports should be filed, were rejected by the Senate and House in the fall of 1975. During hearings on the regulations and the commission budget, Hays got into well-publicized shouting matches with the commission chairman, former Rep. Thomas B. Curtis, R-Mo. (1951-69). *(FEC, Chapter 2, p. 29)*

Buckley v. Valeo

As soon as the 1974 law took effect, it was challenged in court by a diverse array of plaintiffs including Sen. James L. Buckley, Cons-R-N.Y., former Sen. Eugene J. McCarthy, D-Minn. (1959-71), the New York Civil Liberties Union and *Human Events,* a conservative publication. They filed suit on Jan. 2, 1975.

Their basic arguments were that the law's new limits on campaign contributions and expenditures curbed the freedom of contributors and candidates to express themselves in the political marketplace and that the public financing provisions discriminated against minor parties and lesser-known candidates in favor of the major parties and better-known candidates.

The U.S. Court of Appeals for the District of Columbia on Aug. 14, 1975, upheld all of the law's major provisions, thus setting the stage for Supreme Court action.

The Supreme Court handed down its ruling *(Buckley v. Valeo)* on Jan. 30, 1976, in an unsigned 137-page opinion. In five separate, signed opinions, several justices concurred with and dissented from separate issues in the case.

In its decision, the court upheld the provisions of the statute that:

● Set limits on how much individuals and political committees could contribute to candidates.

● Provided for the public financing of presidential primary and general election campaigns.

● Required the disclosure of campaign contributions of more than $10 and campaign expenditures on behalf of the candidate of more than $100.

Spending Limits Overturned

But the court overturned other features of the law, ruling that the campaign spending limits were unconstitutional violations of the First Amendment guarantee of free expression. For presidential candidates who accepted federal matching funds, however, the ceiling on expenditures remained intact. The court also struck down the method for selecting members of the FEC.

"A restriction on the amount of money a person or group can spend on political communication during a campaign necessarily reduces the quantity of expression," the court stated, "by restricting the number of issues discussed, the depth of their exploration and the size of the audience reached. This is because virtually every means of communicating ideas in today's mass society requires the expenditure of money." Only Justice Byron R. White dissented on this point; he would have upheld the limitations. Rejecting the argument that money is speech, White wrote that there are "many expensive campaign activities that are not themselves communicative or remotely related to speech."

Although the court acknowledged that contribution and spending limits had First Amendment implications, it distinguished between the two by saying that the act's "expenditure ceilings impose significantly more severe restrictions on protected freedom of political expression and association than do its limitations on financial contributions."

The court removed all the limits imposed on political spending and, by so doing, weakened the effect of the contribution ceilings. The law had placed spending limits on House, Senate and presidential campaigns and on party nominating conventions. To plug a loophole in the contribution limits, it also placed a $1,000 annual limit on how much an individual could spend independently on behalf of a candidate.

The independent expenditure ceiling, the opinion said, was a clear violation of the First Amendment. "While the ... ceiling thus fails to serve any substantial government interest in stemming the reality or appearance of corruption in the electoral process, it heavily burdens core First Amendment expression," the court wrote. "... Advocacy of the election or defeat of candidates for federal office is not less entitled to protection under the First Amendment than the discussion of political policy generally or advocacy of the passage or defeat of legislation."

The court also struck down the limits on how much of their own money candidates could spend on their campaigns. The law had set a $25,000 limit on House candidates, $35,000 on Senate candidates and $50,000 on presidential candidates. "The candidate, no less than any other person, has a First Amendment right to engage in the discussion of public issues and vigorously and tirelessly to advocate his own election and the election of other candidates," the opinion said.

The ruling made it possible for a wealthy candidate to finance his own campaign and thus to avoid the limits on how much others could give him. The court wrote that "the use of personal funds reduces the candidate's dependence on outside contributions and thereby counteracts the coercive pressures and attendant risks of abuse to which the act's contribution limitations are directed."

Justice Thurgood Marshall rejected the court's reasoning in striking down the limit on how much candidates may spend on their own campaigns. "It would appear to follow," he said, "that the candidate with a substantial personal fortune at his disposal is off to a significant 'head start.'" Moreover, he added, keeping the limitations on contributions but not on spending "put[s] a premium on a candidate's personal wealth."

Federal Election Commission

The court held unanimously that the FEC was unconstitutional. The court said the method of appointment of commissioners violated the Constitution's separation-of-powers and appointments clauses because some members were named by congressional officials but exercised executive powers.

The justices refused to accept the argument that the commission, because it oversaw congressional as well as presidential elections, could have congressionally appointed members. "We see no reason to believe that the authority of Congress over federal election practices is of such a wholly different nature from the other grants of authority to Congress that it may be employed in such a manner as to offend well established constitutional restrictions stemming from the separation of powers," the court wrote.

According to the decision, the commission could exercise only those powers Congress was allowed to delegate to congressional committees — investigating and information-gathering. The court ruled that only if the commission's members were appointed by the president, as required under the Constitution's appointments clause, could the commission carry out the administrative and enforcement responsibilities the law originally gave it.

That last action put Congress on the spot, because the justices stayed their ruling for 30 days — until Feb. 29 — to give the House and Senate time to "reconstitute the commission by law or adopt other valid enforcement mechanisms." As it developed, Congress took much longer than 30 days to act, and instead of merely reconstituting the commission it passed a whole new campaign financing law.

Supporters and opponents of the 1974 law hailed the court's ruling, with each side claiming victory. Common Cause's John Gardner called the decision a triumph "for all those who have worked so hard to clean up politics in this country. The fat cats won't be able to buy elections or politicians any more." Sen. Buckley said the court "struck a major blow for the forces of freedom" by allowing unchecked political spending. But Buckley added that the court had left standing "a clearly unworkable set of ground rules" that Congress would have to revise. (Supreme Court opinion, Buckley v. Valeo, Appendix, p. 120)

1976 Amendments

The court decision forced Congress to return to campaign finance legislation once again. The 1976 election campaign was already under way, but the court said that the FEC could not continue to disburse public funds to presidential candidates so long as some commission members were congressional appointees.

Congress did not begin its work until late February. Although the court extended the original Feb. 29 deadline until March 22, the extra three weeks still did not give Congress the time members wanted to revise the law. One result was that for two months after March 22 the presidential candidates did not receive the federal matching funds they had expected.

President Gerald R. Ford had wanted only a simple reconstitution of the commission, but Congress insisted on going much further and writing an extensive new campaign finance law. The new law, arrived at after much maneuvering and arguing between Democrats and Republicans, closed old loopholes and opened new ones, depending on the point of view of the observer.

In its basic provision, the law signed by the president May 11, 1976, reconstituted the FEC as a six-member panel appointed by the president and confirmed by the Senate. Commission members were not allowed to engage in outside business activities. The commission was given exclusive authority to prosecute civil violations of the campaign finance law and was vested with jurisdiction over

violations formerly covered only in the criminal code, thus strengthening its power to enforce the law.

A major controversy that delayed enactment was the insistence of organized labor that corporate fund-raising activity through PACs be curtailed. Labor was angered by the FEC's controversial SunPAC decision in November 1975. The decision allowed corporate PACs to solicit all employees and stockholders for contributions. Labor PACs had been restricted to soliciting only their members. (PACs, Chapter 3, p. 41)

In mid-March the Senate had reached an impasse. The Democrats were not hesitating to use their overwhelming numerical strength to make changes that would have severely restricted the ability of business to raise political money. The Republicans lacked the strength to fend off the anti-business amendments. But they had the votes to sustain a filibuster and a presidential veto.

At that point, Democratic and Republican leaders drew back from the battle and worked out a compromise acceptable to both sides. Labor won some but not all of its goal. The final law permitted company committees to seek contributions only from stockholders, executives and administrative personnel and their families. It continued to restrict union PACs to soliciting contributions from union members and their families. However, twice a year, union and corporate PACs were permitted to seek campaign contributions by mail only from all employees. Contributions would have to remain anonymous and would be received by an independent third party that would keep records but pass the money to the committees.

The final bill contained another provision prompted by the Supreme Court decision. In addition to finding the makeup of the election commission unconstitutional, the court had thrown out the 1974 law's limitations on independent political expenditures as a clear violation of the First Amendment. Members of Congress feared that the ruling would open a major new loophole. As a result, they inserted a provision in the new bill requiring that political committees and individuals making independent political expenditures of more than $100 swear that the expenditures were not made in collusion with the candidate.

The 1976 legislation also set some new contribution limits: An individual could give no more than $5,000 a year to a PAC and $20,000 to the national committee of a political party (the 1974 law set a $1,000 per election limit on individual contributions to a candidate and an aggregate contribution limit for individuals of $25,000 a year; no specific limits, except the aggregate limit, applied to contributions to political committees). A PAC could give no more than $15,000 a year to the national committee of a political party (the 1974 law set only a limit of $5,000 per election per candidate). The Democratic and Republican senatorial campaign committees could give up to $17,500 a year to a candidate (the 1974 law had set a $5,000 per election limit).

Even after Ford signed the bill May 11 the money could not begin to flow until the president appointed the six members of the commission and the Senate confirmed them. The commission was reconsituted May 21.

Ford, who had been under pressure to veto the bill from business lobbyists and conservatives such as Ronald Reagan, his rival for the Republican presidential nomination, said he approved it only reluctantly. The president's most serious objection was to the provision for veto power by either house of Congress over commission regulations.

"This provision not only circumvents the original intent of campaign reform but, in my opinion, violates the

Constitution," Ford said. "I have therefore directed the Attorney General to challenge the constitutionality of this provision at the earliest possible opportunity."

Despite his reservations, the president said the law was needed "to maintain the integrity of our election process" in this election year. Ford signed the bill several hours after he met with Republican congressional leaders who urged approval. Several of them warned that immediate action was needed to prevent criticism that he was stalling to deprive his political opponents of money.

When the FEC was reconstituted Ford renamed five of the six original commissioners — Democrats Neil Staebler, Robert O. Tiernan and Thomas E. Harris, and Republicans Vernon Thomson and Joan D. Aikens. Thomson was named commission chairman, replacing the controversial Thomas Curtis, who asked not to be reappointed. Ford nominated former Rep. William L. Springer, R-Ill. (1951-73), to fill the slot vacated by Curtis and the Senate confirmed him May 21.

DEBATE ACCELERATES OVER PUBLIC FINANCING

Following the election of Jimmy Carter in 1976, the spotlight in campaign finance quickly focused on extending public financing to House and Senate races. Although a variety of proposals were actively considered during the first three years of the Carter administration, chances of congressional passage appeared rosiest in the opening months of 1977.

The mood in Congress seemed to have changed since public financing of congressional races was last considered in 1974. Leading officials, from the White House on down, were then either opposed or seemingly indifferent to its passage. Presidents Nixon and Ford opposed public financing, as did Rep. Hays, the powerful head of the House Administration Committee, which had jurisdiction over all campaign finance measures. Democratic leaders made no active push to dissuade Hays on the issue.

In early 1977 the climate in Washington was almost completely reversed. President Carter had made the public financing of congressional races part of his election reform package, and House Speaker Thomas P. O'Neill Jr., D-Mass., Senate Majority Leader Robert C. Byrd, D-W.Va., and Hays' successor as House Administration Committee chairman, Frank Thompson Jr., D-N.J., were in support. Prospects for public financing were brightened further by the overwhelming Democratic advantage in the House, far larger than during the 93rd Congress (1973-74) when the House rejected congressional public financing after it had been approved by the Senate.

Carter went on record in favor of congressional public financing during the 1976 campaign, and he underscored his support by making it one of four provisions in an election reform package he unveiled in March 1977.

The president recommended that Congress adopt a matching system of public financing similar to the system used to finance candidates during the presidential primaries, and that the spending ceiling not be set so low that it curbed an adequate presentation of candidates and issues.

He suggested that Congress seek ways to close the court-created loophole that allowed candidates to spend unlimited amounts of their own fortunes if they did not accept public funds.

Carter's proposal called for public financing for congressional primaries and general elections. He urged the members to move quickly, so that public financing could be available for 1978.

The president did not propose any new legislation, since his proposals closely paralleled the provisions in major public financing bills introduced earlier that year in the House and the Senate.

Pro: 'Public Financing Works'

Proponents based much of their argument for congressional public financing on a comparison between the operation of the 1976 presidential campaign, which was conducted with public funds derived from the $1 income tax checkoff, and the congressional races, which relied entirely on private contributions. Public financing cleaned up presidential races, they contended, removing the threat of the influence-buying corporate or individual contributors who dominated the 1972 campaign and others before.

With the presidential race closed to them, the special interest groups gravitated to congressional races and contributed record amounts, a development that drew the ire of campaign finance reformers and fueled their arguments for an extension of public financing. Wrote John Gardner, in a December 1976 article: "A lot of congressmen were bought and sold in 1976, just like the good old days except that the going rates were higher.... The money-heavy special interests couldn't buy themselves a president so they tried to buy as many members of Congress as they could."

Gardner's biting criticism was followed by release of a Common Cause study, which showed that PAC contributions to congressional candidates reached a record $22.6 million in 1976. The total represented an increase of $10 million over interest group giving in 1974.

More than two-thirds of the money was given by labor and business groups. Labor committee contributions amounted to $8.2 million, up from $6.3 million two years earlier. Business giving reached $7.1 million, a dramatic gain from $2.5 million in 1974.

The increase in corporate committee contributions reflected the rapid growth in business political action groups. In 1976 there were 468 corporate committees, 370 of them operating in their first federal election. Most of the remaining money to congressional candidates was provided by medical, dairy and ideological interest groups. Together they contributed $5.7 million in 1976.

Most reformers in Congress did not go so far as Gardner in denouncing interest groups, but they did argue that interest group contributions could look suspicious to the public at a time when Congress was held in low esteem. "More than anything else," observed Rep. Udall, a prime sponsor of congressional public financing legislation, "more than sex scandals or junkets or the issues of pay and fringe benefits — I believe the institution of Congress is damaged, both in public perception and the integrity of its functioning, by the escalating costs of campaigning and the massive amounts of special interest money being pumped into election campaigns."

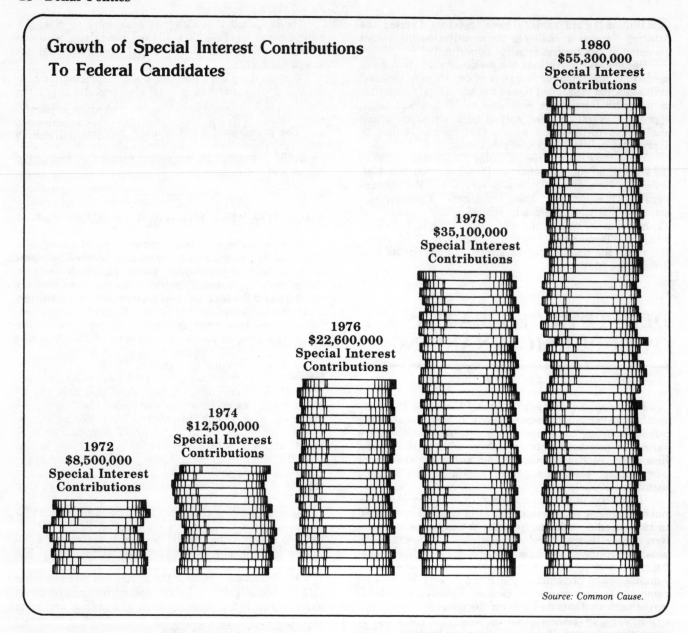

Growth of Special Interest Contributions To Federal Candidates

1980
$55,300,000
Special Interest
Contributions

1978
$35,100,000
Special Interest
Contributions

1976
$22,600,000
Special Interest
Contributions

1974
$12,500,000
Special Interest
Contributions

1972
$8,500,000
Special Interest
Contributions

Source: Common Cause.

While they conceded that the system was not perfect, Udall and his allies claimed that the 1976 presidential election provided a workable model of public financing. They generally agreed with critics who complained that the 1976 general election spending limit of $21.8 million for Carter and Ford was too low, cutting expenditures that could have generated more voter enthusiasm. Proponents of public financing also admitted there needed to be a greater role for political parties in federal campaigns, and public money made more easily available to independent and third party candidates. But these were only refinements, they argued, that could be easily corrected.

"Public financing works," said Udall in March 1977. "We know that it works. Carter and Ford had 40 million contributors last year and the largest was the taxpayer who paid one dollar. The system has proven itself in presidential campaigns and we are now ready to apply it to congressional races."

According to its supporters, public financing in 1976 was a bargain. Using money accumulated through the voluntary income tax checkoff, $72 million in public funds were disbursed in 1976 — $24 million in matching funds to presidential candidates in the primaries, about $4 million to the major parties to hold their national conventions and $43.6 million to Ford and Carter to finance their fall campaigns. According to campaign finance expert Herbert E. Alexander, direct campaign expenditures by presidential and national party committees in the general election were $15 million less than in 1972.

Public financing also encouraged competition, its supporters said. "Under the present system, the money goes to incumbents," noted Fred Wertheimer of Common Cause. In 1976 about 95 percent of the House incumbents seeking re-election won. Even business groups, which had a pro-Republican image, gave nearly all their money to incumbents that year, about half of them Democrats.

Con: 'Incumbents' Protection'

While public financing of congressional races drew strong opposition from Republican leaders and many Southern Democrats, the wide Democratic advantage in Congress kept even the most steadfast foes of federal campaign financing from being very optimistic. "Absent a miracle, you are going to get public financing," Rep. Bill Frenzel, R-Minn., told a March 1977 meeting of PAC representatives. "Whatever strategy you take," he went on to warn, "you better have a fall-back position. You are going to get something."

Although many members of Congress were unenthusiastic about public financing, organized opposition to it was slow to develop. Opponents were placed on the defensive, as advocates of public financing defined the issue as a case of good government against the special interests. Commented Frenzel, PACs had been tainted by "creeping John Gardnerism."

Yet Frenzel and his congressional allies saw little public demand for federal financing. When they returned to their districts, they said no one asked about it, and they cited as evidence of public apathy the low level of participation in the income tax checkoff — 27 percent marked it on their 1976 returns.

Critics of the reforms questioned the argument that public funding would encourage competition. All the assets were with the incumbents, they contended, and would ensure heavy Democratic majorities in Congress. While campaign spending limits would be the same for incumbents and their challengers, incumbents would have the tremendous advantage of up to $1 million each session in congressional perquisites — such as district offices, franked mail and office funds — that could be used to overwhelm any challenger restricted by a spending ceiling. Noting provisions in the House bill, Paul Weyrich, director of the Committee for the Survival of a Free Congress, observed critically: "It's an incumbents' protection bill. What you are really doing is taking $1,150,000 against $150,000."

Critics of public financing claimed the measure was little more than a raid on the public Treasury that they hoped, coming on the heels of a controversial pay raise for members of Congress, would prove unpopular with the public. "This measure," complained Weyrich, "amounts to a welfare bill for members of Congress. They have taken care of themselves one way already with the pay raise, and now they are going to take care of themselves another way with public financing."

Too Many Auditors

Opponents of congressional public financing also expressed concern with the size of the bureaucracy that would be required to implement any plan. They warned that a staggering number of lawyers, accountants and auditors would be needed at both the FEC in Washington and with the individual campaigns.

Altogether, the FEC employed about 200 workers in 1976, many of them to audit matching funds for presidential candidates during the primaries. According to an FEC spokesman, about 12 million pages of information were submitted by the 15 candidates and had to be reviewed by commission staff.

The coverage of congressional races was expected to pose an even greater problem. With hundreds of candidates to audit, the staff of the FEC would have to be drastically expanded. Warned John G. Murphy Jr., a former general counsel for the FEC: "This could be another area where a good idea becomes an unworkable one."

And the problems would not be limited to Washington. Douglas B. Huron, a counsel for the Carter campaign, indicated that in the publicly financed presidential race, Carter employed about 150 lawyers and 80 to 100 accountants around the country to keep his campaign in compliance with the law. Citing the difficulties they experienced, Huron concluded: "It takes more than good faith to comply with this law."

Critics warned that, besides establishing an unwieldy new bureaucracy and creating headaches for the candidates, the extension of public financing to congressional races would cut citizen participation in the campaigns. Again they cited the 1976 presidential experience as an example, when low contribution limits curtailed individual giving and most of the limited public money was plowed by the candidates into media advertising rather than local projects that would enthuse voters at the grass roots. Stated Joan Aikens, a Republican member of the FEC: "1976 was probably the cleanest election ever held and probably the dullest."

Boon to Labor

The final major argument, offered by Republican opponents of congressional public financing, was that the plan enhanced the importance of organized labor, giving Democratic candidates a major boost. Operating nominally non-partisan voter education and registration projects, organized labor could offer valuable assistance to Democratic candidates, which Republican political organizations could not match under the law and corporate PACs would not.

Business groups in 1976 showed neither the unity nor commitment of organized labor and drew a rebuke from Rep. Guy Vander Jagt, R-Mich., chairman of the Republican Congressional Campaign Committee. "Labor has more will to impact elections," he told a group of PAC representatives. "I'm not sure business and industry care as deeply to preserve their point of view as labor."

But even if corporate PACs did want to become more deeply involved with the Republicans, they were threatened by possible lawsuits launched by disgruntled stockholders.

Nonetheless, an extremely wide gap existed between business groups and organized labor concerning their impact on political campaigns. Vander Jagt cited a study that showed organized labor provided nearly $11 million worth of advertisements and other support for Carter in the 1976 general election, while corporate PACs gave Ford barely $40,000 in the same kind of help.

Public financing, Vander Jagt contended, could transfer this disparity to the congressional races. Labor involvement on behalf of the Democrats, he warned, would be like having "two prizefighters against one in 435 districts around the country."

1977: Senate Blocks Action

Despite the high hopes of public financing supporters early in the year, legislation was blocked in 1977 by a filibuster in the Senate and opposition in the House Administration Committee.

The Senate bill would have extended public financing to Senate general elections beginning in 1978. The provisions of the measure were fairly complex. It called for a spending ceiling for each Senate candidate of $250,000 plus 10 cents times the state's voting age population. In only four states would the spending ceiling have been more than $1 million: California ($1.69 million), New York ($1.48 million), Pennsylvania ($1.09 million) and Texas ($1.08 million).

Major party candidates automatically would have received 25 percent of their spending ceiling in federal funds and would have been eligible for matching funds on all individual contributions of $100 or less up to the spending limit. Only contributions received within 14 months of the general election would have been matchable.

Wealthy candidates accepting public financing would have been allowed to spend only $35,000 of their own money. If a candidate intended to exceed either the personal or total spending limit, he would have had to notify the FEC and his opponents. Rival candidates would then have been eligible to spend up to 62.5 percent more than the spending limit in matching funds.

Third party or independent candidates would not have been eligible for automatic grants but could have received matching funds if they raised $100,000 or 10 percent of the spending limit through individual contributions of $100 or less. Money to finance the bill would have come from the voluntary tax checkoff fund. About $20 million would have been needed for each election.

Senate leaders brought the public financing bill to the floor in July, believing that it had the best chance among Carter's reform proposals to win passage.

But they were unable to come close. On the first two cloture votes taken in an attempt to cut off a filibuster by Republicans and Southern Democrats, proponents of public financing fell 11 votes short of the 60 needed to invoke cloture. The third cloture motion was rejected Aug. 2 by a vote of 52-46 (R 4-33; D 48-13). Still eight votes short, the Democratic leadership accepted an amendment to remove the public financing section from the bill.

Left in the bill were revisions to the 1974 campaign reform law, most of which were designed to modify record-keeping problems that had surfaced during the 1976 campaign. Although the House did not take up the bill in 1977, many of the revisions were contained in legislation that cleared Congress in 1979.

With the public financing scheme scuttled in the Senate, attention focused for a brief period on the House, when 155 Democratic members signed a letter in October 1977 asking for prompt action on the legislation. The House plan called for the partial public financing of House general election campaigns beginning in 1978. Like its Senate counterpart, the House bill was complicated. It would have provided up to $25,000 in matching public funds for major party candidates who agreed to limit their spending to $150,000 and to submit to a random post-election audit. A candidate would have begun receiving federal money after first raising $10,000 in contributions of $100 or less, and would have continued receiving public funds in $5,000 increments after raising similar amounts in small contributions. The spending ceiling would have been lifted if one of the candidates exceeded the limit. The "innocent" candidate then would have been entitled to $50,000 more in matching funds.

The bill was referred to the House Administration Committee, and it soon became evident that most of the panel's members were opposed to quick consideration. The bill was effectively gutted when the committee voted to accept an amendment by Mendel J. Davis, D-S.C., to extend public financing to House primaries. All Republican panel members supported the amendment, as did most veteran Northern Democrats.

The bill's supporters argued that the Davis amendment would raise the cost of the program to dramatic — and unacceptable — levels, and would create administrative nightmares. Moreover, it was widely believed that legislation containing public financing of primaries could not pass the House because too many incumbents did not want to face the increased competition the financing might generate. Faced with that situation, and a pending amendment considered to be crippling, committee Chairman Frank Thompson Jr. decided to drop the bill.

1978: Another Defeat

Continuing support from some of the biggest names in Washington — including President Carter and House Speaker O'Neill — was not sufficient to move legislation calling for public financing of congressional elections in 1978. House backers of public financing failed in two parliamentary maneuvers to attach a public financing proposal to campaign finance bills.

Party Spending Bill

The first bill, devised by Democrats on the House Administration Committee, sought to limit PAC contributions as well as contributions from party committees. Democratic proponents contended that lowering those contribution limits provided a needed curb to increasing expenditures by the parties and special interests in House and Senate races. "The presidency can no longer be bought, but House and Senate seats can," said Rep. Thompson.

Democrats cited the proliferation of PACs — up from 608 at the end of 1974 to 1,261 in October 1977 — and increases in PAC and party spending as evidence that concentrated amounts of big money in House races were on the upswing. They noted Common Cause studies that showed interest group spending rose from $12.5 million in congressional races in 1974 to $22.6 million in 1976.

Party spending was also getting out of hand, committee Democrats said, arguing that four special elections in 1977 were little more than auctions. According to FEC figures, Republican Party committees contributed more than $400,000 to House candidates in 1977, compared with $27,000 by Democratic committees. Republicans won three of the four special elections, all seats previously held by Democrats.

Thompson and his allies contended that they had devised the measure on the assumption there was no majority for public financing, and defended it as an effective method of curbing campaign spending. They hoped that it might serve as a bargaining chip to gain public financing.

The White House was kept apprised during drafting of the House bill, but the controversial section on party and PAC limits was devised solely by Democrats on the committee and the majority staff.

Republicans were caught off guard when the bill was unveiled in early March. They had expected a non-controversial measure similar to the 1977 Senate-passed bill.

Yet, while they were initially surprised by the contents of the Democratic bill, GOP leaders reacted quickly with a barrage of criticism. Party spokesmen such as House Minority Leader John J. Rhodes of Arizona and Republican National Chairman Bill Brock denounced the proposed legislation as a blatant Democratic power grab and a vindictive reaction to GOP fund-raising successes. No abuse had been shown under the existing law, they claimed, charging that the Democrats were trying to change the rules in the middle of the election. "It's incredibly piggy," concluded Rep. Frenzel. "It's a punitive, anti-Republican bill."

Angry Republicans, viewing the lower limits as a direct threat to their ability to challenge entrenched Democratic incumbents, were particularly upset with the lids on party spending. These would have reduced from $30,000 to $10,000 the amount national, congressional and state party committees combined could contribute directly to a federal candidate in an election year. The bill also would have lowered from $20,000 to $5,000 the total amount the same party committees could have spent on behalf of a federal candidate in a general election for services such as polling and staff assistance. Transfers between party committees, allowed by existing law, would have been prohibited if they were made as a contribution or expenditure for a candidate. National and congressional committees, which operated under separate contribution limits, would have been combined under one limit.

An analysis of party contributions to House candidates in 1976 and a compilation of party finances for most of 1977 by the FEC showed how seriously the Republicans could have been crippled by the changes. In 1976, 39 percent of the Republican House candidates received more than $10,000 each from party committees. Only 11 percent of the Democratic candidates, in contrast, received at least $10,000 from party sources.

In 1977, while affiliated Democratic committees raised $8 million through most of the year, Republican committees raised more than three times as much, $24.3 million. The cash-on-hand disparity was even greater, with Republican committees enjoying a nearly 10-1 advantage over their Democratic counterparts, $8.2 million to $867,000.

Although they fought hard to restore the higher party contribution and expenditure limits in existing law, committee Republicans spent comparatively little time attacking the proposed cuts in PAC contributions to $5,000 from $10,000 per candidate in an election year.

In part, that lack of opposition was probably due to a realization that the reduction would apply to labor unions, which generally supported Democratic candidates, as well as to GOP-leaning corporate PACs. It was also becoming apparent to Republicans at the time that incumbents, primarily Democrats, were the main beneficiaries of PAC contributions.

Republicans gained an unusual ally when Common Cause announced it opposed the bill. Common Cause feared that the Democrats' proposal would polarize the House on the campaign finance issue, dimming the chances for winning needed Republican votes for a public financing provision they sought to be added to the bill on the House floor. "It's over-partisan," remarked Wertheimer. "They played into the hands of the opponents of public financing."

When the bill was reported in March 1978 by the House Administration Committee, South Carolina's Mendel Davis was the only committee Democrat to join the Republicans in opposition. But there was a fear among many Democrats that the drive for such a controversial campaign finance measure in the midst of an election year might recoil against their party. "The timing is terrible," complained Rep. Edward W. Pattison, D-N.Y. "My opponent will accuse me of taking money away from him."

Others agreed. In an effort to defuse some of the controversy, Thompson offered to restore party spending to its existing level. But for Republicans the Thompson offer was not enough, since it did not restore the provision allowing transfers of funds between different party committees. And in any case most Republicans were in no mood to accept the bill in any form. "The way the initial bill was dropped on us," said Frenzel, "we were past trusting."

By a vote of 198-209, a coalition of Republicans and disgruntled Democrats combined March 21 to defeat the rule to allow floor consideration of the leadership-backed measure. The vote had two practical effects. First, it blocked consideration of the bill's provision to lower the limits on spending by parties and PACs. Second, it killed any hopes of adding to the bill an amendment allowing public financing of House general election campaigns.

FEC Vehicle

In a second attempt to secure a public financing measure, supporters of the concept sought to make a generally non-controversial FEC authorization bill the vehicle for the public financing amendment.

Although some spending and contribution limits were altered, the amendment was basically similar to the public financing proposal that died in the House Administration Committee in 1977. It applied only to House general elections and was voluntary. The plan was scheduled to take effect in 1980.

Proponents made no effort to win a favorable rule for their amendment in the House Rules Committee, where they lacked majority support. Instead, they developed a complex alternative strategy, which hinged on defeating the rule for the FEC authorization bill on the floor and then winning approval of a substitute that would permit consideration of the public financing amendment.

But, by a vote of 213-196 (R 106-30; D 107-166), the House July 19 adopted the rule, refusing to open the FEC authorization measure to the public financing amendment.

The vote on the rule was billed as a clear indication of the strength of public financing forces in the House. "A vote on this rule," Thompson told his colleagues, "is tantamount to your position on public financing."

A diverse House coalition that included a majority of Republicans and Southern Democrats, as well as a significant number of veteran Northern, big-city Democrats, managed to stop the amendment. As in 1977, most Republicans viewed public financing as protection for incumbents and, paradoxically, many Democrats saw it as a boon to challengers.

The vote underscored a growing perception that congressional public financing was one of those "good government" issues that drew widespread praise in the abstract, but fewer votes as a concrete piece of legislation. "Support for public financing has always been very tentative," observed Rep. Pattison. "People make statements for it who are not really in favor of it."

Vigorous White House backing might have made a difference in 1978. But after making public financing of congressional races part of its election law package in 1977, the White House remained well in the background. "It's one of more than several examples that can be cited," said Republican cosponsor John Anderson of Illinois, "where they've paid lip-service to an idea but have not mounted a high-powered campaign behind it."

1979: House Rejection

Public financing of congressional general elections fared no better in 1979. For the third straight year the bill could not overcome determined opposition despite the backing of Carter, the Democratic congressional leadership, the House Democratic Study Group and a host of outside interest groups, led by Common Cause. To underscore its support, the House leadership gave the bill the symbolically important designation HR 1.

Heavy Lobbying

Proponents of HR 1, however, were trying to sell the bill in a climate that had become increasingly partisan. At their national headquarters less than a block from the House office buildings, the RNC and the National Republican Congressional Committee (NRCC) began to mount intensive drives to defeat HR 1. They aimed their lobbying efforts primarily at reducing the measure's GOP support, which included 20 Republican cosponsors (out of 155 House members who cosponsored HR 1).

At a January 1979 meeting, the RNC voted to oppose the bill. After that vote National Chairman Bill Brock worked actively to defeat the measure, writing articles of opposition in party journals and lobbying GOP House members to vote against it. He even threatened a legal challenge if HR 1 were to pass.

In a March letter to House Republicans, Brock warned that passage of HR 1, with its low spending ceilings, would threaten the GOP's survival. HR 1 is "the most blatantly pro-incumbent, anti-challenger bill that Congress has seen," Brock wrote. "HR 1 is a power play by the Democratic majority which seeks to control and stifle Republican challengers' access to the voters. Republicans do not favor suicide. They should not vote for HR 1."

"This is the type of 'reform,'" continued Brock in colorful language, "that Attila the Hun might have offered the hapless peasants who were unfortunate enough to lie in the path of his marauding band."

The NRCC sent a similar message to newspapers across the country. The committee mailed out editorial packages and responded to all pro-public-financing editorials that they saw. "We don't have the votes alone to defeat the bill," NRCC Executive Director Steven Stockmeyer said. "We must go public to bring pressure on the Democrats."

The Republicans were joined in their public lobbying effort by a variety of conservative and business groups that included the National Conservative Political Action Committee (NCPAC) and the Chamber of Commerce of the United States. NCPAC mounted the most visible effort. Beginning in February with a letter written over the signature of Republican Rep. Robert K. Dornan of California, NCPAC sent out nearly 1.5 million pieces of mail with enclosed post cards to be returned to House members.

NCPAC did some targeted media advertising, spending about $12,000 on anti-HR-1 radio and newspaper ads in Democratic Rep. Thomas S. Foley's district in eastern Washington. Foley was chairman of the House Democratic Caucus and had narrowly won re-election in 1978. In addition, the organization printed buttons and bumper stickers with the slogan, "Stop Welfare for Politicians."

The Chamber of Commerce adopted a lower profile but was just as committed as NCPAC to the bill's defeat. The demise of HR 1 was the chamber's No. 1 priority in 1979.

Supporters of HR 1 doubted that a mass mailing campaign alone would sway many votes, but they began letter-writing efforts of their own to show grass-roots support for the measure. Common Cause, which had long advocated congressional public financing, assumed the lead role in mobilizing outside pressure on Congress. It claimed the support of a diverse coalition of more than two dozen national organizations, ranging from the AFL-CIO to the United Methodist Church. Like the NRCC, Common Cause sent editorial packages to newspapers across the country, and it helped to coordinate the local lobbying efforts of the various proponents.

Perhaps the most unorthodox lobbying effort was conducted by Ralph Nader's Public Citizen Congress Watch. The organization encouraged local chapters in about 25 districts to send to their congressmen one-dollar bills with strings attached. The so-called "string campaign" was designed to show that under the existing system large campaign contributors gave with the expectation of having influence with the House member.

Internal lobbying of House members was handled by the Democratic majority on the House Administration Committee, the Democratic Study Group (DSG) and the leadership. Of this triumvirate, the DSG was the nerve center, combating negative accounts of HR 1 with a flow of positive information to House members.

Death Knell

Similar to earlier, unsuccessful versions, HR 1 offered a voluntary plan that would have provided public financing only to House general election campaigns. It was scheduled to take effect in 1980.

When the House Administration Committee markup began May 15, proponents scored an early victory by defeating an amendment to extend HR 1 to cover primary elections. Supporters feared that such a move would weaken severely the bill's prospects for House passage. The committee had adopted a similar amendment in 1977.

Throughout the markup, Republican committee members tried unsuccessfully to amend the bill to aid non-incumbents by lowering the eligibility threshold for participation in the public financing system. Although they were unable to win approval of any of their major amendments, they had no difficulty defeating the motion to report HR 1. It was killed May 24, when the committee voted 8-17 not to report it.

The bill was defeated by the same coalition that had blocked earlier public financing efforts. Eight Democrats defected to join with all nine Republicans in opposing the bill. Chairman Thompson noted that many of the bill's Democratic opponents represented safe, one-party districts and presumably did not want to encourage potential challengers. Two weeks later, House leaders sounded the official death knell when they announced that a whip count showed there were not enough votes to consider other ways of bringing HR 1 to the floor.

PAC Spending Bill

In the wake of the defeat of congressional public financing, supporters of campaign finance reform sought to curb political spending by promoting legislation designed to reduce PAC contributions to House candidates. They met with mixed success. Proponents won House passage of their measure in October 1979, but it died in the Senate the following year. *(PAC spending, Chapter 3, p. 41)*

Supporters of the bill, sponsored by Democratic Rep. David R. Obey of Wisconsin and Republican Rep. Tom Railsback of Illinois, steered it around the hostile House Administration Committee. They won permission from the Rules Committee to offer their measure on the House floor as an amendment to the non-controversial, Senate-passed FEC authorization bill.

The Obey-Railsback bill, which did not apply to Senate candidates, would have prohibited any House candidate from receiving PAC contributions totalling more than $70,000 in any two-year election cycle. It also would have reduced the amount one PAC could give a candidate to $6,000, from $10,000, in primary and general elections combined. Of the $6,000, no more than $5,000 could have been taken from any one PAC in a single election. Candidates facing runoffs would have had an $85,000 aggregate limit and could have accepted up to $9,000 from a single PAC with a $5,000 limitation on any one election.

The House debate on the Obey-Railsback proposal focused on supporters' objections to the recent growth in PAC spending and on the opponents' contention the plan was an "incumbent protection measure." Just under a quarter of all money given to House candidates in the 1978 general election came from PACs. While the share of PAC money in House races increased only slightly between 1976 and 1978 — from 22.4 percent to 24.8 percent — the actual amount given by all PACs to general election House candidates rose from less than $15 million to nearly $23 million.

"We have a new arms race on our hands; only the arms, instead of missiles, are campaign dollars," said Obey. "Whatever business does one year, labor does the next."

But Republicans saw the limitation on PAC spending as a move to thwart challengers. Minority Leader John Rhodes claimed Obey-Railsback "would reduce the ability of the challenger to raise funds in the early stages of a campaign and reduce the ability of PACs to participate in the political process."

Responding to the claim by Minnesota Republican Bill Frenzel that "challengers cannot make a viable challenge without PACs," Indiana Democrat Andy Jacobs Jr. remarked, "PAC contributions don't have the slightest thing to do with challengers or incumbents. PACs are in business to help those who agree with them, whether they are challengers or incumbents." Yet, an FEC study of PAC contributions in 1978 showed that labor, corporate and trade association PACs all gave about three times as much money to incumbents as they did to challengers.

One of the amendments adopted by the House raised the aggregate limit on PAC contributions that could be accepted by one candidate from $50,000, as the original Obey-Railsback plan proposed, to $70,000. It also increased the amount a PAC could contribute to a candidate from $5,000, as originally proposed, to $6,000 for primary and general elections combined.

Raising the aggregate limit may have made the difference in getting the votes to pass the bill. Nearly a third of the House elected in 1978 — 138 — received more than $50,000. But only 51 — 34 Democrats and 17 Republicans — topped the $70,000 mark.

House Speaker O'Neill and Majority Leader Jim Wright of Texas made impassioned pleas on the House floor in an effort to woo Democrats.

"A seat in the House of Representatives ought not to be like a seat on the New York Stock Exchange, up for sale to the highest bidder," Wright said to a chorus of boos from the Republican side.

By a 217-198 vote, the House Oct. 17, 1979, narrowly approved the Obey-Railsback bill. Democrats voted 188-74 in favor, while Republicans lined up 29-124 in opposition.

It marked a major victory for Common Cause and the AFL-CIO. Business groups and conservative organizations, who had lobbied strongly against the bill, were on the losing end. Frenzel, who led the opposition, attributed the bill's passage to pressure from the House leadership. "They felt this was a bill they had to have to protect their incumbents," Frenzel commented. "The leadership flexed its muscle."

But the Obey-Railsback bill stalled in the Senate. Republican Sens. Mark O. Hatfield of Oregon and Gordon J. Humphrey of New Hampshire blocked action on it in the closing months of 1979 by threatening a filibuster. That continuing threat prevailed the following year. Obey-Railsback proponents in the Senate maintained they could obtain the required 60 votes to cut off debate on the second or third try. But opponents claimed nearly unanimous support from the 41 Senate Republicans in the filibuster effort, and that prospect was enough to derail the legislation.

1979 FECA Amendments

In a rare demonstration of harmony on a campaign finance measure, Congress in late 1979 passed legislation to eliminate much of the red tape created by the FECA and to encourage political party activity. Agreement between the two chambers and between members of both parties on the legislation was not difficult because the drafters concentrated on solving the FECA's non-controversial problems.

The Senate passed its version in July, the House in September. Leaders of the House Administration and the Senate Rules committees informally worked out a compromise, which both houses adopted in December, clearing the bill for the president.

Carter's Signature

President Carter signed the legislation in January 1980, although the Justice Department had advised him to veto it. The department's objections focused on a provision barring federal employees from making campaign contributions to their own employers.

A literal reading of the law that existed prior to enactment of the 1979 amendments prohibited campaign contributions from one federal employee to another. But advisory letters from the Justice Department in 1974 and 1977 suggested that such contributions, if they were voluntary, were not prosecutable offenses.

Carter said that the section of the 1979 law represented a "severe infringement of federal employees' First Amendment rights." One apparent White House concern was that it would bar all federal workers from contributing to Carter's re-election campaign.

Democratic and Republican experts on election law legislation in the House and Senate told Carter in a January letter that the provision was intended to be interpreted narrowly so that, for example, it barred only employees of the White House Office from contributing to the re-election-campaign of an incumbent president.

Little Controversy

In putting together the bill, the drafters avoided politically explosive isues such as the public financing of congressional campaigns and cuts in party and PAC spending. Previous efforts in 1977 and 1978 to solve the non-controversial problems of the FECA became embroiled in a fight over these issues and were scuttled.

"The committees of both the House and Senate decided to lay aside the difficult issues on which we enjoy going to war and instead to pass the items in this bill which will simplify and make life easier for the candidates, for the parties, for volunteers and for everybody," Rep. Frenzel told the House in December. "We all knew that these changes had to be made, and now they are being made."

None of the changes was dramatic by itself, but as a whole the amendments constituted a significant overhaul of the FECA. The changes were designed to eliminate the difficulties that had surfaced during the 1976 election. Critics complained the law had imposed too much of a paperwork burden on candidates as well as political committees and that the FECA had stifled volunteer and grassroots party activity by similar red tape or by outright restrictions.

The 1979 amendments reduced the paperwork requirements in several ways. First, the bill decreased the maximum number of reports a federal candidate would have to file with the FEC during a two-year election cycle from 24 to nine. Second, candidates who raised or spent less than $5,000 in their campaigns would not have to file reports at all. In 1978 about 70 House candidates, including five winners, fell below the $5,000 threshold. Previously, all candidates were required to report their finances regardless of the amount. Also, candidates would have to report in less detail. The legislation raised the threshold for itemizing both contributions and expenditures to $200 from $100. *(Summary of major provisions, Appendix, p. 137)*

Party Role

In 1976 political party leaders complained that the FECA almost completely eliminated state and local party organizations from the presidential campaign. With federal funding in effect for the first time that year, there were restrictions on spending and tight limits on additional fund raising by parties and campaign committees.

Because they had only limited federal funds to spend, both the Democratic and Republican presidential campaigns focused on media advertising. At the same time, they cut back expenditures on items such as buttons and bumper stickers that traditionally were used in promoting grass-roots activity.

The 1979 bill permitted state and local party groups to purchase, without limit, campaign materials for volunteer activities to promote any federal candidate. Those items included buttons, bumper stickers, handbills, brochures, posters and yard signs. Also, those party organizations were allowed to conduct, without financial limit, certain kinds of voter registration and get-out-the-vote drives on behalf of presidential tickets.

The incidental mention of a presidential candidate on the campaign literature of local candidates was no longer counted as a campaign contribution. Previously, such references had been counted and that resulted in paperwork problems in reporting those costs to the FEC. Local party groups would be required to report their finances only if annual spending for volunteer activities exceeded $5,000 or if costs for non-volunteer projects were more than $1,000. Before, such groups had to file campaign reports if total spending exceeded $1,000 a year.

Volunteer political activity by individuals was encouraged by raising to $1,000 from $500 the amount of money a person could spend in providing his home, food or personal travel on behalf of a candidate without reporting it to the FEC as a contribution. If the volunteer activity were on behalf of a political party, the person could spend up to $2,000 before the amount was treated as a contribution.

ENTERING THE 1980s: IS DEREGULATION AHEAD?

Nearly a decade of major overhauls and minor tinkering had produced a more smoothly functioning campaign finance system. But it was one that many people agreed still had plenty of kinks in it.

Defenders argued that imperfections should be expected in legislation that rapidly transformed campaign finance at the federal level from a largely unregulated field to one that was strictly regulated. They contended that critics of the system were guilty of overexpectations.

In an article entitled "Reform as Bogeyman: The Law Without a Constituency," former FEC Deputy Staff Director Bill Loughrey wrote: "It was not the intent of this legislation to: reverse the long-term decline of the political parties, assure that campaigns (which have been historically underfunded) are adequately financed, prevent the direct bribery of public officials, or allow campaigns to continue their unregulated, free-wheeling ways of raising and spending funds. Not unexpectedly, observers and critics who erroneously assumed that campaign reform legislation would achieve these goals or cure these ills have been disillusioned."

But defenders such as Loughrey have been in the minority. Critics have become increasingly visible, including some longtime supporters of campaign finance reform who had hoped the law would increase citizen participation and reduce the advantages of the well known and well heeled. Instead, the loopholes that dotted the law had created a system that many felt was something less.

In an April 1981 issue of *Legal Times of Washington*, two former FEC staff members — Carol Darr and Susan Tifft — wrote critically that "The election law has become in effect like tax code, manipulated by those who have the most to gain or lose. The unhappy consequence is a statute that is more loophole than law, and a campaign finance system that gives the American voter the worst of both worlds: the appearance of reform with little of the substance."

The views of Darr and Tifft dovetailed with the conclusions of the 1979 study by the Harvard University Institute of Politics. In reviewing the FECA for the House

Harvard Proposed Campaign Law Changes

In 1979 Harvard University's Institute of Politics released what probably has been the most comprehensive study of the Federal Election Campaign Act (FECA). The study, undertaken for the House Administration Committee, concluded that the FECA has had a major impact on how federal candidates and political parties operate.

The study's major findings were that individual contribution limits have been set too low, forcing candidates to turn to political action committees (PACs) and their own personal wealth; that in enforcing the law, the Federal Election Commission (FEC) has placed extreme burdens on candidates, their committees and contributors; and that the role of political parties has been weakened because of the first two problems.

The Harvard study made the following recommendations:

● The individual contribution limit should be raised from $1,000 to $3,000 per election.
● Contribution limits for individuals should be higher for presidential and senatorial contests than for House races.
● Tax credits for contributions to candidates and parties should be expanded, but the tax credit for contributions to PACs should be eliminated.
● National and state parties ought to be allowed to contribute more than PACs to congressional and senatorial campaigns.
● Local parties should not have to file detailed reports with the FEC if they raise and spend less than $2,000 on federal candidates within their area.
● State party committees should be allowed to spend up to $5,000 on behalf of their candidates without having to file detailed FEC reports.
● Reports filed with the FEC should disclose the names of contributors giving $500 or more, rather than contributors of more than $100.
● Candidates raising and spending less than $5,000 in an election should not have to file detailed FEC reports.

Administration Committee, the Harvard group noted that much of the law either did not work or had unexpected consequences. It pointed to the declining impact of political parties and the increasing reliance of congressional candidates on their personal income or PACs for campaign money. Washington-based PACs, the study maintained, had tended to nationalize campaign fund raising rather than returning it to the grass roots. To remedy the situa-

tion, the Harvard report recommended a strong dose of deregulation and a tripling of the individual contribution limit. (Harvard study, this page)

Some of the recommendations were contained in the 1979 FECA amendments and the mood for further deregulation continued in the early 1980s.

Conservative Initiatives

Throughout the 1970s the impetus for campaign finance legislation came from the political left. But in the early 1980s the conservatives had the votes in Congress to seize the initiative. The spotlight shifted from congressional public financing and PAC spending curbs to other aspects of the FECA. Hearings before the Senate Rules Committee in November 1981 identified several areas of interest, including the existence of the FEC itself.

But there was a general consensus that any changes in the law must take effect after the 1982 political season, so as not to create havoc in the mid-term elections.

A bipartisan task force was appointed by Senate leaders in the summer of 1981 to lay the groundwork for the hearings, which focused on the FECA's application to congressional races. Hearings on the law's operation in presidential campaigns were to wait until 1982, after the Senate Rules Committee had received a report from the Harvard University Institute of Politics on presidential campaign financing.

Contribution Ceilings

Central to any campaign finance debate are the contribution limits. In 1981 an individual could give no more than $1,000 to a federal candidate in any primary, runoff or general election. An individual also could not exceed an aggregate $25,000 in contributions per year to all federal campaigns. A PAC could not give more than $5,000 to a candidate per election. (Limits on campaign contributions, box, p. 26)

These limits were set in 1974. And by 1981 inflation had, in effect, lowered the ceilings by 50 percent, according to Herbert Alexander. One result of this, he said, was increasing independent expenditures.

No limit existed on independent spending. The only restriction was that an independent spender have no contact with the candidate he sought to aid. Independent expenditures surged in the 1980 election season — a development lamented by RNC Chairman Richards.

Although GOP candidates were the major beneficiaries of independent spending, Richards believed that this phenomenon hurt the electoral process because the activities of independent groups such as NCPAC, which spent heavily in the 1980 campaign, could backfire against those they were intended to aid.

Common Cause's Fred Wertheimer suggested that Congress pass legislation granting any candidate confronting an advertising campaign funded by independent expenditures an equal amount of free broadcast time to respond.

A contrary view came from Bill Loughery, who did not see independent spending as a big menace. In a study released in February 1981, he found that relatively few people gave near the individual limit now, suggesting that higher limits would have little impact on those contributions and would not thwart independent spending.

Regardless, sentiment existed in Congress for increasing the individual limit to at least $2,000 per election.

Limits on Campaign Contributions

This table shows the limits on campaign contributions for federal elections. The figures are those in effect following the 1979 amendments to the 1971, 1974 and 1976 financing laws.

Contribution from:	To candidate or his/her authorized committee	**To national party committees[5] (per calendar year)[6]	**To any other committee (per calendar year)[6]	Total contributions (per calendar year)[7]
Individual	$1,000 per election[3]	$20,000	$5,000	$25,000
Multicandidate committee[1]	$5,000 per election	$15,000	$5,000	No limit
Party committee	$1,000 or $5,000[4] per election	No limit	$5,000	No limit
Republican or Democratic senatorial campaign committee,[2] or the national party committee, or a combination of both**	$17,500 to Senate candidate per calendar year[6] in which candidate seeks election	Not applicable	Not applicable	Not applicable
Any other committee	$1,000 per election	$20,000	$5,000	No limit

1. A multicandidate committee is any committee with more than 50 contributors which has been registered for at least six months and, with the exception of state party committees, has made contributions to five or more federal candidates.

2. Republican and Democratic senatorial campaign committees are subject to all other limits applicable to a multicandidate committee.

3. Each of the following elections is considered a separate election: primary election, general election, run-off election, special election and party caucus or convention which, instead of a primary, has authority to select the nominee.

4. Limit depends on whether or not party committee is a multicandidate committee.

**See footnote 6.

5. For purposes of this limit, national party committee includes a party's national committee, the Republican and Democratic Senate and House campaign committees and any other committee established by the party's national committee, provided it is not authorized by any candidate.

6. In 1976 only, and solely in the case of contribution limits established in the 1976 amendments (those indicated by double asterisk), the calendar year extends from May 11 (date of enactment of the act) through Dec. 31, 1976.

7. Calendar year extends from Jan. 1 through Dec. 31, 1976. Individual contributions made or earmarked before or after 1976 to influence the 1976 election of a specific candidate are counted as if made during 1976.

Source: Federal Election Commission.

Critics have contended that the individual limit had not been very cost effective. A candidate was forced to spend the same amount of time with a contributor to raise $1,000 as he did to raise $50,000 or $100,000 from the same person in the past. *(Candidate fund raising, Chapter 4, p. 57)*

Columnist and veteran Democratic campaign manager Mark Shields called this the "ultimate irony" of the 1974 campaign law. "The law that was supposed to diminish the role of money in politics has forced candidates to spend more time and effort raising money," he said.

Many candidates have had to turn to direct mail, since this was the only way that large numbers of small contributors could be reached. But direct-mail fund raising is ex-

pensive and usually most successfully exploited by candidates on the left or right side of the political spectrum, such as George C. Wallace and George McGovern.

Low contribution limits also increased the importance of personal wealth. With individual contributions by outsiders severely limited, the person of independent means becomes a more potent candidate. In response, Democratic Sen. Alan Cranston of California introduced a bill in 1981 that would enable a candidate to accept unlimited amounts of money from any contributor if his opponent spent more than $35,000 of his own money.

And then there are the parties. The existing amount that an individual could contribute to a national party committee in a calendar year was $20,000. While Republicans appeared to be in no hurry to raise that limit, they wanted to be able to contribute more to their candidates. With an effective direct-mail operation tapping small contributors, national Republican committees raised more than $110 million in the 1980 campaign. Relying on a much narrower base of large donors, national Democratic committees raised about one-fifth as much. *(Political parties, Chapter 5, p. 71)*

'Draft' Committees

If Congress did decide to tinker with the contribution limits it could also decide to close the loophole that allowed contributors to donate unlimited amounts of money to "draft" committees. That loophole was underscored by the Supreme Court in October 1981 when it let stand a May 1981 ruling by the District of Columbia federal Court of Appeals that, in effect, told the FEC it had no jurisdiction over committees set up to draft candidates if the committees had no formal connection with a candidate.

The FEC had taken the PAC of the International Association of Machinists to court when it refused to supply information about some $30,000 it gave to nine state draft committees trying to persuade Sen. Kennedy of Massachusetts to seek the 1980 Democratic presidential nomination. The appeals court ruled that the FEC did not have the right to subpoena the Machinists PAC because it had no regulatory power over draft committees.

The Democratic Senatorial and Congressional Campaign committees, in particular, expressed fears that draft committees would proliferate rapidly if the loophole were not closed. "The invitation to subterfuge is patent," explained the leaders of the two committees in a joint statement. "By the mere device of encouraging a 'draft' effort, a putative candidate may wait in the wings while his or her supporters accumulate funds in unlimited amounts and fund an extravagant campaign effort."

But the director of the Machinists PAC, Bill Holayter, doubted this would occur. "Candidates cannot afford to take the risk of joining a subterfuge effort," he said, suggesting that the decision would free only true drafts.

PAC Spending

A stickier question was whether to lift the cap on PAC spending. PACs already had been criticized for their growing influence in elections. Unlike individuals, no aggregate limit on the amount they could contribute existed. Because of the widespread belief among political contributors that the number of candidates helped is more important than the amount contributed to each one, the PAC community had done little to push for raising the $5,000 ceiling. Also, members of Congress very well could be wary of appearing to be aiding PACs by raising the limits.

If a consensus existed on campaign finance regulation, it was that the 1979 Obey-Railsback bill would not be heard from again. Republicans argued that the bill would protect incumbents, who have the advantage of high visibility, and hinder challengers, who need PAC money to make up the difference. Wishing to gain control of the House from the majority Democrats, the Republicans had an interest in looking out for challengers.

Presidential Race Public Funding

The FECA's coverage of the presidential nomination process may also be changed. A limit existed in 1981 on the amount a candidate could spend in each state based on its voting age population. Candidates taking federal financing had to comply with the limits, but doing so made for headaches.

That was especially true in early contests such as the New Hampshire primary, where the ceiling was low ($294,400 in 1980) and the stakes high. Candidates used subterfuges to allow them to spend more money. They might spend the night in neighboring Massachusetts, for example, so they could count the money spent for lodging against their Bay State limit.

After a conference sponsored by the Citizens' Research Foundation, a political-money study group directed by Herbert Alexander, 20 officers of the 1976 and 1980 presidential campaigns called for removing the state caps. In a statement issued in June 1981, the aides deemed the state limits "ineffective and unduly restrictive." David Ifshin, a volunteer lawyer for the Carter campaign, and John Sears, head of the Reagan drive until his February 1980 ouster, were among the signers.

Criticism of FEC

But the immediate target of many legislators is the FEC itself. The unpopularity of the FEC in Congress and the political community was apparent during the 1981 Senate hearings, where few witnesses spoke kindly of the agency. *(FEC future, chapter 2, p. 29)*

Paul Kamenar, an election law attorney, contended that the commission was overly anxious to take petty offenses to court because it had young lawyers eager for trial experience.

Republican Sen. Roger W. Jepsen of Iowa decried the FEC for "unrestrained power," which he said allowed it to operate as "detective, prosecutor and judge." In November 1981, Jepsen sought to limit the FEC to six months' fiscal 1982 funding. But his amendment, attached to the stopgap funding measure for the federal government, lost on the Senate floor, 65-31. The Jepsen amendment sought to grant the agency an authorization only until March 1982 and forbid spending by it beyond that date, pending further congressional action.

Jepsen, who wanted ultimately to abolish the FEC, reasoned that a half-year appropriation would force quicker revamping of the FECA. "Recognize that the simplest law can very often by the best law," Jepsen explained during the hearings. "I firmly believe that returning to a simpler election law will go much further in restoring the public's confidence in their elected officials."

Commissioner John W. McGarry, then the FEC chairman, conceded that the agency had "made some mistakes" in its early years but he expressed confidence that it would function more smoothly in the future.

2

The FEC: A Clouded Future

The Federal Election Commission is an agency that seemingly cannot win. It was created in 1974 to clean up federal campaign financing in the wake of the Watergate scandal. And some believe it has done so. But the FEC hardly has won resounding acclaim. Many in the political community unite in vilifying it.

The FEC is a regulatory body gone amok, critics say. Their main complaints about the commission are: It issues overly restrictive, nit-picking rules. It is beset by inefficient administration and takes too long to complete audits. It shows favoritism in its enforcement actions, especially toward incumbents. One reason given for its alleged kowtowing to Capitol Hill is that the lawmakers gave themselves a stranglehold on it, hobbling the commission structurally when they created it and holding veto power over its regulations.

Unlike most agencies, the FEC has no constituency to stand up for it. Consumer advocates usually support the Federal Trade Commission, farmers sometimes back the Agriculture Department and environmentalists often defend the Fish and Wildlife Service. But when the FEC is attacked, finding allies to defend it is difficult.

Even though Congress holds considerable power over the FEC, legislators are probably the group least satisfied with it. They regard the commission in the same way an exasperated father looks upon a delinquent son.

Congress confronted its problems with the agency in late 1981 but ended up postponing any decisions on what should be done. Unloved and vulnerable, the FEC found itself being held hostage by members pressing for changes in the campaign finance laws before the 1982 elections. Some wanted to abolish the commission outright or give it funding for only six months. Several proposals to relax the law were put forth. Meanwhile, the FEC's bipartisan makeup was in flux, with half of the six commissioners awaiting Senate confirmation as Reagan administration appointees. *(Commission status, box, p. 31)*

'Bunch of Nit-pickers'

While it was unlikely that the FEC would lose its fight for life, especially in an election year, the furor pointed up the extent of the commission's disaffection on Capitol Hill. Rep. Bill Frenzel, R-Minn., ranking minority member of the House Administration Committee (which oversees the FEC) and an expert on election law, offered a typical view.

"The FEC is remorseless in trying to stifle politics," he said in 1980. "If it continues to be so picky, it might find itself with a good deal less authority." By September 1981 Frenzel was saying: "They have become a bunch of nit-pickers."

For the FEC, that reputation was almost unavoidable, in the view of Benjamin M. Vandegrift, a former special counsel with the commission. To comply with its mandate under the law, he said, the FEC must go after even the smallest cases, with the result that "No matter what you do, you make people mad."

Despite the considerable criticism directed at it, the FEC had won praise — sometimes grudging — for helping to clean up politics. Probably no government agency ever can end attempts to curry officeholders' favor with money. The FEC, however, apparently managed to stop the vast, secret transfers of cash that fueled the Watergate abuses. While previous election laws required disclosure, they lacked teeth.

"Before we had this agency, there was no one to enforce campaign finance laws, so nobody took the laws seriously," said Fred Wertheimer, president of Common Cause. "The FEC has changed that."

A former commission chairman, Robert O. Tiernan, said that the agency's biggest strength "has been public disclosure that gives people, through the news media, an idea of who gave to their congressman."

Although many of the FEC's activities attracted disdain, its public records section was regarded by many of its users as well-run and accessible. In addition, the commission had been applauded for its efforts to educate candidates on how to comply with the dauntingly complex election law.

Background

Until the 1970s, the law governing campaign financing was the Corrupt Practices Act of 1925, which set a statutory spending maximum of $25,000 for a Senate race and $10,000 for a House campaign. It went largely unenforced, though, and candidates spent far more than legally allowed. *(History of campaign spending legislation, Chapter 1, pp. 3-24)*

Campaign finance reports were supposed to be filed with the Clerk of the House or the Secretary of the Senate, although compliance with this requirement was lax. Because of the burgeoning cost of political activity, Congress passed the Federal Election Campaign Act of 1971 (PL 92-225), placing limits on expenditures for media advertising and mandating stricter standards for financial disclosure. The torrent of stories about under-the-table political giving in the 1972 presidential campaign was the catalyst for the current era of campaign regulation.

The landmark legislation in 1974 (PL 93-443) placed limits on contributions to federal candidates, required minute disclosure of campaign financial activity and established the FEC to police the law. The commission also was charged with distributing federal money to presidential campaigns.

The commission, in operation just eight months, got a jolt when the U.S. Supreme Court declared it unconstitutional. The Jan. 30, 1976, *Buckley v. Valeo* ruling found, among other things, that the structure of the FEC, an executive agency, violated the separation-of-powers doctrine of the Constitution because four of its six members were appointed by Congress. All should be named by the president, the court said. (*Excerpts from* Buckley v. Valeo *decision, Appendix, p. 120*)

During the more than two months it took to get new legislation (PL 94-283) on the books, the FEC could not operate. As a result, matching funds for 1976 presidential candidates were frozen, and the agency fell far behind in auditing their campaigns.

Reacting to numerous complaints, Congress in December 1979 passed a measure (PL 96-187) to remedy perceived defects in both the law and the workings of the FEC. None of the changes was major. To remedy complaints that the FEC moved too slowly on issuing opinions, for example, Congress mandated that it give an answer within 60 days. Before, no deadlines existed. (*Major provisions of 1971 legislation and later amendments, Appendix, p. 133*)

CONFLICT: A WAY OF LIFE FOR THE FEC

The FEC never can be free of controversy, in the opinion of former Chairman Max L. Friedersdorf, a political veteran who lobbied on Capitol Hill for Presidents Nixon, Ford and Reagan before and after his 1979-81 stint on the commission. He resigned his White House post in late 1981 to become U.S. consul general in Bermuda.

"The election of public officials is by its nature controversial," Friedersdorf said in a 1980 interview. "Politics is a rough, tough game and we have to expect that people will be unhappy with us."

The FEC found this out in one of its earliest rulings, when it outraged organized labor. By a 4-2 vote in November 1975, the commission permitted Sun Oil's political action committee, called SunPAC, to be administered by the corporation and let it solicit voluntary contributions from certain employees as well as stockholders. By clearing up ambiguities surrounding how corporate PACs could be set up, the SunPAC ruling encouraged an explosion of company political committees.

Labor, then predominant in the PAC field, was particularly upset with former Rep. Neil O. Staebler (Mich.,

1963-65), the lone Democrat who had joined the three Republicans in approving the SunPAC opinion. When Staebler's FEC term expired in 1977, labor interests prevailed on President Carter not to reappoint him.

Politics

Nomination to the commission — which is composed of six members, three from each party — is a highly political matter. Republican senators successfully blocked Carter's choice for a GOP vacancy, Sam Zagoria, whom they viewed as too liberal. They almost managed to do the same thing in 1979 to Frank P. Reiche, a Republican whose partisan commitment they also questioned.

On the Democratic side, House Speaker Thomas P. O'Neill Jr., D-Mass., forced Carter to withdraw his backing of Susan B. King, an FEC aide who once worked for the National Committee for an Effective Congress. O'Neill reportedly objected to King as "a do-good, Common Cause type." Carter later named her to the Consumer Product Safety Commission, from which she resigned following the inauguration of President Reagan.

Some critics object to the fact that the commissioners generally have political backgrounds. They say the possibilities for cronyism and indiscretions are great when commissioners are called upon to regulate old friends.

In 1976 the FEC suffered a major embarrassment because of the loose tongue of then-Chairman Vernon W. Thomson, a Republican and former Wisconsin governor (1957-59) and U.S. House member (1961-74). Talking at a cocktail party with a one-time House colleague, Melvin Laird, Thomson let slip that the FEC had subpoenaed records of Democratic senatorial candidate Jim Sasser of Tennessee. Word reached *The Nashville Banner*, which published the story.

While the Justice Department later declined to prosecute Thomson for the breach of confidence, the blot remained on the commission's record. (The FEC cleared Sasser of any violations of federal campaign finance law. Thomson, reappointed by President Carter to succeed Friedersdorf, continued to serve until Reagan gave an interim appointment to Joan D. Aikens in late 1981.)

Having politicians regulate politicians presented an even more acute question in the case of Tiernan, a former House member (D-R.I., 1967-75) who also remained on the commission for most of 1981 after his term expired April 30. He was succeeded by Danny Lee McDonald.

As a commissioner, Tiernan voted on matters affecting campaign debts. But as of June 30, 1981, he still had a debt of $3,929.88 left over from his unsuccessful 1974 race, leaving himself open to conflict-of-interest charges. This made no difference, he asserted, because "I'm eliminating my debt under the law."

In the view of some observers, these kinds of problems indicated that the commission should be reconstituted with a non-political membership. "It shouldn't be a *bipartisan* agency, it should be a *non-partisan* agency," said Herbert E. Alexander, a University of Southern California scholar specializing in campaign finance. "What it needs is constitutional lawyers and political scientists."

The opposing argument was voiced by ex-commissioner Friedersdorf, who lobbied Congress for Presidents Nixon and Ford before leaving the FEC to serve in the Reagan White House. "It's important to have people from

FEC Status Tied to Election Law Revision

The 97th Congress adjourned its first session in December 1981 without having resolved any of the substantive issues that swirled around the Federal Election Commission throughout the year. Stopgap funding for the federal government, including the commission's operations, was provided by continuing resolution, while interim appointments in December assured a full panel of six commissioners as the 1982 elections approached. But it remained for the second session to dispose of the eight-year-old agency's fate.

The postponement of a decision was primarily the work of a bipartisan group in the Republican-controlled Senate, where the FEC's supporters and opponents concentrated their legislative maneuvering in 1981. Among those most active in shaping the non-decision were Majority Leader Howard H. Baker Jr., R-Tenn., Rules Committee Chairman Charles McC. Mathias Jr., R-Md., and Sen. Alan Cranston, D-Calif.

By opening hearings in November on a clutch of proposals to amend the commission's charter, Mathias effectively frustrated the efforts of FEC's most militant critics to kill off the commission before the start of a campaign year. On the very day hearings began — Nov. 20 — the Senate killed, 65-31, a move by Sen. Roger W. Jepsen, R-Iowa, to limit further FEC funding to six months.

Proposed Revisions

At least five specific proposals for revamping federal election law had surfaced when the hearings opened:

● **Eliminate the FEC.** Jepsen, in legislation he planned to introduce, proposed to close the FEC and transfer its functions to the General Accounting Office (GAO) and the Justice Department. An Office of Federal Elections would be created within the GAO to collect disclosure statements and investigate complaints. Also under this plan, federal candidates and political committees would be reimbursed with federal funds for the cost of complying with the law's reporting requirements.

Critics of the proposal said the Justice Department would simply ignore minor election law matters. A similar arrangement with GAO and Justice prevailed in the early 1970s, they said, and it worked poorly.

● **Raise the Ceilings.** Mathias, saying it was "just a vehicle" for discussion, had introduced a bill (S 1851) that would increase the legal limits on giving, which some felt were too low because of the inflation that had occurred since they were set in 1974.

Mathias would lift the cap on individual contributions to a single candidate from $1,000 in a primary and $1,000 in a general election to $4,000 over

an entire campaign. The amount an individual may give to all campaigns would move from $25,000 per year to $40,000.

● **Offset Wealthy Candidates.** Under existing law any person was allowed to spend an unlimited amount on his or her own campaign, thus giving the rich an advantage in politics. As a remedy, a bill (S 1766) drafted by Sen. Cranston would remove any limits on outside contributions to a candidate if his opponent had spent more than $35,000 of his own money on the campaign.

● **End Use of Labor Union Dues.** Unions use members' dues to operate their political action committees (PACs). Sen. Jesse Helms, R-N.C., proposed to outlaw this practice with his bill, S 1550. Corporations still would be able to use company funds to administer their PACs.

● **General Streamlining.** Sen. Arlen Specter, R-Pa., was drafting a bill (S 1899) he introduced after the hearings that would shorten reports that had to be filed within 20 days of an election. Candidates would have to list only donations greater than $1,000. The existing reporting threshold was $200. Specter also would make the full-time FEC commissioners part-time and wipe out state-by-state spending limits in presidential primaries.

Other proposals were likely to result from Rules Committee consideration of a presidential campaign financing study that it had commissioned in mid-1981 for delivery in January 1982. The $100,000 study was assigned to an elections research team headed by Yale political scientist F. Christopher Arterton at Harvard University's Institute of Politics.

FEC Criticized

The Rules Committee hearings demonstrated the unpopularity of the FEC in Congress and the political community. Witness after witness criticized it for alleged nit-picking and over-regulation.

Even those who defended the commission against Jepsen had few kind words for the agency. Sen. Wendell H. Ford, D-Ky., complained that in his 1980 re-election drive he was forced to re-do a campaign finance disclosure statement because a $25 contributor from Chicago had not reported that the city was located in Illinois. Yet Ford said the FEC "has accomplished its most important goal: For the first time the election law is taken seriously."

"No doubt the commission made some mistakes along the way," conceded John W. McGarry, the FEC's 1981 chairman. "We needed an opportunity for maturing."

Jepsen had hoped to speed up the timetable for election law change by limiting FEC funding to six months.

a political background because we deal in the nitty-gritty of politics," Friedersdorf said. "I've been in Washington 20 years and I'm still learning. If I came in here without any knowledge of how politics works, I'd be lost."

A practical question also exists, Friedersdorf noted. "Who else would get confirmed by the Senate? Congress doesn't want naive people regulating them."

Problems

Despite the commissioners' partisan backgrounds and supposed kinship with the world of politics, members of Congress and others in the electoral process never seem to stop grousing about the agency. Besides complaining about its alleged pickiness and inefficiency, they accuse it of protecting incumbents against challengers and of being too much a creature of Congress to be an effective regulator of it.

Over-regulation

The FEC issues rules that are too restrictive, some contend. "Their strict construction, their literal interpretation of the act has had a chilling effect on the constitutional rights," said H. Richard Mayberry, an election law attorney specializing in advising company PACs.

Mayberry pointed to a 1979 decision forbidding Milwaukee-based Rexnord Inc. to use corporate funds for a newspaper ad urging people to register to vote. "They [Rexnord] weren't trying to influence an election," declared Mayberry. "Rexnord said, 'Forget it' about the ad. And free speech is supposed to be constitutionally protected."

As the FEC interpreted the law, the ad could be paid for only by Rexnord's PAC. Corporate funds could be used to encourage voter registration only if the drive were restricted to company stockholders or executives, the FEC ruled. (Six months later, in May 1980, the commission in effect reversed its Rexnord ruling.) *(Commission deadlocks, box, p. 33)*

"There are traditions in politics that you have to accept, and you can't be as narrow and legalistic as the FEC is," said political scientist Alexander. "Take the Okonite case and Congressman Roe. They had no business getting into that stuff."

In July 1976, five weeks after Rep. Robert A. Roe's primary victory and four months before the general election, Okonite Co. ran ads in four newspapers thanking him for his aid in saving the company. The New Jersey Democrat had helped the failing business secure a $13 million federal grant to fund its new employee stock ownership trust. The money enabled Okonite to stay open.

The trouble was that the Okonite ads were paid for with $12,183 in corporate funds. Under federal election law, corporations may not make direct political contributions. Corporate financial influence in elections is legal solely through a separate, segregated fund composed of voluntary donations generally from officers and stockholders — namely, a PAC. (In late 1981 the Athens Lumber Co. of Georgia sued the FEC to test the legality of the ban on corporate contributions.)

The FEC general counsel found in the Okonite case that there was no collaboration between the company and the Roe re-election campaign. Plus, he noted that the ads did not "expressly call for Roe's election." Nevertheless, he concluded, "they unmistakably serve as a tribute to him" and fell within the "ambit" of the law. Okonite paid a civil penalty of $500.

In 1979 the FEC came under fire for its proposed regulations on political debates. Among other things, the regulations permitted news organizations for the first time to sponsor candidate forums. Before, news media sponsorship was considered an illegal corporate contribution.

However, the media, particularly the broadcast industry, objected to a provision in the regulations stipulating that a debate include at least two candidates and not promote one contender over another. They argued that the provision violated First Amendment freedoms.

"The law never intended for the FEC to insinuate itself into regulating the news media," said Steve Nevas, a counsel for the National Association of Broadcasters. The Senate voted down an early version of the regulations. The FEC resurrected them and, although it softened the rules on the media, this did not quiet the objections. In spite of the media protests, Congress cleared the regulations in March 1980.

Another FEC action concerning the media — its inquiry into the promotion of a 1980 *Reader's Digest* story about the involvement of Sen. Edward M. Kennedy, D-Mass., in the 1969 accident at Chappaquiddick — also provoked a large outcry. The Digest sued to halt the probe, which it said infringed its First Amendment rights to advertise the story. But the FEC won approval from U.S. District Court for the Southern District of New York March 19, 1981, to proceed with its investigation into whether the Digest's promotion efforts — it sent out video-

---

The CLITRIM Incident

Although the pamphlet only cost $135 to publish, the Federal Election Commission decided to take its author to court. Shortly before the 1976 election, the Central Long Island Tax Reform Immediately Committee (CLITRIM) distributed the pamphlet on the tax voting record of then-Rep. Jerome A. Ambro, D-N.Y. After Ambro complained, the commission hauled the tax watchdog group into federal court because it had failed to file an FEC financial disclosure report.

Four years and thousands of dollars in legal costs later, Chief Judge Irving Kaufman of the 2nd Circuit Court of Appeals threw out the suit. Kaufman castigated the FEC for violating First Amendment rights, saying, "I find this episode somewhat perverse."

The CLITRIM incident caused an uproar on Capitol Hill. At a fiscal 1981 authorization hearing by the Senate Rules Committee March 26, 1980, Sen. Mark O. Hatfield, R-Ore., blasted the commission for regulatory overkill, at one point sarcastically asking FEC General Counsel Charles Steele where he had gone to law school (Harvard).

Deadlocks on the Election Commission

The National Transportation Safety Board, the Nuclear Regulatory Commission and the Securities and Exchange Commission are five-member boards. With the odd-numbered membership, voting deadlocks are nearly impossible.

That is not true with the Federal Election Commission, which has six members. Three are Democrats and three are Republicans, raising the possibility of a partisan split. (Two ex-officio members, the Secretary of the Senate and the Clerk of the House, do not vote.) Four votes are needed for approval on most questions, meaning that a commissioner from one party must join the three from the other party.

No other federal agency has the direct impact on the political process that the FEC does. And that apparently is why members of Congress, who must run for re-election, gave the commission a built-in deadlock.

Congress' concern over FEC voting blocs was illustrated by the flap that surrounded President Carter's appointment of Republican Frank P. Reiche (pronounced "Richey") as a commissioner in 1979. Conservative GOP senators argued that Reiche, the head of the state election-monitoring agency in New Jersey, was not partisan enough to protect Republican interests. Reiche's nomination was approved only after it weathered a seven-hour filibuster.

As it turned out, however, deadlocks have been infrequent, and tie votes broken by a defector from his or her party have not been that common either. "Before I got here, I imagined there would be a lot of deadlocks," said former White House lobbyist Max L. Friedersdorf in an interview while he was serving as commission vice chairman. "Most decisions, though, are unanimous, 6-0, because the cases are clear-cut. If we have differences, it's usually over interpretation of the law, not due to partisanship."

An example was provided by 1980's advisory opinions (AOs), which are rulings the commission gives to candidates or political committees wanting to know if they legally can take certain actions. Of the 137 advisory opinions issued in 1980, 116 were by unanimous FEC vote, a Congressional Quarterly study found. In the remaining 21 AOs, dissents were filed by one or two commissioners, with Democrats Thomas E. Harris (nine) and Robert O. Tiernan (seven) the most frequent dissenters. John W. McGarry, the third Democrat, dissented only once. And in the five cases where Harris and Tiernan both dissented, it was McGarry's vote, when added to those of the three Republicans, that produced a majority AO. One of these, issued May 1, 1980, overturned the commission's previous ruling of December 1979 concerning the role of Rexnord Inc. in promoting voter registration. *(See p. 32)*

Among the Republicans in 1980, Reiche was the lone dissenter in four cases and he once joined Harris in a minority opinion. Joan D. Aikens and Friedersdorf formed a minority of two in three other cases. (In 1979 Aikens and Friedersdorf had been the most frequent nay-sayers, each voting "no" in nine cases.)

Besides issuing 137 advisory opinions in 1980, the commission considered 20 other requests, 11 of which were withdrawn before final action. The lone 3-3 deadlock that year happened on one of the five remaining cases, on which the commission closed the files for various reasons.

In 1979, too, there had been only one deadlock and that, on the surface, appeared to be a partisan split. It concerned a request by a subsidiary of the Texas Democratic Party, called the Texas Democratic Voter Participation Project, to help five congressional candidates retire their 1978 campaign debts. The April 11 vote was on a straight party line, 3-3, with Democrats voting "yes," Republicans "no." So permission was denied. But the difference between the Democrats and the Republicans turned out to be based not so much on partisanship as on whether regulation or advisory opinion was the best way to decide the question.

Two other seemingly partisan issues cropped up in 1979 and the Democrats won on both. One revolved around a request by the Republican National Committee (RNC) to raise funds in a novel way. The RNC wanted to accept finders' fees from banks in return for soliciting credit card holders from among the party ranks.

By a 4-2 vote, the FEC rejected the proposal, ruling that this would constitute an illegal corporate contribution. Republican Commissioner Vernon W. Thomson joined the three Democrats in that opinion. Reiche, Thomson's replacement, was not a member then.

The other matter involved the National Republican Senatorial Committee's desire to set up individual general election committees for GOP Senate nominees before they were chosen in party primaries. These committees would reserve autumn television advertising time, buy office supplies and take care of similar details for a candidate prior to his or her nomination. The goal was to save time for nominees chosen in September primaries, who have just two months to gear up for the November election.

But the proposal died on a 2-2-1 vote, two votes short of the four necessary for approval. Voting for it were Republicans Aikens and Friedersdorf; voting against were Democrats Harris and McGarry. Republican Reiche abstained and Democrat Tiernan was absent.

Backgrounds of Current Members ...

The Federal Election Commission is composed of six members — three Democrats and three Republicans. Commissioners, who are appointed by the president and confirmed by the Senate, earn $58,500 annually and serve staggered six-year terms.

The commissioners choose one of their colleagues to be chairman for a year. On Jan. 1, the chairmanship changes hands between the two parties. The vice chairman is from the party not holding the chairmanship.

The Republicans

Frank P. Reiche
(Chairman)

Birthdate: May 8, 1929.
Background: Lawyer ... chairman, New Jersey Election Law Enforcement Commission, 1973-79.
Education: Williams College, B.A., 1951; Columbia University School of Law, LL.B., 1959; George Washington University, M.A., 1959; New York University Law School, Master of Laws in Taxation, 1966.
Term Expires: April 30, 1985.

Joan D. Aikens

Birthdate: May 1, 1928.
Background: Fashion consultant and commentator, 1962-75 ...... an original member of the commission ... FEC chairman in 1978-79 ... vice president of public relations firm, 1974-75 ... various positions in Pennsylvania Republican politics.
Education: Ursinus College, B.A., 1950.
Term Expires: April 30, 1983

Lee Ann Elliott

Birthdate: June 26, 1927.
Background: Political consultant ... with American Medical Association, 1951-62; AMA's Political Action Committee (AMPAC), 1962-79; and Bishop, Bryant & Associates, political management consultants, 1979-81.
Education: University of Illinois, B.A., 1949.
Term Expires: April 30, 1987.

---

tapes of a re-enactment of the incident — were an illegal corporate political expenditure.

But the problem with FEC opinions is not only that they are overly restrictive, critics say: It's that they often deal with seemingly picayune matters. One often-cited example is that company and union newspapers are prohibited from running their PACs' endorsements if the publications go to people who cannot legally be solicited for the political fund — such as retirees. "That's ridiculous," as-

serted Alexander.

In 1980 state Sen. Richard C. Bozzuto, a candidate for the Republican Senate nomination in Connecticut, had to ask the FEC if he could distribute pennies as a campaign item. (The answer was yes.)

To critics, the ultimate absurdity was the case of the macadamia nuts. Rep. Cecil Heftel, D-Hawaii, solicited the FEC's assent to give macadamia nuts as gifts to other members of Congress. Heftel was unsure whether he would

... Of the Federal Election Commission

Frank P. Reiche, a Republican, succeeded John W. McGarry as chairman on Jan. 1, 1982. Democrat Thomas E. Harris became vice chairman.

Commissioners Joan D. Aikens, Lee Ann Elliott and Danny Lee McDonald were serving interim ap-

pointments granted by President Reagan after the 1981 session of the 97th Congress adjourned without the Senate's acting on their nominations. Aikens, an original member whose term expired April 30, 1981, was re-appointed to fill a vacancy expiring in 1983.

The Democrats

Thomas E. Harris

John Warren McGarry

Danny Lee McDonald
(Vice Chairman)

Birthdate: May 25, 1912.
Background: Lawyer ... an original member of the commission ... FEC chairman in 1977-78 ... associate general counsel of AFL-CIO, 1955-1975 ... same post for CIO, 1948-55.
Education: University of Arkansas, B.A., 1932; Columbia University School of Law, LL.B., 1935.
Term Expires: April 30, 1985.

Birthdate: June 11, 1922.
Background: Lawyer ... FEC chairman in 1981 ... special counsel on elections to House Administration Committee, 1973-78 ... chief counsel, Special House Committee to Investigate Campaign Expenditures, 1962-72 ... assistant Massachusetts attorney general, 1959-62.
Education: Holy Cross College, B.S., 1952; Georgetown University Law School, J.D., 1956.
Term Expires: April 30, 1983.

Birthdate: Aug. 26, 1946.
Background: Public service ... secretary, Tulsa County (Oklahoma) Election Board, 1974-79 ... general administrator, Oklahoma Corporation Commission, 1979-81 ... adviser to FEC's National Clearinghouse on Election Administration, 1979-80.
Education: Oklahoma State University, A.B., 1971.
Term Expires: April 30, 1987.

be making a political contribution under the law. The commissioners said the gift would not be a contribution.

Once news of the ruling got out, the commission found itself the butt of jokes around Washington. "We're like the National Science Foundation," said Friedersdorf, who was then serving on the commission. "You can always pick out where they're spending a few bucks to study the tsetse fly in Argentina. In any bureaucracy, you always get a few young eager beavers who do that."

But the commission and its defenders point out that under the law the FEC must answer opinion requests (and at least look at enforcement complaints) no matter how trivial or ridiculous the request or complaint might seem to be. Too, the FEC has said that it must discuss such matters because Congress in writing the laws left some areas open for nit-picking debate.

Beyond that, according to its defenders, the commission has a fundamental reason for monitoring campaigns closely — to spur voluntary compliance with the law. The FEC sees itself as a policeman on the corner, the visible deterrent to crime.

"And even in preposterous situations, like the macadamia nuts, principles are lurking," added John G. Murphy, former FEC general counsel and later a professor at Georgetown University Law Center in Washington. Murphy noted that the nuts conceivably could be treated as a contribution — defined in the election law as "anything of value."

"You can open the door to bigger things," contended Murphy. Suppose the nuts were considered a contribution but, because the gift was so insignificant, were permitted to escape FEC restrictions, he said. "Couldn't you then donate desks to a campaign office, which cost a lot of money, without them being considered a contribution? Lawyers are prepared to make these leaps all the time."

But the FEC does not spend most of its time worrying about such matters as macadamia nuts. Often, opinions genuinely are needed in areas where the law is unclear, such as in the SunPAC case. The law, for instance, allows corporate funds to underwrite solicitation of contributions for a PAC. Yet what if a PAC pays for solicitation costs by mistake, which happened with the National Association of Home Builders' (NAHB) political committee? Can NAHB reimburse its PAC? The FEC said it could.

Incumbents

The FEC has shown favoritism in its enforcement actions, particularly toward incumbents, it is alleged. In a March 1980 hearing, Sen. Mark O. Hatfield, R-Ore., accused the FEC of persecuting a New York tax watchdog group called CLITRIM only because a member of Congress had complained about it. Even if the law did require the FEC to look into the matter, Hatfield said, the commission probably would not have taken the group to court if the complaint had come from a non-incumbent. (Box, p. 32)

According to FEC critics, the best evidence of this alleged pro-incumbent tendency is that the commission devotes the majority of its enforcement resources pursuing non-incumbent violators — often those who spend little and receive negligible shares of the vote. The agency has filed civil suits against the Communists, the Socialist Workers, La Raza Unida and the Prohibition Party.

A Congressional Quarterly examination of FEC records for the first three months of 1979 found that most enforcement actions were taken against non-incumbents. Two incumbent senators and six incumbent representatives had been investigated for non-compliance with the election law. The cases were closed after the FEC was satisfied that nothing was amiss.

The number of non-incumbents under investigation in the same period was far greater; eight Senate candidates and 52 House hopefuls were probed. Mostly, the allegations concerned reports that were not filed on time.

While, as with the incumbents, most of these cases ended up without charges of wrongdoing being filed, a few candidates were fined. Allard K. Lowenstein, a one-time House member (D/L-N.Y., 1969-71) trying unsuccessfully for a comeback, paid a $250 civil penalty in 1979 for failing to file a report 10 days before the 1978 New York primary.

The FEC is "there to protect the incumbents," asserted Bill Burt, national director of the Libertarian Party. "A large chunk of our time is spent fulfilling the reporting requirements. It's a hassle and a real expense."

The commission "proceeds against the least powerful and least popular federal candidates ... in effect, it is prosecuting the widows and orphans of the political process," wrote John R. Bolton, an attorney for the plaintiffs of *Buckley v. Valeo*, in *Regulation* magazine.

The FEC's response is that the integrity of the law must be upheld. It points out that non-incumbents are likely to be less sophisticated than officeholders in complying with the law and that non-serious challengers are not going to bother with the paperwork their candidacy requires. Nevertheless, their reporting failures must be followed up.

"It may be that more of these fringe candidates don't know or don't care about filing than is true of incumbents," said one commission lawyer. "But we have no choice."

Probably the most vehement censure the FEC receives comes from groups on the right, who believe the commission tilts to the left. "The FEC obviously is populated by liberals," said Richard A. Viguerie, the direct mail consultant specializing in conservative causes. "It's a potentially dangerous thing and should be abolished."

In the conservative movement, one organization in particular has been the FEC's nemesis — the National Right to Work Committee (NRWC). It has been fighting a series of legal battles with the commission.

The anti-union group won a court order in 1977 forcing the FEC to stop the AFL-CIO from mingling its dues money with contributions to its PAC — the Committee on Political Education-Political Contributions Committee. (A federal appeals court in 1980 scrapped the $10,000 fine levied on the AFL-CIO for the violation, saying that the federation had not broken the law knowingly.)

In similar fashion, the NRWC went to court in 1977 to prod what it viewed as a reluctant FEC into halting a teachers' union fund-raising method, known as the "negative checkoff." The National Education Association's (NEA) PAC had been fed by automatic payroll deductions from union members, who had to take the initiative to ask in writing for a refund.

An FEC spokesman denied that the commission has a pro-union bias. What seemed to the NRWC like foot-dragging was actually the result of time-consuming attempts to reach conciliation agreements with the AFL-CIO and the NEA, he said.

Meanwhile, the FEC and the NRWC were embroiled in a court fight over the right-to-work group's PAC. At issue was the NRWC's refusal on constitutional grounds to disclose its membership roster, as the commission required it to do. On Sept. 4, 1981, a federal appeals court ruled in the NRWC's favor but the FEC was considering an appeal to the Supreme Court.

Administration

The FEC is beset by inefficient administration and takes too long to complete audits, detractors contend. Although the agency improved its past audit performance in the 1980 presidential race, critics complained that it still was not fast enough. If an audit discloses illegal spending or contributions, they argued, the voters should have this information before the election, not afterward when it's too late.

The commission completed the preliminary receipt and expenditure audits of the 1980 Carter and Reagan campaigns within nine months of the primary and general elections. The Carter audit was released in August but dis-

Roles of the Federal Election Commission

Under the law, the Federal Election Commission has four main functions. In fiscal 1981 the FEC had 251 employees and a budget of $9.6 million to carry out those tasks.

● **Public Financing.** The commission certifies presidential candidates' eligibility for matching funds in the pre-convention period. It also makes financial grants to party nominees for the general election campaign and provides partial financing for party nominating conventions.

● **Disclosure.** Federal candidates and political committees must file periodic reports. Reports are to be made available to the public by the commission within 48 hours after their receipt. Campaign finance reports, from 1972 to the present, are available at the FEC's office, 1325 K Street, N.W.

Some visitors object to the commission's location because it borders Washington's pornography zone. But it was chosen for its proximity to the National Press Club, where many Washington news bureaus are housed, and because it is equidistant from the White House and Capitol Hill.

● **Monitoring.** The FEC periodically audits candidates and committees to ensure that they have disclosed the required information. There were 184 audit reports issued in the 1979-80 election cycle. Another 31 were issued in the first nine months of 1981.

If a violation is turned up after a subsequent investigation, the commission may file a civil suit against the offender. Criminal enforcement is handled by the Justice Department, but by 1982 there had been only one such case. Federal law requires that all cases are to be treated as confidential until the commission closes them.

A United Press International (UPI) tally in mid-September 1981 found that the FEC had "closed more than 300 cases since January 1, 1980, more than two-thirds of them without action. Only 78 involved a conciliation agreement in which the candidate admitted guilt, usually a minor technical violation. No penalty was imposed in 12 cases, but in the other 66 fines totaled $147,350."

FEC officials like to emphasize that theirs is "a responding agency, not an initiating agency." In other words, the commission goes after only those cases that have been brought to its attention through its own records review or through a complaint.

The commission is required by law to audit presidential candidate committees receiving matching funds in the pre-convention period, as well as the nominees in the general election who are financed almost completely with federal money. But an FEC policy to audit randomly House and Senate campaigns irked many on Capitol Hill.

For the 1976 election year, 106 congressional candidate committees were audited — in 44 House districts and four Senate races — after a computer picked them at random. No random audits were conducted for 1978 races. The FEC said that it lacked sufficient funds, although some suspect that congressional protests over the policy were part of the reason.

In 1979 amendments to the Federal Election Campaign Act, random audits were banned. Currently the FEC will audit congressional campaigns only after a review shows a lack of compliance. Audits no longer can be authorized by the FEC's administrative staff. Four commissioners must vote to conduct one.

Even so, the *Federal Times* reported Aug. 10, 1981, that the FEC's general counsel had had to warn the commission's staff of 30 auditors to stay away from "invidious excursions," and that as a result "When the auditors party, a mysterious character known as Captain Invidious, in tights and cape, has been known to award prizes to the most aggressive and 'invidious' auditors." The same news story said that 12 members of the commission's audit staff were being fired in the name of efficiency and budget cutting.

● **Guidance.** Interpreting the act is a key part of the commissioners' job. The FEC often is asked for advisory opinions on aspects of the law such as: Is a trucker who hauls mail a federal contractor and thus barred from contributing to a congressman's re-election campaign? The reply was "yes" and that the campaign of Rep. Charles W. Stenholm, D-Texas, would have to refund and disclose the money it already had accepted from the trucker.

Further, the FEC issues regulations implementing the law, which are subject to veto by Congress.

The FEC maintains a staff to deal with questions the public, candidates or political committees have about the law. It is reached through a toll-free telephone line (800-424-9530).

closure of the Reagan audit was delayed until December 1981 by legal challenges.

Reagan lawyers had indicated in papers seeking the injunction that the audit might raise questions of civil or criminal violations of election laws and require repayment

of federal campaign funds. However, the audit when finally made public cleared the Reagan campaign of any criminal wrongdoing. It said the campaign had made a $1.1 million bookkeeping error.

A court fight also was pending over the audit of Sen.

Kennedy's unsuccessful campaign for the Democratic presidential nomination. Kennedy lawyer William C. Oldaker, a former FEC general counsel, criticized the commission for making up its audit procedure as it went along.

The FEC's work on the preliminary 1980 audits had been completed much sooner than it was after the 1976 general election. It was not until mid-1979, a full two-and-a-half years after that election, that the FEC released its audit of President Carter's general election campaign.

After the 1976 audit, the Carter campaign was ordered to pay back $50,000 that the FEC said had been used for improper get-out-the-vote activities and undocumented expenditures. The results for other 1976 contenders took at least a year to release.

FEC supporters pointed to several causes for the delay — the fact that the FEC never had handled a presidential campaign before, the disruptive two-month hiatus caused by the *Buckley v. Valeo* decision, and the lack of cooperation from some candidates.

But Arthur Andersen & Co., a public accounting firm hired to critique the FEC's 1976 campaign auditing performance, faulted the commissioners themselves. According to the Andersen firm, there was a failure to set firm deadlines and insufficient direction of the project. As a result, FEC auditors ended up examining small, inconsequential amounts, Andersen concluded.

As an example of a case where audit results should have been in the hands of voters earlier, critics point to former Pennsylvania Gov. Milton J. Shapp's 1976 bid for the Democratic presidential nomination. The campaign featured a fraudulent fund-raising ploy, yet it was not made public until 1977.

The FEC's answer is that getting audits out much earlier is impractical. "We'd like to make the primary audits available before the general [election], and Arthur Andersen wanted us to do it," said then-Chairman Tiernan. "But, with the size of our staff, doing them that quickly would make for accuracy problems. It's a short time between the conventions and the general."

Beyond the delayed audits lies the broader question of the commission's competence and organization. "The staff is simply not that great," said political scientist Alexander.

Former commission attorney Vandegrift added that "the FEC doesn't draw from law school grads at the top rank, and that's an insoluble problem. Election law is a skill that you can't use to earn a lot on the outside. You're going after people for misreporting $200 — trivial stuff."

Perhaps as a result, the commission has been plagued by staff turnover running upwards of 20 percent yearly. Although the commissioners dismiss this as normal for federal agencies, it is bound to take its toll on expertise.

To many observers, the structure of the commission is flawed. A May 1979 study by Harvard University's John F. Kennedy School of Government found "inefficiency and a lack of clarity and consistency in policy making" because the FEC has no single operating chief. The chairmanship rotates every year, and decision-making is collegial.

"As soon as the staff director gets to know one chairman, he changes," said Vandegrift. "With that arrangement, it can't work." The Harvard study recommended that the law be changed to have the president designate a chairman for four years, perhaps from the party opposite the one controlling the White House. He or she would be responsible for day-to-day management of the agency and would appoint key staffers, subject to the other commissioners' approval.

Hobbled by Congress

Perhaps the FEC's biggest problem is its subordinate position to Capitol Hill. "The leash is tight," said Tiernan. "Clearly, Congress was concerned about a runaway commission. They said, 'We want some reform, but on the other hand ...'"

As Tiernan saw it, the FEC from the outset was "structurally handicapped." By having three commissioners from each party and a rule requiring four votes to pass most motions, there was the built-in possibility of a deadlock.

In practice, however, the FEC has not deadlocked that often, and differences are rarely partisan. Democrat John W. McGarry, the chairman in 1981, generally abstained to avoid 3-3 votes on partisan issues. Tiernan said that he did the same thing during his during his tenure as chairman. While that usually meant the four necessary votes could not be mustered, Tiernan believed that a significant number of tie votes would have rendered a bad precedent. There were 3-3 votes only once in 1979 and 1980, and only twice in 1981. *(Deadlocks, box, p. 33)*

A larger concern for the commission has been trying to regulate the campaigns of members of Congress, who can vote on its budget, conduct oversight hearings on it, tinker with the election law and veto its proposed regulations. While federal agencies often claim they have too little money and staff, the FEC felt it had been singled out for fiscal austerity, long before that was fashionable on Capitol Hill.

Since its inception, the agency's budget request has been chopped by about 20 percent each year. Tiernan warned Congress in 1980 that paring large amounts for fiscal 1981 would hinder the FEC's ability to carry out the requirements of the 1979 amendments and to meet the increased workload of an election year.

One example Tiernan cited was the provision in the 1979 amendments compelling the FEC to answer advisory opinion requests within 60 days. Tiernan said that without additional attorneys other activities would have to be put off. Nevertheless, the FEC subsequently reported that in 1980 it had "issued advisory opinions (not including expedited opinions) on an average of 46 days after receiving a request."

In the FEC's history, three sets of proposed regulations have been vetoed by Congress. The first was in 1975, when the Senate torpedoed rules curbing the use of congressional office accounts, which are used to send out newsletters and pay for other quasi-political expenses using public money.

The second, also in 1975, concerned an attempt by the FEC to end the practice of candidates filing their disclosure reports with the Secretary of the Senate and the Clerk of the House.

The FEC argued that it would be much less cumbersome if reports were filed with the commission alone. House members, however, liked the help the Clerk's office gave them in filing; they voted the regulations down.

The third was in 1979, when the Senate vetoed the FEC's initial debate regulations at the behest of the news media, which did not like the detailed instructions on how such candidate forums should be conducted.

Given its unpopularity and despite the political backgrounds of the commissioners, the FEC's clout in Congress remains quite small. The success of its legislative recommendations is unimpressive. Congress has ignored FEC proposals to grant it a multi-year authorization (it currently has single-year), raise the amounts pre-convention presidential candidates can spend in individual states and make the commission the sole place to file disclosure reports.

"People called the law [establishing the FEC] the congressional retirement act of 1974," said Tiernan. "They said it was like putting the fox in charge of the henhouse. But when we go up to the Hill, all we hear is bitching from those guys."

In 1980 the FEC was the focus of political contention in Congress because of a fight over a plan limiting PAC spending. The so-called Obey-Railsback plan — named after its sponsors, Reps. David R. Obey, D-Wis., and Tom Railsback, R-Ill. — narrowly passed the House in 1979, but died for lack of Senate action. (PAC spending, Chapter 3, p. 41)

FUTURE: FEC FACES POSSIBLE 'FINE-TUNING'

Unloved as it may be, the FEC is widely regarded as a necessary evil, much like a trip to the dentist. Despite threats by some, such as Sen. Roger W. Jepsen, R-Iowa, to abolish the FEC and turn its duties over to the Justice Department and the General Accounting Office, few doubted in early 1982 that it would be around for a long time. For one thing, a move to gut it would generate huge opposition in the press and Congress.

And there was optimism that the FEC would improve with time. Some outside the agency agreed with the commission that it already had improved.

"For what it was mandated to do, I believe the FEC has been functioning well as a young regulatory agency, notwithstanding its staffing and budgetary problems," said Joseph J. Fanelli, president of the Business-Industry PAC.

If its operational failings were corrected — less nit-picking, faster audits — Congress likely would be happier with the FEC. Most incumbents doubted it ever would develop from a necessary nuisance into a powerful agency.

"There exists a strong argument," wrote Yale political scientist F. Christopher Arterton about the FEC, "that the electoral process is of such pivotal importance to a democratic polity that ... a weak regulatory body is highly preferable to a strong one."

Changing the Law

As it fought to hang on to its powers and even its existence, the FEC survived its critics' initial attacks. Hoping to pressure reluctant colleagues into overhauling the Federal Election Campaign Act, Sen. Jepsen and Sen. William L. Armstrong, R-Colo., tried unsuccessfully in late 1981 to restrict the FEC's fiscal 1982 authorization to only six months rather than the normal 12. They were joined in the floor fight by Majority Whip Ted Stevens, R-Alaska, whose participation aroused speculation that the White House was supporting the effort because of the Reagan audit dispute.

Under short-term funding plan, which enjoyed its greatest support among GOP senators, reauthorizing the commission for the second six months would have hinged on action to revamp the election code. If no changes were made by March 1982, the FEC could be put out of business in the midst of an election year. But the chaos in complying with FECA, which still would be in force, made the prospect of losing the FEC a troubling one to many in Congress.

Jepsen and Armstrong had hoped the changes would be in place in time for the beginning of the 1982 election season. Their opponents, while conceding that some changes were necessary, said that such a speedy timetable would not permit thoughtful legislating.

The major issue was not what changes needed to be made in the election law but when to make them. House Administration Committee Chairman Augustus F. Hawkins, D-Calif., and Frenzel, the ranking Republican, opposed the six-month authorization, charging that it would hinder FEC operations.

An examination of the law should proceed more deliberately, they argued. "It took us six months just to take care of the '79 amendments, which were non-controversial," said a Frenzel aide. "It would be too burdensome to get all this done in time for the next election."

Charles McC. Mathias Jr., R-Md., chairman of the Senate Rules Committee, which has jurisdiction over the FEC, bridled initially at the six-month authorization but later tried to work out an accommodation with Jepsen and Armstrong, an aide said. Mathias wanted to postpone work on the election law until early 1982, which would delay any changes until after that year's election. Jepsen nevertheless went ahead in seeking approval of the six-month idea.

The plan brought strong protests from the FEC commissioners. Chairman McGarry said the half-year authorization would hurt the FEC's enforcement efforts. Staff morale would be harmed and year-long contracts for forms, computers and other services would have to be renegotiated, he said.

To Maureen Shea, a lobbyist for Common Cause, the public affairs lobby, a six-month authorization would tarnish the FEC's reputation even more on Capitol Hill. "The FEC wouldn't be able to handle the '82 election well at all, so then people would say, 'Look, I told you so, the FEC can't do its job,'" she said.

The commissioners also were unhappy with the proposed authorization of $9.7 million, which matched the Reagan administration request. That amount was far less than the $11.1 million the FEC sought and only slightly more than the $9.6 million it got in fiscal 1981.

The continuing resolution that Congress approved before adjourning its 1981 session provided temporary funding for the FEC and other agencies whose regular appropriations did not receive final action. The measure allowed the FEC to spend at an annual rate of $8.9 million until March 31, when the continuing resolution was to expire.

Although the Senate killed Jepsen's six-month authorization plan and the FEC received stopgap financing, the 97th Congress put off until 1982 any substantial decisions on revising the election law or the fate of the commission.

Changing the FEC

Strengthening the FEC's internal management powers, curbing some of its enforcement activities and even abolishing it were under consideration as part of the debate.

A likely change was a curb on the way the FEC polices elections. The House Administration Committee in 1981 criticized the FEC's requiring a signed admission of guilt from an election law violator, even when the infraction was inadvertent. As the FEC interpreted the law, it had to obtain this admission.

The most radical proposal remained the one that would eliminate the FEC. Its proponents argued that the Justice Department could handle enforcement, with the General Accounting Office taking care of financial disclosure for all federal candidates. The GAO handled presidential campaign disclosure in the 1972 election.

Two days of Senate hearings in November 1981 by Mathias' Rules Committee showed little support for killing the FEC, but neither did they rule out the possibility that Congress might let the agency expire. There are "very few people who want . . . to be the ones to sink it," Mathias said in an interview.

Most hearing witnesses supported retention of an independent commission and favored a fine-tuning approach. But with others still determined to do away with the FEC, it remained possible that the commission could undergo more than fine-tuning in 1982. "Unless we come forth with some very significant reforms of this commission," said Sen. Hatfield, "there's going to be an ever-increasing demand for its abolition."

3

PACs: Vital Force in Politics

To some, political action committees (PACs) represent a healthy new way for individuals and groups to participate financially in the political process. To others, they are an insidious outgrowth of Watergate-inspired legislation. But all sides agree that PACs are an increasingly important force in the financing of congressional races.

In 1972 only 14 percent of all contributions to House and Senate general election candidates came from PACs. By 1980 the PAC share had swelled to 25 percent. And the total number of PACs, barely 600 at the end of 1974, had eclipsed 2,600 by mid-1981.

Altogether, PACs raised nearly $140 million in the 1980 campaign and contributed $55 million to House and Senate candidates. That figure was more than PACs raised and contributed in the 1976 and 1978 elections combined.

More than two-thirds of the contributions in 1980 went to House candidates, where the campaign budgets were smaller and the opportunities greater for PAC contributions to make an impact.

But with a flock of endangered liberal Democrats providing a target, PAC spending in Senate races also reached a record high. Almost 15 percent of the total campaign receipts of Senate candidates in the general election came from PACs, according to figures compiled by the Federal Election Commission. *(PAC role in congressional elections, 1972-80, graph, p. 45)*

Vehicles for Political Involvement

Traditionally, PACs have steered most of their money to incumbents. Because Democrats held a majority of seats in both houses of Congress until January 1981, their candidates routinely received most of the PAC money. But with the Republican resurgence and the increased willingness of many non-labor PACs to support GOP challengers, it was possible the Democratic advantage could evaporate by the 1982 elections.

PACs have emerged as a major force in congressional races in part because they have been virtually excluded from involvement in presidential campaigns. Since 1976 the general election campaigns of major party presidential candidates have been completely financed by a voluntary income tax checkoff fund, which also has partially financed the pre-nomination campaigns.

Presidential candidates still are allowed to accept indi-

vidual and PAC contributions during the pre-convention stage, but only individual donations are matchable with federal funds. As a result, PACs provided only $2 million in direct contributions to presidential candidates during the 1980 campaign.

The term "PAC" is not precisely defined in the Federal Election Campaign Act (FECA), the law that provides the basic ground rules for the financial conduct of federal campaigns. FECA does define a non-party political committee as any committee, club, association or other group of members that has either receipts or expenditures in a calendar year of at least $1,000, or operates a separate, segregated fund to raise or disburse money in federal campaigns. Committees that fit this definition have come to be known as PACs.

Because corporations and labor unions are prohibited by federal law from using corporate and union treasury funds for political contributions, PACs have become a tightly regulated vehicle for political involvement by business and unions.

Campaign contributions by political action committees must come from voluntary gifts to the PACs. But corporate and union funds may be used to administer PACs and solicit money for them.

Most PACs are affiliated with corporations or labor unions. But there are a large number of political committees affiliated with trade, membership and health organizations and a growing number of independent, non-connected PACs set up by groups interested in a particular cause, such as abortion or the environment.

Impetus for PACs

Labor unions began forming political action committees nearly a half century ago to maximize their influence in the political process. But the real impetus for PAC formation did not come until the 1970s when the federal campaign finance laws were overhauled. Crucial were the 1974 amendments to the FECA, which clamped a $1,000 limit on the amount an individual could contribute to a House or Senate candidate in a primary or general election. PACs were permitted to give $5,000 per election, with no limit on how much a candidate could receive in combined PAC donations.

Overnight, the political landscape was changed. Before 1974 little need existed for PACs outside the labor movement. Individuals — whether business executives or wealthy political philanthropists — could give unlimited amounts to the candidates of their choice. But the 1974 legislation ended this era of unbridled giving and forced wealthy individuals, corporations and other organizations to seek new outlets to remain financially involved in the political process.

The PAC Debate

For many, PACs were the answer. In the wake of the Watergate scandal and the exposure of illegal corporate contributions, they offered a centralized and well-organized way to participate politically.

Foes of PACs, however, view them quite differently. They contend that the committees are a corrupting influence on the political process, filling a vacuum created by the strict federal limitation on contributions and the decline of political parties as basic campaign organizations.

"PACs tilt the system dramatically toward incumbents," complains Common Cause President Fred Wertheimer. "PAC giving is a form of political investment in government decisions."

Critics claim that PAC contributions buy influence. They cite examples such as a June 1979 House amendment to weaken the windfall profits tax, which drew the support of 95 percent of the House members who received more than $2,500 from oil company PACs the previous election.

But PAC defenders contend that any favorable vote in Congress reflects a shared philosophy, not influence-buying. In 1979 Republican William F. Clinger Jr. told a newspaper in his central Pennsylvania district that PACs obtained access to him as a result of their contribution, but that was all. Clinger said, "I've encountered no vote that I've made where I thought, 'Gee, I better vote this way because they gave me $2,000.'"

PAC supporters maintain that the political committees are a practical exercise of their constitutional rights. Explained former Republican Rep. Clark MacGregor of Minnesota, the chairman of the United Technologies Corp. PAC in 1979: "We're talking about voluntary contributions, not windfall profits by some insensitive corporation."

Legislative Background

The legislative groundwork for the PAC boom of the 1970s was laid by the FECA of 1971. When the decade began, the political activities of corporations and unions were tightly restricted.

Corporate gifts of money to federal candidates had been prohibited since 1907 by the Tillman Act. In 1925 the ban was extended by the Federal Corrupt Practices Act to cover corporate contributions of "anything of value." Labor unions were prohibited by the Smith-Connally Act of 1943 and the Taft-Hartley Act of 1947 from making contributions to federal candidates from their members' dues.

The 1971 act modified these bans by allowing the use of corporate funds and union treasury money for "the establishment, administration and solicitation of contributions to a separate, segregated fund to be utilized for a political purpose." Administrative units of those funds became known commonly as PACs.

But the 1971 act did not modify the ban on political contributions by government contractors. This resulted in many corporations holding back from forming PACs. Labor

unions, many of which had government manpower contracts, also became concerned that they would be affected and led a move to have the law changed to permit government contractors to establish and administer PACs. That change was incorporated into the 1974 amendments to the FECA.

SunPAC Decision

But labor's efforts had unexpected consequences. While the easing of the prohibition against government manpower contractors forming PACs removed a headache for organized labor, it also opened the door for the formation of corporate PACs.

Yet in the wake of Watergate many corporations remained skittish about what they were permitted to do. Not until November 1975, when the Federal Election Commission (FEC) released its landmark ruling in the case involving the Sun Oil Company's political committee, SunPAC, did many businesses feel comfortable in establishing PACs.

The FEC decision was in response to a request from Sun Oil for permission to use general treasury funds to create, administer and solicit voluntary contributions to its political action committee, SunPAC. The company also sought permission to solicit its stockholders and all employees for PAC contributions and to establish a separate "political giving program" among corporate employees that could be financed through a payroll deduction plan. Sun Oil indicated that employees would be allowed to designate the recipients of their contributions.

By a 4-2 vote, the bipartisan commission issued an advisory opinion approving the requests, although the FEC emphasized that SunPAC must abide by guidelines ensuring that the solicitation of employees was totally voluntary.

The two dissenting commissioners — both Democrats — objected to the scope of SunPAC solicitations. They argued that because federal law permitted unions to solicit only their members, SunPAC should be restricted to soliciting only its stockholders.

Labor was incensed by the ruling, since it greatly enlarged the potential source of funds available to corporate PACs. The unions pressed hard to have the commission's decision overturned, and they succeeded in the 1976 FECA amendments in having the range of corporate solicitation restricted from all employees to a company's management personnel and its stockholders. Corporations and unions were given the right to solicit the other's group twice a year by mail.

The 1976 amendments also permitted union PACs to use the same method of soliciting campaign contributions as the company PAC used, such as a payroll deduction plan. And the law sought to restrict the proliferation of PACs by maintaining that all political action committees established by one company or international union would be treated as a single committee for contribution purposes. The PAC contributions of a company or an international union would be limited to no more than $5,000 overall to the same candidate in any election no matter how many PACs the company or union formed.

In the short run, the 1976 amendments were a victory for labor, because they curbed some of the benefits for corporate PACs authorized by the FEC's SunPAC decision. But the legislation did nothing to undercut the primary effect of the SunPAC ruling: abetting the formation of PACs within the business community. Moreover, the law explicitly permitted trade associations, membership organizations, cooperatives and corporations without stock to establish PACs. *(Legislative background, Chapter 1)*

Corporate PAC Boom

Prior to the SunPAC ruling, there were more labor than corporate PACs; but that situation changed quickly after the FEC's controversial decision. Within six months of the November 1975 SunPAC opinion, the number of corporate PACs had more than doubled — from 139 to 294 — while only 20 new labor PACs had formed.

After that, the disparity between the number of business and union PACs grew even wider, with corporate PACs numbering 1,251 in July 1981, more than four times the number of labor units (303). These totals did not include the myriad number of corporate PACs that are active only in state and local races and do not have to register with the FEC. *(PAC growth, graph, p. 45)*

Viewed another way, corporate PACs, which represented less than 20 percent of the total number of federally registered political committees in November 1975, comprised nearly half of the total number in mid-1981.

In spite of their fewer numbers, labor PACs were able to run ahead of their corporate counterparts in contributions to federal candidates throughout the 1970s.

Several heavyweight unions provided the edge. In 1978, for example, five labor PACs — affiliated with the United Auto Workers (UAW), the AFL-CIO, the Steelworkers, the United Transportation Union and the Machinists — each contributed between $500,000 and $1 million to congressional candidates. In contrast, no corporate PAC that year gave House and Senate candidates even $200,000. *(Leading PACs in 1980, box, pp. 52-53)*

The situation was similar two years later. The PAC of the Winn-Dixie stores led the corporate category with contributions of barely a quarter million dollars to federal candidates in the 1980 election.

But the financial activity of individual corporations can be understated. While some businesses and labor unions have more than one PAC, most of the state and local labor committees report their financial activity on a single report filed by their international committee. Many of the subsidiary corporate PACs, however, file separately and their reports must be aggregated to obtain the complete campaign finance picture of some corporations.

A prime example is the American Telephone & Telegraph Co. (AT&T). In 1980 it had a PAC for each of its Bell System subsidiaries. While a *Washington Post* study found that none of the 23 subsidiary PACs came close to rivaling the contribution total of Winn-Dixie, the aggregate contributions of the AT&T subsidiaries to federal candidates surpassed $650,000.

AT&T, however, is clearly in a class by itself. Dow Chemical, with eight PACs and $300,000 in donations to federal candidates in 1980, was a distant second in aggregate corporate contributions.

Many of the multiple PACs are subsidiaries concerned only with a region or state — such as the PACs for Pacific Bell Telephone or New York Telephone. They do not provide a national corporation any financial advantage, since a single contribution ceiling applies for each corporation or union regardless of how many PACs it has.

Labor Competes

Altogether in 1978, labor PACs provided congressional candidates $10.3 million, a half million dollars more than the amount provided by corporate PACs. But labor lost its advantage two years later. At the same time that union PACs were increasing their contributions to House and Senate candidates by about 25 percent (to $13.1 million), corporate PACs were nearly doubling their contributions (to $19.2 million). *(1978-80 PAC contributions to House and Senate candidates, p. 47)*

Political experience was one factor in the turnabout. While some corporations were establishing federal PACs for the first time in the late 1970s, many had gained experience by running PACs for years at the state and local level. Other corporations new at the PAC game used 1978 as a trial run and demonstrated far more sophistication in 1980.

But the sheer volume of corporate PACs was probably the deciding factor that enabled the business community to outstrip labor in direct contributions. While the average corporate PAC contributions were smaller — under $1,000

—the category is expanding rapidly. More than 400 corporate PACs were created between December 1978 and December 1980, producing a whole new pool of dollars for political campaigns that even the experienced labor heavyweights could not match. During the same time, only 80 new labor PACs were established, many of them at the local level.

And labor could be at an even greater disadvantage in the future. While there is a finite number of labor unions, most of them already organized, the universe of possible business PACs is huge and relatively undeveloped. The 1,251 corporate units in existence in July 1981 represented only 26 percent of the 4,788 U.S. companies with reported assets of $100 million or more and a paltry 4 percent of the 29,383 companies with reported assets of $10 million or more. Both figures are based on 1977 data published in January 1981 by the Treasury Department.

What is bad news for labor is also bad news for their traditional allies, the Democrats. Throughout the 1970s, the Democrats capitalized on strong labor backing and incumbency to garner the lion's share of PAC dollars.

But the Democrats' fund-raising equation began to break down in 1980 as the party's majorities in Congress dwindled. Incumbency traditionally was the sole reason many business PACs donated to Democratic candidates. As the prospect of a Republican Congress brightened, this lure lost much of its appeal.

Labor support for the Democrats remained solid in 1980, as 93 percent of all direct union contributions went to Democratic House and Senate candidates. But the surge in corporate PAC giving, most of which went to Republican candidates, reduced the overall Democratic advantage. In 1978 Democratic House and Senate candidates received 56 percent of all PAC contributions. Two years later, the Democratic share had fallen to 52.5 percent. *(1980 PAC contributions by category, box, p. 47)*

PAC MONEY: GETTING IT, GIVING IT

Although the law permits corporate PACs to solicit stockholders, very few do. A survey of 275 corporate PACs, coordinated by the Business-Industry Political Action Committee (BIPAC) in 1981, found that only 18 percent of the corporate PACs asked stockholders for contributions.

"Stockholders are a broad and very diverse group," explained Frank S. Farrell, chairman of the Burlington Northern PAC in 1978. "Many of them have differing political complexions and points of view. It's a question of whether it's worth the time and effort."

Corporate Solicitations

Management personnel are the main target for the corporate PACs, but corporations vary widely in how low into the management ranks they reach to solicit. In the late 1970s, General Electric was soliciting its 540 top executives. About two-thirds participated. On the other hand, Lockheed was soliciting its full management group, and approximately 600 — about 5 percent of the number solicited — were contributing.

By the early 1980s, more corporations were following the Lockheed example, soliciting throughout their management ranks. The corporate PACs in the BIPAC survey had an average of 388 donors, giving about $160 apiece.

The frequency of solicitation also differs greatly among corporations. Some solicit annually, others more or less frequently. The primary methods of solicitation are mail, personal contacts, small group presentations and combinations of all three.

Most of the corporations surveyed use payroll withholding plans for their employees to make contributions, although some major companies have held back. They have been concerned that the confidentiality of the contributors might be breached if that information were part of the company's payroll system.

Some corporations permit a PAC contributor to designate which party is to receive the money or to allow the PAC to use it at its discretion. Decisions about which candidates will receive PAC donations are almost always made by special committees of the corporate PAC. But in some instances a PAC may not use a formal committee, instead following the recommendations of the PAC manager, a specialist within the company on politics and government affairs, or the firm's Washington lobbyist.

On the average, the 275 corporate PACs surveyed by BIPAC contributed $471 to House candidates and $824 to Senate candidates in 1980.

Labor Solicitations

Among labor unions less variation exists in solicitation practices. Generally a union business agent or steward will solicit union members in person or in a group on an annual basis, although, according to an AFL-CIO spokesman, more and more unions are using payroll withholding for voluntary political contributions.

If a company uses payroll withholding to collect contributions from its executives, federal law requires that payroll withholding automatically be made available for a union to collect the political contributions of its members who work for the company. If a company does not use payroll withholding, then a union may negotiate for it.

"We're a big unwieldy national organization," observed Bernard Albert, public relations director of the AFL-CIO COPE (Committee on Political Education). Payroll withholding "is just beginning to pick up steam. The big payoff is down the road."

The Steelworkers is one major union that has adopted the plan. It employs a checkoff system that lets union members give either 2 cents a work day or $5 a year to the PAC.

The national boards of union PACs usually contribute to candidates on the recommendations of their local officials. For the AFL-CIO COPE in each state to make a contribution, however, a candidate traditionally has had to receive a two-thirds vote at a state labor convention or from a body designated by the convention.

Machinists' Suit

In October 1979, the International Association of Machinists mounted an assault on the solicitation methods of major corporations. It filed a complaint with the FEC, maintaining that 10 leading corporations — including Dart Industries, General Electric, General Motors, Grumman and Winn-Dixie — were engaging in "inherently coercive" practices to collect PAC contributions from their employees.

The Machinists charged that the companies' solicitation practices were "pregnant with coercion" because the job security of mid-management employees was not protected either by union membership or contracts; employees frequently lacked anonymity — they were sometimes solicited in person and by their supervisors; employees had no control over the distribution of their contributions, which often went out of state; employees rarely declined to contribute. Many employees made contributions in exactly the same amount, which the union contended indicated orchestration by the corporation. The Machinists added that the average amount of contributions to corporate PACs was far greater than the average contribution made by members of the public with comparable incomes.

In summary, the Machinists noted that there was "no possible room for a conclusion that the corporate PACs are

Growth of Political Action Committees, 1974-81

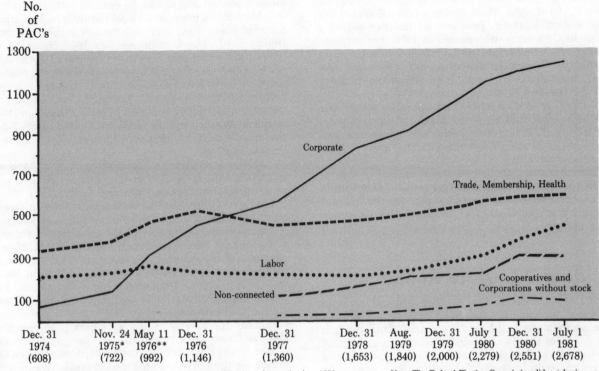

No.
of
PAC's

*Date of SunPac opinion by the Federal Election Commission that prompted the subsequent rapid growth in corporate PACs.

**Effective date of the 1976 amendments to the Federal Election Campaign Act.

Note: The Federal Election Commission did not begin counting PACs of non-connected, cooperatives and corporations without stock in separate catagories until 1977.

Source: Federal Election Commission

PAC Role in Congressional Elections, 1972-80

Political action committee contributions as a share of the total campaign receipts of House and Senate candidates in general elections.

Note: Prior to the 1976 election, campaign spending data were compiled by Common Cause. The Common Cause studies in 1972 and 1974 covered shorter time periods than the FEC surveys. The FEC studies covered the 24 months through the end of the year in which the election was held.

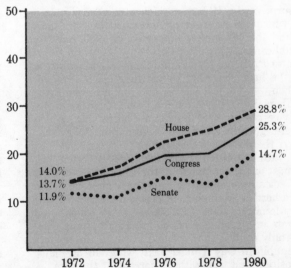

Percent of total
candidate receipts

Source: Federal Election Commission 1976-80; Library of Congress publication by Joseph E. Cantor, 1972-74.

operating with employee contributions that are genuinely free and voluntary political donations."

Corporations saw the union complaint as a thinly disguised effort to drive their PACs out of business, and saw no merit in the charges. Many business officials shared the view of Robert Hibbard, president of the Pennsylvania Chamber of Commerce, who denied in 1979 that corporations were pressuring employees for PAC contributions. "It would hit the paper right away if an employee's arm was twisted," maintained Hibbard. "It would be the dumbest thing for a business to do."

The FEC tended to agree. The commission's general counsel concluded that all of the allegedly coercive practices cited by the union were permissible under the law. And by a 4-0 vote the FEC decided in December 1979 to dismiss the complaint.

Machinists have challenged the dismissal in federal court. But the presentation of oral arguments did not begin until October 1981 and by the end of the year the case was still pending in the District of Columbia federal circuit court of appeals.

Deciding Where to Spend

For PACs, the decision on whether to spend money in a particular campaign involves more than simply winning and losing. Winning is the most important thing, but it is not, as it was for the old Green Bay Packers, the only thing. A lot depends on the candidate's ideology, his standing in Congress and even internal PAC politics. An unsuccessful but attention-drawing challenge to a strong and famous senator may have as much claim on PAC resources as a close House campaign somewhere else.

Most PACs still say, of course, that their primary job is rewarding friends and punishing enemies. "You have good guys and you have bad guys, and we're for the good guys," said William Holayter, political director of the Machinists union.

Not surprisingly, Holayter's idea of a good guy is a Democrat who supports organized labor. Of the 248 candidates he and the Machinists supported in 1980, only six were Republicans.

But most PACs are trying simultaneously to make the "bad guys" a little friendlier by teaching them some respect. "When we were just a lobby and didn't have a PAC, some members didn't pay attention," said Charles Orasin, executive vice president of Handgun Control Inc., which wants stricter government firearms regulation. "Now that we can hurt the members, they listen."

PACs with a particular regional interest often will invest in most of the campaigns in their region, even when victory is certain or defeat a foregone conclusion. The UAW has a hard time staying out of any district in Michigan, its headquarters state. In 1980, the UAW contributed to Democrats in all but one of the state's 19 House elections. The only contest they avoided involved the re-election of Republican Guy Vander Jagt, who had no major party opposition and won with 97 percent of the vote.

For the American Medical Association (AMA), special considerations are professional, not regional. The AMA faces a problem when a doctor runs for Congress, and the group's staff prefers his opponent. "We can be under a lot of pressure from our membership to give to the physician," said an AMA official.

The Human Factor

Deciding on which candidates to help and with how much money is a subjective process. As with other things human, perceptions can be flawed.

Most PACs manage to know who their friends are. But many of them make bad calls on how much support the freinds need. The Communications Workers of America (CWA) still regret that they gave California Democrat Lionel Van Deerlin only $2,000 for his House re-election campaign in 1980. Republican Duncan L. Hunter, lightly regarded early in the year, outspent Van Deerlin and defeated him. "There was a bit of feeling that Van Deerlin wasn't in as much trouble as he was," said Loretta Bowen, the union's political director. "That snuck up on us. We made a mistake."

In the early days of the 1982 campaign, PACs were struggling to make sure that they had the proper intelligence about congressional districts newly drawn all over the country. Often they had to target and then un-target as more information on the new districts became available.

Sometimes, the quality of the candidate or the shape of his district becomes less important to a PAC than the adequacy of his campaign organization. That was the case in Washington's 5th District last year. In light of his narrow 1978 victory, Democratic Rep. Thomas S. Foley seemed highly vulnerable against a well-regarded Republican, John Sonneland.

Many conservative PACs gave heavily to Sonneland. But one "New Right" strategist who thought him a waste of money was Paul Weyrich, executive director of the Committee for the Survival of a Free Congress. "We only gave Sonneland $500 because he had a very poorly run campaign," said Weyrich. "He had no precinct-level organization. We could have put in $1 million, and he still wouldn't have won." In a close race, Sonneland lost.

The Local Connection

Many PACs face the problem of disagreements between their Washington staffs and their local affiliates. Sometimes they are drawn into a race to appease local opinion and are forced to spend far more than they would have liked.

Local considerations also can hinder a PAC's national political objectives. Consider the case of John Glenn, Bob Carr and the CWA, which favors liberal Democrats.

Ohio Democrat Glenn easily won a second Senate term in 1980, outspending his little-known opponent by a margin of 3-1. Although Glenn obviously did not need the money very much, the CWA sent him the full $10,000 allowed by law. Meanwhile, Michigan Democrat Bob Carr, swamped financially and narrowly defeated for a fourth House term, received a mere $400 from the union.

Why did Carr, a solid liberal and friend of the CWA, fare so badly? "We simply ran out of money," said the CWA's Bowen. "We were broke three or four weeks before election day."

But why did they have to give Glenn money they needed elsewhere? "Glenn is close to Marty Hughes, our vice president for Michigan and Ohio, who insisted Glenn get the full 10," said Bowen. "There was not a heck of a lot we could do."

If that sounds unreasonable, it is not uncommon. Ignoring the wishes of the local membership makes for headaches. From the Washington perspective, however, it is important to have local members in a targeted state or

PAC Congressional Contributions:
Corporate Groups Double Their Giving

(In millions of dollars)

Jan. 1, 1977 - Dec. 31, 1978*

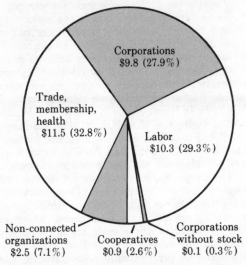

Corporations
$9.8 (27.9%)

Trade, membership, health
$11.5 (32.8%)

Labor
$10.3 (29.3%)

Non-connected organizations
$2.5 (7.1%)

Cooperatives
$0.9 (2.6%)

Corporations without stock
$0.1 (0.3%)

Total PAC contributions: $35.1 million

Jan. 1, 1979 - Dec. 31, 1980*

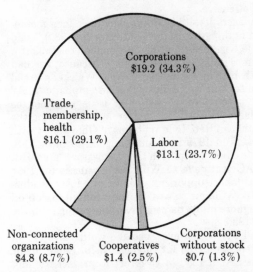

Corporations
$19.2 (34.3%)

Trade, membership, health
$16.1 (29.1%)

Labor
$13.1 (23.7%)

Non-connected organizations
$4.8 (8.7%)

Cooperatives
$1.4 (2.5%)

Corporations without stock
$0.7 (1.3%)

Total PAC contributions: $55.3 million

*Each category's percentage of total PAC contributions to House and Senate candidates during the 1978 and 1980 election cycles is listed in parentheses.

PAC Contributions to House and Senate Candidates in 1980

Type PAC	Total Contributions 1979-80	Increase from 1977-78 cycle	Party Affiliations		Candidate Status		
			Democrat	Republican	Incumbent	Challenger	Open
Corporations	$19.2	+$ 9.4 (+96%)	36%	64%	57%	31%	12%
Trade, Membership, Health	16.1	+ 4.6 +40	44	56	64	23	13
Labor	13.1	2.8 +27	93	7	71	17	12
Non-connected	4.8	2.3 +92	32	68	32	49	19
Cooperative	1.4	0.5 +56	65	35	81	6	13
Corporations without stock	0.7	0.6 +600	56	44	73	17	10
Totals	$55.3	+$20.2 +58	53	47	61	26	13

Source: Federal Election Commission

district because it helps offset the charge that "outside money" is being used to influence an election.

The Loyalty Issue

Some PACs concentrate almost exclusively on rewarding friends and influencing the powerful. Others are more vengeful, willing to spend a great deal of money and effort to make life difficult for members they find personally or ideologically offensive.

PAC managers like to say that they have long memories. "We did nothing for Barry Goldwater (in 1980)," said George Meade, vice president of government relations for the American Trucking Associations, "because we had problems with him in committee. Lowell Weicker's asked us to fund raise, and we've given him an emphatic 'no.' "

Helping a group on a particular issue may not be enough to please its PAC, no matter how important the issue is. Republican Rep. Lyle Williams of Ohio joined with the Steelworkers in 1979 in a suit designed to block U.S. Steel's plans to close two mills in the Youngstown area. But the union PAC still gave to Williams' unsuccessful 1980 challenger, a labor-supporting Democrat. PAC leaders cited a vote by Williams to weaken the windfall tax on oil and chose to ignore his 68 percent favorable rating from the AFL-CIO in 1980.

Nearly all PACs, however, use the word "loyalty" in describing their standards for financial help. Labor spent most of its money in 1980 in an effort to protect friendly Democratic incumbents, many of them moderate and liberal Democrats in Northeastern and Midwestern states. The few Republican beneficiaries of union largesse, such as Sens. Jacob K. Javits of New York and Charles McC. Mathias Jr. of Maryland, had pro-labor records.

But in spite of union assistance, many labor favorites went down to defeat in 1980. Fearful of more congressional losses in 1982, PACs for the major unions began to raise money earlier and to distribute it sooner than ever before. The re-election committees for Democratic Sens. Edward M. Kennedy of Massachusetts and Howard M. Metzenbaum of Ohio, for instance, each raised nearly $100,000 in the first half of 1981 — about two-thirds from labor PACs.

Although labor committees have a tradition of supporting candidates in the early stages of a campaign, spending activity increased dramatically in the first six months of 1981 in comparison with the corresponding period before the 1980 election. An informal survey by Congressional Quarterly's *Campaign Practices Reports* found that the PACs for the Machinists, Steelworkers, United Mine Workers and the National Education Association (NEA) all contributed more than twice as much to federal candidates in the first six months of 1981 than they did in the first half of 1979.

The loyalty standard can create some awkwardness when two of a PAC's best friends run against each other. In 1980 the National Abortion Rights Action League (NARAL) was faced with a dilemma when two of its allies, Javits and Democratic Rep. Elizabeth Holtzman, fought for Javit's New York Senate seat. The PAC solved the problem by giving $5,000 to Javits in the primary and $5,000 to Holtzman in the general election. Javits, beaten for renomination by Alfonse D'Amato, ran on the liberal line in the fall but got nothing from NARAL at that time. D'Amato edged Holtzman by less than 80,000 votes in a bitter contest; Javits finished a distant third.

Access and Influence

In deciding where to invest, PACs spend a lot of time weighing who the future congressional powers will be. The approach for years has been to invest in access and influence and often to ignore real constituent needs.

Democrats have enjoyed an overall financial edge in the past because of incumbency. Republicans are catching up in PAC receipts, due to heavier giving to GOP challengers by corporate and trade association groups.

To be sure, business committees make certain not to neglect powerful Democrats. As the majority party in both houses during the 96th Congress, Democrats — particularly senior ones — benefited from business giving. According to a Common Cause study released in April 1981, 28 Democratic House leaders received an average of $35,000 from corporate and business-related trade association PACs in 1980. House Majority Leader Jim Wright of Texas reportedly drew $155,680 from business-related groups; Rep. Dan Rostenkowski of Illinois, the House Ways and Means Committee chairman, $106,450; and Rep. James R. Jones of Oklahoma, the House budget chairman, $104,851.

The Common Cause figures dovetailed with the conclusions of a study by the liberal Democratic Study Group (DSG) the previous fall. "Business PACs," the DSG concluded, " (give) support to Republican challengers running against Democrats whose seats are not secure, while continuing to buy access to those Democrats who have safe seats and who are generally responsive to business concerns. In other words, help the healthy and shoot the sick."

Other PACs have tried to discipline themselves to ease up on the "access and influence" method and spend their money on candidates who need it. More and more PACs in the business world have been willing to break new ground and support non-incumbents with a free enterprise outlook.

Their willingness to set aside some of their money as "risk capital" was evident in 1980. Although as in earlier years the bulk of corporate contributions went to congressional incumbents, the share given challengers increased from 20 percent of all corporate PAC contributions in 1978 to 30 percent in 1980.

The increased volume of corporate giving in 1980 and the larger share for challengers represented good news for the GOP. Corporate PACs have been less partisan than labor's, but still decidedly Republican in preference. Nearly two-thirds of all corporate PAC contributions in 1980 went to GOP candidates.

Both the National Republican Congressional Committee (NRCC) and the National Republican Senatorial Committee have provided GOP candidates assistance in meeting PAC representatives. For a time in the 1970s, the Republican National Committee even had a PAC division to encourage the formation of business PACs.

As in 1978, much of the corporate PAC money poured into the coffers of GOP congressional candidates late in the campaign. In 1978 many business PACs — some participating in their first campaigns — apparently set aside at least one-third of their budgets for contributions to many Republicans and some moderate Democrats in the final weeks before the election.

In 1980 the late giving spree was even more pronounced. From the beginning of 1979 to Labor Day 1980, corporate PACs contributed nearly $12 million to House and Senate candidates, with slightly more than half the money going to GOP candidates. In the final weeks of the campaign, the business community poured more than $8 million into congressional races, with more than three-quarters earmarked for Republican candidates.

The PACs were guided in their last minute giving by the national party committees and major business organizations such as the Chamber of Commerce. They made available lists of pro-business candidates in close races who needed funds.

While not the only factor in the Republican successes at the polls in 1980, the surge of business PAC money undoubtedly had an effect.

Labor's Consolation

Although labor has taken a back seat to corporations in direct contributions, it still retains several advantages. One is partisan internal communications, a political technique used frequently by labor but sparingly by corporations.

Under federal law, corporations, unions and membership organizations may spend directly from their treasuries to advocate the election or defeat of a candidate. Corporations, though, can direct their appeals only to stockholders, executive and administrative personnel, while unions can communicate only with their members.

Partisan Communications

According to an FEC study, most of the partisan communication money in the 1976 election — 87 percent — went for direct mailings. Other expenses included brochures, phone banks, posters, car stickers and peanuts.

In 1976, labor groups reported spending $2 million on communication with members compared to just $31,045 spent by corporations. The disparity was even greater in 1980. While 57 labor organizations spent close to $3 million, just one corporation made internal communications and their expenditures totaled less than $4,000.

Part of the reason for labor's advantage is that union memberships generally are more cohesive and more easily mobilized through phone banks and targeting techniques than a company's executives and its stockholders, who are scattered throughout the country.

Internal communications have become a traditional way labor can lend additional help to its candidates. Corporations, on the other hand, are more comfortable channeling money through direct contributions.

"I question whether it is our business to educate people (stockholders and executives) on behalf of one candidate with stockholder money," commented Stephen K. Galpin, secretary of the General Electric PAC in 1978. "There is a credibility problem. Would it do any good?"

Among the 10 groups that reported spending the most money on internal communications in 1980, eight were labor groups — including the American Federation of State, County and Municipal Employees ($532,538), the AFL-CIO ($441,064) and the UAW ($402,280). But the front-runner was a membership organization, the National Rifle Association (NRA). After spending about $100,000 to communicate with its members in 1976, the NRA spent more than $800,000 in 1980.

In both 1976 and 1980, most of the expenditures for partisan communications were made in the presidential races rather than in congressional contests. In both years, the major beneficiary was Jimmy Carter. Nearly $1.2 million was spent advocating his election in 1976, and more than $1.5 million promoting his re-election bid in 1980.

In contrast, less than $75,000 was spent each election by groups favoring the Republican presidential candidate. In 1980, much more was actually spent by groups urging the defeat of Republican Ronald Reagan ($254,130) through internal communications than by organizations favoring his election ($64,784).

Unreported Expenditures

While labor's reported expenditures for internal communications have reached seven figures, that amount is just a small portion of the extra help that unions regularly provide the Democratic Party.

Campaign finance expert Herbert E. Alexander wrote in *Financing the 1976 Election* that "only messages sent directly to [union] members and that focused on specific candidates were reported to the FEC. Admonitions to vote Democratic, for example, did not have to be reported, and direct advocacy of a specific candidate did not have to be reported if the basic purpose of the communication was not political or if the total cost did not exceed $2,000. Almost every labor newsletter mailed to members in September and October praised Carter or criticized Ford, and a picture of Carter usually was on the cover. Little of this communication was reported to the FEC, presumably because the material appeared in regular publications that report on union business."

Millions of dollars more were spent in union treasury money for ostensibly "non-partisan" activities such as voter registration and get-out-the-vote drives. Labor unions have become very skilled in these non-partisan techniques, which often are designed to be of particular help to one candidate: An example of this would be a get-out-the-vote drive in an area where pro-labor voters predominate.

Although non-partisan political expenditures do not have to be reported to the FEC, campaign finance expert Michael Malbin estimated in a 1977 *National Journal* article that organized labor the previous year had spent about $11 million on reported and unreported partisan communications, voter registration and get-out-the-vote activities. A significant factor in Carter's victory, the labor expenditures represented about half the amount the Democratic presidential campaign received in public funds for its general election drive that year.

OTHER PACS: INFLUENCE FELT

Corporate and labor units together were responsible for nearly 60 percent of all direct PAC contributions to congressional candidates in 1980. The rest of the money was provided by four other categories of PACs: cooperatives, corporations without stock, trade, membership and health as well as non-connected.

Although numbered among the cooperatives are the lucrative PACs of the Associated Milk Producers and the Mid-America Dairymen, most political committees within the cooperative and corporation without stock categories are relatively insignificant. In mid-1981, the two categories combined had barely 100 PACs, and together they provided only 4 percent of all contributions to House and Senate candidates in 1980.

Trade, Membership and Health PACs

The large group of trade, membership and health PACs, however, is a different story. In the 1980 election they contributed $16.1 million to House and Senate candidates, nearly 30 percent of all PAC gifts. About two-thirds of the contributions from trade, membership and health PACs went to incumbents, and slightly more than half the donations went to Republican candidates.

The trade, membership and health category is a diverse one. Many of the committees within the category — such as the PACs for the National Association of Realtors and the National Automobile Dealers Association — have ties to the business community. The health-related PACs — such as the committees affiliated with the American Medical Association (AMA) and the American Dental Association — also fall into this group. And finally, there are the membership organizations — such as the NRA and the Gun Owners of America — that are rooted in a political ideology or issue.

Like organized labor, the category is anchored by a few heavyweights. In 1978 the AMA PAC ($1.6 million), the Realtors PAC ($1.1 million) and the Automobile Dealers PAC (nearly $1 million) topped all political committees in contributions to House and Senate candidates. These figures represented donations just from the national committees; the totals would have been even higher if the contributions of state affiliates to federal candidates had been included. In 1980 the three were among the top four in total contributions. The Realtors led all PACs with $1.5 million in donations to federal candidates.

The 1975 SunPAC decision — which spurred a rapid increase in the number of corporate PACs — also prompted growth in the number of trade, membership and health PACs. Within six months, nearly 100 new committees were formed. But the creation of trade, membership and health PACs tapered off after that; only 125 new units were established between May 1976 and November 1981.

Strict regulations on the solicitation of contributions has been a major factor in discouraging faster growth. Trade associations raise funds from employees in member corporations. But they must obtain permission from the corporation each year before they may solicit their executive and administrative personnel. The associations maintain this is very costly and want the one-year limitation removed so they can solicit until a corporation withdraws its approval.

Ideological PACs' Influence

About 500 political committees fall into a unique, catch-all category called non-connected PACs. They are independent organizations without a parent body. But the leading non-connected PACs have thousands of contributors who are regularly tapped by direct-mail, fund-raising appeals.

Unlike most other PACs, which are motivated by economic concerns, the principal interests of the leading non-connected PACs are ideological. The most successful ones have been stridently conservative.

According to a *New York Times* analysis published in May 1981, the three PACs that raised the most money in the 1980 campaign were well to the right on the political spectrum: the three were the Congressional Club, formed by backers of Republican Sen. Jesse Helms of North Carolina, which raised nearly $7.9 million; the National Conservative Political Action Committee (NCPAC), which had receipts totaling $7.6 million; and the Fund for a Conservative Majority, an outgrowth of the Young Americans for Freedom, which raised $3.1 million.

Aided by conservative direct-mail, fund-raising expert Richard Viguerie, the Congressional Club and NCPAC have emerged as financial successes by developing mailing lists of more than 300,000 contributors each. In contrast, the leading non-connected PAC with a liberal identification, the National Committee for an Effective Congress (NCEC), has a much smaller mailing list and in 1980 raised less than one-fifth as much as either of the conservative giants.

Altogether, the non-connected PACs collected $40 million in 1980, more than either the corporate ($34.1 million), labor ($25.7 million) or trade, membership and health PACs ($33.7 million). But while the corporate and labor PACs contributed more than half of what they raised to congressional candidates, the non-connected PACs pumped less than $5 million directly into the coffers of congressional candidates, barely 10 cents out of each dollar they collected.

Much of the money raised by the ideological PACs was plowed back into costly direct-mail programs, an expense not incurred by corporate or union PACs. Their administrative costs were covered by the corporation or union, and they were able to raise money from members, employees or stockholders without expensive mass appeals.

With the rest of their funds, the leading non-connected PACs found several ways to become involved in congressional campaigns. In addition to making direct contributions or independent expenditures, some hired national experts on polling, media and other facets of modern-day campaigning which they made available to their candidates. Other PACs sponsored candidate training schools and provided research information from their Washington offices.

Since the ideological PACs were not restrained by affiliation with a parent organization that depended on access to members of Congress, they took greater risks than other PACs in supporting non-incumbents. In 1980 more than two-thirds of all direct contributions from non-connected PACs to House and Senate candidates went to challengers or candidates for open seats. All the other PAC categories channeled a majority of their donations to incumbents.

Most of the recipients of these direct contributions from non-connected PACs were Republicans. Two-thirds of all their donations in 1980 went to GOP candidates, an even higher share than was given by corporate PACs (64 percent). *(1980 PAC contributions by category, box, p. 47)*

But the ideological committees made their greatest mark on the 1980 campaign through independent expenditures that benefited Republicans, in particular. The independent spending route was particularly enticing to the well-heeled conservative PACs since it was not subject to the legal ceilings on direct contributions. PACs can independently spend an unlimited amount in a federal race as long as they do not make contact with the candidate that they favor. *(Independent spending for or against candidates, Chapter 6, p. 79)*

ATTEMPTS TO CURB SPECIAL INTERESTS

Even before the 1980 election, leading Democrats were concerned about the financial success of corporate and conservative PACs. In 1979 they moved to pass legislation that would curb contributions by PACs to House candidates.

While the proposal drew bipartisan support — Democrat David R. Obey of Wisconsin and Republican Tom Railsback of Illinois were the principal co-sponsors — it received most of its backing from the Democratic Party and its traditional allies, such as the AFL-CIO and the public affairs lobby, Common Cause. Republican leaders as well as business groups and conservative organizations strongly opposed the measure.

The Obey-Railsback bill was unveiled on the heels of the release of a Harvard University study of federal election laws. The study, commissioned by the House Administration Committee, concluded that the post-Watergate revisions designed to clean up campaign finance had a number of unintended consequences, including a decline in grass-roots fund raising and a burgeoning role for PACs.

"PACs have increasingly supplanted other sources of money in politics and candidates for Congress have become increasingly dependent (on them)," the study explained. "If one of the original intentions of campaign finance reforms was to limit the appearance of special interests in the political process, the law has, in practice, had the opposite effect. (Details of Harvard study, p. 25)

Obey-Railsback Bill

Armed with the conclusions of the Harvard study, Obey and Railsback bill introduced their bill in the House in July 1979. In its original form, the bill cut in half the maximum amount a PAC could contribute to a candidate to $2,500 per primary, runoff or general election, and proposed a limit of $50,000 on the total amount a candidate could accept from all PACs during a two-year election cycle. Previously, there had been no limit. The measure applied only to House campaigns, where most PAC money was spent.

With prospects of House passage uncertain, the sponsors subsequently revised their plan by raising the contribution limit to $3,000 per election for each PAC and increasing the total a candidate could receive from all PACs to $70,000. Candidates with runoffs could receive up to $85,000.

The bill also called for a 30-day limit on any extension of credit above $1,000 by PACs, political consultants and other vendors of media advertising or direct mail. The provision was aimed particularly at curtailing the role of large campaign specialists such as Viguerie.

But at the heart of the bill were the PAC limitations, and both sides agreed that passage of Obey-Railsback could bring major changes in fund raising for House campaigns. Nearly one third of the House was elected in 1978 with the help of PAC contributions that exceeded the $50,000 cutoff proposed in the original bill and nearly one-eighth won office with PAC help that exceeded $70,000.

Pros and Cons of PAC Giving

Supporters of Obey-Railsback claimed that the growth in PAC contributions was undermining the effectiveness and integrity of Congress. "PAC giving is giving with a purpose," declared Obey. "It is money given by groups who then follow up their contribution with lobbying activities in behalf of their particular interests."

PACs were a "centrifugal force," Obey argued, that pulled members of Congress away from broad consensus-building and toward narrowly defined goals. He warned that action must be taken quickly before PACs became too powerful to curb. Proponents of Obey-Railsback maintained that PACs were fueling a political arms race, with the cost of congressional campaigns escalating out of control.

But opponents of the measure countered that more money was needed in politics, not less. "More dollars were spent on fireworks last year than all congressional elections combined," claimed Rep. Guy Vander Jagt, R-Mich.

Rather than be restricted, opponents contended that PACs should be encouraged. Although most PAC money went to incumbents, they claimed that Obey-Railsback was an "incumbent protection measure." Critics of the bill contended that PAC contributions were vital to challengers, particularly in the important early stages of a campaign when most of them had little name recognition and fund raising was difficult.

Opponents also doubted that Obey-Railsback would bring the new emphasis on small contributors that proponents anticipated. Instead, they saw a rise in wealthy candidates who would finance their own campaigns, a movement by many PACs into independent expenditures to avoid the limits on contributions and more burdensome paperwork and bureaucracy.

Finally, Republicans maintained that while Obey-Railsback effectively curbed direct contributions — the staple of corporate PACs — it did nothing to restrict the huge labor expenditures for internal communications and "non-partisan" activities.

Death in Senate

Although opponents succeeded in delaying floor action for a time, the House passed the compromise measure on Oct. 17, 1979, by a vote of 217-198. A large majority of Northern Democrats supported the bill; most Republicans and Southern Democrats opposed it.

House passage proved to be the high-water mark for the drive to curb PAC spending. The bill quickly bogged down in the Senate. Republican Sens. Mark O. Hatfield of Oregon and Gordon J. Humphrey of New Hampshire blocked action in the closing months of 1979 by threatening a filibuster. The threat continued the following year, stalling the proposal.

One drawback for Obey-Railsback was that most of its supporters also backed public financing of congressional races. Although the House Administration Committee had rejected legislation in May 1979 that would have established public financing for House general election campaigns, opponents were afraid that passage of the PAC limitation bill could renew interest in public financing.

Also many senators feared that passage of Obey-Railsback would set a precedent that could lead to PAC spending ceilings in Senate races. Supporters of the bill felt compelled to emphasize that they had no plan to put a cap on PAC spending in Senate elections because they consid-

Leading PACs in 1980 Election...

...In Gross Receipts and Expenditures

Committee and Affiliation	Category	Receipts	Expenditures
1 Congressional Club	N	$7,873,974	$7,212,754
2 National Conservative Political Action Committee	N	7,600,637	7,464,533
3 Fund for a Conservative Majority, The	N	3,163,528	3,150,496
4 Realtors Political Action Committee (National Association of Realtors)	T	2,753,139	2,576,077
5 Citizens for the Republic	N	2,356,751	2,384,210
6 Americans for an Effective Presidency	N	1,920,377	1,874,312
7 UAW Voluntary Community Action Program (United Auto Workers)	L	1,792,406	2,027,737
8 American Medical Political Action Committee (American Medical Association)	T	1,728,392	1,812,021
9 Committee for the Survival of a Free Congress	N	1,647,556	1,623,750
10 National Committee for an Effective Congress	N	1,570,788	1,420,238
11 Gun Owners of America Campaign Committee	T	1,414,951	1,398,670
12 Committee for Thorough Agricultural Political Education (Associated Milk Producers Inc.)	Co	1,323,567	1,274,931
13 Texas Medical Association Political Action Committee-TEXPAC (Texas Medical Association)	T	1,286,003	1,237,893
14 Automobile and Truck Dealers Election Action Committee (National Association of Automobile Dealers)	T	1,271,857	1,392,745
15 ILGWU Campaign Committee (International Ladies' Garment Workers' Union)	L	1,256,116	925,065
16 Transportation Political Education League (United Transportation Union)	L	1,162,113	1,196,241
17 AFL-CIO COPE Political Contributions Committee (AFL-CIO COPE)	L	1,129,378	1,196,938
18 Americans for Change	N	1,072,549	1,061,123
19 NRA Political Victory Fund (National Rifle Association)	T	1,044,879	1,125,123
20 California Medical Political Action Committee (California Medical Association)	T	1,039,172	895,350

Categories: Co - Cooperative; L - Labor; N - Non-connected; T - Trade, membership, health

*Statistics are based on interim reports for the 1979-80 election cycle filed with the Federal Election Commission.

...In Contributions to Federal Candidates

Committee and Affiliation	Category	Expenditures
1 Realtors Political Action Committee (National Association of Realtors)	T	$1,546,573
2 UAW Voluntary Community Action Program (United Auto Workers)	L	1,422,931
3 American Medical Political Action Committee (American Medical Association)	T	1,360,685
4 Automobile and Truck Dealers Election Action Committee (National Association of Automobile Dealers)	T	1,035,276
5 Machinists Non-Partisan Political League (International Association of Machinists and Aerospace Workers)	L	847,608
6 Committee for Thorough Agricultural Political Education (Associated Milk Producers Inc.)	Co	740,289
7 AFL-CIO COPE Political Contributions Committee (AFL-CIO)	L	715,327
8 Seafarers Political Activity Donation (Seafarers International Union of North America)	L	686,748
9 United Steelworkers Political Action Fund (United Steelworkers of America)	L	681,370
10 National Association of Life Underwriters PAC (National Association of Life Underwriters)	T	652,112
11 American Dental Political Action Committee (American Dental Association)	T	648,875
12 MEBA Political Action Fund (Marine Engineers Beneficial Association)	L	615,295
13 American Bankers Association BANKPAC (American Bankers Association)	T	593,910
14 Transportation Political Education League (United Transportation Union)	L	583,969
15 Active Ballot Club (Food & Commercial Workers International Union)	L	569,775
16 Carpenters Legislative Improvement Committee (United Brotherhood of Carpenters & Joiners of America)	L	554,175
17 ILGWU Campaign Committee (International Ladies' Garment Workers' Union)	L	493,810
18 CWA-COPE Political Contributions Committee (Communications Workers of America)	L	449,520
19 NRA Political Victory Fund (National Rifle Association)	T	434,303
20 National Committee for an Effective Congress	N	427,387

ered it to be less severe a problem than in House campaigns.

Although Senate proponents predicted that they could obtain the required 60 votes to cut off debate on the second or third try, opponents claimed nearly unanimous support from the 41 Senate Republicans in the filibuster effort. And that prospect was enough to derail the legislation.

Liberal PACs Compete

The conservative Republican gains in 1980 interrupted, at least temporarily, attempts to curb PAC spending. Senate Minority Leader Robert C. Byrd introduced a version of Obey-Railsback at the beginning of the 1981 session and several moderate House members introduced a PAC limit bill later in July. But neither measure sparked much enthusiasm, and no action had been taken on either by the end of the session.

The attitude in the House was summarized by the new House Administration Committee Chairman, Augustus F. Hawkins, D-Calif. "What we need is relief from controversy," he remarked. Under Hawkins' predecessor, Democrat Frank Thompson Jr. of New Jersey, the committee was a principal spawning ground for campaign finance legislation. But the Abscam-tainted Thompson and many of his liberal allies were beaten in 1980.

Flattery Through Imitation

With the political climate no longer favorable for legislative remedies, Democratic leaders were faced with the problem of what to do next. By early 1981 their answer was obvious. If they couldn't curb the PACs, they would copy them.

Within several months of the 1980 election, five major new liberal PACs had been formed. While they differed in their goals and their leadership — political consultants started two of them, the leading Democratic presidential hopefuls for 1984 were behind two more and a party elder statesman began the other — their rhetoric was similar.

Through all their fund-raising appeals sounded the refrain that liberal causes were imperiled by the Republican capture of the Senate and the White House in 1980 — and by the chance that the GOP could win the House in 1982.

NCPAC figured as the arch-villain in virtually all the liberal money pitches. Unfailingly, their financial pleas cited the superior financial power of NCPAC and other "New Right" groups, whose treasuries were much fatter.

The new PACs with the most ambitious fund-raising objectives, the Progressive Political Action Committee (PROPAC) and Independent Action, were founded by political consultants who specialized in direct mail. Victor Kamber's PROPAC expressed hopes of raising $1.5 million for the 1982 campaign, while Roger Craver's Independent Action set a budget goal of $2 million. Kamber previously had done most of his work for labor PACs, while Craver's clients had included the DNC and independent presidential candidate John B. Anderson.

Democrats for the '80s, created by former New York Gov. Averell Harriman and his wife, Pamela, was expected to raise most of its money at social events that drew wealthy, longtime Democratic contributors. This was the traditional fund-raising method for establishment Democrats such as the Harrimans.

Sen. Kennedy's Fund for a Democratic Majority and former Vice President Walter F. Mondale's Committee for the Future of America were widely perceived as vehicles for their sponsors' presidential ambitions. Kennedy's PAC planned to raise funds by tapping the mail list of 1980 contributors to the senator's White House campaign, while Mondale's relied more heavily on fund-raising events. By mid-1981 the Kennedy PAC had raised $252,532, while Mondale's had garnered $217,081.

John Anderson established his own PAC as well. But the National Unity Committee's initial fund-raising efforts were modest. They took in less than $20,000 in the first half of 1981.

Among the new liberal PACs, PROPAC was at the bottom of the list with barely $100,000 in receipts by mid-1981. But what PROPAC lacked in money, it made up for with combativeness. On the heels of an early 1981 NCPAC advertising attack on Sen. Paul S. Sarbanes, D-Md., PROPAC launched a counterattack on the conservative committee in Maryland newspapers and *The New York Times*. Taking a page from NCPAC, the liberal committee announced plans to target conservative incumbents in 1982. *(Attack on Sarbanes, p. 88)*

Two other organizations were established to combat the "New Right" — former Democratic Sen. George Mc-Govern's Americans for Common Sense and television producer Norman Lear's People for the American Way. These two, though, were not PACs and planned to fight conservatives through media ads about specific issues.

Fund Raising

But the new liberal groups, struggling against the financial and technical advantages of the right, had a long way to go. In the first half of 1981, only the liberals' one big established PAC, the National Committee for an Effective Congress (founded in 1948), had passed the half-million-dollar mark in fund raising. And it just barely made it.

During the same period, Helms' Congressional Club raised a whopping $2.5 million, while NCPAC took in another $2 million. "The New Right is light years ahead," observed Herb Alexander. "They've been at it for years, and it's unrealistic to think the liberals can get near them soon."

While the liberals still had to go through the long task of assembling contributor lists, the conservatives had theirs in hand and some believed that the liberals would never catch up. "If you want to get money from the ones on the street during Vietnam," explained Viguerie, "you have to realize that they're 28, 30, 32 now and spend their money buying shoes for the kids every four months. By the time the kids are gone, those people have turned conservative."

Liberal PACs argued that a conservative White House and Senate had sufficiently energized fellow believers to make their financial plans successful. They maintained that liberals were eager to give, pointing to the $8.6 million that Anderson raised through individual contributions for his independent presidential quest in 1980. *(1980 presidential campaign costs, p. 9)*

But the New Right clearly had momentum. Conservatives, long regarded as bloody but unbowed losers, had their political appetites whetted by the victory of Reagan and many of his Republican allies in 1980. "Everyone's mailings have gone through the roof since November," Viguerie told *The Washington Post* in March 1981. "Conservatives, in our lifetime, have never had any victories before, and they are excited and enthusiastic."

PRESIDENTIAL PACs: REAGAN LEADS THE WAY

In establishing PACs, Kennedy and Mondale were merely following the lead of Ronald Reagan, who launched the Citizens for the Republic after his unsuccessful presidential bid in 1976.

From the beginning, the Reagan PAC operated with a scope that dwarfed any imitators. Possessing a $1 million surplus from 1976 and a mailing list of more than 100,000 names, Reagan created his PAC in early 1977. By the time it was operating in full swing, it employed a staff of nearly 30, a crew of consultants and a cartoonist. With a multimillion-dollar budget, the Santa Monica, Calif.-based organization emerged as an off-year refuge for many longtime Reagan advisers, including Lyn Nofziger, who headed the PAC in 1978.

Citizens for the Republic relied heavily for money on its carefully developed mailing list, but augmented it with fund-raising events and campaign management workshops around the country. By the end of 1978 the Reagan PAC had spent $4.5 million and still had more than $200,000 left in its treasury.

Presidential Hopefuls Compete

An FEC study found that in 1978 the Citizens for the Republic exceeded all other non-party PACs in gross receipts and expenditures. But because of its high overhead, its level of contributions to federal candidates trailed PACs established earlier by large business and labor organizations.

Yet the size and scope of the Reagan effort was unprecedented for a presidential hopeful in a midterm election. Citizens for the Republic listed contributions to 400 Republican candidates across the country: 25 running for the Senate, 234 for the House, 19 for governor and 122 for other offices, which ranged from lieutenant governor of California to clerk of Clinton County, Mo. Reagan's wide-ranging activities also extended into intra-party affairs, with contributions to candidates for several state chairmanships.

Citizens for the Republic clearly overshadowed the other PACs formed by presidential hopefuls in 1978 — the John Connally Citizens Forum, George Bush's Fund for Limited Government and Robert Dole's Campaign America. The Connally PAC listed contributions to only 80 candidates, the Bush PAC to 51 and the Dole PAC to 17.

The Bush and Dole groups had limited objectives, serving primarily as speaking bureaus for their sponsors. Connally's PAC had more ambitious ideas, but fell short of its projected $1 million budget when it encountered difficulty in developing a reliable base of direct-mail contributors.

Unlike Reagan, the other GOP hopefuls had to form their PACs from scratch. Both Bush and Dole, former RNC chairmen, relied extensively on personal contacts with business leaders around the country to raise money. A Bush PAC spokesman claimed funds were raised by the "rifle shot technique," which consisted of Bush's brother or some other aide on the telephone.

Altogether the four PACs spent more than $5.6 million during the 1978 campaign, most of it eaten up by heavy start-up and operating costs and unitemized travel expenses. Of the $809,330 the PACs listed on their campaign spending forms as contributions, more than two-thirds went to House and Senate candidates. The remainder went to candidates at the state and local level and various party organizations.

A substantial minority of the contributions were made by providing in-kind services rather than direct donations. Forty percent of the contributions listed by the Citizens for the Republic, for example, were in the form of in-kind services, such as television and radio tapes by Reagan, travel expenses for a Reagan appearance and polling data commissioned by the PAC.

New Route to White House

While PAC spokesmen stressed that the basic purpose of their organizations was to help Republican candidates in 1978, there was little doubt that they also had 1980 on their minds. "The PACs are a new way a presidential candidate can pick up chits," observed Steve Stockmeyer, the executive director of the National Republican Congressional Committee in 1978.

The PACs were a logical extension of the traditional non-presidential election year appearances by White House hopefuls at fund-raising dinners along the "rubber chicken" circuit. When Richard M. Nixon, for example, was laying the groundwork for his 1968 presidential campaign, he traveled 30,000 miles on behalf of GOP congressional candidates in 1966. His travels, plus the salary and expenses of one assistant, cost $90,000.

While all of the 1980 Republican hopefuls made their greatest efforts in their home states — Texas for Bush and Connally, Kansas for Dole and California for Reagan — they showed particular interest in contests in the early presidential primary states.

New Hampshire, traditionally the first primary state, got special attention from the presidential PACs that belied its small size. Led by a $5,000 contribution from the Citizens for the Republic, all four PACs gave to Gordon Humphrey, the upset Senate winner over Democratic incumbent Thomas J. McIntyre. The Bush PACs contribution of $500 was sent two weeks after the election, the PAC's only post-election contribution.

The GOP PACs also funneled most of their donations to conservative non-incumbents. None of the PACs listed a contribution to prominent moderate Republicans such as Sens. Mark O. Hatfield of Oregon or Charles H. Percy of Illinois, who were seeking re-election in 1978. The small number of contributions to moderate Republican candidates came from the Bush and Dole groups.

Bush lent campaign assistance to Reps. William S. Cohen of Maine (in his successful Senate race), William A. Steiger of Wisconsin, who died after winning re-election, and Illinois' John Anderson, later Bush's rival for the GOP presidential nomination. Dole campaigned for two Republican House members endorsed by the UAW, Elwood Hillis of Indiana and Matthew J. Rinaldo of New Jersey.

Like the other Republican PACs, the Citizens for the Republic made its greatest effort on behalf of challengers and candidates for open seats. In House races, GOP opponents of Democratic members elected in 1974 and 1976 were major recipients. But the Reagan group provided a lot of other help to long-shot candidates.

The other three Republican PACs worked more closely with the RNC and its congressional, senatorial and gubernatorial affiliates in determining which candidates to support.

The presidential PACs represented a significant new Republican fund-raising source in 1978. Not only did the White House hopefuls make contributions, but their appearances raised millions more for GOP candidates and the party. Spokesmen for the Bush and Connally PACs both claimed that fund-raising appearances by their sponsors helped raise upwards of $2.5 million for Republican candidates in 1978. While the possibility existed that presidential PACs could pose a threat to the financial base of traditional party organizations, friction appeared to be minimal in 1978. "We're not in competition with them to raise money," explained Stockmeyer, "but we're gleefully joining with them to give it. They've opened a new area of candidate money."

Of the Republican PACs active in 1978, only the Citizens for the Republic remained in operation afterward, and it on a somewhat scaled-down basis. With Reagan mounting his own presidential campaign, the PAC raised "only" $2.4 million in 1979-80. In the first six months of 1981, it had collected about $600,000 more.

Although some of the presidential PACs were short-lived, there was agreement among their directors that a PAC is a necessity for a presidential hopeful under the existing campaign finance law. No longer are candidates permitted to tap sympathetic individuals or groups for large donations, nor can they count on a single aide or their congressional staff to handle scheduling requests throughout the increasingly long presidential campaigns. "The law forces top national candidates into PACs," observed Paul Russo, the executive director of Dole's Campaign America. "How else would you pay for travel?"

Another PAC spokesman agreed with Russo, but put it more bluntly: "Any potential candidate has to ally himself with this type of structure," he said. "They have to move around the country and meet party leaders. The law forces us to set up dodges called PACs."

4

Washington Fund-Raisers

When Mark Green headed up Ralph Nader's Congress Watch in Washington, he used to say that no one knew more than he did about the influence of campaign money on Congress. And as a co-author of the book *Who Runs Congress?*, Green helped popularize the idea that special-interest political action committees (PACs) "own" Congress.

But when Green decided to run in 1980 for Congress himself, from New York's 18th District, he scheduled a modest $100-a-head fund-raising dinner, and guess who was invited: mentor Ralph Nader, economist John Kenneth Galbraith, a lot of liberals . . . and a passel of PACs.

Green explained in an interview, "I have to raise money now. . . . Otherwise, it would be like playing tennis and refusing to hit the ball." Ironic as this may sound, Green's fund-raising efforts simply provided evidence that he had learned the elementary lesson of modern campaign finance: Get the Washington money.

The most popular way to do that is to throw a party and offer potential donors the opportunity, for a price ranging from $100 to $1,000 a head, to sip cocktails, munch canapés, and mingle with members of Congress and their staffs. The donors usually are lobbyists who buy their tickets with money from PACs organized by businesses, labor unions or trade associations.

As political campaign costs have escalated and PACs have proliferated, Washington fund-raisers have kept pace, becoming a commonplace institution in the capital. Almost every available source agrees that there are more Washington fund-raisers — perhaps double the number in 1976 — that ticket prices have soared, and that they are scheduled earlier in each campaign cycle. Because fund-raisers are not just attended by representatives of special interests, but also frequently are organized by them, they are more than just another campaign endeavor. Directly or indirectly, they are lobbying events as well.

While many in Washington see that as harmless, or even a beneficial stimulant to the political process, an outspoken minority thinks this trend has brought fund raising and law making too close for comfort. Lobbyists, these critics say, use their fund-raising prowess to win extraordinary access to members of Congress. At the same time, legislators may be tempted to abuse their lawmaking power to extract campaign contributions from the people who petition them for help.

"It's not a question of buying [votes]," said Fred Wertheimer, president of Common Cause. "It's a question of relationships that get built, obligations and dependencies that get established. . . . It puts PACs at the head of the line, as opposed to the great bulk of a congressman's constituents."

The Washington fund-raiser is a "phenomenon that is getting bigger and bigger and bigger," remarked Joseph S. Jenckes, a lobbyist for Abbott Laboratories. "If I don't get 400 invitations in a year, I'd flip. No, maybe more."

"They are awfully numerous," agreed Rep. Thomas S. Foley, D-Wash., who, as chairman of the House Democratic Caucus during the 96th Congress and majority whip during the 97th, attended a fair number of fund-raisers himself. "For the people who are going to these things, it must get very tiring."

There are good reasons for the proliferation of fund-raisers. Most obviously, candidates for federal office are finding they need more and more money to wage a campaign these days, more than they can easily raise from contributors in their own states.

House candidates in 1978 spent $88 million, up 44 percent from 1976. Republican and Democratic House candidates on the average spent $107,795 on their races. But close races cost a lot more. In the 74 districts where the winner received 55 percent or less of the vote, the average combined campaign cost for the candidates was $448,000.

Running for the Senate was even more expensive. A total of $65.5 million was spent on 35 Senate contests in 1978, up from $38.1 million for 33 seats in 1976. Moreover, 21 Senate candidates spent more than a million dollars compared to 10 in 1976.

"As long as there's a source of money somewhere else, why take it all out of your district?" commented Jay Stone, an aide to Rep. Henson Moore, R-La. In Moore's district, he noted, funding sources in 1980 were milked dry by a high-priced gubernatorial campaign and a spate of local races — as well as by the 1982 Senate and House races.

Impact of Campaign 'Reforms'

Ironically, the passage in 1971 and 1974 of a series of comprehensive reforms in the federal election process may have been the single most significant reason for the increasing popularity of Washington fund-raisers. The laws allowed corporations and unions to become campaign contributors through the vehicle of political action committees and at the same time restricted the amounts individual donors could give. *(PACs, Chapter 3, p. 41)*

PACs flourished — increasing from none in 1972 to 608 by the end of 1974, and to more than 2,600 by mid-1981. Cash-hungry candidates eagerly reached out to them. Because the highest concentration of PACs is in Washington, the Washington fund-raiser became a logical way to get money from them. The candidate needed simply to schedule a party, charge for the tickets, and convince as many PACs as possible to attend.

"PAC money," explained Common Cause's Wertheimer, "is the cheapest and the easiest money to get if you're an incumbent." *(Incumbents and challengers, box, p. 66)*

"Washington is not full of big Republican givers," commented independent political consultant Robert J. Perkins, who organizes fund-raisers for Republican politicians. "But the concentration of PACs is greater here than anywhere else. So Washington fund-raising events concentrate on PACs."

Early Bird Fund-raisers

As the competition for PAC dollars has become more intense, candidates have begun to schedule their fund-raising events earlier and earlier in the election cycle. Cocktail parties and receptions for the 1982 election began to occur almost immediately after the debts were paid off for the 1980 election.

Once a member decides to hold a Washington fund-raiser, he or she has plenty of places to turn for logistical help. A member's congressional staff can lend a hand, though federal law forbids a staffer from helping out during office hours or even while physically in the office. The House and Senate party campaign committees also can be of some assistance. They can provide candidates with advice, mailing lists, and help with planning and organizing an event and making follow-up telephone calls to the targets of the candidate's invitations — all at no cost to the candidate.

So great has the demand for fund-raising dates become that the Democratic and Republican congressional campaign committees even play traffic cop. To avoid scheduling conflicts, every three to four weeks they mail out complete listings of upcoming Washington fund-raising events.

A lot of candidates, though, want more specialized help. Some will seek out professional fund-raisers who — for a fee — will do all the work of organizing and putting on the event. *(People, box, pp. 60-61)*

Help from Lobbyists

More often, though, incumbents find that they can get the same kind of help — at no cost — from lobbyists. Lobbyists can help in a number of ways. They can donate mailing lists for the invitations, and then make the follow-up telephone calls to push for the ticket sale. Or, a lobbyist actually can throw the fund-raiser, hosting it as well as donating the organizing time, the food and drinks, the mailing list and even the location. Inevitably, the lobbyists who help out also turn out to have a professional interest in the member's legislative activities.

Rep. Joseph P. Addabbo, D-N.Y., chairman of the House Appropriations Subcommittee on Defense, raised $23,375 in 1979 at a fund-raiser heavily attended by defense contractors. The assistant treasurer of the effort was James McDonald, a lobbyist for Northrop Corp., the huge aircraft and weaponry company. McDonald said he has been helping the chairman organize fund-raisers since 1972, because "Joe Addabbo and I have been friends for 15 years." He said he only handles "a small part" of Northrop's Washington interests.

McDonald also helped raise money for Rep. Leo C. Zeferetti, D-N.Y., and half a dozen others, he said, and for many years was a principal fund-raiser for former Rep. Thomas Morgan, D-Pa. (1945-77), chairman of the House Foreign Affairs Committee. Other examples:

● Abbott Laboratories' Jenckes helped organize a $150-a-head breakfast prior to the 1980 elections for Rep. James R. Jones, D-Okla., a key member of the Ways and Means Committee, which handles much of the health legislation of concern to Abbott. Jenckes also helped out Rep. Tom Loeffler, R-Texas, and Sen. John Glenn, D-Ohio. Glenn and Loeffler both come from states where Abbott has plants.

● William R. Edgar, vice president for government relations of the General Aviation Manufacturers Association, called colleagues to solicit support for Rep. Robert Duncan, D-Ore., chairman of the House Appropriations Subcommittee on Transportation. Duncan's campaign was unsuccessful.

● Robert Barrie, lobbyist for General Electric, and Thomas H. Boggs, whose clients include several energy giants, were co-hosts for a $1,000-a-head dinner in March 1980 for Sen. Mike Gravel, D-Alaska, chairman of subcommittees on energy taxation and water resources. Gravel also lost his bid for re-election.

● Lucinda Williams, a lobbyist for the Federation of American Hospitals and active on many members' fund-raising steering committees, frequently assists members who work on committees handling health legislation. In 1979 her beneficiaries included Ways and Means member Ken Holland, D-S.C., and the Commerce Committee's James D. Santini, D-Nev.

● Jack H. McDonald, a former congressman (R-Mich., 1967-73) turned lobbyist — his clients include American Express Co., Burroughs Corp. and the Sugar Association — helped promote a successful event for Rep. Guy Vander Jagt, R-Mich., of the tax-writing Ways and Means Committee. He said he also had aided at least five other members of congress. "I just work for my friends," McDonald said. "In a lot of cases, I've never lobbied them."

"Beyond the $100 or $200 you can give to a candidate, the more important thing is helping him arrange his fund-raiser," said Linda Jenckes, lobbyist for the Health Insurance Association of America. "It's a double way to say, 'Thank you, and I hope you get elected.'" She added: "Those that don't get this kind of support get the message: 'Hey, maybe I'm not doing a good job.'"

Hits, Flops and Power

Though there may be many reasons why a particular fund-raiser turns out to be a hit or a flop, some factors clearly are more important than others. Perhaps the key consideration is the power of the candidate for whom the fund-raiser is being thrown, and the candidate's willingness to use that position of influence to promote ticket sales.

For this reason, junior members and challengers often do better staying away from the Washington fund-raiser altogether. They usually are better off raising their money in some other way. For the more senior members, on the other hand, the longer they have been around and the more powerful their committee assignments, the better are the odds of turning an evening of handshakes and cocktails into a tidy list of contributors.

"The number of people who think you are wonderful tends to increase as you climb the ladder," explained veteran fund-raiser Leslie Israel, who was labor coordinator of the Kennedy for President campaign. One way incumbents try to take maximum advantage of their seniority is by targeting their invitations to the lobbyists and PAC officials they feel are least able to turn them down.

"The most important thing is your list," Response Marketing's Bradley Sean O'Leary explained. "You've got to reach everyone who would have the faintest reason for wanting to have your candidate elected." Lists, often in the form of computer tape, can be borrowed from lobbyists or bought from professionals. Perhaps the most popular is a PAC list available, free, to almost any member of Congress from the political arm of the American Trucking Associations.

While some lists are accorded a certain mystique or financial value (the truckers report donations of their list as an in-kind contribution worth $20, while the Americans for Constitutional Action value theirs at $1,200), most experts agree all are the same basic roster of PACs with a history of attending fund-raisers. Usually the list is supplemented with names of the congressman's friends and official contacts, and targeted to PACs interested in issues in which the lawmaker has made a name for himself.

Just as important are the follow-up telephone calls that are made after the invitations have gone out, preferably by close friends or influential associates of the invited guests. If the checks still do not seem to be pouring in, a candidate can up the ante by scheduling a second, more intimate gathering with a few lobbyists who might be willing to pay for his company.

In February 1980, for example, officials of energy PACs got a letter from General Electric lobbyist Robert Barrie reminding them of an upcoming fund-raiser for Gravel. Noting that at a price of "only $200" this was likely to be a large, impersonal affair, Barrie invited his friends to "make the night better for Mike" by attending a more exclusive dinner later in the evening, at $1,000 per guest.

Tailored to Transportation

An example of a fund-raising effort carefully tailored to exploit a member's legislative position was a pair of Washington events prior to the 1980 election thrown by Duncan, then chairman of the House Appropriations Transportation Subcommittee. Duncan traditionally ran shoestring campaigns against token opposition. In 1980, however, he faced a stiff primary challenge from Ron Wyden, a 30-year-old lawyer who was executive director of Oregon's Gray Panthers organization.

To put together an invitation list for his $250-a-head affairs, Duncan's executive secretary, Helen Burton, said she began with a variety of PAC mailing lists, including one from the American Trucking Associations. She added the addresses of officials of groups that had invited Duncan to speak at their conventions, business cards collected by Duncan from people who had come to see him on issues, and the names contained in a card file of contacts maintained by Thomas J. Kingfield, staff assistant of Duncan's subcommittee.

Among those making follow-up phone calls urging attendance were Duncan's legislative assistant on transportation Terry Scannell and lobbyists for the Marine Engineers Beneficial Association and the General Aviation Manufacturers Association.

Not surprisingly, about two-thirds of the proceeds from the 1979 event ended up coming from transportation PACs and individuals interested in transportation matters. "I guess it's pretty heavy with transportation people," conceded Burton, "although the transportation people did not come through as heavily as I expected they would." Duncan managed to sweeten the pot a bit with a third event, a

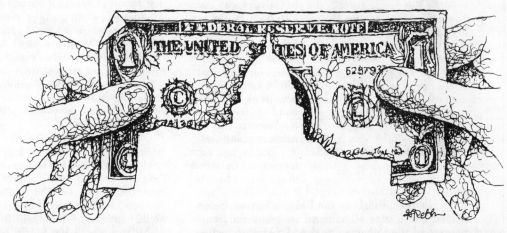

$1,000-a-plate dinner with transportation and timber representatives at the home of lobbyist and former Rep. Lloyd Meeds, D-Wash. (1965-79). Nevertheless, the aggressive, well-planned campaign of the youthful Wyden was successful and Duncan was defeated handily in the primary election.

Getting the Best Buy

When PAC officials or lobbyists try to decide whether to buy a ticket to a fund-raiser, they often act just like any other consumer: They try to figure out ahead of time what they will get for their money.

There are two basic reasons for purchasing a fund-raiser ticket. A group can base its buying decisions on the chance of winning future access to a member, or on the hope of an ideological return.

Those more interested in access buy tickets so that their candidates — if later elected — presumably will meet them at the door and welcome their future lobbying pitches.

Fund Raising for Profit or Politics ...

Charlene Baker Craycraft does it for conservatives. Victor Kamber does it for labor. Thomas H. Boggs does it for friends. Nancy Cole does it for money. What all of them do is arrange fund-raising events, using their inside knowledge of Washington to help steer millions of interested dollars into the coffers of congressional candidates.

Tom Boggs is one of a handful of Washington lawyer-lobbyists who have become almost as legendary for their ability to corral dollars as for their knack at shaping federal law. This group of "superheavies," as one fund-raising expert described them, includes lawyers and lobbyists of such high-powered firms as Patton, Boggs and Blow; Williams and Jensen; Charls E. Walker Associates; and Timmons and Co.

Helping to arrange fund-raisers not only boosts their stock with members of Congress, but it also

Thomas H. Boggs

gives them a valuable status among their fellow lobbyists. Boggs was born into politics, the son of House Majority Leader Hale Boggs, D-La. (1941-43; 1947-73), and Rep. Lindy Boggs, D-La., who took her husband's place after he disappeared in an Alaskan plane crash. Boggs' law firm lobbies for a string of clients that includes General Motors Corp., Chrysler Corp., Exxon Corp., Pepsico, Pillsbury and Ralston Purina. He also helped the Carter administration lobby for Senate passage of the Panama Canal and SALT II treaties.

In a 1980 interview, Boggs said he was involved at the time as a coordinator or participant in the campaigns of 25 or 30 candidates, ranging from Sens. Russell B. Long, D-La. ("the easiest" to raise money for) to Patrick J. Leahy, D-Vt., and John A. Durkin, D-N.H. ("the toughest" — Durkin lost). For Senate candidates, Boggs will help arrange fund-raisers not only in Washington, but also in New York, Chicago, Los Angeles and Dallas.

Boggs "has the ability to convince his clients and his friends of their need to contribute to an individual or the party," Robert C. McCandless, a member of the Democratic National Committee's finance council, told *The Washington Post* in 1979. "You've got to be able to tell your clients that if they're going to do business in this town, they better make certain contributions to the party in power."

Boggs, however, said he does not solicit or receive much campaign money from his law firm's clients, because they usually are too conservative for the candidates he favors. Mostly, he raises money from other lobbyists and their political action committees. Federal records also show he had given more than $7,000 of his own money by mid-1980 for that year's election.

Boggs said "people like me frankly resent" the growth of for-profit fund-raising companies, especially when these professionals ask him to help out as a volunteer. "These are hard political dollars to raise, and you don't like seeing them going to people who basically are just getting a percentage."

J. D. Williams, whose law firm represents such clients as Litton Industries, Brown and Root, and American Medicorp, said there are "numerous, frequent" occasions when he will help a candidate with a bit of advice — or a few phone calls to his highly reputed list of lobbying contacts. "If it's somebody that I want to give to, I give to them personally and a lot of times we will make recommendations to clients, suggestions as to where they perhaps want to consider giving," Williams said.

Williams' firm also maintains its own PAC, financed by the partners, which donated to at least 22 candidates in the 1980 elections. And Williams gives liberally from his own pocket — more than $10,000 to 1980 campaigns as of mid-May 1980, according to FEC records.

Victor Kamber probably is the best known money raiser for organized labor, putting on 12 to 15 fund-raisers a year for House and Senate candidates. Formerly political operative for the AFL-CIO Building and Construction Trades Department, he opened his own office as a consultant in 1980 but said he would continue to do unpaid fund raising for friends — his own and labor's. His loyalties are mostly to Democrats, though sometimes he harvests campaign money for Republicans. He raised $40,000 for then-Sen. Jacob K. Javits, R-N.Y., at a $1,000-a-head dinner prior to the 1980 election. In 1979 he did one for Sen. Bob Packwood, R-Ore., raising some hackles among Oregon labor groups who were still waiting to see who the Democratic challenger would be. Kamber explained that the Packwood event was designed to alert Republicans that they, too, can reap financial rewards for helping labor on its major issues.

Kamber favors public financing of congressional elections to end reliance on special interest money, but "as long as that's the system we have, and as long as the other side is doing it, I'm going to do the best job I can."

Several fund-raising professionals offer their services only to candidates of one party. Bradley Sean

... The Experts Candidates Call for Help

O'Leary, president of the Response Marketing Group, works exclusively for Republican senators, and says they get a hefty discount from his usual commercial marketing work. Prior to the 1980 election, O'Leary stated as his goal "control of the U.S. Senate for the Republican Party. That's all I'm interested in. I make more money at the other things I do, but that's the only way I can afford to do the political things." O'Leary sees the Washington fund-raiser as one part of a two-year-long candidate marketing plan; his program for a campaign often will run to more than 400 pages and include mail solicitation and other techniques.

Among Democrats, the most experienced free-lance arranger is probably Esther Coopersmith. Sen. William Proxmire, D-Wis., once called her "the den mother of all political fund-raisers." Coopersmith does not charge for her labors. In the 1980 elections, she raised money for Sen. Alan Cranston, D-Calif., as well as the unsuccessful campaigns of President Carter and Democratic Sens. Gaylord Nelson, Wis.; Birch Bayh, Ind.; and Frank Church, Idaho.

She boasts of "the great gift God has given me" for raising money. She first used that gift at the age of 17 in an Estes Kefauver campaign. Coopersmith came to Washington in about 1956, and was a pioneer of the use of political celebrities and rarely glimpsed private homes to lure donors. "If I went into this as a business, I'd really be paid very, very well," she said.

The Americans for Constitutional Action may be the foremost conservative political group in the field of fund-raising events. ACA Chairman Charlene Baker Craycraft will organize 20 or 30 events a year, usually upon request from candidates who score well in ACA's annual conservative vote rating.

ACA has a $100,000 annual budget for compiling its ratings and helping candidates find money, she said. In the 1978 election, it raised about $700,000 for conservative candidates, about 90 percent of that through Washington fund-raisers. Craycraft is inclined to scoff at "instant experts" who raise money only for pay (often they "can't get past the secretary" of a potential donor), and at members who rely on informal groups of lobbyists to drum up donations (they are too busy to devote full time to fund raising).

Several firms in Washington will arrange all or part of a fund-raiser for a fee. Nancy Cole of Fundraisers Unlimited is a 10-year veteran who will work for anyone, regardless of party. Her list of about 20 campaigns for which she worked in the 1980 election included those of Reps. Tom Bevill, D-Ala.; Matthew J. Rinaldo, R-N.J.; and Charles Wilson, D-Texas. She also worked for the unsuccessful campaigns of then-Reps. Bob Carr, D-Mich., and John Buchanan, R-Ala. She also said she prefers to

Lawyer-lobbyist J. D. Williams, center, and his wife at a party with Vice President Walter F. Mondale during the Carter administration.

handle the entire event, from preparing a mailing list and organizing a committee of lobbyist-helpers, to booking the caterer and collecting the checks. She charges about $2,000 on top of expenses.

Two newer entries in the field are PAC Associates and PAC Information Services, both organized within the year before the 1980 elections. They have computerized lists of PACs, broken down by area of interest and past giving, and offer services ranging from direct mail solicitation and targeted invitations to "full service" fund raising.

William P. Steponkus of PAC Associates, who has worked for Republicans in Congress and the White House, said his firm handles only GOP clients. The company was involved in a dozen 1980 campaigns, including those of Guy Vander Jagt, R-Mich., and Henson Moore, R-La. Steponkus said the typical price of preparing and sending invitations to an extensive, tailored list of PACs is around $5,000, including postage.

Michael deBlois of PAC Information Services said his group is non-partisan, a claim supported by his list of Senate clients in 1980. PAC Information Services also will arrange fund-raisers outside of Washington. "For a senator sitting on the Finance Committee, for example, there may not be much interest in that committee assignment in his state, but there would be in Chicago or New York," deBlois said. "We go where the greatest potential dollars are."

Crab Soup or Liz Taylor, In Fund Raising...

Walter Mondale may have been the vice president to you, but to a fund-raising expert during the 1980 campaign he was a great gimmick. Like crab soup, Liz Taylor or a day at the circus.

With hundreds of congressional candidates competing every election year to attract paying guests to Washington fund-raising events, it is no longer enough to offer tiny meatballs, watery cocktails and the over-familiar atmosphere of the Democratic or Republican clubs on Capitol Hill, say experts in the field.

While the biggest draw is still the opportunity to bend the ears of members of congress and their staffs, fund-raisers say, it helps to have a celebrity, an exclusive location, an unusual menu or a bit of song and dance — a gimmick.

"On July 4 last year, Americans spent $610 million on fireworks," said Bradley Sean O'Leary, president of Response Marketing Group in Washington. "That's compared to about $400 million spent every two years to elect a Congress. I've got to say that cracking the entertainment dollar is easier than competing for the political dollar. If you give them more bang for the buck, you have a better chance at those dollars."

O'Leary is remembered in fund-raising circles as the man who had John Wayne enter a 1972 Nixon-Agnew fund-raiser riding shotgun on a stagecoach drawn by four white Belgian horses. Wayne's dramatic entrance brought the entire, formally attired crowd to its feet, jumping onto table tops and cheering wildly.

Regional Themes

Probably the most common gimmick in Washington these days is a party with a regional theme. Ted Miller, general manager of the Capitol Hill Club, said he would suggest ham and bourbon for a Kentucky congressman, salmon and crab for an Alaskan, and, of course, chili for a Texan. Nevada Democrat James Santini evokes the Wild West with an annual banquet of buffalo, quail, venison and other game, while Louisianan John B. Breaux, D, feeds his contributors Cajun food.

Marty Russo, D-Ill., who is of Italian descent, featured Italian food. William H. Gray III, D-Pa., who is black, set one end of a banquet table with ribs, black-eyed peas and collard greens, the other end with roast beef. Barbara A. Mikulski, D-Md., served Maryland fried chicken and crab soup, while William Lehman, D-Fla., imports stone crabs from a famous Miami restaurant. In a more homey touch, Don Bailey, D-Pa., had various ethnic groups from his district bring in their traditional dishes for a fund-raising potluck.

Rep. Tony Coelho, D-Calif., topped the usual limits for freshman fund-raisers by distributing individual bottles of California wine, each labeled with the names of Coelho and the contributor.

Clowns, Midgets and Showgirls

One of the more unusual non-culinary gimmicks is Rep. Andy Ireland's, D-Fla., annual trip to the circus. When the Ringling Bros. and Barnum & Bailey Circus, which winters in Ireland's district, comes to Washington, the congressman books a block of tickets, puts up a tent beside the D.C. Armory, and arranges for clowns, midgets and showgirls to come over and entertain the crowd before showtime. At $250 for a lobbyist and his family, the event brings in about $20,000, according to an Ireland aide.

Rep. James J. Howard, D-N.J., once rented a boat and cruised his fund-raiser down the Potomac River. House Majority Leader Jim Wright's, D-Texas, annual, multi-candidate soiree, which Common Cause has dubbed "the Super Bowl of fund-raisers," is usually an opportunity to see members of Congress let down their hair. In 1980 Rep. Howard provided the entertainment, singing his version of the mining song "Sixteen Tons" — bewailing the "Sixteen Hours" in a congressman's workday.

When Rep. Bella S. Abzug, D-N.Y. (1971-77), ran for the Senate in 1976, she rented a theater and showed her husband's film of a trip 10 congress-

"This town works on personal relationships," fund-raiser Israel said. "Anytime there's an opportunity to develop those relationships, it's a plus.

"The most anybody figures they can get in this business is access. You can't buy a vote. What you can do is say, 'Listen, I've helped you. Now let me make my case, and then you can make up your mind at least having heard my side of the story.' "

Officials of the American Trucking Associations' PAC, for example, go to almost every fund-raiser they are invited to. "We're not that interested in whether the man's a liberal, conservative, Democrat or Republican," said lobbyist John M. Kinnaird. "We're just interested in whether he is friendly or has an open mind on the issues we're concerned with."

On the other side are the groups hoping to funnel their contributions so effectively that the balance of thought in Congress eventually will be tipped toward their point of view. For example, BIPAC — the Business-Industry PAC — intended to dole out its 1980 campaign war chest of

...Candidates Find You Gotta Have a Gimmick

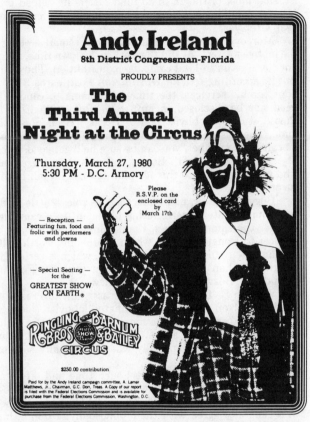

Poster for Rep. Andy Ireland's Circus Fund-raiser

women took to China — home movies at up to $100 a head.

Star Quality

A star of show business or politics, or an invitation to a rarely viewed home, usually will draw a crowd in Washington.

Sen. Edward M. Kennedy, D-Mass., can count on plenty of takers when he opens his home for a fund-raiser, as he has on a few occasions. Wealthy Washington socialite Anna C. Chennault sometimes opens her plush penthouse for Republican candidates. And few people turn down invitations to the home of Sen. John W. Warner, R-Va. Before their separation, his wife, actress Elizabeth Taylor, was a tireless fund-raiser for GOP causes.

"She must have a heart of gold," a political action committee director remarked. "Sure, she choked on a chicken bone. She must eat 6,000 chickens a year."

For Democrats, former national party Chairman Robert S. Strauss is close to the top as a fund-raiser. A June 1979 "Mo Udall Birthday Party" in Tucson, Ariz., featuring Strauss, raised about $50,000, more than double the take at a Udall fund-raiser five months later in Washington.

One of the more profitable Washington fund-raisers by a challenger was held by Democrat Gene Wenstrom of Minnesota, who advertised Mondale as his star attraction. The vice president canceled at the last minute, but was booked for a later date. The guests got rain checks.

Fund-raisers: No Fun

Despite all the efforts to find gimmicks, fun fund-raisers are the exception rather than the rule, say many of the lobbyists who attend them. More often than not, the food, surroundings and company are predictable, and the events are all in a monotonous day's work.

"The food is generally all the same," said a lobbyist for a major corporation. "I don't think people go for the food. If they think that's why a guy does or doesn't show up, they're nuts."

In his 1978 campaign, Sen. Mark O. Hatfield, R-Ore., sensed the general distaste for conventional fund-raisers and found a way to cash in on it. He staged a $100-a-plate dinner without the dinner. He simply sent donors an engraved china plate.

$250,000 based solely on which candidate was "more business-oriented," according to the PAC's president, Joseph Fanelli. Candidates are judged on the basis of business groups' vote ratings and consultations with local businessmen, he said. "Since we don't lobby, we don't even think about access."

More often, the decision whether or not to buy is based on a combination of ideological compatibility and access. For example, Rohm and Haas Co.'s $10,000-a-year PAC account will go toward the support of "members who sup-

port our point of view," said Kenneth E. Davis, the chemical and plastics firm's director of government relations. "For those who support our point of view, they don't need to ask. Our natural inclination is to give to their campaigns."

However, "some members from marginal districts might come to us and ask to see it their way, and half the time we'll sympathize with them. We might need access to a guy or a committee report or some information. There are a lot of off-the-book relationships we have with guys whose business record with the Chamber of Commerce is a zero," Davis said.

Although back in the district a member might charge as little as $10 or $25 for a fund-raiser, Washington ticket prices rarely go below $100 each and often are much more, reflecting what the market will bear. A typical ticket that was $100 in 1977-78 was running $200 to $250 in 1979-80, lobbyists reported. The price of admission to a fund-raiser for an incumbent senator can cost as much as $1,000 a head.

The cost of throwing a fund-raiser in the Republicans' Capitol Hill Club or the Democrats' National Democratic Club can run as low as $15 a person for a simple reception with a bar and hors d'oeuvres, or as high as $50 a head for exotic food and a fancier bar, according to Ted Miller, general manager of the Capitol Hill Club.

Though a freshman incumbent's fund-raiser may typically rake in $8,500 or less, the take for a more senior member generally ranges between $15,000 and $60,000.

Fringe Benefits

Many PAC officials and lobbyists buy tickets to fund-raisers and then do not show up. But those who do get more than just clam dip and a weak drink. They can see and be seen by the member throwing the event, make business contacts, meet other lobbyists — and maybe even get in some legislative lobbying on the side.

Most lobbyists agree that it is bad form to buttonhole a member at his own fund-raisers, although the practice is not unheard of. However, the other senators and House members in attendance — invited to the reception as window dressing — are considered fair game.

"On a matter of great importance, it's unlikely you would go to a guy at his own fund-raiser and tell him you need his vote," said Rohm and Haas' Davis. "It's really amateurish and not the way to win his respect. If you have to go to the guy's fund-raiser to ask him for his vote, then you're already too late. You should have known before buying the ticket that he would give you his vote."

For the other incumbents in attendance, on the other hand, the rule seems to be that that is what they are there for. "I can be as direct as I want with those fellows because it's just like meeting someone at a cocktail party," Davis said. "If a guy can get his entire state delegation, or a whole bunch of senators to attend, that sets up a great opportunity to get to meet a guy you've been trying to reach for three weeks but you can't get past his legislative assistant," explained a transportation lobbyist.

Joseph Miller, who lobbies for the Marine Engineers Beneficial Association, said perhaps one fund-raiser out of four will produce a lobbying opportunity or a tidbit of intelligence; more often, he said, attendance is simply "showing the flag. It's telling the guy you cared enough to come."

Canapés and Conflicts

In the view of some lobbyists and members of Congress, the fund-raising minuet of lobbyists and candidates unduly influences the making of the nation's laws and creates frequent opportunities for conflicts of interest. Exactly what a lobbyist buys for his $250 ticket to a fund-raiser is disputed. At the most, it appears to assure access; at the least, it seems to give some peace of mind.

But in many cases the relationship is more complex — especially when a lobbyist actually organizes a fund-raiser or works on a fund-raising steering committee. Such assistance often blossoms from a one-time favor into a perennial relationship. Thomas Boggs, the Washington lawyer-lobbyist, said most of the 25 to 30 fund-raisers he helped organize for candidates in 1980 were for people he had helped year after year.

Moreover, according to an FEC spokesman, so long as the lobbyist asserts he did the work on his own time, it does not count as an in-kind campaign contribution. Thus while Boggs, according to *The Washington Post*, earns $165 an hour for his services, the time he donates to candidates need not be disclosed in any way. "Put yourself in his shoes," a fellow lobbyist said of Boggs. "He is one smart dude. There is nothing in it financially for him, but when he calls that member, you can be sure he'll get good access. My surprise is not with Boggs, but with the congressman who would let him do this for him. It's not illegal, but it's surprising."

Boggs, however, maintains that his role is little different from an entertainer offering his talent to a campaign. "Under the campaign laws, Frank Sinatra can donate his services to Ronald Reagan, which is probably worth half a million dollars for a one-night concert, which is certainly a lot greater than the $1,000 maximum you can give to a candidate," Boggs said in an interview.

William E. Timmons, a former assistant to Presidents Ford and Nixon and now a Washington lobbyist, said, "If I were a member, I would be more appreciative of a fellow who spent some time and effort at it, as opposed to just giving some money, especially when it's usually someone else's money."

But Timmons does not feel such time and effort are rewarded with extra influence. "I just think the rising costs of a campaign mean politicians have got to appeal to those who generally agree with their philosophy. I don't think there's anything sinister in that. I think that's just democracy working," he said.

Lawyer J. D. Williams, another well-known fund-raiser, said the fund-raising partnership of candidates and lobbyists is beneficial because "you not only get people's financial support, but you can develop relationships where you can get a lot of advice on how to be an effective member of the House, and how to advance your career and your constituents' interests."

Others are not as comfortable with this relationship between candidates and lobbyists. One representative of a major corporation pointed out that lobbyists on a company payroll must either take time off without pay or risk violating the law against corporate campaign contributions. "I just don't think that's a valid thing for us to be doing. I don't mind putting in a good word for some of my friends ... but where do you stop?"

A lobbyist who fought for a bill to contain hospital costs in 1979 — and lost — complained that an opposing lobbyist, Lucinda Williams of the Federation of American Hospitals, was helping to arrange fund-raisers for key congressmen during deliberations on the bill. "I happen to believe it's a good way to buy votes and make friends," the lobbyist said. "But who's to say her clientele wouldn't vote that way anyway?"

"I'm not helping anybody that I wouldn't have helped anyway," Williams replied. Noting that fund-raisers may take months to set up, she added, "How am I to know if the vote on whatever issue will be the same week?"

The Goldschmidt Fund-Raiser That Wasn't

A fund-raiser thrown by Rep. James J. Florio, D-N.J., prior to the 1980 elections, illustrates why fund-raisers are so popular with members of Congress and lobbyists alike.

The members' influence in writing laws may help persuade lobbyists to buy tickets. Lobbyists often willingly buy the tickets because they feel this may give them a favored status with the member in the future. Sometimes, though, this hoped-for relationship can go awry. A lobbyist may send his money to the wrong man. Or, occasionally, an influential Washington name may be misused, accidentally or otherwise. The Florio episode is a case in point.

As chairman of the House Commerce (now Energy and Commerce) Subcommittee on Transportation, Rep. Florio had jurisdiction over several key aspects of national transportation policy. The invitation to his March 10 fund-raising reception featured the seal of the Transportation Department and the message: "The Secretary of Transportation, Honorable Neil Goldschmidt, cordially invites you to join him for a reception for Congressman Jim Florio."

To a lobbyist interested in transportation matters, the presence of Goldschmidt alone was a sure-fire draw. But the invitation also was good for Florio's image because it made him appear so powerful that the transportation secretary would want to sponsor a fund-raiser for him. In the world of Washington influence peddling, a transportation lobbyist would think twice before ignoring such an event.

The strategy apparently worked, for Florio. The fund-raiser brought in $26,900 for his campaign.

But it was less of a success for at least one lobbyist, Frank P. Gallagher, president of the New Jersey Bus Association. He heard about the fund-raiser from American Bus Association (ABA) Governmental Affairs Director David H. Miller, who got the invitation at ABA's Washington headquarters.

Florio's subcommittee at the time was considering legislation authorizing funds for the completion of the Northeast passenger rail corridor. The subcommittee planned New Jersey field hearings on the legislation and Gallagher wanted to testify because the bus industry competes with passenger rail service in the Northeast corridor.

Despite the ticket purchase, however, Florio turned down Gallagher's plea. Buses, Florio told Gallagher, were under the jurisdiction of the Public Works Subcommittee on Surface Transportation, chaired by fellow New Jersey Democrat James J. Howard. Gallagher wrote Miller to thank him for the information about the Florio fund-raiser. He then told him of his failure to change Florio's mind. Finally, he added: "If you receive any invitation for a Jim Howard fund-raiser, please let us know."

Goldschmidt was secretary of transportation during the Carter administration. Although it appeared that he had sponsored the Florio event, in fact he was only an invited guest at a function put on by Florio's campaign committee. "There was some confusion about the fund-raiser because it gave the impression that Mr. Goldschmidt was the sponsor," a Transportation Department spokeswoman said. "Mr. Goldschmidt has never given a fund-raiser."

Florio's office referred the matter to campaign treasurer Tom Cucinotta, who said he had never seen the invitation and had played no role in its design. When a reporter described the invitation to him, he said: "There was a picture of the Transportation Department seal at the top? That doesn't sound too cool." Cucinotta added: "There was never any intention to convey the impression that he [Goldschmidt] was sponsoring the event. I guess I'd have to offer an apology if this impression was given."

The Secretary of Transportation

Honorable Neil Goldschmidt

cordially invites you

to join him

for a reception

for

Congressman Jim Florio

on March 10, 1980

at

The Reserve Officer's Club

One Constitution Avenue, N.E.

6 - 8 p.m.

RSVP
Envelope Enclosed

Price
$250 per person

While Incumbents Rake the Money In...

October 17, 1979 — A lively crowd circles the hors d'oeuvre table in the Presidential Room of Washington's Mayflower Hotel, paying homage (at $1,000 a head) to Sen. Warren G. Magnuson, D-Wash., then chairman of the Senate Appropriations Committee and Senate president pro tempore.

Many of the Senate's big names are here — Kennedy, Byrd, Cranston, Jackson — surrounded by a Who's Who of Washington lobbyists. Brock Adams, former secretary of transportation and Washington state congressman, and now a lobbyist, mugs for a Seattle TV crew, pulling out his checkbook and signing over $1,000 to the Magnuson campaign.

The take for the evening: About $125,000.

April 17, 1980 — Magnuson's challenger, Washington Attorney General Slade Gorton, waits with his wife at the doorway to the Republican Capitol Hill Club. The contributors, who have paid $100 a head, trickle in, perhaps 30 paying guests, a few Republican senators, and enough non-paying friends to put a small dent in a huge round of beef.

Later, one of the lobbyists in attendance will implore a reporter not to use his name because "I don't want the company to get in trouble with Warren Magnuson. And I want to keep my job."

The take: $3,525.

Although the incumbent Magnuson, an old-fashioned New Deal, pork-barrel politician, lost in the 1980 election to the moderate Republican Gorton, his fund-raising experiences still serve as examples of one of the advantages of incumbency.

High Card

If campaign fund raising is a deck stacked against challengers, the Washington fund-raiser is one of the highest cards an incumbent can hold.

According to a Federal Election Commission study of the 1978 elections, political action committees give $3 to incumbents for every $1 they give challengers. And while there are no official figures to measure it, incumbents almost certainly get the lion's share of the money passed out at capital fund-raisers.

"Non-incumbents who come to Washington are frequently disappointed and, indeed, to a degree embittered by the lack of interest in their efforts here, because this town is just geared toward incumbents," said J. D. Williams, a lawyer-lobbyist and one of the city's best-known fund-raisers. "It's not a town of gamblers. Or even speculators."

Charlene Baker Craycraft, who organizes fund-raisers for the conservative Americans for Constitutional Action, estimates that of the 250 PACs she can count on to help conservative candidates, perhaps 25 will assist a challenger. "Washington really is a city full of people who want to get a little bit of mileage out of their contributions," she said.

The most valued mileage is the chance to talk to a powerful incumbent, and to have him remember that you helped his campaign. Because the number of PACs has grown, experts say there is more money for everyone in the capital, including non-incumbents. And some PACs, perhaps an increasing number, are more concerned with a candidate's philosophy than his power.

The Business-Industry PAC, for instance, which does not lobby, gave two-thirds of its money in the 1978 election to non-incumbents. The National Conservative PAC organized about 25 fund-raisers prior to the 1980 elections, almost all for challengers because, explained Chairman John T. Dolan, "By and large, we're more interested in changing the Congress than preserving it. And we're not interested in access."

But traditionally, Washington donors have preferred to use their money to build up useful friendships with members who have proved their value.

Rule of the Game

"Our basic rule," said John M. Kinnaird, vice president for government relations of the American Trucking Associations, "is that we normally would support the incumbent unless he's been totally anti-trucking in everything he's done. Why? Well, you avoid a lot of political problems. And then, why not

Since fund-raising and legislating seasons coincide, the timing may be happenstance, but sometimes it can be convenient for the lobbyist. For example, former building trades representative Victor Kamber's $1,000-a-head fund-raiser for then-Sen. Jacob Javits, R-N.Y., a member of the Labor and Public Welfare Committee, came when the committee was mulling an occupational safety bill the union hotly opposed.

One senior House Democrat, however, said most members are extremely sensitive to the possibility of seeming to be unduly influenced by lobbyist-contributors. "There is a

very fine line in this business between soliciting support and engaging in even jocular attempts to gain favors in exchange for campaign contributions," he said. "Most members would not want the contribution if they thought it meant they were guaranteeing their support for a particular position, even if they already held that position."

Pressure from Members

From the lobbyists' point of view, sometimes the lawmaker exploits their relationship. A lobbyist invited to Rep. Duncan's 1979 fund-raiser was chagrined that the

...Challengers Often Find It More Difficult

support him? He's been there. You've gotten to know him. You've got that relationship. You just don't want to gamble on it. I don't."

"Challengers definitely have to work harder because before you give him money he has to establish his credibility by giving you an idea of what he's interested in and his stand on the issues," said another Washington lobbyist. "But the main reason incumbents get the money as opposed to challengers is that you don't want to alienate the incumbents."

The Washington fund-raiser is especially important to incumbents because it is a card that can be played early in the campaign. PACs that normally make their major giving decisions later on, usually have enough loose money so their Washington representative can attend fund-raisers early in the off-election year. This gives the incumbent a head start on the money necessary to reserve television time, hire a direct-mail specialist, and get a campaign organized.

One Challenger's Story

By most conventional wisdom, Slade Gorton represented the most credible challenger Magnuson had had in his seven races for the Senate. He was popular in the state, an energetic campaigner facing a 75-year-old incumbent, a moderate conservative running against a man long identified with government spending and regulation.

But in the race for dollars, Gorton gave himself an early handicap by declaring he would not accept any money from PACs. His intent was to dramatize Magnuson's reliance on PAC money; and he probably realized he could not compete with the incumbent in soliciting such safe-money bettors. Nonetheless, when Dallas Salisbury, an old friend who now runs an insurance research firm in Washington, proposed a Washington fund-raiser, Gorton went along.

Salisbury followed standard procedure, borrowing a mailing list from the Republican Senatorial Campaign Committee and cross-checking it with a PAC directory purchased from a local press. He sent out about 3,000 invitations, then rounded up some friends — mostly lawyers and lobbyists — to make more than 800 follow-up phone calls.

He ran into two problems, neither one unexpected. First, many lobbyists were not willing to come if their PACs could not pick up the tab. And second, many said they did not want to take on the chairman of the Appropriations Committee unless they were pretty sure he was going to lose. "They said, 'Are you out of your mind?' " Salisbury recalled on the evening of the fund-raiser.

Gorton said even some of the Republican senators who showed up to lend credence to his event "say they can't walk by [Magnuson] without him chewing their ears off." Two lobbyists who did attend both stressed afterwards that they had paid from their own pockets, as a personal gesture, after meeting Gorton and liking him. Both said their firms were contributing to Magnuson.

Though the Gorton fund-raiser did not raise much money, Salisbury said that — along with a fund-raising lunch in New York that raised an equivalent amount — it made Gorton's trip worthwhile. And he said it established some future contacts, useful especially when Magnuson seemed to be in trouble.

Still, as of March 31, 1980, according to FEC reports, Gorton's entire campaign had raised $82,191, about two-thirds of Magnuson's haul that one evening in October 1979.

Magnuson's event — sponsored by about 30 senators and promoted by a group of aides and lobbyists — drew money from scores of PACs and executives with interests before Appropriations and the Commerce Committee he used to chair. Magnuson's administrative assistant, Michael Steward, nevertheless disparaged the notion that his legislative power gave the senator a fund-raising advantage.

"I would presume it's because Magnuson has a strong record and people that are contributing to his campaign think he's the best candidate," Steward said.

---

invitation arrived shortly after his group had testified before Duncan's subcommittee, requesting an increase in the annual appropriations bill. The subcommittee did not mark up the bill until after Duncan's event.

That "made it uncomfortable," the lobbyist said. "Whether or not there was any pressure, we felt we should go." Duncan's executive secretary, Helen Burton, said the fund-raiser unavoidably had been rescheduled from an earlier date and its time was "rather fortuitous. . . . If they didn't want to participate, they didn't have to," she said. "If that is a problem, no one told me about it."

Rep. James M. Hanley, D-N.Y., chairman of the Post Office and Civil Service Committee, staged a June 1979 fund-raiser a few weeks after his committee drafted a bill to increase federal postal subsidies. The lion's share of the $40,000 he raised came from representatives of postal unions, magazine publishers, direct mail outfits and other groups with a special interest in the postal issues.

Hanley later announced he would retire at the end of 1980. An aide said the congressman had not decided what to do with the $39,812 in his campaign account, although under existing law he could declare it as income and keep

Getting the Money for an Expensive Race

On a damp April evening in spring 1980, Rep. Robert K. Dornan, R-Calif., looked out at the faces crammed tightly into the McLean, Va., basement of direct mail wizard Richard A. Viguerie, and was pleased.

"Because of people like Richard Viguerie, because of people like you," he told the admiring faces, "we have raised more money in the off-year than any other congressman in the history of America."

On Dornan's left stood singer Pat Boone, who came as a personal favor to Dornan. Next to Boone stood Viguerie, who had opened up his home for this fund-raiser as "just one of those things I try to do to help the conservative movement."

For the price of a $100 ticket, the several hundred guests were able to crowd the basement bar, snack at hors d'oeuvres and oysters, and knock off prodigious quantities of smoked salmon, chicken curry on rice, salad, coffee and pastries. They were allowed to poke their noses into every corner of Viguerie's oversized suburban home, shake hands and chat with the candidate, and get a pep talk from Boone. The reward: an estimated $50,000 in campaign funds.

The fund-raiser was just one part of a strategy Dornan expected to produce $600,000 by the end of May 1980. Through March, Dornan said he had raised about $450,000, most of it from direct mail campaigns by two firms — one of them Viguerie's. These donations were being augmented by at least four fund-raisers, Dornan said.

In 1978 Dornan's 27th District had been the site of the closest, most expensive race in California that year. Dornan spent $291,762 to squeak to a 51 percent to 49 percent victory over Democratic opponent Carey Peck. Peck had spent $308,017 on the campaign, much of it raised with the help of his actor father, Gregory Peck.

For 1980 Dornan said he wanted to be better prepared. "Peck said he's going to raise $600,000," Dornan said. "I said, 'Richard [Viguerie], let's get going.'" Although the figures were high, they were not out of line with the costs of a close House race. The 1978 Dornan-Peck contest illustrates the skyrocketing costs of federal campaigning.

Federal Election Commission figures show that House candidates in 1978 spent $88 million on the November ballot, a 44 percent increase over the $60.9 million in 1976 expenditures. Moreover, spending on House elections between 1972 and 1978 rose 34 percent over the increase in the Consumer Price Index, according to a Harvard University study.

Together Dornan and Peck spent $599,779 in 1978, an average of $299,889 each. Not long ago a campaign in which two House candidates spent even a quarter million dollars was considered expensive. In 1972, 24 districts had campaigns that large. In 1976, 63 campaigns passed the $250,000 mark. By 1978, nearly a third of the House contests — 129 — cost more than $250,000.

A principal reason is that close races cost a lot of money, particularly in suburban districts such as Dornan's.

In individual spending, the Dornan-Peck race also was part of the growing tendency toward expensive House races. In 1976, there were just 15 House general election candidates whose individual campaigns cost more than $250,000. In 1978, the figure was 81.

For Dornan, the re-election costs are moving in a direction opposite to those of many colleagues; as a rule, the longer a member is around the House, the less costly a re-election campaign becomes. Members who were first elected in 1976, as was Dornan, spent an average of $143,000 to win re-election in 1978. For the 216 representatives elected before 1974, the average campaign cost just $87,000.

Fund-raisers would seem to be a good way to raise campaign dollars. Ticket sales for the Dornan reception in Viguerie's home were brisk. The party cost Dornan nothing because Viguerie donated the food and drink, and the site. On the other hand, direct mail campaigns have expensive printing and postage costs, and only a small percentage of the letters produce a cash return.

Dornan's campaign finance reports, filed with the Federal Election Commission, confirm that impression. Through March 31, 1980, according to the reports, the Dornan campaign had raised $439,537 — most of it presumably by direct mail. His expenses for the same period, however, were $404,078.

"Does Dornan really have $450,000 on hand?" opponent Peck asked in a telephone interview. "His direct mail expenses are sky-high. I think his overall totals are very impressive, but after expenses, what he's raised is much less than the figures."

Viguerie maintained nonetheless that direct mail was working much better for Dornan than were the Washington fund-raisers. "One gosh awful lot of work went into that reception compared to what was raised," Viguerie said. "The fund-raiser is the old way to raise money. Direct mail is one of the key components of the campaign of the future."

"I suspect that the average reception probably will raise only two to three dollars for every dollar spent," Viguerie said. By comparison, he maintained that Dornan's direct mail campaign was netting six to seven dollars for every dollar spent. The reason, he said, was that direct mail campaigns return again and again to the same contributors, asking for more money. The people who give once, Viguerie said, are likely to give every time they're asked.

it, or give it to a charity. Another congressman who retired, Commerce Committee Chairman Harley O. Staggers, D-W.Va., raised $72,095 in October 1979 at a Washington fund-raiser. An aide said Staggers mailed all the money back to contributors. Staggers' fund-raiser came at a time when his committee and its subcommittees were weighing major bills on railroads, communications and health, and when he was expected to be a conferee on a bill governing the Federal Trade Commission. His event was heavily attended by groups interested in all of those bills.

"There's always a little pressure" to buy a ticket, commented one business lobbyist. "On the few occasions when the incumbent himself calls, you are under a lot of pressure to ante up.... Sometimes, I've had to sell my whole [PAC] committee on switching its position and giving to a guy, if I've felt his pitch was so strong that I felt that to say, 'no,' would really harm our interests," he said.

Other lobbyists said it is not unusual for members of Congress to prime the pump before a fund-raiser with not-so-subtle reminders of their past favors for interest groups. Sen. Gravel, for example, preceded his 1980 election fund-raiser invitation with a series of letters, on official stationery, to energy PACs, reminding them of his staunch opposition to an oil windfall profits tax as chairman of the Finance energy subcommittee.

Rep. Charles H. Wilson, D-Calif., invited donors to an April 1980 fund-raiser with the assurance that he would be moving to a position of "even greater influence" in Congress — referring to his growing seniority on the House Armed Services and Post Office committees. The fund-raiser came a few days after Wilson's attorneys had won a two-week delay in House disciplinary proceedings against the congressman. Nevertheless, Wilson lost in the California primary.

An energy lobbyist recounted an even less subtle come-on from a high-ranking member of the House Ways and Means Committee when the lobbyist visited the member's office to discuss a tax issue. "The first question out of his mouth was, 'You guys got a PAC?' It was sort of like that was the entry fee.... We said, 'Yes, we do, and we're still making up our minds,' and then we dropped it...."

Several lobbyists say they find fund-raising solicitations especially annoying when they come from members who face little or no opposition for re-election. Rep. Richard Bolling, D-Mo., who faced token opposition and had had no serious contest since 1964, held a fund-raiser at the Democratic Club in October 1979, and a fund-raising dinner hosted by lobbyist and former Rep. Meeds in February 1980.

"Because a lot of [a member's] friends in interest groups have been asking what they can do to help ... sometimes he'll hold an event just to get them off his back," said labor political operative Kamber.

Constituent Loyalty

As a central feature of the larger phenomenon of PAC giving, the Washington fund-raiser also is subject to another criticism — that "nationalization" of campaign financing weakens a lawmaker's loyalties to his constituents back home. According to a 1979 Harvard University study, "As Washington has become the best place to raise campaign funds, a concomitant concern is the increasing detachment of candidates from their constituents."

One lobbyist who has worked and raised money for members of the House said reliance on Washington money is an increasingly touchy issue with incumbents. "It's something most of them are very, very careful about," she said. "But the fact of life is that they cannot raise enough money back home to wage an effective campaign."

Fund-raiser Statistics Hard to Uncover at FEC

Federal election law makes it difficult for the public to learn key details about congressional fund-raisers — including when and where they take place, who organizes them, who supplies the mailing lists for the invitations, who attends them and even who pays for the food and drinks. An examination by Congressional Quarterly of hundreds of campaign spending reports filed with the Federal Election Commission (FEC) indicates that while many candidates make it their business to detail how they raise their campaign dollars, others do not bother.

In its original form, the FECA of 1971 required each candidate for federal office to report to the FEC on a special form "the total amount of proceeds from the sale of tickets to each dinner, luncheon, rally and other fund-raising event." However, because all major campaign donors had to be listed on another FEC reporting form as well, many candidates simply did not file the special fund-raising event form. Because of FEC's limited staff, the requirement was not vigorously policed. And Congress voted to drop the separate form in 1979 amendments to the 1971 law. "One of the reasons they were dropped is that the commission found very little use for them," commented FEC spokesman Fred Eiland. "We're more concerned with full disclosure than with how the money was raised."

Campaign law also permits an individual to spend up to $1,000 on a candidate's campaign for food, beverages and "invitations" — including the cost of mailing lists and postage — without that money being counted as a reportable contribution. The reporting threshold originally was $500 but was raised to $1,000 in the 1979 amendments. In-kind contributions by an individual — such as the donation of one's time or home — do not have to be counted at all in computing money spent.

The net effect of the law is that a lobbyist can organize and hold a fund-raiser in his or her home and provide guests with up to $1,000 in food and drink without the event appearing in the candidate's FEC reports and without the lobbyist appearing in the reports as a contributor to the candidate's campaign.

Because of the criticism Washington fund-raising sometimes attracts, it often is a sensitive subject with members of Congress and those who attend the functions. Frequently reporters are barred, or at least discouraged, from attending; members do not put out press releases to their hometown papers announcing their fund-raisers or boasting of their success.

Rep. Don J. Pease, D-Ohio, was embarrassed in his 1978 campaign when a reporter for his hometown paper attended his Washington fund-raiser and wrote about the lobbyists in attendance. Pease started thinking there might be something to the criticism, and in 1980 he decided to forgo a Washington fund-raiser and work harder to gain individual donations from his district.

"I know it is true in most cases when members say they can accept money from a PAC and then turn around and vote against them," he said. "But I think there's still sort of an unspoken *quid pro quo* of some kind. Whether it's lending an ear, or more than lending an ear, I don't know." Pease said he found many of his colleagues also feel "uncomfortable" about Washington fund-raisers, but view them as "necessary evils" in these days of high-cost campaigning.

Despite the problems, the Washington fund-raiser is an institution that promises to continue playing a major role in the political process, if only because there is no consensus for an alternative. Common Cause, organized labor and many liberal congressmen have long argued that the answer is public financing of congressional elections, similar to that now available for presidential campaigns. They argue public financing would reduce the reliance on "interested" money.

At the other end of the spectrum, some conservatives, such as John T. Dolan of the National Conservative PAC (NCPAC), argue that the solution is to lift limits on individual donations to reduce dependence on special interest money. Asked if he considered the growth of Washington fund-raisers — and PAC spending in general — a healthy thing, Dolan said: "No, I guess I really don't. By mandating artificially low campaign spending limits, we have mandated precisely the thing the reformers were opposing. Now, their solution [public financing] is more poison."

The Harvard study leaned a long way in Dolan's direction by proposing that the limit on individual donations be raised from $1,000 to $3,000 per election. "In effect, the current law forces candidates to turn to corporate and labor PACs as well as to their personal bank accounts for the needed funds no longer available through the parties and from individual contributors," the study said. "At the same time, the limits on amounts individuals can contribute directly to candidates have served primarily to divert money into channels of organized giving." The report said raising the individual donation limit "would provide the best means to limit the potential influence of political action committees and personal wealth while simultaneously improving the flow of money into campaigns."

5

The Parties and Campaign Laws

In pure dollars and cents, the Democratic and Republican party organizations resemble David and Goliath. Even though Republicans have long been outnumbered by Democrats in Congress and state legislatures, the GOP towers over its rival in financial resources.

In the 1980 election cycle, the major federal-level Republican committees reportedly raised about $120 million, six times the total amount raised by their Democratic counterparts. And that degree of dominance is unlikely to end soon. Studies by the Citizens' Research Foundation show that Republican national committees perennially have been better off financially than Democratic national committees.

For example, in 1963 national Republican groups raised $3.3 million in contrast to $2.2 million for Democratic national committees. In 1971 the Republican committees collected $11.5 million, while the Democratic committees raised only $2.8 million.

The disparity has grown even wider since passage of the Federal Election Campaign Act (FECA) amendments in 1974. The legislation placed a cap on how much individuals and Congress could contribute to national party organizations.

Under the FECA, individuals may give $20,000 per year to a national party committee and $5,000 to any state or local party committee. However, an individual's aggregate contribution in one year to parties, political action committees (PACs) and federal candidates cannot exceed $25,000.

PACs may give $15,000 a year to a national party and $5,000 to any state and local party. Their aggregate annual contribution is not limited.

The Republicans adjusted effectively to the declining influence of "fat cat" contributors by placing a heavier emphasis on direct mail contributions. By 1981 the Republican National Committee (RNC) claimed that it had a list of more than one million contributors, with most direct mail donors sending $25 or less.

The Democrats, shackled throughout the 1970s by a multimillion-dollar debt incurred in the 1968 campaign, were slow to emulate the Republicans. Without the money to launch an extensive direct mail effort, the federal-level Democratic committees were forced to rely on pre-FECA fund-raising techniques — large donor programs and special events such as $500 or $1,000 per plate dinners. Large contributors have enabled the Democratic Party to stay financially afloat, even though they cannot be as generous to the party as they were before 1974.

GOP, DEMOCRATS COPE WITH THE LAWS

Each party has a welter of special committees set up to support its candidates. In all, the Republicans have six and the Democrats, nine.

Most of them give relatively little money. The Thomas P. O'Neill Jr. Congress Fund, set up by the House Speaker, disbursed only $1,500 to Democrats through August 1980, and the Republican National Hispanic Assembly, geared toward boosting the GOP's vote among Hispanics, gave a mere $150 to one candidate during that period.

But it is the six main national bodies — three for each party — that pack the heaviest financial weight. The Republicans' biggest givers are the RNC, the National Republican Senatorial Committee (NRSC) and the National Republican Congressional Committee (NRCC), which handles House candidates.

The Democrats have the Democratic National Committee (DNC), the Democratic Senatorial Campaign Committee (DSCC) and, for the House, the Democratic Congressional Campaign Committee (DCCC).

The DNC and the RNC have the broadest scope, dealing with both presidential and congressional races. The four other committees are dedicated solely to House or Senate candidates. In addition to giving money, the DNC and the RNC also run the national party conventions, and they push nationwide voter registration and Election Day get-out-the-vote drives.

GOP Advantage

The Democratic Party committees have portrayed themselves as poverty-stricken underdogs in an unfair battle with a money-bloated GOP. "We don't have the luxury of our Republican cousins to give the maximum to everybody," remarked DNC Treasurer Peter Kelly in 1980.

One reason the Democrats are behind financially is that their party is more prone to internal quarreling, which takes its toll. DNC fund raising was hindered in early 1980 by the divisive struggle for the Democratic presidential nomination between President Jimmy Carter and Sen. Edward M. Kennedy of Massachusetts, Democrats say. Although the DNC ultimately raised more than $12 million during the election year, three-quarters of it was not available until after July 1 when early planning should have been completed.

Also casting a large cloud over DNC fund-raising plans has been the party's decade-old debt. Nearly all of that obligation was incurred in 1968 from the expenses of the Democratic convention and the party's assumption of the leftover debts from the presidential campaigns of Hubert H. Humphrey and Robert F. Kennedy. "We cannot establish credibility as a party back in business until we make a major effort to pay off our debt," DNC Treasurer Evan Dobelle told Congressional Quarterly in 1978.

But the debt has been reduced only gradually. Initially $9.3 million, the indebtedness was whittled down by annual fund-raising telethons from 1972 through 1975. The DNC also settled part of its debts by paying some of its creditors 20 to 25 cents for each dollar owed. The Federal Election Commission (FEC) has strict regulations about how debts by political committees to corporations may be settled.

By December 1976 the DNC debt was reduced to $2.4 million. By paying off creditors — primarily airlines and telephone companies — in small increments since then, the DNC had trimmed the lingering debt to about $600,000 by late 1981.

However, the Republican financial lead has little to do with the Democratic debt or the GOP being the so-called "party of the rich." The GOP's advantage owes more to better planning. Their committees have a large, ongoing direct mail solicitation program that the Democrats have been unable to approach.

As Herbert E. Alexander, a University of Southern California political scientist, pointed out in 1980, "The Republicans are more professionalized than the Democrats at fund raising. They're able and willing to do prospecting [for mail contributors].... The Democrats haven't exploited their majority in Congress."

Ideology also is a factor in the Republican committees' financial edge. "The Republicans are a far less diverse party," explained former DNC political strategist Karl Struble. "The conservatives are in control there, and they can appeal to ideological zealots. Look at [President Gerald R.] Ford, who was a moderate. He did not do well at all in direct mail."

Three factors encouraged the GOP's direct mail push in the late 1970s. One was the FECA with its strict contribution limits. Another was the loss of the White House and with it access to some major donors. A third factor was congressional passage in 1978 of legislation giving national party committees special low rates on third-class bulk mail. (*Legislative history, box, p. 77*)

Fund-Raising Methods

Direct mail provides much of the revenue for the three national GOP groups. In 1980, the NRSC, for example,

had a base group of 350,000 donors culled from mailing lists it rented from *Business Week,* a magazine read by many corporate executives who traditionally vote Republican.

Ironically, direct mail's use as a political fund-raising device was first exploited in 1972 by a Democrat — George McGovern, the party's presidential nominee. The South Dakota senator appealed to liberals by letter and raised 40 percent, or $12 million, of his general election campaign receipts that way.

The Democrats continue to emphasize large fund-raising events, and only in the mid-1970s did the party organization begin to use direct mail. Observers attribute the delay to the man who chaired the DNC from 1972 to 1976, Robert S. Strauss, who managed President Carter's reelection campaign.

"Bob Strauss believed in those old-style fund-raisers where you go to the big contributors," said Fred Wertheimer, president of Common Cause, the public affairs lobby, and an expert on campaign finance.

According to an audit of DNC financial activity in 1980, 61 percent of the $26.5 million raised by the national committee from 1977 through 1980 came from major donors. Only 30 percent was raised through direct mail. And actually more money was raised by the DNC through direct mail in 1976 than 1980.

DNC Chairman Charles T. Manatt placed a new emphasis on direct mail fund raising after his election in early 1981. Manatt, a former chairman of the party's National Finance Council, hired the direct mail firm of Craver, Matthews, Smith, which had worked for independent presidential candidate John B. Anderson in 1980.

The firm's early efforts pointedly sought to tap displeasure with the conservative policies of the Reagan administration and its allies. Large mailings decried proposed cutbacks in the Social Security system, while smaller mailings signed by former Interior Secretary Cecil Andrus, Atlanta Mayor Maynard Jackson and former Assistant Secretary of Education Liz Carpenter sought to exploit liberal dissatisfaction with the new Republican administration on issues such as the environment and civil rights. Still, party officials only expected to raise $1 million from direct mail in 1981, compared with the $15 million that the RNC projected that it would raise from its established program.

Apart from dinners and direct mail, the parties employ a variety of devices to spur donations. A popular method among Democrats was to sell paintings furnished by sympathetic artists such as Peter Max and Lowell Nesbitt.

But probably no project was more unusual than the DNC's proposed "VIP tour" of Egypt and Israel. For $10,000 an individual or $15,000 a couple, an interested Democrat would receive private meetings with Israeli Prime Minister Menachem Begin and Egyptian President Anwar Sadat. The assassination of Sadat in October 1981 forced postponement of the trip.

Both parties have elite groups of contributors who, in return for their generosity, can attend social functions and seminars hosted by party notables. At the beginning of the 1980s the DNC had the National Finance Council for individuals who give $5,000 annually, and the Business Council for donations of at least $10,000 annually. Among congressional clubs was the Democratic House and Senate Council, with members paying $1,500 a year to belong.

Republicans had several groups. The top RNC club was the Republican Eagles, which cost $10,000 annually to belong. The Republican Senatorial Trust cost $5,000 to join, and the Republican Senatorial Inner Circle required a $1,000 contribution. Most of the groups had several hundred members each.

Legislative Maneuvering

To some Democrats, the disparity in party financing has the elements of a conspiracy. They note that former RNC Chairman Bill Brock, when he served as a senator from Tennessee (1971-77), was the prime advocate of the provision in the 1974 law that permitted big spending by party committees. Before 1974, there was not so much of a need for such party efforts for candidates because no limits existed on what private contributors could give.

A small group of Democratic activists who follow the intricacies of campaign finance say most Democrats are unaware of the challenge they face from national GOP money.

"The Republicans set out in 1974 to win control of the Senate, and it's incredible what they have been able to do," said one Democratic election law analyst. "The Democratic incumbents were a bunch of prima donnas who did not want to join with others to help themselves. Those Democrats don't know what's going on."

House Democratic leaders were more aware of the building GOP advantage, but were too heavy-handed in their attempts to curb it. In early 1978, Democrats on the House Administration Committee proposed cutting back from $30,000 to $10,000 the amount national, congressional and state party committees combined could contribute directly to a federal candidate. Under the FECA each of the three committees may give $5,000 for a primary election and another $5,000 for the general election. The Democratic plan would have allowed the national party committee and the party's congressional campaign committee combined to make a maximum contribution of $5,000 in one election year. A state party committee would have been able to give no more than $5,000 in one election year.

But with Republicans solidly opposed to any party spending limits and many Democrats fearful that it would emerge as a campaign issue to hurt them, the legislation was defeated. (*Legislative background, Chapter 1*)

MAJOR PARTY SUPPORT OF CANDIDATES

Under the landmark 1974 election law that established the existing campaign finance rules, party organization spending enjoys a privileged spot. The amount that party committees can spend on candidates is far higher than the amounts that can be spent by individuals and non-party political action committees (PACs).

To many Democrats, the Republicans are circumventing the original intent of the law, passed by a Democratic Congress that believed the existing situation allowed rich Republicans to "buy" elections. The law placed a lid of $1,000 on what an individual could give to a campaign per election, and $5,000 for a PAC. National party committees,

on the other hand, could spend up to $34,720 for a House seat in 1980 and as much as $987,548 for a Senate seat. (*Expenditure ceilings, box, p. 75*)

To assist their presidential nominees, the national party committees were each permitted to spend $4.6 million in 1980. The money could not be contributed to the candidate, but it could be spent in conjunction with him. State and local parties were allowed to spend unlimited amounts to conduct voter registration, get-out-the-vote and other grass-roots activities. (*Presidential general election spending, Chapter 7, p. 91*)

But only the Republicans have been able to capitalize on these advantages. Democratic Party committees were not able to come up with enough money to give anywhere near the maximums. To be sure, the campaign war chests of Democratic officeholders were hardly bare. The mere fact that they controlled Congress in the past gave Democrats the edge with money provided by PACs. "It [our prosperity] is widely interpreted as an advantage, but it just gets us into a competitive position," commented Steven F. Stockmeyer, executive director of the NRCC in 1978.

In 1980, 93 percent of the contributions to congressional candidates by labor union PACs went to Democrats. And Democratic candidates snared about 40 percent of the political gifts made by business and trade association PACs. "The only place to make up that gap is through the parties," Stockmeyer said. (*PACs, Chapter 3, p. 41*)

Many Democratic candidates have another advantage over Republicans, GOP officials contend. "Our financial capability is not the advantage for us that incumbency is for the Democrats," remarked Charles Black, the Republican National Committee (RNC) campaign director in 1978. The Democrats still control the House and about two-thirds of the Senate seats up in 1982. The advantages of incumbency — use of the franking privilege for mail, public exposure, extensive staff — are significant.

In any event, Black noted, contributions by party committees account for a small share of congressional candi-

Election Spending by Political Parties

(Jan. 1, 1979, through Sept. 30, 1980)

	Receipts	Amount Spent on Federal Candidates	Amount Spent on Federal Candidates 1977-78	Share Given to Candidates			Number of Candidates	Average Amount Spent Per Candidate
				Open	Challengers	Incumbents		
REPUBLICANS								
National Republican Senatorial Committee	$10,444,980	$3,275,887	$3,055,400	33.2%	59.8%	7.0%	35	$93,596
National Republican Congressional Committee	11,952,900	1,981,150	2,656,845	20.3	18.8	60.9[1]	267[1]	5,255[1]
Republican National Committee	34,013,804	581,792	1,242,225	32.2	54.5	13.3	97	5,998
DEMOCRATS								
Democratic Senatorial Campaign Committee	438,958	363,000	427,000	11.0	14.2	74.8	26	$13,961
Democratic Congressional Campaign Committee	1,383,211	334,244	537,438	21.2	18.9	59.9	138	2,442
Democratic National Committee (Democratic Services Corp.)	6,015,352	374,174	133,129	22.3	20.9	56.8	56	6,682

1. Figures based on reports filed through Aug. 30; report for Sept. 1980 was incomplete.

Source: Compiled from Federal Election Commission summaries and committee reports filed with FEC.

dates' receipts. In 1976, for instance, only 7.8 percent of the receipts of House general election candidates came from party committees, according to figures compiled by the FEC. In the 1976 Senate general election, party committees gave only 3.6 percent of the candidates' receipts. Those figures did not change appreciably between that election and the 1980 races.

House Races

In the 1980 election cycle, the NRCC raised about $27 million; its Democratic counterpart about $1.65 million. The disparity between the two figures encouraged the Republicans to think boldly.

The GOP House campaign committee has been working for years to perfect a check list that can gauge the vulnerability of an incumbent Democrat. It looks at how many staffers he has, their salary levels, the number of newsletters he sends to constituents, his constituent services, his age and how often he returns home. It no longer targets first-term Democrats almost automatically, the way it did in 1976, when it was embarrassed by managing to defeat only two of them. In 1978 the Republicans targeted the 58 open seats and came up with a net increase of 11.

Essentially, the 1980 Republican strategy was to focus on what they believed were vulnerable Democratic-held seats, most notably those of senior Democrats such as Interior Committee Chairman Morris K. Udall of Arizona and Agriculture Chairman Thomas S. Foley of Washington, who both represented relatively conservative districts. The GOP had mixed success. Udall and Foley won, but the Republicans showed a net gain of 33 seats, raising hopes that the party could win control of the House in 1982.

The Federal Rules on Party Spending

In campaign finance jargon, the funds political parties spend are known as "section 441a(d) money," named after the section of the 1974 law that allows national and congressional party campaign committees to contribute to federal candidates.

In an effort to increase the influence of party organizations, the law allows them to spend more than either individuals ($1,000 per election) or nonparty political action committees (PACs, $5,000 per election).

In 1980 the national party limits ranged from $34,720 for a House election to $502,524 for a Senate seat from California, the most populous state. Maximums vary in Senate races according to the population of a state.

Two Ways to Aid

Technically, party money is given in two ways — as a "direct" or as a "coordinated" expenditure.

Direct contributions, as the name implies, are funds a party committee sends directly to a candidate to do with as he or she pleases. With coordinated spending, the national party becomes, in effect, a senior partner in a candidate's campaign. The party pays for services the candidate requests, usually polling or television ad production, but has a say in how the money is spent.

For example, the Democratic National Committee in September 1980 paid $269,280 to Cambridge Survey Research in Massachusetts to do polling for 22 Democratic Senate candidates. The DNC was controlled by President Carter, whose personal pollster, Patrick Caddell, owned Cambridge.

Some candidates believe this setup allows the parties too much opportunity to impose their views on the campaign. For example, the National Republican Congressional Committee cut off Maryland state Del. Raymond E. Beck in 1980, reportedly because it disapproved of the way he was running his congressional campaign. Beck, who was challenging incumbent Democrat Beverly B. Byron, displeased the committee by not hiring professional political staffers, according to one source.

The ceilings for coordinated spending are far higher than those for direct giving, which is why the financially superior GOP — at least in Senate races — channeled vast sums into these tandem expenditures.

Coordinated spending is preeminent in Senate elections, Republican campaign officials say, because purchases of polling and advertising are more important for contests that span an entire state. House per-election costs are less. The financially disadvantaged Democrats perform a negligible amount of coordinated spending.

Spending Restrictions

Here is a review of the federal restrictions on party spending:

Senate and At-Large House Limits. For Senate coordinated funds, national party committees could spend in 1980 an amount equal to the voting age population of a state multiplied by two cents, adjusted for inflation — or $29,440, whichever was higher. Coordinated money may not be used for primaries.

Fourteen states had $29,440 ceilings on coordinated funding by the national committees. California, because of its large population, had the largest allowable coordinated amount, $485,024.

Direct party contributions were another matter. A national committee and its senatorial campaign committee together may give a maximum of $17,500 in direct aid to a Senate candidate during the calendar year he or she is seeking election. Thus, in California, GOP Senate candidate Paul Gann could have benefited from a total of $502,524 in national Republican funds ($485,024 plus $17,500).

State parties may, if they choose, also spend two cents times the voting age population. Gann, then, could have been helped by another $485,024 from the California Republican State Committee in coordinated spending, bringing the total allowable party spending for him to $987,548.

But most state committees do not have this kind of money, and the law allows the national party to pick up their share — which is what the National Republican Senatorial Committee does. By using the California state party's authorization, the national group was able to give Gann $521,755 overall. The less well-off Democrats did very little coordinated spending.

Identical rules on coordinated giving apply to House candidates in states with only one House seat, because they must campaign statewide like Senate contenders.

House Limits. For a House candidate in a state with more than one district, the national committees in 1980 could not spend more than $14,720 in coordinated funds. In direct funds, each of the national party committees could give $5,000 to a candidate in both the general and primary election — for a total of $10,000 per committee.

So, for example, Republican Ed Weber, who was challenging Rep. Thomas L. Ashley of Ohio, theoretically was eligible for $34,720 in national party aid. That amount is based on $14,720 in coordinated funds, $10,000 from the House party committee and another $10,000 from the Republican National Committee.

The Republicans have had enough money to be extremely generous. The Republican House committee gave a direct $4,000 contribution to most general election candidates in 1980. Anything beyond that was dictated by the circumstances of the race. But if a Republican challenger's prospects were chancy, the committee might give him just $2,000 and see how he did before committing more money.

Most incumbent Republicans who asked could get the full $4,000. The exception was Florida's Richard Kelly, who, after he was linked to the FBI's Abscam bribery probe, resigned from the House Republican Caucus and was disowned by the party. Kelly lost in the Florida Republican primary.

With less money available, the Democratic House committee gave money according to the strength of the incumbent Republican or financial need. The NRCC was expecting to have an even larger campaign chest in 1982, which would enable them to give up to $6 million to House candidates — about double their contributions in 1980.

Senate Races

The GOP Senate committee had a similarly large advantage over its Democratic rival in 1980, reportedly raising $20 million to the Democrats' $2 million. The Democratic Senate committee was able to give barely $1 million to its candidates, while the NRSC donated $6 million. Aiming to tighten its control of the Senate, the GOP was eyeing nearly $10 million in gifts to party Senate candidates in 1982.

Despite the Republicans' party financing advantage, Democrats generally have kept pace with their opponents through their candidates' own private fund raising. According to the FEC, Democratic Senate general election candidates raised $5.6 million more than GOP contenders in 1980.

But the NRSC had plenty to give to the large crop of Republican challengers. The Senate Republican committee allocated funds to challengers based on the vulnerability of Democratic incumbents, according to a four-point scale. Democrats considered the most vulnerable, such as Sen. Frank Church of Idaho, got a "1," while incumbents considered safe, such as Arkansas Democrat Dale Bumpers, got a "4."

With this in mind, the group, as of Sept. 30, 1980, had spent $126,363 on St. Louis County Executive Gene McNary, who was running against incumbent Missouri Democrat Thomas F. Eagleton, a "1." Whereas, former Kentucky state Auditor Mary Louise Foust was thought to have little chance against Democratic Sen. Wendell H. Ford, a "4," so she got nothing through September. Both Eagleton and Ford retained their seats.

Other considerations enter into distributing funds, such as the rules governing how much can be spent in particular states. That apparently was why California Republican Paul Gann was a major beneficiary of party spending, even though he was a long shot to topple incumbent Democrat Alan Cranston, who won. California has the highest ceiling. "Republicans have it to spend, and they don't want to look cheap in a high-visibility state like California," commented one Republican activist.

The top beneficiary of GOP money in 1980 was New York's Alfonse M. D'Amato, who upset Sen. Jacob K. Javits, R-N.Y., in the GOP primary. D'Amato received $775,000 from the NRSC. Javits, an earlier recipient of $15,000 from the committee, stayed in the race on the Liberal Party line, but got no more NRSC money.

Republican Initiatives

In addition to traditional campaign spending, the parties provide candidate services. Virtually all the federal-level committees operate schools to teach office-seekers how to run a campaign.

The parties also aid candidates with research, usually in two forms — opposition research and precinct targeting. With the first the party dredges up unfavorable information about a candidate's adversary. The other provides a computer analysis of voting patterns and party registration that helps a candidate know where to concentrate his energies.

With its larger budget, staff and technological expertise, the Republicans can offer its candidates far more services than the Democrats. The GOP has also found sophisticated and innovative ways to use the FECA. For example, FEC regulations permit state parties to spend as much as the national party in behalf of Senate candidates, but many state groups, Republican as well as Democratic, lack the funds to do it.

But the national committees can pick up both their own share and the state committee's share, if a state body agrees to let the national groups act as its "agent."

In this way, the NRSC has nearly doubled the amount it has spent for some candidates. The committee had "agency agreements" in 33 of the 34 states electing senators in 1980. Indiana was the exception; the state party said that it was wealthy enough to support its Senate contender, Rep. Dan Quayle.

The DSCC challenged this arrangement in 1980 as a violation of federal campaign laws, contending it was merely a device to circumvent the spending limits on the national committee. Although the FEC had allowed the arrangements, the U.S. Court of Appeals for the District of Columbia ruled in favor of the Democrats in October 1980.

But the Supreme Court granted a 90-day stay of the lower court's order, which permitted the Republicans to continue their spending through the election. On Oct. 27, the Democratic Senatorial Campaign Committee asked the court for an expedited determination, which was denied. The Supreme Court finally decided the case in November 1981, ruling 9-0 in favor of the NRSC and its "agency agreements."

"The legislative [congressional] discussion of preserving a role for political parties did not differentiate between the state and national branches of the party unit," wrote Justice Byron R. White in the decision.

White added that "effective use of party resources in support of party candidates may encourage candidate loyalty and responsiveness to the party."

"Indeed," White concluded, "the very posture of this case betrays the weakness of . . . [the Democrats'] argument — an argument that, at bottom, features one of the two great American political parties insisting that its rival requires judicial assistance in discovering how a legislative enactment operates to its benefit."

Reshaping GOP Image

As part of its effort to boost its numbers in Congress, the RNC and the two Republican congressional committees mounted in 1980 a television campaign with the slogan "Vote Republican. For a Change." It cost $8 million. The series, which began April 1 and was aired until Election Day, blamed the nation's economic and energy woes on the quarter-century of Democratic hegemony in Congress.

Parties Benefit from Mail Subsidy Bonanza

An "apple pie and motherhood" bill designed to encourage more people to vote was given final approval in the closing hours of the 95th Congress in 1978. Tacked on to the hard-to-oppose legislation was a multimillion-dollar subsidy for Democratic and Republican campaign committees.

The bill prevented states from using as evidence of residency for tax purposes the vote of an American living overseas. Sponsors said many Americans living abroad did not vote out of fear of having to pay additional taxes.

Attached to the voting rights bill as cleared was a provision the Congressional Budget Office (CBO) estimated would cost taxpayers $2.5 million in 1979 and $4.7 million in 1980 in subsidized mail rates for Democratic and Republican national and state campaign committees.

The House added the mail subsidy to S 703 as passed by the Senate. The Senate accepted the House amendment Oct. 13, 1978, by voice vote, clearing the bill for the president.

In remarks entered in the *Congressional Record,* Claiborne Pell, D-R.I., urged the Senate to accept the provision because it "will provide a measure of relief to the financially burdened political process."

The subsidy provision entitled certain "qualified political committees" to use low-cost mail rates available to other non-profit organizations. Those "qualified" committees would include any "national committee" or "state committee" as defined by the federal election law, but not non-party or "candidate" committees such as the "Jones for Congress Committee."

Theoretically, the provision could provide subsidies to minor parties such as the Libertarian and U.S. Labor parties. But for practical purposes, the principal beneficiaries of the subsidy provision were the Democratic and Republican party committees.

The bill specifically stated that the term "qualified political committee" included "the Republican and Democratic Senatorial Campaign committees, the Democratic National Congressional Committee, and the National Republican Congressional Committee." Support for the bill was, as one advocate described it, "a bipartisan effort."

Mary Maginnis, a CBO analyst, said her cost projections were based exclusively on costs resulting from use of the subsidy by Republican and Democratic campaign committees. She said CBO assumed costs from other party committees would be "negligible."

"In most states only the Republican and Democratic parties would be included," she said.

David L. Shurtz, who worked on the bill for Charles E. Wiggins, R-Calif., said, "It's obvious the Democratic and Republican campaign committees were the authors of this thing. . . . They were looking for a nice convenient noncontroversial bill" to which they could attach the provision. (Wiggins supported the provision, but opposed the bill.)

The non-profit mail rates sought by the Republican and Democratic campaign committees provided that letters may be sent for 2.7 cents a letter, rather than at the 8.4 cents-a-letter rate paid by the committees using third-class bulk rate. (In late 1981 the postal commission had special rates varying from 1.8 to 3.8 cents per letter, depending upon the amount of pre-sorting.)

No one opposed the provision on either the House or Senate floor. But Sen. Robert P. Griffin, R-Mich., inserted comments opposing the provision in the *Congressional Record* as part of the Senate debate. "This provision is an attempt to extend the public financing arrangement already in effect. . . ," Griffin said. "The bill would extend this subsidy to the most politically active committees of our political parties. These committees send out millions of pieces of mail each year — and every piece of mail sent by these committees would be subsidized. . . ."

Griffin noted that reduced postage rates already were available to groups such as Common Cause, the National Right to Work Committee and labor unions. He charged that the unions "routinely use this special postage rate for blatantly political mailings."

The two major parties apparently decided they wanted a piece of the action. Thomas J. Josefiak, legal counsel to the National Republican Congressional Committee, said GOP supporters of the subsidy recognized that unions, which primarily support Democratic candidates, were qualified for the special mail rates and wanted to "provide both parties with equal footing."

Former Wiggins' aide Shurtz had a different view: "The history of this is that labor has been getting an incredible windfall. But the Republican view was that since the Democrats were getting the benefits through labor, Republicans should get them by hook or by crook."

Asked why Congress had not prohibited those organizations from using the subsidized rates rather than expanding the rates to include partisan political committees, Josefiak said the idea would have found little support on Capitol Hill. He said the provision was not expanded to include local committees in addition to the state and national committees because while "in theory it should apply across the board, Congress wouldn't pass that kind of broad subsidy."

The Republican Party and conservative groups have made widespread use of mass mailings, while the Democrats only recently have begun to get more heavily involved in mass mailing fund raising.

In one 1980 Republican television ad, an actor who resembles House Speaker Thomas P. O'Neill Jr. drives a car that runs out of gas after he ignores warnings from a passenger.

In one spot, an actor who resembled House Speaker O'Neill drove a car that ran out of gas after he ignored warnings from a passenger. In another, two blue-collar workers derided the Democrats' handling of the economy and how their paycheck had shrunk.

This flaunting of the GOP label and appeal to traditional Democratic voters marked a change for a party that long has labored under an upper-crust, country-club image. The last time something similar occurred was in 1946 when the GOP sought to exploit post-World War II economic dislocations with the slogan, "Had Enough?" and won control of both chambers.

The Republicans' 1980 ads were credited with helping the party win the presidency and majority control of the Senate, and encouraged the GOP to mount a $9 million encore in 1982. Boosting an incumbent rather than challenging one, the Republicans were clearly upbeat in their advertising that began airing in 1981. This positivism was underscored in the slogan: "Republicans. Leadership that works for a change."

The Democrats counterattacked in October 1981 by writing the heads of the two television networks running the ads, asking that the GOP commercials either be withdrawn or the Democrats be granted time to respond. Essentially acknowledging that they did not have the money to buy their own ads, the Democrats' lawyer indicated that time be given the Democrats under the "fairness doctrine" of the Federal Communications Commission (FCC).

Drawing less controversy was about $120,000 in expenditures by the RNC for radio ads in 1981 to promote President Reagan's tax cut plan. The ads marked an unusual foray by a national party into the field of lobbying.

A party usually finds it easier to raise money when it occupies the White House, but extra expense also is involved. About 10 percent of the RNC's $20 million budget in 1981 went for White House support — namely, paying for campaign-related travel by President Reagan, Vice President George Bush and other White House officials.

In another effort to boost the number of Republicans in the House, the GOP pumped a comparatively large amount of money into key state legislative races in 1978 and 1980. The goal was to get Republican control of legislatures so GOP candidates would be favored when those bodies started redrawing House districts in 1981 based on 1980 census data.

The RNC's local elections division, with a staff of 30, gave $1.5 million to state candidates and provided an array of technical services. The DNC did relatively little in this regard and gave no money directly to legislative candidates.

The heavy emphasis on state legislative races, which RNC Chairman Brock labeled his top priority in 1980, was possible because of the increased resources available to the GOP House and Senate committees.

The Republican state legislative drive was only moderately successful, but it enhanced the GOP position in a number of states and strengthened ties between the state and national parties.

Initiatives Rebuffed

Republicans sought approval for two other money-raising ventures, but both were turned down:

● The RNC wanted to fatten its coffers by enlisting Republicans as credit card customers for banks. Under the plan, the committee would furnish banks its mailing lists and get a fee for each party member who signed up.

The six-member FEC turned down the proposal in mid-1979 by a 4-2 vote. The three Democrats on the commission were joined by one Republican, Vernon W. Thomson, in disapproving the plan; Republican commissioners Joan D. Aikens and Max L. Friedersdorf voted in favor of it.

According to the FEC majority, the bank fees would be the same as legally prohibited corporate political contributions. The RNC said the fees were a "commercial transaction."

● Because winners of September 1980 primaries had to scramble to get ready for a general election only two months off, the National Republican Senatorial Committee sought to set up "prepackaged" campaigns for them.

During the summer, when the Republican candidates' attention was fixed on getting the nomination, the committee wanted to rent office space, explore the records of potential Democratic foes for weaknesses, buy air time for ads and perform other chores.

The FEC turned down the proposal in March 1980 on a party-line vote. All three Republican commissioners favored it, but two of the Democrats voted "no." The third Democrat, Robert O. Tiernan, abstained. Motions need four votes to pass.

Both parties, however, have found exceptions to the current limits on how much they can accept from donors. Through a 1976 amendment to the FECA, Republicans received corporate contributions for a special fund to pay off the mortgage on their national party headquarters and accepted gifts from individuals for that purpose that exceeded the limits.

In line with several earlier rulings, the FEC confirmed that the DNC could accept contributions in excess of the current limits to pay off their debt that was incurred before the limits went into effect in 1975.

6

The Search for Loopholes

"Money," the saying goes, "is the mother's milk of politics." Thanks to a quirk in campaign finance law, some candidates were nourished more heartily than others during the 1980 campaign. A notable surge in independent expenditures before the elections benefited Ronald Reagan and other, particularly Republican, candidates.

Political spending by individuals or committees without the knowledge or consent of a candidate, or his campaign, was not subject to the contribution limitations imposed by the campaign finance laws of the 1970s. This loophole, deriving from the Supreme Court's 1976 *Buckley v. Valeo* decision, provided a previously little used device for contributors to circumvent the legal limits on campaign financing.

According to the existing law in 1980, a candidate could accept up to $1,000 from an individual contributor and $5,000 from a political committee in each election. Primary and general elections counted as separate contests. The Democratic and Republican nominees for president, who each received $29.4 million in public financing for the general election, generally could accept no outside contributions during the fall campaign, except for the very limited purpose of paying for the campaign's legal and accounting costs.

1980 Figures Show Increase

Sidestepping these general campaign restrictions, independent spending figures during the 1979-80 election cycle towered over any similar figures for previous elections. In 1980 independent expenditures exceeded $16 million, more than eight times greater than the $2 million figure for 1976.

Presidential Expenditures

Of that 1980 total, $13.7 million was spent on the primary and general presidential campaigns in both parties. Prior to this election, independent spending had taken up a minuscule share of overall campaign financing; but independent spending accounted for about 10 percent of the total expenditures for the 1980 presidential election, and nearly 90 percent of the independent figure was spent on behalf of one candidate: Republican Ronald Reagan. About $12.2 million went toward promoting his presiden-

tial candidacy. Independent presidential candidate John B. Anderson came in a distant second to Reagan, with almost $200,000 in independent expenditures made in his behalf, followed by Sen. Edward M. Kennedy, D-Mass., with $77,000 and incumbent President Jimmy Carter with almost $46,000. *(See table, p. 82)*

Both in 1976 and 1980 the Carter camp made it clear it disliked independent expenditures. John D. White, the president's handpicked chairman of the Democratic National Committee, said he feared that independent spending would lead to a "distortion of the fund-raising process." In 1976 Carter was aided by a minor amount of independent spending, mostly from the United Auto Workers ($27,064), but he actively discouraged this type of political spending.

Observers, however, painted that as a tactical move aimed at keeping the level of GOP independent spending low. "If Carter were going great guns using this loophole, the Republicans could easily top him," explained one political operative who had worked for Carter. "The Republicans always could blast us out of the water on money."

And blast they did, despite Carter's efforts at downplaying independent giving. Unlike Carter, Reagan did not strongly disavow independent efforts. But according to a *Washington Post* article that appeared prior to the 1980 election, Reagan advisers were concerned over the huge sums being expended over which they legally could exert no control. The advisers reportedly feared that Reagan would be charged with trying to buy the election.

Congressional Elections

The total amount of independent expenditures spent to influence congressional races was tiny in comparison with the presidential election figures. Spending for and against House candidates totaled $684,727, and similar independent expenditures in Senate races totaled $1.7 million. Congressional candidates themselves spent nearly $250 million on their election campaigns, which meant that independent efforts represented only about 1 percent of the total spending figure. But the amount of money spent to hurt candidates, through so-called negative campaigns, was significant in the congressional elections. Final FEC figures for congressional and presidential campaigns showed $2.2 million was spent in attempts to defeat, rather than promote, 65 federal candidates. The amount represented 14 percent of the $16 million spent independently of candidates, leaving $13.8 million spent to promote candidates. But the negative expenditures played a greater role in the elections than their percentages would imply, because more than half of them were funneled into just six Senate races.

Of the $2.2 million, $1.2 million was spent in attempts to defeat Democratic senators Frank Church of Idaho, John Culver of Iowa, George McGovern of South Dakota, Alan Cranston of California, Birch Bayh of Indiana and Thomas F. Eagleton of Missouri. All but Cranston and Eagleton were defeated. *(See Target '80, box, p. 87)*

Top Independents

The leaders among independent spenders were the non-connected political action committees (PACs), which the FEC describes as "non-party political ideological committees and committees sponsored by particular issue groups." The most powerful groups that played a part in the 1980 election fell to the right of the political spectrum. Rich individuals who traveled this route were few, but those who did gave to both liberal and conservative candidates.

Topping the FEC's list of the highest independent givers with $4.6 million was the Congressional Club, the North Carolina-based organization that served as the political apparatus of conservative Republican Sen. Jesse Helms. The National Conservative Political Action Committee (NCPAC), which was noted for its negative advertising blitz against the six liberal Democratic senators, came in second with $3.3 million listed in expenditures. Next came the Fund for a Conservative Majority with reported expenditures of $2 million. These three groups were "New Right" PACs that had existed for several years prior to the 1980 election. Because they aided more than one candidate, federal law allowed them to accept up to $5,000 per giver.

Americans for an Effective Presidency and Americans for Change, both organized in 1980, followed in total independent expenditures, with $1.2 million and $700,000 respectively. Former Nixon White House assistant Peter M. Flanigan and former Air Force Secretary Thomas Reed, who had been chairman of Reagan's 1970 gubernatorial

campaign in California, created Americans for an Effective Presidency. Americans for Change was headed by Sen. Harrison "Jack" Schmitt, a Republican from New Mexico.

The two temporary groups raised most of their money through personal requests to longtime Republican contributors, whereas the three established ideological PACs generally used the more impersonal direct mail solicitation technique.

Texas industrialist Cecil R. Haden, who donated more than five times as much as any other individual, was next to Americans for Change in total expenditures with his "once-in-a-lifetime" donation of nearly $600,000. A *New York Times* article quoted the 81-year-old businessman as saying, "I've helped elect the quarterback.... Now it's up to the others to elect the other people to play with him." After investing $182,726 in former Texas Gov. John B. Connally's short-lived presidential campaign, Haden spend $413,221, mainly on newspaper advertisements, to elect Reagan.

The individual with the second-largest independent expenditure was Stewart R. Mott of New York, a descendant of the founder of General Motors, who spent $90,000 in behalf of John B. Anderson and $20,000 promoting Kennedy. Norman Lear, the California television producer of "All in the Family," spent $108,302 on Anderson, the third-highest individual independent expenditure.

These three were the only individuals spending more than $100,000 in independent expenditures during the 1979-80 election cycle. One reason for the reticence of the rich to make independent expenditures, according to NCPAC's Director John T. "Terry" Dolan, could stem "from their not knowing how to do it and maybe not even knowing it exists."

But the biggest deterrent could be the extensive reporting requirements for federal political financing. Individuals must report each independent expenditure exceeding $250. "I consider that a major breach of my privacy so I choose not to be involved." said one big giver to McGovern's 1972 presidential campaign.

Also the stigma attached to being a so-called "political fat cat" reportedly has dissuaded many of the rich from pursuing the independent route. Such large-scale spending raises suspicions of influence-seeking, such as the "ambassador auction" under the Nixon administration. A $250,000 donation for Nixon's 1972 re-election, for instance, made New Yorker Ruth Farkas the envoy to Luxembourg, according to testimony in the Nixon impeachment inquiry.

MURKY LEGAL AREA: INDEPENDENT SPENDING

Independent spending must be for a communication — usually broadcast spots, print ads, brochures, bumper stickers or buttons — and must be done without consultation with the candidate it is designed to help. From the contributor's viewpoint, direct donations offer much more convenience; he only has to write out a check to the candidate or the campaign. In contrast, to make an independent expenditure, the contributor must go through the trouble of drawing up ads, buying publication space or air time, as well as filling out FEC reports. Also, for the duration of the

Independent Spending Divided by Candidate Type

Candidate Type	Democrats				Republicans			
	For	*No.*	*Against*	*No.*	*For*	*No.*	*Against*	*No.*
House	$190,615	91	$ 38,023	32	$ 410,478	205	$ 45,132	6
Senate	127,381	24	1,282,613	15	231,678	58	12,430	5
Presidential	123,058	2	736,796	3	12,537,522	3	65,040	2
Total	$441,054	117	$2,057,432	50	$13,179,678	266	$122,602	13

The table shows how the $16 million in independent expenditures made during the 1979-80 election cycle was divided among Senate, House and presidential candidates. According to federal election law, an independent expenditure is money spent to support or defeat a clearly identified candidate. Such an expenditure must be made without cooperation or consultation with the candidate or the candidate's campaign. The columns titled "For"

show expenditures to support a candidate; those entitled "Against" refer to spending meant to defeat a candidate. The "No." columns indicate the number of candidates to whom the spending was directed.

Because some candidates had expenditures made both for and against them, the figures for the total number of candidates are smaller than the sums of the "No." columns.

Candidate Type	Others					
	For	*No.*	*Against*	*No.*	*Total*	*No.*
House	$ 479	1	$ 0	0	$ 684,727	321
Senate	0	0	0	0	1,654,102	89
Presidential	271,978	7	11,050	2	13,745,444	15
Total	$272,457	8	$11,050	2	$16,084,273	425

campaign, he must scrupulously avoid any association with the candidate he supports to avoid charges of collusion.

There are distinct disadvantages to this indirect support from the candidate's point of view, too. Generally, candidates prefer to control all spending designed to help them, and, by definition, they cannot control independent activity.

The practice is a reaction to the ceilings placed on direct contributions in 1974. Before then, financial limits were nominal and seldom enforced, allowing big campaign donors to give as much as they wanted straight to a candidate.

"With no caps, there would be no need for independent expenditures," said NCPAC's Dolan. "Otherwise, we could work through [a candidate's] campaign. We'd say,

'Here's $10,000, and you should spend it this way.'"

Also helping to squeeze money into independent activity were the 1976 amendments to FECA. They banned the formation of subgroups to get around the direct contribution limit of $5,000 that each committee can give one candidate. In other words, a PAC no longer could split into four subsidiaries and give a total of $20,000 to its favorite politician, according to the amendments.

Origins of System

Independent spending used to be an occasional undertaking reserved for politically minded millionaires and small interest groups.

Where Independent Funds Were Spent in 1980 Campaign

Presidential	For	Against	Total
Ronald Reagan (R)	$12,246,057	$ 47,868	$12,293,925
Edward M. Kennedy (D)*	77,189	491,161	568,350
Jimmy Carter (D)*	45,869	245,611	291,480
John B. Connally (R)*	288,032	——	288,032
John B. Anderson (I)*	199,438	2,635	202,073
Senate			
Frank Church (D-Idaho)*	1,945	339,018	340,963
John C. Culver (D-Iowa)*	59,584	186,613	246,197
George McGovern (D-S.D.)*	3,553	222,044	225,597
Alan Cranston (D-Calif.)	2,285	192,039	194,324
Birch Bayh (D-Ind.)*	1,027	180,723	181,750
Thomas F. Eagleton (D-Mo.)	22,910	101,794	124,704
House			
Robert W. Edgar (D-Pa.)	39,182	30	39,212
Jack M. Fields (R-Texas)	38,376	——	38,376
Carey Peck (D-Calif.)*	37,734	——	37,734
Harold S. Sawyer (R-Mich.)	14,219	13,912	28,131
Charles E. Grassley (R-Iowa)*	27,799	——	27,799
Harold Volkmer (R-Mo.)	26,917	——	26,917
Robert F. Drinan (D-Mass.)†	——	23,147	23,147
W. J. "Billy" Tauzin (D-La.)	22,535	——	22,535

*Indicates losers
†Indicates retired

Source: Federal Election Commission

In 1968 liberal philanthropist Mott spent $100,000 for newspaper ads trying to persuade Nelson A. Rockefeller, then governor of New York, to run for president. In 1972, with the Vietnam War still going, and President Nixon up for re-election, the General Motors heir spent $50,000 to publicize a statement Nixon had made in 1968: "Those who have had a chance for four years, and could not produce peace, should not be given another chance." The Vietnam conflict also precipitated the formation of numerous peace groups that bid to mobilize public opinion both for and against candidates.

In 1972 Environmental Action began its "Dirty Dozen" effort, designed to highlight the records of 12 members of Congress that the conservationist group deemed pro-pollution. Posters, press conferences and paid advertisements vilified the dozen as enemies of the environment. Although the effectiveness of the campaign was disputed, the novelty caught the eye of many other groups and probably helped to set a trend in political tactics.

Congress planted the seeds of the current era of independent spending when, distressed by the large television costs of the 1968 presidential race, it passed the Federal Election Campaign Act of 1971. That measure imposed ceilings on spending for media advertising. Media were required to get certificates from candidates stating that their ads did not exceed the spending limits.

The crucial element, though, was the law's treatment of independently placed ads opposing a candidate. People who took out such negative ads were compelled to certify that they had no affiliation with the targeted candidate's opponent. Otherwise, the opponent would have the cost of the ad counted toward his limit, even though he had nothing to do with it.

The entire certificate system came into question when

Top Independent Spenders in 1980 Campaign

Political Committees: Independent Expenditures For and Against Candidates

Congressional Club	$4,601,069
National Conservative Political Action Committee	3,307,962
Fund for a Conservative Majority	2,062,456
Americans for an Effective Presidency	1,270,208
Americans for Change	711,856
NRA Political Victory Fund	441,891
Christian Voice Moral Government Fund	406,199
1980 Republican Presidential Campaign Committee	314,740
American Medical Political Action Committee	172,397
Gun Owners of America Campaign Committee	119,891

Individuals: Independent Expenditures For and Against Candidates

Cecil R. Haden	$ 599,333
Stewart Rawlings Mott	110,179
Norman Lear	108,301
Richard M. DeVos	70,575
Jay Van Andel	68,433
Theo N. Law	66,230
David B. Melville	35,159
Henry C. Grover	29,076
Michael Rosen	25,940
Dwight G. Vedder	20,000

Source: Federal Election Commission

The New York Times refused to accept ads listing members of Congress who voted against President Nixon's busing proposals. The ads had no accompanying certificates of non-affiliation. In a 1973 case growing out of this episode, *ACLU v. Jennings*, the U.S. District Court for the District of Columbia held the media limits unconstitutional.

Partly with this in mind, Congress in 1974 passed the landmark legislation setting ceilings across the board for all kinds of campaign activity, while repealing the specific limit on media. Also capped were independent expenditures, which the lawmakers limited to $1,000 yearly on behalf of a candidate.

But an ideologically diverse group led by the conservative Sen. James L. Buckley, Cons./R-N.Y., and the liberal Sen. Eugene J. McCarthy, D-Minn., contested the statute in court on grounds that it abridged freedom of speech by restricting what someone could spend on a candidate.

In *Buckley v. Valeo*, the Supreme Court agreed with Buckley and McCarthy, at least as far as independent expenditures were concerned. If an independent spender had no dealings with a candidate, the justices said, then the object of the 1974 amendments had been attained — corruption would not be a problem. By this reasoning, the court upheld limits on the supposedly more corruption-prone direct contributions. In a dissenting opinion, however, Justice Byron R. White said permitting independent spending would result in "transparent and wide-spread evasion of the contribution limits." *(Excerpts from* Buckley v. Valeo *decision, p. 120)*

Spending and Controversy Grow

The outpouring of independent money in 1980 precipitated a parallel outpouring of controversy over the

'Draft' Decision Underscores Loophole

In October 1981 the Supreme Court brought attention to a campaign finance loophole that allowed contributors to donate unlimited amounts of money to political committees organized to "draft" candidates to run for office. By refusing to reconsider a case the Federal Election Commission (FEC) brought against the Machinists Non-Partisan Political League (MNPL), the political arm of the International Association of Machinists and Aerospace Workers, the high court let stand a May 19, 1981, ruling by the District of Columbia U.S. Circuit Court of Appeals. In effect, that court told the FEC it had no jurisdiction over committees set up to draft candidates, if the committees had no formal connection with a candidate.

The commission took the MNPL to court when the union refused to supply information about some $30,000 it gave to groups trying to persuade Sen. Edward M. Kennedy, D-Mass., to seek the Democratic presidential nomination. The appeals court ruled the FEC did not have the right to subpoena the MNPL because it had no regulatory power over draft committees.

Reactions to the Supreme Court decision were mixed. Critics focused on the prospect of draft committees raising and spending unlimited amounts drafting candidates and giving them early public exposure.

Particularly upset were some Democrats, who were struggling to maintain hold of the House of Representatives and to prevent further losses in the Senate in 1982. They reasoned that incumbents would be hurt most by the decision.

Calling it "another decision that has reduced the FEC's ability to control [campaign spending]," Victor Kamber, founder of the Progressive Political Action Committee (PROPAC), said the decision could help well-heeled groups such as the National Conservative Political Action Committee (NCPAC). Kamber added, however, he did not disagree with the appeals court's finding.

MNPL Director Wiliam Holayter, however, did not believe the decision would have much effect. "Candidates cannot afford to take the risk of joining a subterfuge effort," he said, suggesting the decision would only free true draft efforts. Holayter added that aggressive independent groups such as NCPAC had been willing in the past to test the limits of federal election laws.

Whatever effect the decision had, the Senate was likely to look at the issue as part of its ongoing study of the FEC and the election law. *(Future of the FEC, p. 29)*

practice. Its backers lauded independent expenditures as a cornerstone of the constitutional right of free speech. "It's not a loophole, it's clearly a First Amendment question," said John Bolton, a Washington attorney for the plaintiffs in *Buckley v. Valeo.*

"If it's your money, you should be able to spend it any way you want to," said Henry C. Grover, a public relations man and one-time Texas state legislator. Grover independently spent $29,076 to benefit Connally's 1980 push for the Republican presidential nomination. He also spent $63,000 in Reagan's behalf in 1976.

"Independent expenditures are a good safety valve for people to vent their emotions," said Herbert E. Alexander, director of the Citizens' Research Foundation and a University of Southern California political scientist. "What if there had been financial limits put on the [anti-Vietnam War] peace movement?"

But others condemned independent expenditures as a means of subverting the 1970s federal election reforms. "This could crush the system of regulation," said Fred Wertheimer, president of Common Cause, the public affairs lobby. "I'm not sure the [Schmitt effort] fit within the parameters of the *Buckley* decision. A separate track wasn't what the Supreme Court was talking about."

Supreme Court Consideration

Two sets of cases before the Supreme Court in 1982 challenged the legality of independent expenditures. Three of the five highest independent committee givers — Americans for Change, Americans for an Effective Presidency and the Fund for a Conservative Majority — were before the court defending their right to support independently the candidates of their choice.

One provision of the Revenue Act of 1971, the law that set up a federal fund to finance presidential campaigns, limited to $1,000 the amount any "unauthorized" political committee (that is, a committee other than the candidate's official campaign unit) could spend in behalf of a presidential candidate who accepted public financing. This provision did not take effect until the first publicly funded presidential campaign in 1976, so the Supreme Court did not address it in its *Buckley* decision in January of that year. In that ruling, however, the court did find that Congress violated the First Amendment when it tried to limit independent expenditures.

After Americans for Change, Americans for an Effective Presidency and the Fund for a Conservative Majority announced plans to raise and spend millions in behalf of Reagan and other conservative candidates in 1980, Common Cause went to court seeking to enforce the $1,000 limit on "unauthorized" PAC spending. Common Cause was joined by the FEC.

The PACs responded by challenging the $1,000 spending limit as a violation of their First Amendment rights. A three-judge federal court on Sept. 30, 1980, agreed with the PACs in a ruling that Common Cause and the FEC appealed to the Supreme Court in *Common Cause v. Schmitt, FEC v. Americans for Change.*

In their briefs, Common Cause and the FEC argued the spending limit was an essential part of the system for public financing of presidential campaigns, "minimizing the risk that publicly funded candidates will become beholden to fundraisers who amass and control large political funds for the candidate's benefit." Common Cause also claimed that the independent groups were not truly autonomous. For example, it contended that the association developed between Thomas Reed of Americans for an Effective Presidency and Reagan during his 1970 gubernatorial campaign precluded the group's claim of independence.

Charging that such "million-dollar shadow campaigns" jeopardize the independence of the candidates they favor, Common Cause argued the Supreme Court should uphold the spending limit as it applied to PACs supporting publicly financed presidential candidates.

The American Civil Liberties Union (ACLU) disagreed and filed an *amicus curiae* brief with the high court. ACLU lawyer Philip Lacovara said that just because political committees are viewed as "sophisticated" they should not be denied rights accorded individuals.

By a 4-4 vote, the Supreme Court in a decision announced Jan. 19, 1982, upheld the lower court's finding. Although the court's even division meant the case had no weight as legal precedent, the practical effect was to leave independent committees free for the present to spend unlimited amounts in presidential campaigns.

Restrictions Difficult

Other people were trying to limit independent expenditures in different ways. "You have to include independent expenditures in regulations somehow; you can't regulate everybody else and let them do their thing," said Rep. Tom Railsback, R-Ill., a devotee of campaign spending lids. The only good aspect of independent spending, he added, was that it helped challengers take on entrenched incumbents.

Broadcast Regulations

Railsback suggested one method to control independent expenditures might be to limit the use of broadcast time for paid political ads, thus constricting a major outlet of independent spending. Another remedy, proposed by Common Cause's Wertheimer, would be passage of a law requiring that any candidate faced with an independent spender's advertising campaign on television or radio be entitled to an equal amount of free broadcast time to respond.

In a September 1981 *New York Times* Op-Ed article, Wertheimer criticized the absence of accountability when independent groups organize potent advertising campaigns to advance or hurt the cause of candidates. Of a 1981 NCPAC advertising campaign aimed at unseating Sen. Paul S. Sarbanes, D-Md., Wertheimer said, "Unlike the campaign of any opposing candidate, however, this one was run by a group that did not have to provide voters with constructive policy alternatives and did not have to assume responsibility at the ballot box for the consequences of its actions." Passage of a law such as he suggested would entitle the candidate to respond to attacks without heavy expense, he maintained.

Sen. Barry Goldwater, R-Ariz., asked the Federal Communications Commission (FCC) to study how the political broadcasting laws, designed to afford candidates and their opponents equal time on and reasonable access to the airwaves, should apply when PACs that are independent of candidates' campaigns buy television and radio time to support or oppose particular candidates.

In February 1981 the commission issued the report, focusing on the 1980 election, in which it concluded that "application of existing political broadcasting laws generally proceeded smoothly."

The longstanding equal-time provision of the Federal Communications Act specified that if a candidate was allowed to use the airwaves, then the broadcaster had to provide an equal opportunity to the candidate's opponents. Appearances on genuine news shows were exempt.

In September 1980 the Carter/Mondale Re-Election Committee asked the FCC for a declaratory ruling that a broadcast "use" — the appearance of a candidate's face or voice in an ad — by independent committees supporting Ronald Reagan's election entitled Carter to free equal time. The Carter committee argued that spending limits imposed by campaign laws and acceptance of public campaign financing made it impossible for the committee to purchase its equal opportunities.

The FCC disagreed. Congress' primary purpose in enacting the equal-time provision was to prevent favoritism by broadcasters among candidates, the FCC concluded. It said it was not the broadcaster's function to equalize the relative financial resources of competing candidates. The commission emphasized that stations airing independent ads supporting Reagan would have to sell equivalent time to the Carter campaign, or to independent groups backing his candidacy.

In its later 1981 report, however, the FCC pointed out that Congress might consider the basic question of whether a political broadcast involving the appearance of a candidate who had not authorized or exercised any control over that appearance actually constituted a "use" triggering the equal-time rule. The report also posed the question of whether independent groups should have other candidate advantages, such as reasonable access to paid and free time.

In response to a NCPAC inquiry to the FCC, the commission in November 1981 issued a staff ruling that independent political committees did not enjoy the same "reasonable access" to the airwaves guarantees accorded to federal candidates themselves.

Internal Revenue Ruling

Another bid to curb independent spending concerned an Internal Revenue Service private letter ruling, issued March 21, 1979. The action disallowed tax credits for contributions that went to NCPAC's Target '80 campaign because, according to the IRS, the program sought only to defeat the six senators. NCPAC appealed the matter unsuccessfully within the IRS.

The IRS letter ruling applied only to the one NCPAC contributor who was the subject of the agency's action, according to NCPAC's attorney, J. Curtis Herge. The IRS disputed that interpretation.

Sen. Bob Packwood, R-Ore., also apparently was upset by the ruling that "seriously jeopardizes our constitutionally protected rights of political expression." In February 1981 he introduced legislation to change the tax code to "make unmistakably clear the intent of Congress to maximize participation in the democratic process by actively encouraging individuals to make contributions to the candidates, parties, and political organizations of their choice." The ACLU supported the bill.

Lifting Limits

Raising the caps on direct contributions, which were set in 1974, also was suggested as a third possible means of stemming the growth of independent expenditures. Herbert Alexander pointed out that "$1,000 in 1974 dollars is meaningless — it's worth less than $500." This option was proposed to the Senate Rules Committee during its consideraton of campaign finance law revisions in late 1981. *(See Chapter 2, p. 29.)*

Treading Carefully

Because of the controversy surrounding independent expenditures, most such spenders get lawyers' advice before taking a single step. A talk with an independent spender is as much about the law as it is about politics.

NCPAC, for instance, solicited guidance from the FEC on nine different courses it was thinking about pursuing. Under one proposal, NCPAC wanted to hire a consultant with a husband employed by a Republican Senate candidate whose Democratic foe the group opposed through independent spending. The FEC said it could hire her provided that the couple had no professional dealings with each other.

Like many independent expenditors, philanthropist Mott feared that the FEC could end up viewing the rule against collusion too narrowly. In February 1980 he held a fund-raiser for John Anderson, he said, but in March and April he kept clear of personal contact with the Anderson campaign while he boosted it with independent spending. "I had to check I.D.s before I talked with anyone to ensure they weren't with Anderson," he recounted.

Later in the campaign Mott was back in touch with the candidate because, wishing to have Anderson's ear, he no longer intended to use independent expenditures. He hoped that "the slate is wiped clean."

A desire to avoid legal problems played a role in Environmental Action's scrapping its "Dirty Dozen" campaign. According to group official Peter Harnik, "It became difficult to guarantee that our people were not strategizing with campaign people."

HARMFUL OR HELPFUL, THE PRACTICE CONTINUES

There was disagreement over whether independent expenditures always helped the intended beneficiary, or instead, due to the no-contact rule in particular, they inadvertently could hurt the very candidate they were meant to help.

Impact of NCPAC

Taking some of the credit for the 1980 Republican victories were representatives from New Right groups such as NCPAC and conservative fundamentalists from groups such as the Moral Majority. They claimed the 1980 election established them as a credible force in American politics.

But Republican Party officials and many of the candidates who ousted liberal Democrats said the New Right's role was minimal, and in some cases harmful. They attributed the victories to more familiar factors: fresh but experienced candidates, generous doses of party financing, a popular presidential candidate atop the ticket and a throw-the-incumbents-out mood.

Evangelical groups — particularly the Moral Majority, but also the Christian Voice and the Religious Roundtable — relied mostly on rallies, leaflets and word of mouth, often centered on churches, to spread their political message. Of the three, only Christian Voice made independent expenditures according to the FEC report. The group spent more than $400,000 in behalf of Ronald Reagan, its only beneficiary.

NCPAC, however, was the second highest independent giver and its role in the defeat of Sens. Bayh, Culver, Church and McGovern was highly publicized — much to the group's delight.

If NCPAC was a factor in the election, the group was collecting few thank-you notes from the Republicans it claimed to have helped. Republican Rep. James Abdnor, who unseated McGovern in South Dakota, not only belittled NCPAC's influence, but filed a complaint with the Federal Election Commission charging NCPAC had used his name without authorization. "I don't think if NCPAC had not existed it would have made any difference in the outcome," said his press secretary, Jane A. Boorman.

GOP Rep. Charles E. Grassley felt the same way about his defeat of Culver in Iowa, said press secretary Beverly Hubble. And Bill Fay, an aide to Rep. Steven D. Symms, R-Idaho, who beat Church, contended NCPAC's efforts on Symms' behalf backfired. Fay said NCPAC made "erroneous charges" that gave Church something to talk about. "I think if anything, groups such as NCPAC probably hindered Steve Symms," Fay said. Dan Quayle, the Republican representative who replaced Bayh in Indiana, concurred.

Among those most disgruntled by news coverage attributing the election outcome to the the New Right was the Republican Senatorial Campaign Committee, which believed its campaign operation had been overshadowed. *(See Chapter 5, The Parties and Campaign Laws, p. 71.)*

Both NCPAC and the Republican Senatorial Campaign Committee commissioned post-election polls, which they hoped would shed light on the factors affecting the outcome.

Risk Is Worth It

Many ideological groups appeared to believe the risk of hurting the candidate was worth taking.

"You see, no candidate wants to discuss abortion," said Bea McClellan, president of the Life Amendment PAC of Oregon. "That's why we have to make sure it's one of the issues." The group expended $1,500 on behalf of successful Republican House candidate Denny Smith and an equal amount on behalf of another Oregon contender — this one unsuccessful — Michael Fitzgerald.

But Texas' Henry Grover defended his individual spending in another way. According to him, his activity for Connally was a matter of regional savvy. "I knew Texas better than anybody in that campaign," he said. But NCPAC's Dolan said he thinks polling is vital before doing any independent spending, "because it's more objective than talking to your friends."

One critical key to successful independent spending appears to be monitoring a favored candidate's progress. An example was the 1980 New Hampshire primary, when Reagan appeared threatened by a hard-charging George Bush. With Reagan nearing the crucial first-in-the-nation primary's $294,000 spending lid, the Fund for a Conservative Majority leaped in with an estimated $60,000 for advertising and leafletting.

NCPAC's Target '80 Techniques

As "Sweet Georgia Brown" played in the background, the basketball player showed South Dakota television viewers his dribbling artistry. "Globetrotter is a great name for a basketball team," said the advertisement's narrator. "But it's a terrible name for a senator." The alleged junketeer was Sen. George McGovern, D-S.D., who was running for re-election in 1980.

More than a year in advance of the same 1980 election, Idaho voters already were seeing television advertisements that showed empty Titan I missile silos in the state. These ads were designed to attack Sen. Frank Church, D-Idaho, by portraying him as opposed to a strong national defense.

Three senators including Church, Birch Bayh, D-Ind., and John C. Culver, D-Iowa, were derided through an advertising "baloney" blitz. These ads featured slices of baloney with multimillion-dollar price tags equaling the amount of deficit spending the target senator purportedly voted for. "One very big piece of baloney is Birch Bayh telling us he's fighting inflation," the announcer said.

All these ads were part of a nationwide media campaign to defeat six Democratic senators in 1980. Known as Target '80, the controversial independent spending drive was mounted by the National Conservative Political Action Committee (NCPAC), with some help from state-based organizations such as the Anybody But Church (ABC) Political Action Committee and Target McGovern.

NCPAC's independent expenditure efforts were the most visible — and the second most expensive — in the 1979-80 election cycle. NCPAC spent $3.3 million in its independent efforts, of which $1.2 million was spent against the candidacies of the six incumbents. In addition to McGovern, Church, Culver and Bayh, NCPAC targeted Alan Cranston, Calif., and Thomas F. Eagleton, Mo. All but Cranston and Eagleton were defeated.

Dolan Cites 'Dirty Dozen'

Precedents for the 1980 NCPAC endeavor were found in groups of varying philosophy. The "Dirty Dozen" campaign in the early 1970s, in which Environmental Action targeted for defeat twelve members of Congress who showed low ratings on key environmental votes, caught the attention of NCPAC Chairman John T. "Terry" Dolan. Of Environmental Action and its Dirty Dozen program he said, "What they have done is given us legitimacy, certainly." Anti-abortion forces claimed that leafletting of church parking lots in 1978 provided the crucial margin to dislodge liberal Sen. Dick Clark, D-Iowa.

While the effectiveness of these programs was questioned by some observers, both received wide-spread attention in the political community and helped to foster negative endeavors such as NCPAC's Target '80.

According to Dolan, NCPAC chose its 1980 targets on the basis of the political vulnerability and liberal ideology of the incumbent, the nature of the state and the availability of attractive challengers. "Our goal is a conservative Senate, and this is the best way to get it," he said.

Machiavellian Methods

But some critics characterized NCPAC's methods as Machiavellian. Several of the targeted senators asserted that the groups had distorted their voting records and stances on issues.

Church said in an *Idaho Statesman* article that the Titan I empty-silo ads were misleading because Titan I missiles had been replaced by another generation of missiles. "These charges cannot be characterized as healthy, honest political debate," he said.

While Church's reaction was no surprise, Idaho Republicans reportedly were not enthusiastic about the negative campaign against Church. Dennis Olsen, the Idaho GOP chairman, declined to say whether the NCPAC and ABC efforts against Church were welcome or unwelcome. "Any effort by any group to inform the public as to Church's voting record on significant issues will be helpful," he said. "The public reaction will be positive if the facts are correct."

John T. "Terry" Dolan

And in McGovern's South Dakota, Republicans were open about their displeasure with the independent expenditures. "I don't think you can defeat George McGovern by standing up cussing him," said Dan Parrish, the South Dakota Republican chairman.

Nevertheless, McGovern's campaign registered a shift away from its candidate after harshly anti-McGovern advertising appeared in South Dakota in 1979. According to administrative assistant George V. Cunningham, the senator's "favorability rating" dropped about 20 percent during NCPAC's pre-primary activities.

"It was sort of like a pack of jackals around an elk," said Cunningham. "They pull him down, then the bear comes in and eats him."

NCPAC Attacks, PROPAC Counters

Before the 1980 election had cooled down, the National Conservative Political Action Committee (NCPAC) began targeting the liberal senators it hoped to unseat in 1982. NCPAC launched its attack early in 1981 with the above newspaper advertisement against Maryland Democrat Paul S. Sarbanes. A new liberal group, Progressive Political Action Committee (PROPAC), promptly responded with ads defending Sarbanes and criticizing what it called NCPAC's "scare campaign." A sample PROPAC ad is shown at the right.

That amounted to a 20 percent spending hike for Reagan. And Bush could do nothing about it.

1982 Election

Despite any negative reaction to its efforts, NCPAC held a news conference one week after Election Day during which it announced a list of "potential targets" for 1982.

The list was headed by liberal Democrats such as Kennedy; Sarbanes; Howard M. Metzenbaum, Ohio; and Donald W. Riegle Jr., Mich.; but it also included moderates such as Henry M. Jackson, Wash.; Daniel P. Moynihan, N.Y., and Republican Lowell P. Weicker Jr., Conn.

Other conservative PACs began raising money again almost immediately, and by mid-1981 NCPAC and Helms' Congressional Club had raised more than $2 million.

Conservative groups in early 1981 launched a negative advertising campaign against Sen. Sarbanes. NCPAC's anti-Sarbanes television ad, which aired in Maryland, starred a beefy construction worker whose facial expression changed from calm to disgust as a voice-over denounced Sarbanes' alleged liberalism. But later in the year it appeared that the media campaign might have backfired. Some observers maintained that Sarbanes had become a sort of *cause célèbre*, rallying Democrats and liberals who hoped to stop NCPAC's advance through their own fund raising.

NCPAC was blunted in its effort to mount negative campaigns against Kennedy and three other prominent Democrats up for re-election in 1982 — Sen. John Melcher of Montana and Reps. Jim Wright of Texas and James R. Jones of Oklahoma. By late fall of 1981, NCPAC had been unable to buy time for its controversial ads from television stations in any of the three states. Stations said that the ads were inaccurate, that it was too early for 1982 politicking or that they sold time only to candidates.

In connection with these rejections, NCPAC's Dolan in December 1981 said he was planning to sue several Democrats, including Kennedy, Melcher and Wright, as well as numerous broadcast stations for conspiring to violate his First, Fifth, and Fourteenth Amendment rights.

Spokesmen for the Democrats named by Dolan acknowledged to *The Washington Post* that their representatives had called television stations, alerting them of the consequences of airing ads that contained errors or distortions, but all maintained nothing was improper about that.

Liberal Counter-groups

The New Right tactics alarmed a number of liberals and inspired the creation of counter-groups. Not long after the election, five new liberal political action committees had been formed. All had as their main goal economic support of liberal candidates. But only one of the five planned to concentrate on independent expenditures aimed at vilifying conservatives it deemed vulnerable in 1982. That one was Victor Kamber's Progressive Political Action Committee (PROPAC), formed in 1981.

Due to its association with NCPAC and its controversial Target '80, the independent expenditure concept had a particularly bad name among many liberals PROPAC hoped to tap for funds. Sensitive to this, the organization defended negative independent spending as a necessary evil. "Nobody likes it, but the right wing has developed it extensively," said a PROPAC representative. "So where it needs to be done, we will have to do it."

Like NCPAC, PROPAC prepared its own "hit list" of conservatives to challenge in 1982. Beginning in December 1981, PROPAC began an advertising campaign designed to unseat four conservative Republican senators, including North Carolina's Helms. "We plan to use Terry Dolan's exact logic that we're only exposing [the legislators'] records," Kamber explained. PROPAC's campaign, costing an initial $30,000 to $50,000, targeted Sens. Helms, Schmitt, Orrin G. Hatch, Utah, and S.I. "Sam" Hayakawa, Calif.

The group also planned to do some positive independent spending to aid endangered moderates and liberals. Money it spent to counter NCPAC's charges against Sarbanes was counted as an independent expenditure for the Maryland incumbent.

Kamber, listed as PROPAC treasurer, was a one-time Young Republican official who went to work for the AFL-CIO Building Trades Department in 1974 and gradually began shifting toward the Democratic Party. In 1980 he began his own business, and in 1981 he organized PROPAC.

The group hoped to raise $1.5 million by early 1982, spending the bulk of it independently. As of mid-1981 and after two mailings, it had raised $105,224. That figure placed it behind the other new liberal committees.

Parties Seek Control

The growing clout of the conservative PACs understandably concerned Democratic Party officials, who viewed NCPAC and its allies as a disrupting influence in congressional races. In early 1981 Democratic National Committee (DNC) Chairman Charles T. Manatt named New York lawyer and former Kennedy adviser Theodore C. Sorensen to head a party panel that would explore ways to curb independent spending.

Manatt invited the Republican National Committee (RNC) to participate in a joint study of the independent spending question, but RNC Chairman Richard Richards declined. Instead, the RNC set up its own committee in June 1981 with the broader mandate of reviewing and recommending changes in the federal election law and the presidential nominating process. Republican National Committeeman Ernest Angelo of Texas was named the committee chairman.

But Richards did voice concern that the conservative PACs were loose cannons in Republican campaigns. While their negative advertising might soften up Democratic incumbents, Richards warned, the conservatives were prone to overdo their attacks and ultimately might prove an albatross to GOP candidates.

At the urging of Reagan political adviser Lyn Nofziger, Richards met privately in May 1981 with conservative PAC leaders, including Dolan, Tom Ellis, the director of the Congressional Club, and Richard A. Viguerie, a direct mail fund raiser for conservative causes.

Richards asked the conservative PACs not to make independent expenditures in campaigns where GOP candidates or Republican state chairman objected to their involvement.

But the conservative groups expressed little interest in an agreement. "Our conclusion," said Dolan the following month, "is that we cannot have any kind of formal agreement from a legal point of view, nor would we want to from a political point of view."

With hopes of an agreement dashed, Richards began issuing public warnings. In July 1981 he urged NCPAC to stay out of the 1982 Massachusetts Senate race, indicating that attacks on Kennedy would backfire against his Republican challengers.

The System in Operation

7

Like the country itself, diversity is the byword in describing the various systems of campaign finance in the United States.

There is no uniform national system that governs all candidates for political office. A presidential candidate must abide by different rules than an individual seeking a seat in Congress. And a congressional candidate is bound by a separate campaign finance law than someone running for a governorship or a state legislative seat.

Presidential politics has been governed by a system of public financing since 1976. There is nearly full federal funding for major party candidates in the general election, with partial public financing in the primaries. House and Senate campaigns, however, remain totally bankrolled by private contributions. The variety of state laws affecting gubernatorial and legislative campaigns reflects a mixture of the two systems.

The disparity in campaign financing methods at the state level was evident in the two gubernatorial contests held in 1981. While New Jersey offered major party candidates public funds, Virginia employed a free-wheeling system of private financing that enabled corporations to give directly to candidates and permitted individuals to contribute without limit.

PUBLIC FUNDING OF PRESIDENTIAL CAMPAIGNS

No aspect of campaign finance has changed more dramatically in the last decade than the way presidential campaigns are funded. And the impact has been far-reaching.

Presidential candidates operated under a wide-open system until 1976 that permitted multimillion-dollar contributions by individuals and unlimited spending by candidates. But the Watergate scandal changed all that. In 1980 candidates were conducting the second presidential campaign under the Federal Election Campaign Act (FECA), which provides public financing for presidential elections.

The law tightly restricts contributions and, to win observance of expenditure limits, offers major party candidates a sizable carrot in the form of federal money. In addition, the Democratic and Republican national committees are provided funds to conduct their parties' national conventions.

Basic Provisions

The major provisions of public funding for presidential campaigns were passed in 1974 with amendments adopted in early 1976. Parts of the law were declared unconstitutional in the January 1976 *Buckley v. Valeo* Supreme Court decision. But the court upheld contribution limits, including the provision that a candidate accepting federal money may spend no more than $50,000 out of his own pocket. Acceptance of public funds, the court ruled, also obligated a candidate to obey the spending ceilings imposed by Congress. *(Legislative background, Chapter 1)*

Yet if a candidate decides not to accept the federal money — as former Texas Gov. John B. Connally did in 1980 — he is still bound by the provision limiting individual contributions to each candidate to $1,000 and political action committee (PAC) donations to $5,000 during the nominating process. No longer can candidates garner hundreds of thousands of dollars from a few wealthy contributors, although a candidate refusing federal funds could spend as much as he likes out of his own pocket.

For the primaries, there is a partial system of public funding. To qualify, candidates are required to raise $5,000 in 20 or more states in individual contributions not exceeding $250. Only money collected after Jan. 1 of the year prior to the presidential election counts. Upon qualifying, candidates can have contributions of $250 or less matched by the government on a dollar-for-dollar basis up to one half of the national spending ceiling. The 1974 law set the ceiling at $10 million with a cost-of-living adjustment each election.

By 1976 inflation had raised the ceiling to $10.9 million. By 1980 it had increased to $14.7 million, enabling candidates to qualify for nearly $7.4 million in matching funds. Additionally, candidates can spend 20 percent beyond the spending ceiling (or $2.9 million in 1980) for fund-raising costs. And they are permitted to spend an unlimited amount for legal and accounting costs.

In spending their money, candidates accepting public financing during the nominating process must watch not only the national spending ceiling but also individual state ceilings. The state limits are based on voting age population multiplied by 16 cents with adjustments for inflation. In 1980 they ranged from $294,400 in the smallest states and territories (such as New Hampshire) to $3.9 million in California. However, candidates cannot spend the maximum in each state because an aggregation of the state spending totals is more than twice the national ceiling.

In the general election, there is nearly full public financing for major party candidates, with private campaign fund raising permitted only to cover legal and accounting costs incurred in complying with the law. The 1974 law set the general election stipend for the major party candidates at $20 million.

But like the matching fund allotment, it is adjusted each election for inflation. In 1976 Democrat Jimmy Carter and Republican Gerald R. Ford each drew $21.8 million in public funds to run their general election campaigns. Both Carter and Republican nominee Ronald Reagan received $29.4 million from the federal treasury in 1980. *(Presidential limitations and public funding, box, p. 93)*

Third party and independent candidates can receive some public money only if they draw at least 5 percent of the national popular vote. No candidate came close to qualifying in 1976. But in 1980 independent John B. Anderson received almost 7 percent of the vote, and collected about $4 million in federal funds after the election.

Public funds come from voluntary income tax checkoffs and are maintained in a special treasury called the Presidential Election Campaign Fund.

Individual taxpayers may annually designate $1 on their federal tax return to the fund. Couples filing jointly may designate $2.

In 1976, $72 million was disbursed from the fund — $24 million in pre-convention matching funds, $4 million to

the Democratic and Republican parties to hold their national conventions, and almost $44 million to Carter and Ford to run their fall campaigns.

In 1980 inflation helped push federal disbursements over $100 million — with $31 million going to pre-convention candidates in matching funds, $8 million to the two major parties for convention funding and $63 million to Carter, Anderson and Reagan for their general election campaigns.

Although the checkoff rate has gradually increased since the fund was first established in the early 1970s, in no year have more than 30 percent of federal taxpayers designated their tax dollars for it. Still, the fund has remained financially viable. At the end of October 1981, $114.3 million was left in the special treasury.

Political Ramifications

The FECA has won praise from public financing advocates. They claim that it has cleaned up presidential politics by controlling spending and by driving out influence-seeking "fat cats" and special interest groups.

They argue that the law encourages candidates to run tightly organized, efficient campaigns and spurs creativity in fund raising and campaign management.

Critics counter that the FECA is producing presidential campaigns that are underfinanced and overregulated. The contribution and spending ceilings are too low, they contend, forcing candidates to run highly centralized campaigns that curtail grass-roots activity.

Opponents argue that the major beneficiaries of the FECA are lawyers and accountants, whose skills are needed to comply with the detailed provisions of the law. "If General Washington had to fight the Revolutionary War like we fight our political campaigns," observed political consultant Bob Keefe at an American Enterprise Institute (AEI) conference in 1979, "we'd still have a king."

Spending Curbed Temporarily

The FECA did temporarily succeed in curbing the sharp increase in campaign spending. According to Herbert E. Alexander in his book *Financing the 1976 Election*, spending for both the pre-convention and general election phases of presidential campaigns jumped by $47 million from 1968 to 1972 (from $91 million to $138 million), but by only $22 million from 1972 to 1976 (to $160 million).

The elimination of extensive private contributions from the fall campaign tended to reduce general election spending, while the addition of matching federal funds helped to swell spending in the pre-convention phase. Before the FECA, pre-convention spending never execeeded $50 million. In 1976 the major party contenders spent $72 million.

In 1980 presidential campaign spending shot upward again, reaching — according to Alexander — about $250 million. Besides inflation, Alexander attributed the sharp increase in 1980 presidential spending to the fund-raising success of Connally, Anderson and third party candidates, greater activity by the major parties at the national, state and local levels and significant independent expenditures on behalf of Reagan.

Nearly one half of all spending in the presidential race came during the pre-convention stage. Major contenders for the Democratic and Republican nominations spent $107 million. About $10 million — including funds raised

privately by host city committees — was spent conducting the major party conventions. The rest of the money was pumped into the general election campaign.

Presidential Primaries

Over the decade since 1971, three major factors have been at work to dramatically overhaul the presidential nominating process. One has been the FECA, which through public funding and strict contribution limits has reduced the advantage of well-known members of the Washington power structure by removing their ability to easily tap wealthy contributors.

The second factor has been the proliferation of presidential primaries. As the number of primaries has increased from 17 in 1968 to 37 in 1980, their role in the nominating process has changed from advisory to prime determinant.

The third factor, the declining influence of the party hierarchy, has been a manifestation of the first two. As primaries have grown more important in delegate selection and small individual contributors in campaign finance, the role of party leaders in the nominating process has declined.

Under the existing system, it would be virtually impossible for a candidate to avoid the primaries and rely on the support of party leaders to win his party's nomination, as Democratic Vice President Hubert Humphrey did in 1968. And it would be virtually impossible now for a candidate to wait until the primaries had begun and then launch a whirlwind, multimillion-dollar campaign as Democratic Sen. Robert F. Kennedy of New York did the same year.

The first two elections under the FECA have shown that a candidate must start early and do well in the early primaries, caucuses and straw polls.

The Great Equalizer

Before the FECA, the well-known Washington politician — supported by party leaders and large contributors — had the inside track in mounting a successful presidential campaign. But the new campaign law has helped to change that by prohibiting large contributions and making donations from PAC and party sources unmatchable for public funds. The FECA has served as a great equalizer, giving a big boost to politicians outside the Washington power structure such as Jimmy Carter.

As a former governor of Georgia, Carter was not well known to national party leaders or major contributors when he launched his first presidential campaign in November 1974. But he had the time to criss-cross the country and raise the small chunks of money that would earn him matching federal funds.

"It is fair to say," wrote Alexander in 1981, "that the Federal Election Campaign Act opened up the electoral process to some candidates who otherwise might not have had staying power in the pre-nomination contests."

Small Contributors Emphasized

Before 1976 all campaign money was raised privately, often in large chunks from wealthy contributors or interest groups. But that changed with the FECA. In the 1976 pre-convention period, 36 percent of the funds received by prominent candidates was public money. With Connally

Presidential Spending Limits and Public Financing

(In millions of dollars)	1976	1980
Nominating Process		
Maximum federal matching funds per candidate	$ 5.5	$ 7.4
Prenomination campaign spending limit	10.9	14.7
Additional expenditures for fund raising	2.2	2.9
General Election		
Public grant to major party nominees	21.8	29.4
National party spending limits	3.2	4.6

Source: Citizens' Research Foundation

declining to accept federal funds, that figure fell to 29 percent in 1980. But small individual contributions remained the linchpin of fund raising in the pre-convention stage.

Because only individual contributions are matchable, they represented more than 90 percent of all privately raised net receipts in 1980. Candidates experimented with a variety of ways to raise small chunks of matchable funds, but generally focused on personal solicitation, direct mail, dinners and concerts.

Fund-raisers for Democratic Sen. Edward M. Kennedy of Massachusetts, however, found another lucrative way to draw individual contributions. They sold artwork. The pieces, designed especially for the campaign by prominent artists such as Andy Warhol and Jamie Wyeth, were sold to contributors for a specified, "suggested" donation determined by an art appraiser. While the cost of the artists' materials counted against the $1,000 individual contribution limit, their time and effort was considered a voluntary activity by the Federal Election Commission (FEC) and not subject to the limit.

PACs: A Small Role

Besides freezing out wealthy "fat cats," the FECA has limited the role of political action committees (PACs) and party organizations in the presidential nominating process. Money from those sources is not matchable with public funds.

PAC giving to candidates in the nominating process did increase from less than $800,000 in 1976 to nearly $1.6 million in 1980. But the latter figure still represented less than 2 percent of the candidates' total net receipts.

In both elections PACs were cautious, frequently hedging their bets by giving to several candidates and holding back their heaviest giving until it was apparent who would win. In the first half of 1975, for example, Carter's long-shot campaign received only one PAC donation totaling $500. But in June 1976, after he had wrapped up the nomination, Carter collected more than $200,000 in PAC money.

The story was similar in 1980. Through February, Reagan had drawn less than $30,000 from the PACs. But from March on, when it was apparent he was far ahead of his other GOP rivals, PAC donations began to pour into his campaign headquarters. By summer he had received more than a quarter million dollars in additional PAC money.

President Carter was the prime beneficiary of PAC largesse in 1980. Altogether, he collected about a half million dollars from them (or about 3 percent of his net receipts). As the incumbent, he was able to draw contributions from a diverse range of corporate and labor PACs, including the political arms of the Chrysler Corp. and the United Auto Workers (UAW).

Both Reagan and Connally received nearly $300,000 from PACs, with the Texan relying heavily on money from corporate groups. Many of the PACs gave to several candidates. The political committee of the UAW, for instance, contributed to both Carter and Kennedy, while the PAC affiliated with the Grumman Corp. gave to virtually all the major contenders including Reagan and Kennedy.

Parties: A Smaller Role

Party sources are playing an even smaller role than PACs in the restructured world of presidential campaign finance. Passage of the FECA has ensured candidates of their independence from party sources.

While state and local party organizations can still serve as forums for presidential candidates in meeting party activists, they provide virtually no cash. Altogether, party committees provided major party candidates barely $15,000 during the nominating process, with most of the total split about evenly between Carter and Kennedy.

Much more than that came out of the pockets of the presidential contenders. Candidates contributed or lent their pre-convention campaigns more than $700,000, with most of that accounted for by a large loan from Connally to his campaign. Still, the $50,000 limit on candidate contributions prevents any candidate accepting public funds from largely bankrolling his own campaign as New York Gov. Nelson A. Rockefeller did in 1964 and 1968.

Press Reimbursements

In searching for money, some campaigns found another way to increase gross income — bill the news media for traveling with the candidate. The Kennedy operation was probably most adept at the practice. From December 1979 through February 1980, the campaign received more than $200,000 a month from the traveling press corps.

In theory, billing of the press was to be limited to reimbursing the campaign for the amount that the campaign paid for providing transportation for reporters traveling with Kennedy. But for items such as chartered airplanes and buses it was difficult to determine an exact transportation cost for each reporter. As a result, when a reporter accompanied the candidate on chartered planes, the campaign billed the media on a formula that added a fixed percentage to first-class air fare.

No effort was made by the Kennedy campaign to determine whether the press corps was, in fact, paying more than the actual cost of its transportation. But Kennedy officials claimed that the formula had not resulted in added usable campaign income.

In March 1980 Kennedy's campaign abandoned its chartered jet in favor of flying on commercial airlines. Reporters traveling with Kennedy then were required to pay airlines directly for their tickets, resulting in a drop in reimbursements from $216,000 in February to $39,000 in March.

Impact on Campaigns

The law has caused numerous changes in the nominating process, but probably none has been so unwelcome to candidates and campaign officials as the extensive disclosure requirements. To comply with the detailed provisions, campaigns spend hundreds of thousands of dollars apiece. Lawyers and accountants have become the most valuable members of campaign organizations, and their knowledge of the law is considered a basic ingredient in building a successful operation. They are often the first people hired by a presidential candidate.

Compliance Hassles

Officials with the short-lived 1976 presidential campaign of Democratic Sen. Henry M. Jackson of Washington were flabbergasted to find during a crucial stage that $70,000 in checks could not be deposited because the campaign did not have required disclosure information on the contributors.

In 1976 the law required candidates to report the names and addresses of contributors of more than $100 as well as their occupations and places of business. Expenditures over $100 had to be itemized with the amount, date and purpose of the transaction.

Congress amended the FECA in December 1979 to eliminate some of the red tape and paperwork. The 1979 amendments reduced the number of reports required and raised the level of reportable contributions and expenditures from $100 to $200.

Yet many campaign officials remained unhappy with the law and its enforcement. In responding to one inquiry in July 1979, Reagan treasurer Bay Buchanan tersely accused the FEC of making "a hypertechnical case out of disclosure, fit only for the aficionados of election law administration."

Other campaigns also have complained about FEC nitpicking, and in April 1981 the counsels for nine 1980 presidential campaigns and lawyers for the Democratic and Republican national committees wrote to the commission complaining about its audit process. (Criticism of FEC, Chapter 2, p. 29)

The FECA's supporters contend that the law has discouraged sloppy bookkeeping and wasteful management.

But critics maintain that in emphasizing small donors the law has increased the effort needed to raise campaign funds and has forced campaigns to divert an inordinate amount of their time and money to minor details. According to Republican Rep. Richard B. Cheney of Wyoming, President Ford's chief of staff from 1975 to 1977, compliance with the law may mean that a candidate is "better equipped to serve as director of the Office of Management and Budget than as president."

More Professional and Centralized

A major effect of the FECA has been the increasing professionalization of presidential campaigns. No longer just hobbies for political activists, they are evolving into businesses with the jargon of major marketing campaigns.

"When you have the Federal Election Commission requiring a lawyer and accountant to be prominent in your campaign, you have a businesslike approach," claimed campaign consultant Lance Tarrance, a national pollster for Connally in 1980.

Inflation has accentuated the need for good management. A $1,000 contribution in 1975 was worth only $641 in 1980, but the cost of campaign necessities had skyrocketed. Campaign finance expert Herbert Alexander reported that while the consumer price index had increased by about 40 percent between 1976 and 1980, the cost of producing direct mail appeals was up as much as 50 percent, the cost of making television commercials had doubled and the cost of chartering a jet on the East Coast for candidate travel had almost tripled.

With a limited amount of money to spend, the law has encouraged candidates to run highly centralized campaigns out of a national headquarters. Grass-roots activity is discouraged because any expenditure by an affiliated local group counts against the candidate's spending ceiling. Button and bumper stickers are the first items to be dropped, as candidates husband their money to afford travel, advertising and direct mail.

"The experience of the Ford campaign in 1976," observed Cheney at an AEI conference in 1979, "showed conclusively that it was much easier to discourage grass-roots activity than it was to control it or report it..."

"Given a choice between local spontaneity and enthusiastic participation or control over spending," Cheney concluded, "the cautious campaign manager has little choice but to opt for activities which are 'controllable.'"

Longer Campaigns

The growth in the number of primaries as well as the need to tap large numbers of small contributors has forced all candidates, not just the long shots, to organize and begin raising money early.

For decades the planning for major presidential campaigns has required several years of lead time. Preparations for New York Gov. Rockefeller's 1964 presidential campaign, for example, were under way by the summer of 1962.

But there is little doubt that the visible, public side of campaigns is longer than ever before. Even before Republican Rep. Philip M. Crane of Illinois formally began the 1980 campaign by announcing his presidential candidacy in August 1978, four other GOP contenders — including Reagan — had opened a new era in the history of presidential campaigning by establishing their own PACs. The PACs coordinated traveling and speechmaking in 1978 for the Republican presidential hopefuls and made contributions to GOP congressional candidates.

PACs operated by George Bush, Connally and Sen. Robert Dole of Kansas terminated after the 1978 election but Reagan's PAC, Citizens for the Republic, is still in business. It was joined in early 1981 by two new PACs formed by Kennedy and former Vice President Walter F.

Spending Money Early

One of the major criticisms of the presidential nominating process is that it encourages candidates to spend heavily in the early delegate selection events, giving short shrift to the primaries and caucuses that follow.

That complaint is borne out by the state spending totals that the Democratic and Republican candidates reported to the Federal Election Commission (FEC) in 1976 and 1980. Candidates spent heavily in the important Iowa caucuses and the New Hampshire primary, but steadily decreasing amounts in later primary and caucus states.

The chart shows the amount of money candidates collectively spent for each vote in a sampling of delegate selection events from the beginning of the nominating process to the end. For both elections, the findings are limited to candidates who accepted public financing. Other contenders did not have to report their state-by-state spending to the FEC.

	1976	1980
Iowa (Jan.)	$9.46	$13.89
New Hampshire (Feb.)	7.22	8.90
Florida (March)	2.02	2.21
Wisconsin (April)	1.15	1.36
Nebraska (May)	1.30	0.45
California (June)	0.68	0.23

Mondale, both regarded as 1984 Democratic presidential hopefuls. *(Presidential PACs, Chapter 3, p. 55)*

While Kennedy did not have a PAC before launching his 1980 campaign, he was the target of a controversial "draft" movement. Dozens of committees formed across the country in 1979 urging Kennedy to seek the Democratic nomination. Because he was not a declared candidate and did not authorize the draft effort, the draft committees were not bound by contribution or spending limits.

The FEC sought to curb the draft committees by challenging contributions made by the political arm of the International Association of Machinists to a number of the draft committees that exceeded $5,000 apiece, the limit PACs may contribute to a candidate. But the Supreme Court rejected the FEC challenge in October 1981, ruling that the commission had no jurisdiction over the draft committees. *(See box, Chapter 6, p. 84)*

The formation of PACs and draft committees represents a new opening phase in what has become longer and longer presidential campaigns. In June 1979 there already were seven major announced candidates for president compared with six in June 1975, one in June 1971 (Sen. George McGovern of South Dakota, the eventual Democratic nominee), and none in June 1967.

Even well-known candidates running in the 1980 election who delayed their formal announcements until late 1979, felt compelled to form campaign committees months earlier to do necessary organizational and fund-raising work. The campaign committee for Republican Sen. Howard H. Baker Jr. of Tennessee was established in January 1979; the Reagan and Carter committees in March.

While qualifying for public financing was more time-consuming than difficult for most candidates, it represented a milestone for any campaign. According to former North Carolina Gov. Terry Sanford, a 1976 Democratic presidential aspirant, qualification for matching funds is viewed as a "license to practice," and campaigns are not taken seriously by the media until they have qualified.

The law encourages candidates to qualify early by setting Jan. 1 of the presidential election year as the date when the FEC is permitted to begin certifying candidates for matching funds.

Value of Early Success

The need for early money has been accentuated by the increasing importance of preliminary events in the nominating process. The growth of primaries, with many of the later ones scheduled on the same days, has increased the value of a strong showing in the opening round of states.

Candidates who do well in the important early events win favorable media attention; that in turn can boost fund raising and create a bandwagon effect that propels them into the later primaries. Conversely, a candidate who does not do so well in the early events usually does not have a chance to recover. He or she acquires a losing image and fund raising often dries up.

In 1980 four of the six major Republican contenders and one of the three prominent Democratic candidates had withdrawn from the race by the end of April — a time when more than half the primaries remained. As in 1976, the nominees in 1980 were the candidates who had won most of the important early events.

Presidential campaigns have grown so lengthy that the first indications of candidate strength no longer occur in New Hampshire's traditional first-in-the-nation primary in February, but in the myriad straw polls and public opinion surveys that are taken in the year before the election. Candidates have responded by spending heavily not only in early delegate selection contests such as the January Iowa caucuses and the New Hampshire primary but for non-binding straw polls.

Carter and Reagan, for instance, reported spending more in Florida than any other state in 1979. Carter invested $500,000, and Reagan $300,000, with most of the money earmarked to win straw votes taken by their parties at November state conventions. For all the other candidates who listed their state allocation figures, Iowa was the prime target in 1979.

Priorities Pre-determined

While it would seem that campaigns face a difficult choice between saving their money for a long campaign or spending heavily in the early events, realistically there is little choice because a candidate must do well early.

According to the law, a candidate who draws less than 10 percent of the vote in two consecutive primaries becomes ineligible to receive matching funds 30 days after the second primary. The only way then for a candidate to regain eligibility is to receive 20 percent of the vote in a

later primary. But with the strict contribution and spending limits, it is virtually impossible to mount a comeback.

As Carter's Cinderella campaign in 1976 illustrated, the FECA tends to work to the advantage of front-runners. Not only did his victorious campaign through the primaries elicit a groundswell of matchable, individual contributions, but the law curbed the ability of his better-known rivals to quickly collect the large sums of money that they would have needed to successfully challenge him.

"A vital part of the Carter success story is the FECA," Herbert Alexander has written. "Without stringent contribution limits, better-known candidates who had connections with wealthy contributors could have swamped Carter; and without federal subsidies, Carter would have lacked the money to consolidate his early lead."

As a consequence, the need for early success leaves candidates with little flexibility in developing strategy. "You can't pick and choose," declared Rick Stearns, director of delegate selection for Kennedy's 1980 presidential campaign. "It makes early states far more important."

Instead of developing grand strategies, campaign managers are left to wrestle with tight budgets. Good fund-raisers and finance officials are as valuable now as big money contributors were in the past. "The system has forced the development of a much more careful set of priorities," explained campaign consultant John Deardourff.

Campaigns must be particularly careful how they budget their limited resources in the primary and caucus states. Many candidates have complained that the state spending limits are unrealistically low. They maintain that the ceilings do not take into account a state's political importance or its delegate selection system.

The formula establishing the state limits is based solely on voting age population. The ceilings are not raised for primary states, even though Congressional Quarterly found that in 1976 candidates on the average spent about $5 in every primary state for every $1 that they spent in a caucus state.

Nor are adjustments made for traditionally important states such as New Hampshire. Even though nearly all major candidates make a big effort in New Hampshire, it has the same spending ceiling as Guam.

The 1980 New Hampshire expenditure limit of $294,400 left most candidates searching for loopholes to spend as much as they possibly could. Candidates stayed overnight in neighboring states, placed New Hampshire staff members on their national headquarters' payroll and purchased advertising time on Boston television stations. Boston television reaches most New Hampshire households, and nearly the entire advertising cost could be charged against the Massachusetts limit.

Another loophole was independent expenditures. According to Alexander, Reagan was boosted in New Hampshire by the Fund for A Conservative Majority, which independently spent more than $60,000 on the Californian's behalf. (In other primary states, the conservative PAC reportedly spent more than a half million dollars for Reagan.)

Both Carter and Reagan, victorious in New Hampshire, exceeded the state limit and were fined by the FEC. But it apparently was money well spent. "Political reality is that New Hampshire has traditionally been the most important primary in the nation," wrote Cheney. "In 1976, 1,500 votes in New Hampshire (Ford's margin of victory over Reagan) were far more important to President Ford and Governor Reagan than were a million votes in California in June." *(Cost per vote, box, p. 95)*

And, reflecting this reality, the candidates reported spending almost twice as much money in New Hampshire in 1980 as they did in California.

Free Enterprise Option

Rejecting public funds frees a candidate to spend as much as he wants in New Hampshire or any other state. But in the first two elections under the FECA, only Connally took that course. The Texan indicated that public financing was alien to his free enterprise beliefs. Yet he also believed that the only way he could defeat Reagan for the Republican nomination in 1980 was to spend as much as he could in the early primaries.

But freedom from the spending ceilings proved to be no bargain, because he still was bound by the strict contribution limits. Connally was able to raise more money than all other candidates in 1979 and he finished the campaign with more than $12 million in net receipts. But failing to beat Reagan in any state, he saw private contributions dwindle. Without the prospect of public money, he withdrew from the race in March with a campaign deficit of nearly $2 million.

Reagan campaign officials also had weighed the possibility of financing their campaign without public funds, but reluctantly decided in January 1980 to take the federal money. "It's impossible to run a good campaign in 35 primaries [sic] if you take matching funds," said Reagan's national political director, Charles Black in explaining the dilemma. "It means you can't make the maximum effort in the middle and late primaries."

Big Spending Early...

The propensity to spend quickly means that the survivors of the early primaries and caucuses often find themselves facing months of delegate selection events ahead, with little cash on hand or their spending totals approaching the national ceiling. Usually there is no choice but to reduce spending, target particular primaries and hope that their momentum and favorable media exposure will carry them to victory in the other states.

Fortunately for the front runners in 1976 and 1980, they had virtually knocked out their rivals in the opening round of primaries. If their races had remained close, the decision to spend early could have backfired.

Led by Reagan, the major presidential contenders spent money at a much faster rate in 1980 than 1976. According to a June 1980 report by the Campaign Finance Study Group of Harvard University's Institute of Politics, Reagan had spent about one-third of the national limit by the end of 1979 (compared with 6 percent by the end of December 1975), and had spent more than two-thirds of the ceiling by the end of March 1980 (compared with about 40 percent at a similar date in 1976).

Reagan approached the spending ceiling at a quicker pace than any of his 1980 rivals, but his pattern was followed by others. The Harvard group reported that all three of the best-financed candidates in 1980 — Reagan, Bush and Carter — had all spent more than 50 percent of the national limit by the end of March. None of the candidates in 1976 had spent 50 percent of the ceiling until the end of April.

The Harvard group attributed the quickened spending pace to the growth in primaries (up from 30 in 1976 to 37),

a sharp increase in campaign expenses (on items such as office space, printing and advertising) that exceeded the inflation rate, and the need to do well early.

... Austerity Later

"In terms of finances, the later primaries are given short shrift by the contenders," the Harvard group noted, "especially by those who pursue a strategy of early victory and thereby run the risk of being unable to expend sufficient funds in the latter stages."

That analysis certainly applied to Reagan in 1980. His campaign already had begun to cut back spending by the end of March, earlier than any of the other major candidates still in the race.

In spite of a heavier schedule of primaries that month, Reagan's campaign spending in March was 41 percent less than in February. His monthly staff payroll of more than a half million dollars was sliced in half.

Also, Reagan ran a limited advertising campaign in the April Pennsylvania primary and had no television at all in the May Texas primary. Bush, who spent heavily in both, won in Pennsylvania and did better than expected in Texas. But in spite of the spending advantage Bush was unable to break Reagan's momentum.

Campaign Loans, Debts

The early spending in 1980 forced some candidates into a precarious financial position. At the end of 1975, Democratic Rep. Morris K. Udall of Arizona had the largest campaign deficit, about $330,000. Entering 1980, Reagan, Baker, Kennedy and Crane had outstanding debts that dwarfed Udall's. By the end of March, the situation had worsened for most candidates, with four contenders showing outstanding debts of $1 million or more.

Facing sizable deficits, loans played an important part in most candidates' campaign financing. Altogether, more than $15 million worth of loans, either from lending institutions or from individuals, were taken out by the major contenders. After the primaries, both Reagan and Carter held unity dinners with their defeated rivals to help pay campaign debts.

Candidates needed to rely on loans because the flow of contributions fluctuated sharply with their success or failure at the polls. Bush, for example, collected $2.4 million from individuals in February, the month after his well-publicized victory in the Iowa caucuses. But after his loss in New Hampshire he received less than $1 million in individual donations in March.

The fluctuation was even more dramatic for John Anderson. In January, when even the candidate jokingly referred to himself as "John Who," his campaign for the Republican nomination raised less than $150,000 from individuals. In February the figure rose to $426,000.

And following close second-place finishes in the Massachusetts and Vermont primaries, he received more than $2 million in individual contributions in March. That was more than any other candidate raised from individuals during the month.

Presidential General Elections

At first glance, it would appear that the financing of general election campaigns is quite simple. The major party nominees who accept public funding — and all of

Blackjack Stevens?

What do Jimmy Carter, Ronald Reagan, Lord Robert Benedict and Earl Vern Blackjack Stevens have in common? According to the Federal Election Commission (FEC), all were candidates for president in 1980.

In January 1980 the FEC counted about 200 presidential hopefuls. The list included the major Republican and Democratic contenders. But most of the candidates were political unknowns who did not appear on a single state primary or general election ballot in 1980.

All it takes to become a presidential candidate in the eyes of the FEC is to designate a campaign committee and bank account and to file a statement of candidacy or acknowledge the committee. The lenient requirements produced a 1980 campaign field that included a television repairman, a trucking magazine publisher, a self-described "prophetess," a former movie critic for the Beloit *Daily News* and a convict serving a life term for airplane hijacking.

Fund-raising techniques for these lesser lights varied. One contender held a $1-a-plate dinner that was attended by two people, the candidate and his campaign manager. Another unveiled a grandiose scheme to raise $25 million through contributions of one dollar apiece.

But probably the most unusual plan to raise money in a hurry was unveiled by a candidate who was more modestly bidding for the vice presidency. He offered pre-paid interviews at $50 a minute.

them did in 1976 and 1980 — automatically receive a stipend from the Presidential Election Campaign Fund shortly after their nomination. The only private campaign money they are allowed to raise must be earmarked for costs in complying with the law, which in the last election amounted to less than $2 million for each campaign. Reagan also raised several hundred thousand dollars to cover planning during the transition period.

Yet the money directly controlled by the candidates represents just the tip of the iceberg. There are a variety of other sources that pump money into the presidential campaign, and in 1980 they exceeded the nearly $60 million in federal money provided Carter and Reagan.

According to Herbert Alexander, an estimated $25 million was spent by the political parties on behalf of their nominees, with most of the party spending by GOP committees at the state and local level. Labor, corporations and trade associations spent nearly $20 million more, with the bulk of the money disbursed by unions in communicating with their members and organizing voter registration and get-out-the-vote drives on behalf of Carter.

Independent expenditures exceeded $10 million, with Reagan the prime beneficiary. And nearly $20 million more was spent by Anderson and his third-party colleagues.

Although both Carter and Reagan received an equal amount of public money, Reagan's edge among party sources and independent spenders gave him a financial advantage in 1980 that labor's work for Carter could not offset.

But public financing has helped the Democrats by curbing GOP access to big contributors. According to Alexander's Citizens' Research Foundation, Republican presidential nominees consistently outspent their Democratic adversaries when campaigns were privately funded, sometimes by margins exceeding 2-1.

Public Financing

Carter and Reagan each received $29.4 million in federal funds in 1980. That may seem like a lot, but it was only half the amount raised privately by President Nixon in 1972. While critics have complained that Nixon's scandal-tinted re-election drive amassed a campaign chest far beyond his needs, there have been numerous complaints that public financing does not provide the candidates enough money.

"If it's a landslide situation for either candidate, like it was for Richard Nixon in 1972, it won't make much difference how much money anybody spends," explained Alexander in 1976. "But if you have a very tight campaign in October and November, the candidates are going to be hobbled. . . . That [money provided by public financing] is a paltry amount to run a national campaign."

The limited amount of money leaves little room for waste or strategic errors. Party committees are left with playing a major role in grass-roots organization. In 1980 Carter and Reagan both poured over half their federal money into media advertising and hundreds of thousands of dollars more into polling. Even then, candidates had to depend heavily on attracting free media exposure from carefully scheduled campaign events.

Although incumbent presidents were beaten in both 1976 and 1980, there are advantages to occupying the White House: a presidential staff whose work is partly political; access to news coverage; the convenience of Air Force One for travel; and the ability to take action on policy issues that may arise during the campaign.

On a 1976 campaign trip by President Ford to Oregon, for instance, the expenses of only two of the 20 White House staff members and other government employees were paid for by the president's campaign committee. Daily expenses of the other 18 were paid by the government. They included three press officers, four secretaries, three stenographers, a Navy cameraman, an Army communications technician and six transportation office employees. The salaries of all 20 were also paid by the government during the trip.

GOP Committees Boost Reagan

One of the major criticisms of the FECA during the 1976 campaign was that the tight budgets forced campaigns to underfinance or ignore completely local organization and the staples of grass-roots enthusiasm — such as buttons, bumper stickers, yard signs and posters.

Part of the problem was that the FECA prohibited money raised in the pre-convention stage from being used in the general election campaign. With spending limits, state headquarters had to be closed after each primary. "It was hardly surprising, then," noted ex-Ford aide Richard Cheney, "that with only a little more than two months for the [1976] general election campaign, we found it difficult to spend money on organizational efforts at the state and local level when we had dismantled the nucleus of our organization at the end of each primary campaign. It made a lot more sense to spend it on media."

Party organizations could not pick up the slack. In 1976 the national committees were permitted to spend only $3.2 million in privately raised funds in behalf of their parties' presidential tickets, and state and local parties were not permitted to spend more than $1,000 apiece.

Neither national party spent the full $3.2 million. After the Watergate scandal, the Republican National Committee (RNC) was uncertain how to interpret some of the rulings of the new FEC, and was fearful of violating them. As a result, the RNC displayed an overabundance of caution and spent barely $1 million, much of it establishing telephone banks for Ford.

The Democratic National Committee (DNC) was more eager to help Carter, but fell short of spending its allotment. The DNC spent $2.8 million on behalf of the presidential ticket for a variety of projects that ranged from get-out-the-vote drives to radio tapes. The expenditure total included more than $200,000 in FEC-approved spending by state and local Democratic committees on behalf of the financially-troubled DNC.

To encourage more party activity at the grass-roots level, the FECA was amended in 1979 to permit state and local parties to spend unlimited amounts to conduct voter registration and get-out-the-vote drives and to organize other volunteer projects. But the parties still are prohibited from spending money to hire workers, mount a direct-mail campaign or use some other method of mass communication to benefit the presidential ticket.

"We're putting money back on the street," explained Bob Moss, former counsel for the House Administration Committee and one of the architects of the amendments. "We're trying to get people back into the political process."

Under the FECA, individuals may give $20,000 a year to a national party committee and $5,000 to any state or local party committee. However, an individual's aggregate contribution in one year to parties, PACs and federal candidates cannot exceed $25,000.

PACs may give $15,000 a year to a national party and $5,000 to any state and local party. Their aggregate annual contribution is not limited.

In 1980 the national committees were allowed to spend $4.6 million on behalf of their party's national ticket. While the money could not be transferred directly to the candidate or to state or local committees to fund grass-roots activity, it could be spent in conjunction with the candidate.

The RNC had no trouble raising its allotment. By setting aside $5,000 out of every contribution to the party of $10,000 or more, it had raised $4.6 million for Reagan by the time of his nomination at the GOP convention in July.

The heart of RNC activity was "Commitment '80," an ambitious grass-roots program worked out by RNC Chairman Bill Brock and Reagan campaign officials to mobilize thousands of Reagan volunteers to knock on doors and deliver campaign literature, identify Reagan supporters and then get them to the polls on Election Day. The program also involved state and local parties, which with the help of campaign appearances by Reagan and his run-ning-mate, George Bush, raised more than $10 million for the national effort. One massive party fund-raiser — that was held in Texas in September 1980 and featured appearances by Reagan and Bush — collected close to $3 million.

The GOP's financial success enabled them to easily dwarf their Democratic counterparts. With a slimmer financial base, the variety of Democratic Party committees felt a keener battle for campaign dollars. Even with an incumbent president as a fund-raising draw, the DNC failed to raise its alloted $4.6 million. And, according to Alexander, Democratic state and local committees could raise only $3 million to help the Carter-Mondale ticket.

Independent Expenditures: Reagan Ally

Another boon for Reagan was the extensive independent expenditures made on his behalf. Altogether, a variety of groups spent $12.3 million to promote Reagan. Most of it was spent during the general election, and more than two-thirds was provided by three "New Right" PACs — the Congressional Club ($4.6 million), the Fund for a Conservative Majority ($2.1 million) and the National Conservative Political Action Committee ($1.9 million). Only $45,869 was spent independently on behalf of Carter.

The independent expenditures added a significant new element to the general election campaign, because they presented the opportunity for groups to circumvent the strict contribution limits and spend unlimited amounts of money. But they were also viewed warily by Reagan officials because their independent supporters had to spend their money without consultation with Reagan or his managers.

While the Supreme Court had sanctioned independent spending in its January 1976 *Buckley v. Valeo* decision, the "loophole" was used sparingly in 1976 because many political groups were cautious about testing it. Attitudes had changed, though, by 1980 and conservative groups saw independent spending as a way to promote Reagan.

In the summer of 1980 the conservative PACs plus two new pro-Reagan groups — the Americans for Change and the Americans for an Effective Presidency — announced plans to independently spend up to $70 million to help Reagan. While their spending goal was subsequently reduced drastically, their independent effort threw a scare into the Carter campaign.

The Carter-Mondale Presidential Committee, the FEC and Common Cause launched separate — and (by the end of 1981) unsuccessful — legal assaults on the independent spenders. Common Cause feared that independent spending would wreck the system of presidential public financing and contribution caps, and claimed that the independent groups were not truly autonomous.

Both Common Cause and the Carter campaign contended that unrestricted independent spending was prohibited by the section of the FECA that provides government funding to presidential nominees. They interpreted that provision as limiting one group's independent expenditures to $1,000 in behalf of a major party nominee.

The FEC joined Common Cause in launching a legal challenge against several of the pro-Reagan independent spenders. Their case was heard by the Supreme Court in late 1981. (Independent expenditures, Chapter 6, p. 79)

Labor: Democratic Counterweight

Against the pro-Reagan blitz by Republican committees and independent spenders, the Democrats could re-

Retroactive Funding

The Democratic and Republican presidential nominees each received $29.4 million in federal funds to run their 1980 general election campaigns.

Third party candidates received no public money during the campaign, but independent John B. Anderson qualified for federal funds after the November election by appearing on the ballot in at least 10 states and drawing more than 5 percent of the national popular vote.

The amount of public money Anderson was eligible to receive was based on a formula comparing his vote to the average vote for the Democratic and Republican candidates. No candidate could receive more than $29.4 million in post-election public funds.

The following chart, detailing a range of possible post election subsidies, was based on computations by the Anderson campaign before the election. Anderson's actual vote and post-election subsidy is shown in boldface type.

Percentage of Vote

Dem-Rep.Average	Anderson	Post-Election Subsidy
47.5%	5.0%	$ 3,094,737
45.8	**6.6**	**4,242,304**
45.0	10.0	6,533,333
42.5	15.0	10,376,470
40.0	20.0	14,700,000
37.5	25.0	19,600,000
35.0	30.0	25,200,000
32.5	35.0	29,400,000

spond with only one effective counterweight, organized labor.

Alexander estimated that the unions spent about $15 million on partisan communications with its members, voter registration and get-out-the-vote activities on behalf of Carter's re-election bid in 1980.

Although the Teamsters and several other unions backed Reagan, labor spending easily exceeded the estimated $11 million disbursed by the unions to boost Carter four years earlier.

Corporations have a similar right to communicate with their executives and stockholders and organize "non-partisan" registration and get-out-the-vote drives. But they have been reluctant to act.

Part of the reason is that corporate executives and stockholders are scattered throughout the country and are not so easily mobilized as union members. Corporations have preferred to make direct contributions through their PACs to candidate and party committees. (PACs, Chapter 3, p. 41)

Third Parties

Possibly no group has been more sharply critical of the FECA than independent and third party candidates. Unlike the major party nominees, they must comply with the disclosure requirements and contribution limitations of the law without any assurance of receiving public money.

Third parties that receive at least 5 percent of the national popular vote in one election can qualify for some federal funding before the next general election. But no third parties reached this threshold in 1976.

Consequently, third party and independent candidates in 1980 were eligible to receive some federal funding only after the November election, and then only if they appeared on the ballot in 10 or more states and drew at least 5 percent of the vote. (Retroactive funding, box, this page)

But Anderson found that even the prospect of retroactive funding was not enough to obtain needed bank loans in the late stages of the 1980 campaign. Large banks considered his independent candidacy too poor a risk.

"If the FECA has done nothing else," admitted RNC general counsel Ben Cotten in 1980, "it has institutionalized the two-party system."

Bucking the System

Challengers of the two party system have perenially operated at a financial disadvantage. Prominent third party candidates such as former President Theodore Roosevelt in 1912, Sen. Robert M. LaFollette of Wisconsin in 1924 and former Alabama Gov. George C. Wallace in 1968 were significantly outspent by their major party rivals.

For the most part, even the most heralded independent and third party movements have operated outside the political mainstream, where they have lacked the lucrative financial sources available to the major parties.

According to political scientist Louise Overacker, Roosevelt and LaFollette each spent less than $1 million. But Roosevelt was popular with important segments of the nation's business community and raised more than three-quarters of his $665,000 campaign chest in contributions of $5,000 or more from just 18 individuals.

Stressing populistic themes, both LaFollette and Wallace were less popular with big money donors and were forced to rely heavily on small contributors. More than half of LaFollette's modest $235,000 campaign fund came either in contributions of less than $100 or collections from rallies.

With an estimated 750,000 contributors, Wallace had a much larger base of support. But like LaFollette, he placed a similar emphasis on grass-roots fund raising. According to Herbert Alexander, about three-quarters of the estimated $7 million collected by Wallace's 1968 campaign came in contributions of less than $100.

With the $1,000 limit on individual donations, the FECA has forced third party candidates in recent years to follow the Wallace example.

In 1976 they were not very successful. A FEC report showed that all third party candidates combined raised barely $2 million for the entire campaign, a minimal sum compared with the $43.6 million in federal grants given the major party nominees. Independent entry Eugene J. McCarthy, the former Minnesota senator and most prominent of the "minor" candidates, raised less than $500,000.

But two factors improved the fund raising totals of independent and third party candidates in 1980. One was the presence of Anderson as an independent candidate. The second was the ability of the Libertarian Party to exploit a loophole in the FECA.

Anderson Candidacy

According to its 1980 year-end report to the FEC, Anderson's independent campaign netted about $14 million. That was the most money ever raised by a candidate bucking the two-party system.

Anderson's report indicated that he had collected $8.6 million in individual contributions, $4.2 million in public money (although the FEC in October 1981 asked that $645,000 be returned), and more than $700,000 from PACs and other committees. Most of the latter sum was a transfer of surplus funds from Anderson's Republican primary campaign. Not included in the net receipts were more than $2 million in loans, obtained from thousands of contributors after efforts to obtain large bank loans failed.

Anderson emerged as a fund-raising success because he was able to establish a level of viability during his well-publicized campaign for the GOP presidential nomination. His independent venture — officially titled the "National Unity Campaign for John Anderson" — benefitted from a mailing list of nearly 100,000 contributors built up during his Republican primary campaign. It served as the backbone of an extensive direct-mail effort, which was a basic source of campaign revenue.

The Anderson campaign also experimented with other methods of raising money, ranging from the formation of a national finance council for $1,000 contributors (like philanthropist Stewart Mott and businessman Stanley Marcus) to local garage sales, bike-a-thons and the sale of shirts and Frisbees. Hollywood entertainers such as actor Ed Asner and producer Norman Lear were also enlisted for special events and an arts committee was formed to solicit the creation of original artwork for sale by the campaign.

But from the start, his independent campaign was at a financial disadvantage. While the publicly financed major party candidates did not have to worry about fund raising and could pump their money into media advertising, Anderson had to plow much of his revenue back into direct mail, ballot drives and other start-up costs.

Alexander estimates that Anderson spent $3 million on direct mail and $2 million on his successful drive to get on the ballots in all 50 states and the District of Columbia. Included in ballot costs were legal fees, as Anderson's attorneys criss-crossed the country to research state requirements and fend off court challenges brought by worried Democratic officials.

Most of the rest of Anderson's money was eaten up by organizational expenditures for phones, staff salaries and travel. According to Alexander, this left barely $2 million for media advertising — a drop in the bucket compared to the approximately $20 million that Carter and Reagan each spent on media advertising in the fall campaign.

Anderson's fund-raising operation, however, was boosted by several significant decisions. One by a federal district court in New York in June 1980 enabled Anderson and third party committees to send campaign mail at the same low rate for third-class items (3.1 cents at the time) as was established earlier for Democratic and Republican party committees. Before the ruling, Anderson had been required to pay 8.4 cents per piece.

Another decision in September, this time by the FEC, recognized Anderson as a third party for the purpose of receiving retroactive federal money. Running as an independent four years earlier, McCarthy had been denied similar status. Like Anderson, he had hoped to use the prospect of post-election financing as collateral to fund a late media drive.

But in October 1976, the FEC denied McCarthy's request on a 3-3 party-line vote. All three Republican commissioners voted in favor of McCarthy, while all three Democratic commissioners voted against him. As in 1980 the Democrats feared that a well-financed and well-publicized independent would draw more votes from Carter than the Republican candidate.

Anderson also duplicated another element of McCarthy's financial strategy by seeking approval from the FEC to receive individual contributions of up to $20,000, the annual limit for individual donations to political parties. While Anderson and McCarthy each maintained that they were not forming third parties, they claimed that their needs were the same as a political party's. The FEC, however, denied both requests.

The Libertarian Loophole

Although they did not enjoy the fund-raising capabilities of the Anderson campaign, the fledgling Libertarian Party in 1980 took advantage of a loophole in the FECA that enabled it to tap millions of dollars from one of its wealthiest supporters. The Libertarians nominated him for vice president.

As an individual, New York chemical engineer David Koch could have donated only $1,000 to the party's presidential ticket. But the *Buckley* decision removed FECA restrictions on how much a candidate not receiving federal funds could spend on his own behalf, viewing the provision as a violation of First Amendment rights.

In an open letter to Libertarian convention delegates, Koch pledged to contribute $500,000 to the national campaign if nominated for vice president. The offer was persuasive as Koch was an easy winner on the first ballot.

While emphasizing that Koch was a longtime party member who would be an articulate candidate, Libertarian leaders did not hesitate to admit that he was nominated primarily because of his wealth. "The reason he offered his candidacy was to circumvent the FECA," explained the party's national director Chris Hocker. "That is why he is the vice presidential nominee."

Koch proved to be even more generous than he promised, providing the Libertarian ticket, headed by California lawyer Ed Clark, with $2.1 million of the $3.5 million it raised. Koch's personal contributions dwarfed other fund-raising sources, including monthly mailings to party sympathizers and conference phone calls by Clark and Koch with potential donors.

Other Parties: Slim Budgets

Lacking a financial angel like David Koch, other third parties had to operate on much smaller budgets. Fairly typical was the Citizens Party, which was formed in 1979 as a coalition of dissident liberals and populists.

While the Citizens Party established dozens of state affiliates around the country, its 1980 presidential ticket headed by environmentalist Barry Commoner raised less than $25,000. The party collected some money through direct-mail appeals but lacked the start-up capital necessary to develop a large fund-raising apparatus.

"The election system is set up so you cannot function without money," explained Bill Zimmerman, the national manager of the Commoner campaign in 1980. "We have a program, a candidate and a national organization. But we don't have a campaign."

SPENDING ON SENATE AND HOUSE CAMPAIGNS

As in the presidential campaign, spending for seats in Congress in 1980 increased to about $250 million. But while the cost of those seats reached a record level, the rate of growth in expenditures actually tapered off. Between 1976 and 1978, spending by Senate general election candidates soared by 72 percent, while expenditure totals for House general election candidates jumped 44 percent.

Between 1978 and 1980, spending still increased. But the growth rates were not so dramatic. Expenditures by House candidates increased 33 percent to $117.3 million — slightly above the 25 percent increase in the consumer price index from January 1978 to January 1980. But spending by Senate general election candidates rose by only 18 percent to $77.5 million.

Several factors were at work in curbing the increases in congressional spending. For one, the presidential campaign apparently deflected some money from the congressional races. Secondly, there was a rise in independent expenditures, with groups and wealthy individuals pumping their money directly into congressional races rather than making contributions to candidates. And third, there were no blockbuster Senate campaigns to compare with North Carolina Republican Sen. Jesse Helms' $7.5 million effort in 1978. Preliminary figures from the FEC indicated that none of the Senate general election candidates spent more than $4 million in 1980.

Yet even with the growth rate for congressional spending slowing down, the FEC reported that in 1980 nearly a quarter billion dollars ($242.2 million actually) was spent in primaries, runoffs and general elections by candidates seeking a seat in Congress.

Of the millions of dollars fed into congressional races, nearly equal amounts went to Democratic and Republican candidates. Incumbents in both parties, however, were clearly better financed than their challengers, although they were the ones who needed money the least.

According to political scientist Barbara Hinckley, voters usually have a firm opinion about incumbents that is not significantly altered by campaign spending. The level of spending, however, does affect the prospects of challengers and candidates for open seats. "Spending is particularly important for nonincumbents and especially challengers," wrote Hinckley in her book, *Congressional Elections*. "It significantly increases recognition and affects the vote."

Contribution Sources

The FECA has drawn about the same complaints from congressional candidates that it has from presidential aspirants. They criticize the bookkeeping requirements, the low contribution limits and the longer campaigns that have resulted since the law was passed.

But unlike presidential aspirants, congressional candidates are neither bound by spending ceilings or faced with the option of public financing. Their fund-raising practices have been less drastically altered by the FECA.

Both in the pre-FECA election of 1972 — when Common Cause made a study of campaign contributions — and in 1976 — when the FEC made its most detailed analysis of congressional campaign financing — individual contributions provided a clear majority of funds for House and Senate candidates. The studies showed PACs becoming a greater fund-raising source under the FECA, while parties declined. But neither source rivaled individual contributions as the principal provider of congressional campaign money. *(Source of receipts for congressional candidates, 1976-78, box, p. 103)*

Both the Common Cause and FEC studies showed distinct differences in fund raising by House and Senate candidates. House candidates relied more on small givers as well as party committees and PACs for their contributions. Senate candidates more extensively tapped the big givers, particularly those donating $500 and more.

Although the amount spent by Democratic and Republican House candidates in 1976 was nearly identical, the FEC study revealed a significant disparity in their sources of funds. GOP candidates placed a greater reliance on small donors and party committees than their opponents. Democratic candidates relied more heavily on contributions from non-party sources — such as organized labor — and loans and contributions by candidates to their own campaigns. The FEC found in 1976 that Democratic and Republican candidates received money in nearly equal proportions from large contributors giving more than $100.

PAC and Party Activity

Virtually locked out of a significant role in presidential campaigns, PACs have assumed an increasingly important place in congressional contests. In 1978 PACs provided 20 percent of all contributions to House and Senate general election candidates. In 1980 the PAC share had grown to 25 percent, with the sharpest growth in PAC activity in Senate contests. *(PACs, chapter 3, p. 41)*

The battle for control of the Senate, coupled with the conservative assault on liberal Democratic senators, were major factors in the increased PAC activity. According to a study by *The Washington Post* in December 1980, six Senate candidates received more than $500,000 apiece from PACs. Four of them were conservative Republicans challenging vulnerable Democratic incumbents — Charles E. Grassley against Sen. John C. Culver in Iowa, James Abdnor against Sen. George McGovern in South Dakota, Steven D. Symms against Sen. Frank Church in Idaho and Dan Quayle against incumbent Birch Bayh in Indiana.

Helped by the PAC largesse, all four GOP challengers won. Their victories enabled the Republicans to win control of the Senate for the first time in a quarter century.

But Republican Party committees deserved at least as much credit as the PACs for GOP congressional gains in 1980. The role of the parties in financing House and Senate campaigns has tended to decline in the last decade, but party organizations still enjoy a privileged position under the FECA.

While individuals and PACs are tightly limited as to how much they can directly contribute to a candidate,

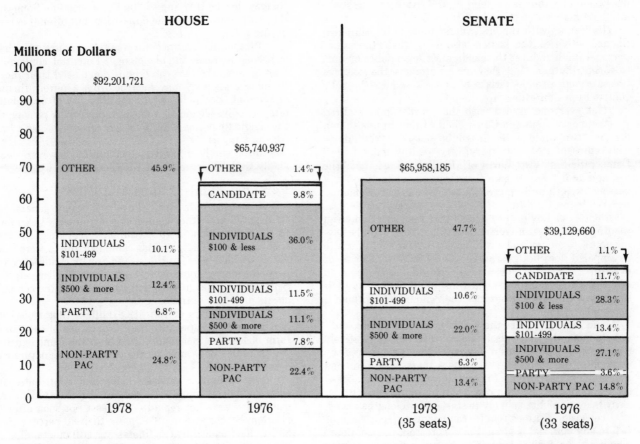

Source of Receipts for Congressional Candidates*

HOUSE   **SENATE**

Millions of Dollars

1978   *1976*   *1978 (35 seats)*   *1976 (33 seats)*

HOUSE 1978: $92,201,721 — OTHER 45.9%, INDIVIDUALS $101-499 10.1%, INDIVIDUALS $500 & more 12.4%, PARTY 6.8%, NON-PARTY PAC 24.8%

HOUSE 1976: $65,740,937 — OTHER 1.4%, CANDIDATE 9.8%, INDIVIDUALS $100 & less 36.0%, INDIVIDUALS $101-499 11.5%, INDIVIDUALS $500 & more 11.1%, PARTY 7.8%, NON-PARTY PAC 22.4%

SENATE 1978: $65,958,185 — OTHER 47.7%, INDIVIDUALS $101-499 10.6%, INDIVIDUALS $500 & more 22.0%, PARTY 6.3%, NON-PARTY PAC 13.4%

SENATE 1976: $39,129,660 — OTHER 1.1%, CANDIDATE 11.7%, INDIVIDUALS $100 & less 28.3%, INDIVIDUALS $101-499 13.4%, INDIVIDUALS $500 & more 27.1%, PARTY 3.6%, NON-PARTY PAC 14.8%

* Data include only figures for candidates running in general election. Figures for 1978 include repaid loans; in 1976 repaid loans were excluded.

NOTE: For 1978, the Federal Election Commission failed to itemize contributions from individuals of $100 or less, contributions from candidates and loans.

Candidate category in 1976 includes loans from the candidate to his campaign.

Party figures include direct contributions to the candidates plus expenditures made on behalf of the candidate by the party.

Source: Federal Election Commission 1976 & 1978 Reports on U.S. Senate and House Campaigns Financial Activity.

national party committees were permitted to spend up to $34,720 for each of their House candidates in 1980, and as much as $987,548 for each Senate seat.

But only the well-financed Republican committees (the RNC, the National Republican Congressional Committee and the National Republican Senatorial Committee) were able to capitalize on this advantage. Their financially hard-pressed Democratic counterparts were unable to raise enough money to come anywhere near the maximums.

The disparity was noted in a Congressional Quarterly study, which found that through September 1980 the Republican Senate committee already had given more than $100,000 to eight GOP candidates. In contrast, Democratic committees had not given even $40,000 to any one of the party's Senate entries. *(Party spending, Chapter 5, p. 71)*

Wealthy Candidates

One of the major differences between presidential and congressional races is the role of the wealthy candidate. In the publicly financed presidential nominating process, a candidate can contribute only $50,000 to his own campaign. In privately financed House and Senate contests, a candidate can reach as deeply into his own pocket as he wants.

It has not always been that way. The FECA amendments passed in 1974 limited the amount House candidates could contribute to their own campaigns to $25,000, and set a $35,000 ceiling for Senate candidates. But even before that provision was to take effect, it was ruled unconstitutional by the Supreme Court in the 1976 *Buckley* decision. The court ruled that "the candidate, no less than any other person, has a First Amendment right to engage in the discussion of public issues and vigorously and tirelessly to advocate his own election."

In keeping with the law's intent to clean up campaign finance activities, the justices also wrote that "the use of personal funds reduces the candidate's dependence on outside contributions and thereby counteracts the coercive pressure and attendent risks of abuse to which the act's contribution limitations are directed."

Not everyone agreed with the court's opinion. Fred Wertheimer of Common Cause claimed that in less than a decade, "two kinds of people will be elected — candidates who represent PACs and very, very wealthy individuals." Democratic Sen. Carl Levin of Michigan added that "the loophole that the Supreme Court carved out for people of personal wealth undermines the whole reform movement."

While most political observers were not so strident as Wertheimer or Levin, they agreed that the court had given wealthy contenders a tremendous advantage. Simply having access to money and a willingness to pour a lot of it into a campaign does not guarantee victory in November — or even in a primary. But wealthy candidates are able to afford expensive, professional consultants and plan their strategy with greater assurance than candidates without a personal fortune.

And money enables the wealthy, but unknown, candidate to make the first splash in a crowded field of relatively obscure contenders. Often the races that attract wealthy candidates are for open seats where there is no ordained successor. While dozens of potential candidates may jockey for position, the one who can begin his campaign with an early television blitz is likely to start several lengths ahead.

Television stations require campaigns to pay their bills before any material is aired. For this reason, the candidate who has the ability to loan or contribute a sizable sum can purchase expensive television advertising whenever he wants. Those who are less well-off financially are forced to wait until the money comes in.

"The advantage of personal wealth in a campaign is amplified in the pre-nomination stage," observed Herbert Alexander, "because the voters don't take their cues from the party and are more open to a variety of appeals."

There are several examples of candidates who began early with little name recognition, but went on to be elected using their personal fortunes. They include Democratic Sen. Howard M. Metzenbaum of Ohio, who finally won on his third try in 1976 after winning two primaries but losing the general elections; Democratic Sen. Lloyd Bentsen of Texas, who was first elected in 1970; and former Democratic Gov. Milton J. Shapp of Pennsylvania, who also was first elected in 1970. Shapp reportedly once said, "I'm not trying to buy the election, I'm trying to sell myself."

As the campaign progresses, especially after the primary, the advantage of personal wealth diminishes. Candidates without a personal fortune then have greater access to other sources of money, particularly from party coffers; the field is smaller, making it easier for voters to draw clear distinctions between the candidates; and more free publicity is available as the general election draws nearer.

There are many cases where a rich candidate was able to clear out the primary field, but then lost in the general election. Metzenbaum, a wealthy parking lot magnate, is a prime example.

While being able to bankroll a large portion of one's own campaign has many advantages, there are clearly several disadvantages. The most obvious and frequently encountered is that it opens the self-financing candidate to charges that he is trying to "buy" the election. Sometimes the charge comes from the opposition, but often it is raised by the media.

Another disadvantage for wealthy candidates is that it is harder to raise outside money. Potential contributors often assume the rich candidates don't need their money. In some cases that may be true from a purely financial standpoint. But politically, a healthy list of contributors often can give a campaign more credibility by proving that the candidate not only has a fat war chest, but also a broad base of support.

Most slimly financed candidates, however, would gladly trade their problems for those of the wealthy.

Personal Funds: Loans and Gifts

According to the FEC, House and Senate general election candidates either loaned or contributed $12.8 million to their campaigns in 1976 (the only year the FEC made such a study). The personal campaign funds were about evenly divided between House and Senate candidates, with personal money comprising 12 percent of all receipts by Senate candidates in 1976 and 10 percent of the campaign chests of House entries.

Three-quarters of the $12.8 million that House and Senate candidates put into their own campaigns was in the form of loans, either made directly to the campaign from the candidate or secured by the candidate's signature from a bank.

The difference between loans and contributions in some candidates' minds was not very big. Most loans from candidates were not repaid — at least not soon after the election. By the end of 1976, more than 80 percent of the $9.5 million loaned by candidates was still outstanding. By comparison, other sources loaned $1.4 million to House and Senate campaigns in 1976. By the end of the election year, half of this amount had been repaid.

On the House side, there were 155 candidates who either contributed or loaned their 1976 campaigns amounts ranging from $10,000 to $507,000. A majority were challengers, who found fund raising difficult against entrenched incumbents.

On the Senate side, Pennsylvania Republican Rep. John Heinz dwarfed all other wealthy candidates. He pumped more than $2.6 million of his personal fortune from the family food processing empire into his successful 1976 campaign for the Senate seat vacated by Hugh Scott. All of the money Heinz poured into his campaign was in the form of non-interest bearing loans. But two years later, none of the money had been repaid and Heinz doubted that it ever would.

Heinz's Democratic opponent, Rep. William J. Green, collected nearly $1.3 million. But without a large fortune to tap, he had to spend much of his time raising money. *(House and Senate Candidate Receipts and Expenditures, 1976-78, Appendix, p. 139)*

The Heinz and Green campaigns at times looked like a study in contrasts. With a larger budget, Heinz often used a chartered jet, which cost $500 per hour to operate, and a helicopter, at $200 per hour, to quickly navigate the state. Green usually had to rely on commercial airlines to get from one end of Pennsylvania to the other. Once on the ground he would be driven in a private car.

Congressional Campaigns: Not Lavish

Though congressional campaigns that spend hundreds of thousands of dollars dominate the headlines, most House candidates actually run "mom and pop" operations, low on both money and professionalism.

This was the assessment of pollster Peter D. Hart, whose firm — with the help of Decision Making Information — conducted a post-election survey of 1976 congressional candidates and campaign officials for the Federal Election Commission (FEC).

The survey was undertaken to gauge candidate reactions to the 1971 Federal Election Campaign Act, amended by Congress in 1974 and in effect for the first time in 1976. The law increased candidate reporting requirements and set limits on personal and group contributions.

Nearly 40 percent of the 2,150 candidates in House and Senate primary and general elections in 1976 were contacted. The results of the extensive survey were released the following April.

Not surprisingly, most candidates said that fund raising was difficult, citing the public's perception of their candidacy as a sure winner or loser as the major problem. Fund raising was a far more significant problem for challengers than incumbents. Barely one-tenth of incumbents mentioned fund-raising problems as opposed to nearly two-thirds of the challengers.

The campaign finance law got mixed reviews. Democratic candidates, who on the whole were more successful, rated the law more favorably than Republican or independent candidates.

"The act tended to be created with the entire perspective that everyone is running a $1 million campaign," said Hart. "But the basic fact is that most candidates are running mom and pop campaigns. Most regulations are stultifying for these people."

In particular, candidates were critical of the extensive paperwork needed to comply with the law. They targeted that as the major area for change. Other complaints were voiced about the difficulty in interpreting FEC regulations, the problems in fund raising caused by contribution ceilings and the built-in assistance for incumbents.

Challengers have contended that contribution ceilings magnify the advantages that wider name recognition and office perquisites give to incumbents. Even a majority of incumbents (50 percent) agreed that the act increased their advantage in running for re-election. According to the survey, 93 percent of congressional incumbents won re-election in 1976.

Besides getting reactions to the campaign finance law, the FEC obtained demographic information on the candidates. It found that the median age for congressional candidates in 1976 was 46, that 90 percent were male and that the vast majority of all candidates (71 percent) lost their primary or general election races.

There were far more Democratic than Republican candidates — 49 percent Democratic, 32 percent Republican and 19 percent independent — a disparity due in part to a larger number of contested primaries on the Democratic side.

Heinz's large war chest also enabled him to finance a late media blitz. Although many of the Philadelphia media dollars were wasted on voters in New Jersey and Delaware, Heinz could afford it as he needed to keep his losses low in the Philadelphia area.

Answering criticism of his personal spending, Heinz noted that being able to contribute unlimited amounts to one's own campaign "had been the law for about 200 years of American history." Added Heinz's campaign treasurer in 1976, Stewart Dalzell: the FECA has "made it much, much more difficult to raise money.... If the challenger is not a millionaire, he has an enormous problem — probably insuperable. In our case, we are lucky because Congressman Heinz was lucky — to be born rich."

Senate Spending

The relationship between money, incumbency and victory is much weaker in the Senate than it is in the House. Barely half of the senators seeking re-election in 1980 were able to hold their seats, even though 84 percent of them (21 out of 25) outspent their challengers.

Senators represent larger and more diverse constituencies than House members. Frequently lacking the personal rapport that congressmen can develop with a smaller electorate, they are inviting targets for well-funded challengers and hostile single-issue groups.

Conservative PACs, led by the National Conservative Political Action Committee (NCPAC), pumped more than $1.2 million into negative campaigns against six liberal Democratic senators. Four lost — Church, Culver, McGovern and Bayh. Only Alan Cranston of California and Thomas F. Eagleton of Missouri survived.

But the re-election prospects of all four were precarious even before the negative independent expenditures began. The prime example was McGovern, who spent far more than any other Senate candidate in 1980 — nearly $4 million — but still was overwhelmed by a challenger who he outspent by a margin of about 2-1.

And McGovern's example was not so unusual. Six other incumbent senators were beaten in 1980, even though they outspent their challengers. Expecting tough re-election fights, most senators began raising money earlier than ever before. The early Senate activity paralleled the presidential campaign, where the low contribution limits forced intensive fund-raising activity in 1979.

"It's become almost imperative for senators to spend the fifth year of their terms [in an effort] to sew up the following year's election," said Herbert Alexander.

Aware of the unexpected losses in 1978 of Democratic Sens. Dick Clark of Iowa and Thomas J. McIntyre of New Hampshire, even heavy favorites began raising money early for 1980. The fortunate ones used early fund-raising success to dissuade formidable challengers from entering the race. The less fortunate at least had some early money available.

The increasing competitiveness of Senate races has been a major factor in their increased cost. Million-dollar Senate campaigns, once a rarity, are fast becoming the norm. Preliminary figures from the FEC indicated that in 1980, nearly half of the major party general election Senate candidates had campaign expenditures that exceeded $1 million. The 31 general election candidates were joined by seven primary losers in eclipsing the $1 million threshold.

That was the largest group of big Senate spenders ever. In 1978, 21 general election candidates, as well as four primary losers, spent more than $1 million in their campaigns. In 1976 there were 10 general election candidates with expenditures reaching seven figures, seven in 1974 and four in 1972.

Yet while there were a lot of big spenders in 1980, none came close to matching the record $7.5 million spent by North Carolina Republican Sen. Helms' re-election effort in 1978. Derisively nicknamed the "six million dollar man" by his Democratic opponent, Helms raised most of his huge budget in contributions of $100 or less that were solicited by mail. Much of his money was plowed back into fund raising, largely orchestrated by conservative direct-mail expert Richard A. Viguerie.

House Fund Loophole

The U.S. House retained for itself in 1979 a campaign fund loophole through which unspent campaign money could pour into the pockets of retired members.

Legislation overhauling the Federal Electric Campaign Act had the effect of exempting only the 434 House members who were sitting in early 1980 once they were former legislators from a provision prohibiting the conversion of money collected for federal election campaigns to personal use.

The result was that those 434 House members could accumulate campaign money — even if they had no election opponents — and then could use it for their personal expenses by paying income taxes on it after they left Congress. The bill stated that no one — including members of Congress, former members and candidates for Congress — could use campaign funds for personal purposes. But fearing objections from some House members, drafters of the provision specifically exempted the 100 senators and 434 representatives then sitting in Congress.

The exemption meant that the sitting 534 members were controlled by their own chambers' rules on the use of campaign funds. Senate rules prohibited personal use of campaign funds by former senators as well as incumbents. So the bill's loophole was of no benefit to the senators.

But the House rule barring the conversion of campaign funds to personal use applied only to sitting members and not former members. So the loophole, coupled with the House rule, meant that the 434 representatives would be free after they left Congress to spend leftover campaign money. Only House members elected in 1980 and after would be barred from converting campaign funds to personal use when they became ex-members.

A survey of 1980 House retirees by the Scripps-Howard News Service found that at least 10 former members took at least several thousand dollars with them. Democrat Mendel J. Davis of South Carolina led the way, pocketing $45,047.

House Spending

The correlation between incumbency, spending and electoral success is much stronger on the House side, where more than 90 percent of all incumbents were re-elected in 1980. But it is becoming more costly each election to keep the equation intact.

Not long ago two candidates together spending a quarter million dollars for a House seat was considered an expensive campaign. In 1972 just 24 districts saw contests of that size or greater. By 1978 nearly a third of the House contests — 129 — had more than $250,000 spent on them.

As in all political races, inflation has been a major factor in increased spending. But as in the Senate, the competition for House seats has grown more intense.

Million-dollar campaigns are still unusual at the House level. There were only two candidates spending more than $1 million in 1980 — Republican Robert K. Dornan of California, whose expenditures surpassed $1.9 million, and Democrat Jim Wright of Texas (the House majority leader), who spent more than $1.2 million.

But there were 28 other candidates in 1980 who spent at least a half million dollars, according to preliminary figures from the FEC. In some cases the high spending became a campaign issue and backfired. A bare majority of the big House spenders (16) won in 1980.

Expensive campaigns often share several characteristics. One is that the elections usually are close. Second, one or both of the candidates usually face primary opposition. Third, the campaigns extend over a long period of time. And fourth, many of the most expensive contests are for the open seats where party control is more likely to shift.

In the costliest House campaigns of 1980, however, the latter characteristic did not hold true. Fourteen of the candidates spending more than $500,000 were challengers,

12 were incumbents, while only four were seeking an open seat. Seven of the incumbents and seven of the challengers were actually paired in the same races, lending credence to Barbara Hinckley's thesis that incumbent spending is frequently related to the challenger's level of spending.

"Spending does not help incumbents," she wrote in *Congressional Elections*. "Incumbents' spending tends to be reactive; it increases or decreases in response to the spending of the challenger...incumbents' spending makes little difference to their recognition or the vote."

District Differences

The average cost of a campaign is affected partly by the location and size of the district. A Congressional Quarterly study of 1978 FEC figures showed that largely suburban districts had the most expensive campaigns that year. Urban districts were the least costly, with rural districts falling in between.

In 88 districts where 60 percent or more of the population lived in suburban areas, the average combined cost for the general election candidates was $197,000. The average campaign cost in 90 districts with predominantly rural population was $176,000.

And in 79 districts with at least 60 percent urban population, the combined cost dropped to an average of $155,000. The remaining 178 districts were mixed among the three categories.

Social and economic factors play a role in the higher cost of campaigns in suburbs. Candidates in suburban areas often have to contend with thousands of new voters each election due to migration from the cities. Those voters do not have the same familiarity with the candidates that it found in more stable rural areas. Studies have found that partisan allegiance often lessens with a move to the suburbs, creating more marginal and competitive seats. Further, television and radio advertising are essential to campaigning in many suburban districts. But the cost is high and much of the advertising money is wasted on voters in adjoining districts.

In rural districts, the larger size is the biggest factor in keeping costs high. Traveling in the district costs more, and television and radio spots often have to be placed in more than one media market to cover the district.

Candidates running in urban districts do not have to worry about transportation costs and often forgo media campaigns because of the prohibitive cost for the limited value. Further, fewer of the urban districts share the competitive nature of the suburban or rural districts. Often the parties in control have dominated the area for years, with the incumbent drawing only token opposition.

'Price of Admission'

The "price of admission" to the House skyrocketed during the 1970s. The "Watergate Class," first elected in 1974, got to Congress by spending an average of $106,000 per winning candidate. Two years later the average freshman spent $141,000 to win his first election to the House. In 1978 the cost had shot up more than 60 percent, as the average price of a winning campaign for a freshman was $229,000.

The spiralling costs and the access of incumbents to campaign money have discouraged many potential candidates from even seeking a seat in Congress. One Pennsylvania legislator, interviewed by Congressional Quarterly in 1978, thought that he could be re-elected to the state legislature for about $10,000. He estimated that a challenge to the incumbent House member in his area would cost $150,000. "That district used to get by on $20,000 to $30,000 per year," he said. "But because the incumbent will set the pace, whoever challenges him will have to match it if he is serious about winning."

While the cost of getting elected the first time is expensive, figures from the FEC indicated that it costs relatively less the longer one stays in office. By the time they have reached their fourth term, many House members are considered safe and often do not draw strong opponents. In most cases an incumbent can avoid elaborate, expensive campaigns because his opponent will not be able to raise enough to outspend the incumbent. The odds in that case strongly favor the higher-spending incumbent.

Unopposed Incumbents

Many House members face little or no opposition. But lack of competition does not always discourage the incumbent from raising and spending large sums. In 1978, 26 members had no primary or general election opposition whatsoever. Yet they raised more than $1.8 million and spent more than $1.2 million.

Incumbents gave several reasons for such seemingly unnecessary spending. Often the previous election was close, and the campaign plan for the coming year was based upon the last battle. Others believed it necessary to put on a campaign simply to remind voters who there representative was.

And ambition for higher office was another reason many incumbents raised a lot even when there was no opponent. Often a high spending campaign against no opponent is actually the first phase of a bid for another office. Such a campaign keeps the candidate's name in the public eye and demonstrates his ability to tap financial resources. In some states it has been permissible to gain the added benefit of transferring leftover funds to a new campaign for a different office.

THE STATES: A PATCHWORK SYSTEM

Nearly every state in the nation now requires its candidates for statewide and legislative office to report their campaign receipts and expenditures. Yet, ironically, while advocates of campaign finance reform have succeeded in the post-Watergate years in getting disclosure laws on the books, the usefulness of the data is limited.

It still remains almost impossible to compile figures on state-level spending that can be compared vaildly from one state to another or aggregated on a national basis.

The basic problem is an absence of national uniformity. There is no clearinghouse such as the FEC — which monitors financial activity in presidential, Senate and House campaigns — to establish national guidelines or to compile figures on state-level races.

Each state has its own system. There is no common definition of basic terms such as "receipt" and "expenditure," nor agreement on when candidates should file their first and last campaign reports.

Campaign Receipts and Expenditures . . .

The following figures on receipts and expenditures in 1978 gubernatorial contests were compiled by Congressional Quarterly from data provided by state election officials and candidate committees and newspaper articles.

Unlike House and Senate campaign figures, which are tabulated by the Federal Election Commission, there is no national uniformity in the compilation of gubernatorial campaign figures. Each state has its own system and, as a result, comparison of figures between one state and another can be misleading.

One of the major problems in comparing figures between states is that no common definition exists for the terms "receipts" and "expenditures." Some states, for example, include loans and transfers to and from committees affiliated with a candidate in total receipts and expenditures, thus inflating the totals. Other states did not. The totals below are based on each state's definition.

Also, reporting periods differ widely. Some states require candidates to report financial activity only after the primary and general elections, while others require reports to be filed throughout the election year.

Most states provided Congressional Quarterly either state-produced summaries on 1978 gubernatorial campaign spending or copies of each candidate's report. But access to information in some states was difficult.

For example, Maryland and Tennessee required that reports be inspected in person.

A footnote number appears next to the name of each state explaining the source of information:

[1] Figures reported by state officials or listed on either the year-end or most recent candidate reports;

[2] Figures computed by Congressional Quarterly from reports provided by state officials. (In Illinois, New Mexico and Texas, state election officials advised using figures only for the candidates' major statewide committees, although figures from smaller affiliated committees were available);

[3] Figures provided by campaign officials or consultants;

[4] Figures appearing in newspaper articles.

The primary vote percentages are taken from *Weekly Report* articles that appeared throughout 1978 on gubernatorial primary results. The percentages are not official.

The general election vote percentages are official and appeared in the March 31, 1979, *Weekly Report*, pp. 576-82.

Only candidates who received at least 5 percent of the general election vote are included.

An asterisk (*) indicates an incumbent. A double asterisk (**) denotes that the percentage is for a primary runoff. A dash (—) indicates that the candidate was unopposed in the primary.

	Percent of Primary Vote	Percent of General Vote	Receipts	Expenditures
ALABAMA[4]				
James (D)	55.2**	72.6	$1,955,332	$2,386,383
Hunt (R)	82.3	25.9	519,290	520,143
ALASKA[1]				
Hammond (R)*	39.3	39.1	692,647	740,611
Croft (D)	36.1	20.2	449,489	474,281
Hickel (R write-in)	39.2	26.4	761,285	873,413
Kelly (I)	—	12.3	317,937	319,475
ARIZONA[1]				
Babbitt (D)*	76.8	52.5	532,629	525,122
Mecham (R)	44.1	44.8	NA	NA

Note: In New York, Carey had $1.9 million worth of non-monetary transactions that were not included in his totals.

	Percent of Primary Vote	Percent of General Vote	Receipts	Expenditures
ARKANSAS[2]				
Clinton (D)	59.4	63.3	743,232	709,234
Lowe (R)	—	36.7	105,108	171,382
CALIFORNIA[2]				
Brown (D)*	77.4	56.0	4,898,367	4,786,274
Younger (R)	40.1	36.5	3,457,892	3,408,840
Clark (I)	—	5.5	365,885	361,317
COLORADO[1]				
Lamm (D)*	—	58.7	446,922	429,579
Strickland (R)	59.0	38.5	548,480	547,906
CONNECTICUT[1]				
Grasso (D)*	67.5	59.1	726,260	726,260
Sarasin (R)	—	40.7	877,504	869,451

...For 1978 Gubernatorial Contests

	Percent of Primary Vote	Percent of General Vote	Receipts	Expenditures		Percent of Primary Vote	Percent of General Vote	Receipts	Expenditures
FLORIDA[1]					**NEW MEXICO**[2]				
Graham (D)	53.5**	55.6	2,772,057	2,766,040	King (D)	61.0	50.5	423,700	403,334
Eckerd (R)	63.7	44.4	3,330,527	3,329,579	Skeen (R)	80.0	49.5	431,284	446,285
GEORGIA[2]					**NEW YORK**[2]				
Busbee (D)*	72.5	80.7	378,988	323,206	Carey (D)*	51.8	50.9	6,232,270	6,868,583
Cook (R)	87.6	19.3	77,550	62,063	Duryea (R)	—	45.2	4,407,939	4,394,517
HAWAII[1]					**OHIO**[2]				
Ariyoshi (D)*	50.3	54.5	1,717,472	1,911,367	Rhodes (R)*	67.6	49.3	2,320,776	2,311,115
Leopold (R)	91.6	44.3	114,611	113,957	Celeste (D)	84.3	47.6	2,306,153	2,326,120
IDAHO[2]					**OKLAHOMA**[1]				
Evans (D)*	—	58.8	376,336	377,847	Nigh (D)	57.7**	51.7	839,939	827,737
Larsen (R)	29.0	39.6	266,230	265,872	Shotts (R)	76.9	47.2	548,306	500,448
ILLINOIS[2]					**OREGON**[2]				
Thompson (R)*	—	59.0	2,340,032	2,794,833	Atiyeh (R)	46.1	54.7	659,006	650,902
Bakalis (D)	82.7	40.1	1,523,664	1,533,739	Straub (D)*	51.4	44.9	496,444	521,300
IOWA[1]					**PENNSYLVANIA**[2]				
Ray (R)*	87.3	58.3	521,102	532,357	Thornburgh (R)	31.9	52.5	2,789,172	2,667,285
Fitzgerald (D)	55.1	41.0	242,220	241,691	Flaherty (D)	44.7	46.4	1,535,646	1,539,898
KANSAS[2]					**RHODE ISLAND**[2]				
Carlin (D)	54.8	49.4	334,196	327,558	Garrahy (D)*	—	62.8	313,432	446,696
Bennett (R)*	68.1	47.3	482,856	492,257	Almond (R)	—	30.7	108,633	103,132
MAINE[2]					Doorley (I)	—	6.5	22,435	27,295
Brennan (D)	51.5	47.7	278,639	256,278	**SOUTH CAROLINA**[1]				
Palmer (R)	48.4	34.3	235,876	239,446	Riley (D)	53.3**	61.4	886,376	880,888
Frankland (I)	—	17.8	146,984	189,542	Young (R)	51.3	37.8	291,448	289,634
MARYLAND[3]					**SOUTH DAKOTA**[2]				
Hughes (D)	37.4	71.0	1,007,682	1,006,007	Janklow (R)	50.6	56.6	240,259	235,274
Beall (R)	57.1	29.0	NA	NA	McKellips (D)	49.1	43.4	451,036	450,919
MASSACHUSETTS[3]					**TENNESSEE**[3]				
King (D)	50.9	52.5	1,819,247	1,480,953	Alexander (R)	85.0	55.6	NA	2,073,436
Hatch (R)	56.0	47.2	1,270,816	1,313,413	Butcher (D)	40.8	44.0	NA	4,688,206
MICHIGAN[2]					**TEXAS**[2]				
Milliken (R)*	—	56.8	1,804,956	1,774,394	Clements (R)	73.0	50.0	7,783,081	7,593,625
Fitzgerald (D)	38.9	43.2	1,766,640	1,766,640	Hill (D)	51.4	49.2	3,493,944	3,589,532
MINNESOTA[1]					**VERMONT**[1]				
Quie (R)	83.3	52.3	1,043,334	1,026,425	Snelling (R)*	—	62.8	68,677	62,649
Perpich (D)*	79.8	45.3	618,604	564,789	Granai (D)	65.0	34.1	31,189	49,920
NEBRASKA[2]					**WISCONSIN**[1]				
Thone (R)	45.1	56.0	634,288	629,125	Dreyfus (R)	58.8	54.4	559,967	557,078
Whelan (D)	79.6	44.0	275,617	277,985	Schreiber (D)*	60.3	44.9	751,376	858,704
NEVADA[2]					**WYOMING**[2]				
List (R)	88.9	56.2	1,012,937	952,879	Herschler (D)*	65.3	50.9	310,403	281,732
Rose (D)	50.4	39.7	847,083	888,083	Ostlund (R)	58.7	49.1	394,423	373,441
NEW HAMPSHIRE[1]									
Gallen (D)	73.4	49.4	235,509	232,178					
Thomson (R)*	59.4	45.4	298,128	290,522					

Some states, for instance, require candidates to report their financial activity only after the primary and general elections. Others require reports to be filed throughout the election year and sometimes even beyond that, when thousands of dollars in contributions are received and late bills are paid.

About half the states have contribution limits. Ten have provisions for publicly financed gubernatorial races, and four make legislative candidates eligible for state money. *(State campaign finance laws, table, pp. 112-116)*

Because each state has its own system, the only accurate comparisons can be made between candidates in a single state. Even then the seriousness of the primary opposition facing each candidate affects comparison.

Big Spenders Usually Win

Given these caveats, Congressional Quarterly surveyed spending in the 36 gubernatorial races held in 1978, and found — as in House contests — a definite relationship between incumbency, spending and winning.

Most incumbents seeking re-election won, with almost two-thirds outspending their challengers. In open seat contests where an incumbent was not running, the candidate with the highest expenditures won almost three-quarters of the races.

Republican candidates had larger expenditures in 17 states, Democratic candidates in 16. In Alaska, former Gov. Walter J. Hickel, a Republican running as a write-in candidate, outspent his major party rivals. In Arizona and Maryland, expenditure totals were not available for the Republican general election candidates. *(1978 gubernatorial spending, box, pp. 108-109)*

In Minnesota, Republican challenger Albert H. Quie succeeded where John Connally failed. Quie ousted Democratic Gov. Rudy Perpich in part because he declined to participate in the state's public financing system, as Connally had done in the presidential race. Perpich accepted public funds and was restricted to a $600,000 spending ceiling for the primary and general elections.

By not participating, Quie was ineligible to collect nearly $200,000 in state money. But he was able to outspend Perpich by nearly a half million dollars.

No Uniform Standards

The difficulty in making more sweeping statements about gubernatorial campaign spending was illustrated by the major differences in the way information on financial activity was reported in 1978 by the two largest states — California and New York.

The California Fair Political Practices Commission presented detailed information in two large books on campaign contributions and spending that covered races for state offices, legislative seats and ballot measures. One book was for the primary, the other for the general election.

The commission consolidated the receipt and expenditure totals for Democratic Gov. Edmund G. Brown Jr. and his Republican challenger, Evelle J. Younger, so they included not just the activity of their major statewide committees but also small affiliates such as "Filipino Americans for Brown — Northern California Region" and "Drycleaners Committee to Elect Evelle Younger."

The California commission clearly explained its methodology in tabulating receipts and expenditures. Transfers of funds between a candidate's various committees were deducted from the total figures, and loans received during the primary and general election periods were reduced by loans repaid during the same periods.

In its summary of 1978 campaign spending in California, the commission indicated that the victorious Brown was the only Democratic gubernatorial candidate in at least the last 20 years to outspend a Republican opponent. But the combined disbursements of $8 million represented only a small fraction of the $58 million spent for all state offices, legislative seats and ballot issues. Brown and Younger actually spent less during the general election than four tobacco companies expended in their successful campaign to defeat a state anti-smoking initiative.

In contrast to California, the New York State Board of Elections published neither a book nor a summary on spending in the 1978 gubernatorial race. Instead, the board supplied summary pages of each report filed by the major campaign committees for Democratic Gov. Hugh L. Carey and his unsuccessful Republican challenger, Perry B. Duryea. There were eight reporting periods between May 15, 1978, and May 15, 1979.

Because neither candidate provided a final total of their receipts and expenditures, Congressional Quarterly had to tabulate the figures using information from each report. Unlike California, no adjustments were made in the Carey and Duryea totals for loan repayments or transfers.

Using this methodology, Carey's total receipts amounted to $6.23 million, which included $3.38 million in contributions, $2.65 million in loans and nearly $240,000 in transfers. Duryea's smaller war chest of $4.41 million relied more on transfers from committees than on monetary contributions and loans.

Not included in the receipt or expenditure totals of either candidate were non-monetary transactions for in-kind services. They particularly would have inflated Carey's final totals if they had been included. Carey listed nearly $1.9 million in non-monetary transactions for the campaign; Duryea about $60,000.

Also not included in Carey's contribution total was a beginning cash balance of more than $600,000, which either was a surplus from his 1974 race or the product of early campaign activity. While large, Carey's opening cash balance was not unique. Several other incumbents began their 1978 campaigns with large war chests, notably Republican James R. Thompson of Illinois and Democrat J. Joseph Garrahy of Rhode Island. They both had beginning cash balances of more than $100,000.

Detailed Explanations

There are more states that offer data on gubernatorial campaign activities in the do-it-yourself manner of New York than the carefully tabulated style of California. Generally, Western states provided the most comprehensive information, with Alaska by far the most detailed.

The Alaska Public Offices Commission produced an extensive book on 1978 campaign and lobbying activity that covered both the primary and general elections. The commission broke down total contributions to gubernatorial candidates by amount — personal, $100 or less, more than $100 — and by source, within the state or outside.

Total expenditures for each candidate were broken down into two major categories — media and non-media. Media expenses were subdivided into areas such as television, radio, newspaper and production, while non-media disbursements were arranged in areas such as travel, salaries and office expenses.

On a cost-per-vote basis, the 1978 Alaska gubernatorial campaign was probably the most expensive in the nation. The vast size of the state, the absence of concentrated media markets and the inflated prices in Alaska helped drive up campaign costs. Nonetheless, the amount of financial activity was astronomical.

Altogether, candidates in Alaska had total expenditures of more than $3.2 million, an average of more than $10 per vote. Slightly more than half the money went for media expenses.

But even the Alaska level of spending paled in comparison to the gubernatorial campaigns of wealthy Democrat John D. "Jay" Rockefeller IV, a nephew of the late New York governor. Rockefeller reportedly spent at least $4 million in seeking the governorship of West Virginia in 1972 and 1976, and nearly $12 million more to retain it in 1980. His re-election effort was reportedly the costliest statewide race in the nation's history, and featured hundreds of thousands of dollars in advertising on Pittsburgh and Washington, D.C, television stations.

While supporters of former GOP Gov. Arch A. Moore Jr. sported bumper stickers that read, "Make Him Spend It All, Arch," Rockefeller won re-election with 54 percent of the vote.

State Campaign Finance Provisions

State	Tax Provisions	Individual Contribution Limits	Expenditure[1] Limits	Reporting Provisions	Elections Commission	Ethics Commission
Alabama	None	None	None	After each election	None; secretary of state	Administration, depository, advisory opinions, investigations
Alaska	Credit: $100	$1,000 per year to a single candidate	None	Before and after election	Administration, depository, advisory opinions, investigations	None
Arizona	Deduction:$100	None	None	Before and after election	None; secretary of state	Hearings, investigations; reports filed with secretary of state
Arkansas	Deduction: $25	$1,500 per election per candidate	None	Before and after election	Certification, vote canvass; secretary of state	Personal financial disclosure by officials
California	Deduction: $100	None	None	Before and after election	Administration, investigations, hearings, enforcement; secretary of state	Administration, investigations, hearings enforcement
Colorado	None	None	None	Before and after election	None; secretary of state	None; statements filed with attorney general
Connecticut	None	Gov.: $2,500; Amount differs for other offices; $15,000 total per primary or general election	None	Before and after election	Administration, advisory opinions, investigations; secretary of state	Administration, advisory opinions, hearings, investigations, enforcement
Delaware	None	$1,000 per candidate for statewide elections; $500 in all other elections	None	Before and after election	None	None
Florida	None	$3,000 per candidate for statewide candidates; $1,000 for legislative candidate	None	Before and after election	Violations hearings; secretary of state	Advisory opinions, hearings, investigations
Georgia	None	None	None	Before and after election	Administration, advisory opinions, hearings, investigations	None
Hawaii	Deduction: $500 aggregate if to candidates abiding by spending limits; $100 per candidate; $2 checkoff for public campaign fund	$2,000 per candidate per election	Gov.: $1.25 per voter in preceding general election; amount differs for other offices	Before and after election	Administration advisory opinions, hearings, investigations enforcement, depository	Advisory opinions, hearings, investigations

State	Tax Provisions	Individual Contribution Limits	Expenditure¹ Limits	Reporting Provisions	Elections Commission	Ethics Commission
Idaho	Credit: Half of political contribution up to $5; $1 checkoff to political party	None	None	Before and after election	None; secretary of state	None
Illinois	None	None	None	Before and after election	Administration, investigations, hearings; secretary of state	Investigations, hearings
Indiana	None	None	None	Before and after election	Administration, audits, investigations, hearings, depository	Advisory opinions, hearings, investigations
Iowa	Deduction: $100; $1 checkoff to political party	None	None	Before and after election (quarterly reports)	Administration, depository, investigations	None
Kansas	None	$2,500 to candidate for statewide office; $500 for state legislative office	None	Before and after election	None; secretary of state	Administration, advisory opinions, hearings investigations
Kentucky	Deduction: $100; $1 checkoff to political party	$3,000 per candidate per election	None	Before and after election	Administration, depository, audits, hearings, investigations, enforcement	None
Louisiana	None	None	None	Before primary; before and after general election	Advisory opinions, investigations, depository	Advisory opinions, hearings, investigations
Maine	Deduction: $100; $1 add-on designated to political party	$1,000 per candidate per election; $25,000 total	None	Before and after election	Depository, advisory opinions, audits, investigations, hearings; secretary of state	Advisory opinions, audits, investigations, hearings
Maryland	Deduction: $100; $2 add-on for public campaign fund	$1,000 per candidate per election; $2,500 aggregate limit	Gov./Lt. Gov.: 10 cents per resident for primary and general elections; amount differs for other offices	Before and after election	Administration, depository, audits, enforcement	Review, audit, hearings, advisory opinions, investigations
Massachusetts	$1 add-on for public campaign fund	$1,000 per candidate per year; also to political parties and political committees	None	Before and after election	Administration, advisory opinions, audits, hearings, investigations, depository, enforcement	Advisory opinions, hearings, investigations
Michigan	Deduction: $50; $2 checkoff for public campaign fund	$1,700 per statewide candidate per election	Gov.: $1 million for primary and general election	Before and after election	None; secretary of state	Advisory opinions, hearings, investigations

State	Tax Provisions	Individual Contribution Limits	Expenditure[1] Limits	Reporting Provisions	Elections Commission	Ethics Commission
Minnesota	Credit: Half of political donations up to $50 if candidate abides by spending limits; $2 checkoff to political party or general campaign fund	Gov.: $60,000 in election year, $12,000 in a non-election year; amount differs for other offices	Gov.: $600,000; amount differs for other offices	Before and after election	Administration, depository, audits, advisory opinions, investigations, enforcement	Advisory opinions, administration, investigations, hearings
Mississippi	None	None	None	Before and after election	None	Administration, investigations, hearings
Missouri	None	$10,000 per candidate; $50,000 total per year	None	Before and after election	None; secretary of state	None
Montana	Deduction: $50; $1 add-on for public campaign fund	Gov./Lt. Gov.: $1,500; other statewide offices: $750	None	Before and after election	Administration, depository, advisory opinions, investigations, hearings	None
Nebraska	None	None	None	Before and after election	None; secretary of state	Advisory opinions, investigations, hearings, enforcement
Nevada	None	None	None	Before and after election	None; secretary of state	None
New Hampshire	None	$5,000	None	Before and after election	None; secretary of state	None
New Jersey	$1 checkoff for public campaign fund	Gov.: $800 per candidate per primary or general election	General election: 70 cents per voter in last presidential election - maximum $2.1 million per candidate; primary: 35 cents per voter in last presidential election - maximum $1.05 million	Before and after election	Administration, depository, audits, advisory opinions, investigations, hearings, enforcement	Advisory opinions, investigations, hearings
New Mexico	None	None	None	Before and after election	None; secretary of state	None
New York	None	$150,000 total per year	None	Before and after election	Administration, depository, advisory opinions, audits, hearings, investigations, enforcement	Advisory opinions, hearings, investigations
North Carolina	Deduction: $25 $1 checkoff for political party or unspecified	$4,000 per candidate per election	Media limit: 10 cents per voter	Before and after election	Administration, depository, audits, investigations, hearings	Advisory opinions, investigations
North Dakota	None	None	None	Before and after election	None; secretary of state	None

State	Tax Provisions	Individual Contribution Limits	Expenditure[1] Limits	Reporting Provisions	Elections Commission	Ethics Commission
Ohio	None	None	None	Before and after election	Hearings, investigations; secretary of state	Advisory opinions, hearings, investigations, depository
Oklahoma	Deduction: $100; $1 checkoff for public campaign fund	$5,000 per statewide candidate, organization, or political party; $1,000 to candidate for local office	None	Before and after election	Administration, depository	Hearings, investigations; administration
Oregon	Credit: Half of political contributions up to $25	None	None	Before and after election	None; secretary of state	Advisory opinions, hearings, investigations
Pennsylvania	None	None	None	Before and after election	None; secretary of commonwealth	Investigations, hearings, advisory opinions
Rhode Island	$1 checkoff to political party or non-partisan general account	None	Gov.: $400,000 for general election, $100,000 for primary; amount differs for other offices[2]	Before and after general or special election	Administration, depository, advisory opinions, hearings, investigations, enforcement	Advisory opinions, hearings, investigations, depository
South Carolina	None	None	None	After election	Administration, certification, ballots	Advisory opinions, hearings depository, investigations
South Dakota	None	$1,000 per year for statewide candidates; $250 per year for county and legislative offices; $3,000 for political party	None	Before and after election	Administration; secretary of state	None
Tennessee	None	None	None	Before and after election	Certification of ballot; secretary of state	None
Texas	None	None	None	Before and after election	None	None
Utah	Deduction: $50; $1 checkoff to political party	None	Media limit: Gov. $100,000; amount differs for other offices	Before and after election	None; secretary of state	None
Vermont	None	$1,000 for statewide offices and legislature	None	Before and after election	None; secretary of state	None
Virginia	None	None	None	Before election	Administration	None
Washington	None	None	None	Before and after election	Administration, depository, hearings, investigations; secretary of state	Hearings, depository, administration, investigations

State	Tax Provisions	Individual Contribution Limits	Expenditure[1] Limits	Reporting Provisions	Elections Commission	Ethics Commission
West Virginia	None	$5,000 per election	None	Before and after election	Advisory opinions; secretary of state	None
Wisconsin	$1 checkoff for public campaign fund	$10,000 total per year to candidates for state and local office and committees; amount differs by office	Gov.: $221,075 for primary; $515,875 for general election	Before and after election	Administration, depository, audit, advisory opinions, hearings, investigations	Hearings, depository, enforcement administration, investigations
Wyoming	None	$1,000 per candidate for two-year campaign period; $25,000 total	None	After each election	None; secretary of state	None

▣ Indicates states with provisions for public financing of gubernatorial candidates in general election campaigns.

[1] Although other states may still have expenditure limits in the books, only those states that provide for public financing of candidates or political parties are permitted expenditure limits as a result of *Buckley v. Valeo*, decided in 1976 (424 U.S. 1).
[2] The Rhode Island expenditure limits are from 1974. Cost-of-living increases based upon the Consumer Price Index have applied since June 30, 1975.

SOURCES: Citizens' Research Foundation, Council on Governmental Ethics Laws.

Appendix

The Law: Tested and Changed

Congress in early 1972 cleared the first comprehensive political campaign financing law since the unenforced Corrupt Practices Act of 1925. The Supreme Court Jan. 30, 1976, held unconstitutional major portions of the legislation, called the Federal Elections Campaign Act of 1971, which had been amended in 1974.

A suit challenging the constitutionality of provisions of the law had been brought by James L. Buckley, Cons-R-N.Y., then a senator, and by Eugene J. McCarthy, D-Minn., who retired from the Senate in 1971 and ran for president as an independent candidate in 1976. The suit challenged provisions of the law that set campaign contribution and spending limits and that established disclosure requirements. It also challenged the appointment by Congress of some of the members of the Federal Election Commission, which was charged with administering the act. Moreover, the suit challenged the constitutionality of provisions that authorized public financing of presidential campaigns and of party nominating conventions.

The Supreme Court held in the case, *Buckley v. Valeo* [Francis R. Valeo was then secretary of the Senate], that the Federal Election Commission was improperly appointed since four of its six members had been appointed by Congress. Appointment of some of the panel's members by Congress, rather than by the president, the court ruled, was unconstitutional. In its opinion, the court pointed to the "concern of the Framers of the Constitution with maintenance of the separation of powers. . . ." Article II, Section 2, Clause 2 of the Constitution provides that officers of the United States be appointed by the president (with the advice and consent of the Senate in the case of superior officers). The court did not accept the argument of the appellants that the commission, because it oversaw congressional as well as presidential elections, could include members appointed by Congress. However, the court held that the commission's past actions had de facto validity.

Court Findings

The Supreme Court upheld the act's limits on the size of individual and political committee campaign contributions. The challengers had contended that limits on how much individuals and groups could give to political campaigns violated their First Amendment right to freedom of speech. The court, with two justices dissenting, held that such limits entail "only a marginal restriction upon the contributor's ability to engage in free communication."

The court also sustained the act's provisions for public disclosure of campaign contributions. The challengers had not attacked disclosure directly but had claimed that the law hurt minor party and independent candidates by requiring that too much be disclosed.

Provisions of the act limiting expenditures for presidential, Senate and House campaigns were found unconstitutional except in the case of presidential candidates who accepted federal matching funds. The court said that although both contribution and spending limits have First Amendment implications, the act's "expenditure ceilings impose significantly more severe restrictions on protected freedom of political expression and association than do its limitations on financial contributions." The court also ruled against the act's limits on how much of his own money a candidate for federal office could spend on his campaign. Another spending limit found to be unconstitutional was one on independent expenditures — the amount groups or individuals who were not candidates could spend in advocating a candidate's election so long as the expenditures were not controlled by or coordinated with the candidate.

The court upheld public financing of presidential elections and national party nominating conventions and asserted that the use of public money to subsidize candidates did not favor established parties over new parties or incumbents over challengers. The formula for distributing the public funds, the court said, "is a congressional effort, not to abridge, restrict or censor speech, but rather to use public money to facilitate and enlarge public discussion and participation in the electoral process." The act's provisions for matching federal grants to finance presidential primary campaigns was also upheld.

Action by Congress

The court's ruling put immediate pressure on Congress to pass new legislation to provide a flow of federal funds to the 1976 presidential candidates. Congress responded to the Supreme Court's decision with a major revision of the campaign finance law. The new measure, the Federal Election Campaign Act Amendments of 1976, was signed into law by President Ford May 11 of that year. The law reconstituted the Federal Election Commission with all six of its members nominated by the president and confirmed by the Senate and with its enforcement powers strengthened. Some changes were made in the definitions and limits on campaign contributions although the aggregate contribution limit for individuals was not changed. The new law placed restrictions on the fund-raising activities of corporate and union political action committees.

Disclosure provisions were amended to require candidates and political committees to keep records of contributions of $50 or more rather than $10 or more as provided in the 1974 law. It also required political committees and individuals making an independent political expenditure of more than $100 to file a report with the commission. Presidential candidates who accepted public financing were limited to spending no more than $50,000 of their own or their family's money. The new law did not change the public financing provisions for presidential campaigns or spending limits for presidential campaigns.

Shortly before the 1980 presidential election year began, Congress enacted the 1979 amendments to the FECA, without opposition in either house. President Carter signed the bill into law on Jan. 8, 1980. The amendments were designed to be "non-controversial" to ensure passage, and many of the provisions resulted in technical fine-tuning of the FECA after flaws and problems with it became obvious during the 1976 and 1978 elections. The new law's significance was that it represented some backtracking from the earlier stringent reform positions and some lightening of the burdens upon practitioners. Yet some changes were extensive. Essentially the bill simplified record keeping and public reporting requirements, increased the permissible role of state and local political parties, and refined the procedural requirements of the enforcement process.

In the pages that follow are excerpts from the *Buckley v. Valeo* decision, as well as summaries of the major provisions of the 1971 Federal Election Campaign Act, the related 1971 Revenue Act, and the FECA amendments of 1974, 1976 and 1979.

Buckley v. Valeo
January 30, 1976

Following are excerpts from the Supreme Court's opinion, decided Jan. 30, 1976, on the constitutionality of the Federal Election Campaign Act of 1971, as amended in 1974, and from the opinions, dissenting in part and concurring in part, of Chief Justice Warren E. Burger and Associate Justices Byron R. White, Thurgood Marshall, Harry A. Blackmun and William H. Rehnquist:

Nos. 75-436 and 75-437

James L. Buckley et al.,
Appellants,
75-436 *v.*
Francis R. Valeo,
Secretary of the United
States Senate,
et al.

On Appeal from the United States Court of Appeals for the District of Columbia Circuit.

James L. Buckley et al.,
Appellants,
75-437 *v.*
Francis R. Valeo,
Secretary of the United
States Senate,
et al.

On Appeal from the United States District Court for the District of Columbia.

PER CURIAM. [MR. JUSTICE STEVENS took no part in the consideration or decision of these cases.]

These appeals present constitutional challenges to the key provisions of the Federal Election Campaign Act of 1971, as amended in 1974.

The Court of Appeals, in sustaining the Act in large part against various constitutional challenges, viewed it as "by far the most comprehensive reform legislation [ever] passed by Congress concerning the election of the President, Vice-President, and members of Congress." ... The Act, summarized in broad terms, contains the following provisions: (a) individual political contributions are limited to $1,000 to any single candidate per election, with an overall annual limitation of $25,000 by any contributor; independent expenditures by individuals and groups "relative to a clearly identified candidate" are limited to $1,000 a year; campaign spending by candidates for various federal offices and spending for national conventions by political parties are subject to prescribed limits; (b) contributions and expenditures above certain threshold levels must be reported and publicly disclosed; (c) a system for public funding of Presidential campaign activities is established by Subtitle H of the Internal Revenue Code; and (d) a Federal Election Commission is established to administer and enforce the Act. ...

... On plenary review, a majority of the Court of Appeals rejected, for the most part, appellants' constitutional attacks. The court found "a clear and compelling interest," 519 F. 2d, at 841, in preserving the integrity of the electoral process. On that basis, the court upheld, with one exception, the substantive provisions of the Act with respect to contributions, expenditures and disclosure. It also sustained the constitutionality of the newly established Federal Election Commission. The court concluded that, notwithstanding the manner of selection of its members and the breadth of its powers, which included nonlegislative functions, the Commission is a constitutionally authorized agency created to perform primarily legislative functions. The provisions for public funding of the three stages of the Presidential selection process were upheld as a valid exercise of congressional power under the General Welfare Clause of the Constitution, Art. I, § 8.

In this Court, appellants argue that the Court of Appeals failed to give this legislation the critical scrutiny demanded under accepted First Amendment and equal protection principles. In appellants' view, limiting the use of money for political purposes constitutes a restriction on communication violative of the First Amendment, since virtually all meaningful political communications in the modern setting involve the expenditure of money. Further, they argue that the reporting and disclosure provisions of the Act unconstitutionally impinge on their right to freedom of association. Appellants also view the federal subsidy provisions of Subtitle H as violative of the General Welfare Clause, and as inconsistent with the First and Fifth Amendments. Finally, appellants renew their attack on the Commission's composition and powers.

At the outset we must determine whether the case before us presents a "case or controversy" within the meaning of Art. III of the Constitution. Congress may not, of course, require this Court to render opinions in matters which are not "cases and controversies." ... We must therefore decide whether appellants have the "personal stake in the outcome of the controversy" necessary to meet the requirements of Art. III. ... It is clear that Congress, in enacting [the Federal Election Campaign Act], intended to provide judicial review to the extent permitted by Art. III. In our view, the complaint in this case demonstrates that at least some of the appellants have a sufficient "personal stake" in a determination of the constitutional validity of each of the challenged provisions to present "a real and substantial controversy admitting of specific relief through a decree of a conclusive character, as distinguished from an opinion advising what the law would be upon a hypothetical state of facts." *Aetna Life Insurance Co.* v. *Haworth*, [1937]. . . .

I. Contribution and Expenditure Limitations

The intricate statutory scheme adopted by Congress to regulate federal election campaigns includes restrictions on political contributions and expenditures that apply broadly to all phases of and all participants in the election process. The major contribution and expenditure limitations in the Act prohibit individuals from contributing more than $25,000 in a single year or more than $1,000 to any single candidate for an election campaign and from spending more than $1,000 a year "relative to a clearly identified candidate." Other provisions restrict a candidate's use of personal and family resources in his campaign and limit the overall amount that can be spent by a candidate in campaigning for federal office.

The constitutional power of Congress to regulate federal elections is well established and is not questioned by any of the parties in this case. Thus, the critical constitutional questions presented here go not to the basic power of Congress to legislate in this area, but to whether the specific legislation that Congress has enacted interferes with First Amendment freedoms or invidiously discriminates against nonincumbent candidates and minor parties in contravention of the Fifth Amendment.

A. General Principles

The Act's contribution and expenditure limitations operate in an area of the most fundamental First Amendment activities. Discussion of public issues and debate on the qualifications of candidates are integral to the operation of the system of government established by our Constitution. The First Amendment affords the broadest protection to such political expression in order "to assure the unfettered interchange of ideas for the bringing about of political and social changes desired by the people." *Roth* v. *United States* . . . (1957). . . . "[T]here is practically universal agreement that a major purpose of th[e] Amendment was to protect the free discussion of governmental affairs, . . . of course includ[ing] discussions of candidates. . . ." *Mills* v. *Alabama* . . . (1966). . . .

The First Amendment protects political association as well as political expression. The constitutional right of association explicated in *NAACP* v. *Alabama* . . . (1958), stemmed from the Court's recognition that "[e]ffective advocacy of both public and private points of view, particularly controversial ones, is undeniably enhanced by group association." Subsequent decisions have made clear that the First and Fourteenth Amendments guarantee "freedom to associate with others for the common advancement of political beliefs and ideas," a freedom that encompasses "[t]he right to associate with the political party of one's choice." *Kusper* v. *Pontikes* . . . (1973). . . .

It is with these principles in mind that we consider the primary contentions of the parties with respect to the Act's limitations upon the giving and spending of money in political campaigns. Those conflicting contentions could not more sharply define the basic issues before us. Appellees contend that what the Act regulates is conduct, and that its effect on speech and association is incidental at most. Appellants respond that contributions and expenditures are at the very core of political speech, and that the Act's limitations thus constitute restraints on First Amendment liberty that are both gross and direct.

In upholding the constitutional validity of the Act's contribution and expenditure provisions on the ground that those provisions should be viewed as regulating conduct not speech, the Court of Appeals relied upon *United States* v. *O'Brien* . . . (1968). . . .

. . . Even if the categorization of the expenditure of money as conduct were accepted, the limitations challenged here would not meet the *O'Brien* test because the governmental interests advanced in support of the Act involve "suppressing communication." The interests served by the Act include restricting the voices of people and interest groups who have money to spend and reducing the overall scope of federal election campaigns. Although the Act does not focus on the ideas expressed by persons or groups subjected to its regulations, it is aimed in part at equalizing the relative ability of all voters to affect electoral outcomes by placing a ceiling on expenditures for political expression by citizens and groups. . . .

. . . A restriction on the amount of money a person or group can spend on political communication during a campaign necessarily reduces the quantity of expression by restricting the number of issues discussed, the depth of their exploration, and the size of the audience reached. This is because virtually every means of communicating ideas in today's mass society requires the expenditure of money. The distribution of the humblest handbill or leaflet entails printing, paper, and circulation costs. Speeches and rallies generally necessitate hiring a hall and publicizing the event. The electorate's increasing dependence on television, radio, and other mass media for news and information has made these expensive modes of communication indispensable instruments of effective political speech.

The expenditure limitations contained in the Act represent substantial rather than merely theoretical restraints on the quantity and diversity of political speech. The $1,000 ceiling on spending "relative to a clearly identified candidate," . . . would appear to exclude all citizens and groups except candidates, political parties and the institutional press from any significant use of the most effective modes of communication. Although the Act's limitations on expenditures by campaign organizations and political parties provide substantially greater room for discussion and debate, they would have required restrictions in the scope of a number of past congressional and Presidential campaigns and would operate to constrain campaigning by candidates who raise sums in excess of the spending ceiling.

By contrast with a limitation upon expenditures for political expression, a limitation upon the amount that any one person or group may contribute to a candidate or political committee entails only a marginal restriction upon the contributor's ability to engage in free communication. A contribution serves as a general expression of support for the candidate and his views, but does not communicate the underlying basis for the support. The quantity of communication by the contributor does not increase perceptibly with the size of his contribution, since the expression rests solely on the undifferentiated, symbolic act of contributing. At most, the size of the contribution provides a very rough index of the intensity of the contributor's support for the candidate. A limitation on the amount of money a person may give to a candidate or campaign organization thus involves little direct restraint on his political communication, for it permits the symbolic expression of support evidenced by a contribution but does not in any way infringe the contributor's freedom to discuss candidates and issues. While contributions may result in political expression if spent by a candidate or an association to present views to the voters, the transformation of contributions into political debate involves speech by someone other than the contributor.

Given the important role of contributions in financing political campaigns, contribution restrictions could have a severe impact on political dialogue if the limitations prevented candidates and political committees from amassing the resources necessary for effective advocacy. There is no indication, however, that the contribution limitations imposed by the Act would have any dramatic adverse effect on the funding of campaigns and political associations. The overall effect of the Act's contribution ceilings is merely to require candidates and political committees to raise funds from a greater number of persons and to compel people who would otherwise contribute amounts greater than the statutory limits to expend such funds on direct political expression, rather than to reduce the total amount of money potentially available to promote political expression.

The Act's contribution and expenditure limitations also impinge on protected associational freedoms. Making a contribution, like joining a political party, serves to affiliate a person with a candidate. In addition, it enables like-minded persons to pool their resources in furtherance of common political goals. The Act's contribution ceilings thus limit one important means of associating with a candidate or committee, but leave the contributor free to become a member of any political association and to assist personally in the association's efforts on behalf of candidates. And the Act's contribution limitations permit associations and candidates to aggregate large sums of money to promote effective advocacy. By contrast, the Act's $1,000 limitation on independent expenditures "relative to a clearly identified candidate" precludes most associations from effectively amplifying the voice of their adherents, the original basis for the recognition of First Amendment protection of the freedom of association. . . .

In sum, although the Act's contribution and expenditure limitations both implicate fundamental First Amendment interests, its expenditure ceilings impose significantly more severe restrictions on protected freedoms of political expression and association than do its limitations on financial contributions.

B. Contribution Limitations

1. The $1,000 Limitation on Contributions by Individuals and Groups to Candidates and Authorized Campaign Committees

Section 608 (b) provides, with certain limited exceptions, that "no person shall make contributions to any candidate with respect to any election for Federal office which, in the aggregate, exceeds $1,000." The statute defines person broadly to include "an individual, partnership, committee, association, corporation, or any other organization or group of persons." . . . The limitation reaches a gift, subscription, loan, advance, deposit of anything of value, or promise to give a contribution, made for the purpose of influencing a primary election, a Presidential preference primary, or a general election for any federal office. . . . The $1,000 ceiling applies regardless of whether the contribution is given to the candidate, to a committee authorized in writing by the candidate to accept contributions on his behalf, or indirectly via earmarked gifts passed through an intermediary to the candidate. . . . The restriction applies to aggregate amounts contributed to the candidate for each election — with primaries, runoff elections, and general elections counted separately and all Presidential primaries held in any calendar year treated together as a single election campaign. . . .

Appellants contend that the $1,000 contribution ceiling unjustifiably burdens First Amendment freedoms, employs overbroad dollar limits, and discriminates against candidates opposing incumbent officeholders and against minor-party candidates in violation of the Fifth Amendment. We address each of these claims of invalidity in turn.

(a) . . . [T]he primary First Amendment problem raised by the Act's contribution limitations is their restriction of one aspect of the contributor's freedom of political association. The Court's decisions involving associational freedoms establish that the right of association is a "basic constitutional freedom" that is "closely allied to freedom of speech and a right which, like free speech, lies at the foundation of a free society. . . . In view of the fundamental nature of the right to associate, governmental "action which may have the effect of curtailing the freedom to associate is subject to the closest scrutiny." NAACP v. Alabama, supra. . . . Yet, it is clear that "[n]either the right to associate nor the right to participate in political activities is absolute. . . ." Civil Service Comm'n v. Letter Carriers . . . (1973). Even a " 'significant interference' with protected rights of political association" may be sustained if the State demonstrates a sufficiently important interest and employs means closely drawn to avoid unnecessary abridgment of associational freedoms. . . .

Appellees argue that the Act's restrictions on large campaign contributions are justified by three governmental interests. According to the parties and amici, the primary interest served by the limitations and, indeed, by the Act as a whole, is the prevention of corruption and the appearance of corruption spawned by the real or imagined coercive influence of large financial contributions on candidates' positions and on their actions if elected to office. Two "ancillary" interests underlying the Act are also allegedly furthered by the $1,000 limits on contributions. First, the limits serve to mute the voices of affluent persons and groups in the election process and thereby to equalize the relative ability of all citizens to affect the outcome of elections. Second, it is argued, the ceilings may to some extent act as a brake on the skyrocketing cost of political campaigns and thereby serve to open the political system more widely to candidates without access to sources of large amounts of money.

It is unnecessary to look beyond the Act's primary purpose . . . in order to find a constitutionally sufficient justification for the $1,000 contribution limitation. Under a system of private financing of elections, a candidate lacking immense personal or family wealth must depend on financial contributions from others to provide the resources necessary to conduct a successful campaign. The increasing importance of the communications media and sophisticated mass mailing and polling operations to effective campaigning make the raising of large sums of money an ever more essential ingredient of an effective candidacy. To the extent that large contributions are given to secure political quid pro quos from current and potential office holders, the integrity of our system of representative democracy is undermined. Although the scope of such pernicious practices can never be reliably ascertained, the deeply disturbing examples surfacing after the 1972 election demonstrate that the problem is not an illusory one.

Of almost equal concern as the danger of actual quid pro quo arrangements is the impact of the appearance of corruption stemming from public awareness of the opportunities for abuse inherent in a regime of large individual financial contributions. . . .

Appellants contend that the contribution limitations must be invalidated because bribery laws and narrowly-drawn disclosure requirements constitute a less restrictive means of dealing with "proven and suspected quid pro quo arrangements." But laws making criminal the giving and taking of bribes deal with only the most blatant and specific attempts of those with money to influence governmental action. And while disclosure requirements serve the many salutary purposes discussed elsewhere in this opinion, Congress was surely entitled to conclude that disclosure was only a partial measure, and that contribution ceilings were a necessary legislative concomitant to deal with the reality or appearance of corruption inherent in a system permitting unlimited financial contributions, even when the identities of the contributors and the amounts of their contributions are fully disclosed.

The Act's $1,000 contribution limitation focuses precisely on the problem of large campaign contributions — the narrow aspect of political association where the actuality and potential for corruption have been identified — while leaving persons free to engage in independent political expression, to associate actively through volunteering their services, and to assist to a limited but nonetheless substantial extent in supporting candidates and committees with financial resources. Significantly, the Act's contribution limitations in themselves do not undermine to any material degree the potential for robust and effective discussion of candidates and campaign issues by individual citizens, associations, the institutional press, candidates, and political parties.

We find that, under the rigorous standard of review established by our prior decisions, the weighty interests served by restricting the size of financial contributions to political candidates are sufficient to justify the limited effect upon First Amendment freedoms caused by the $1,000 contribution ceiling.

(b) Appellants' first overbreadth challenge to the contribution ceilings rests on the proposition that most large contributors do not seek improper influence over a candidate's position or an officeholder's action. Although the truth of that proposition may be assumed, it does not undercut the validity of the $1,000 contribution limitation. Not only is it difficult to isolate suspect contributions but, more importantly, Congress was justified in concluding that the interest in safeguarding against the appearance of impropriety requires that the opportunity for abuse inherent in the process of raising large monetary contributions be eliminated.

A second, related overbreadth claim is that the $1,000 restriction is unrealistically low because much more than that amount would still not be enough to enable an unscrupulous contributor to exercise improper influence over a candidate or officeholder, especially in campaigns for statewide or national office. While the contribution limitation provisions might well have been structured to take account of the graduated expenditure limitations for House, Senate and Presidential campaigns, Congress' failure to engage in such fine tuning does not invalidate the legislation....

(c) Apart from these First Amendment concerns, appellants argue that the contribution limitations work such an invidious discrimination between incumbents and challengers that the statutory provisions must be declared unconstitutional on their face. In considering this contention, it is important at the outset to note that the Act applies the same limitations on contributions to all candidates regardless of their present occupations, ideological views, or party affiliations. Absent record evidence of invidious discrimination against challengers as a class, a court should generally be hesitant to invalidate legislation which on its face imposes evenhanded restrictions....

There is no such evidence to support the claim that the contribution limitations in themselves discriminate against major-party challengers to incumbents. Challengers can and often do defeat incumbents in federal elections....

...The charge of discrimination against minor-party and independent candidates is more troubling, but the record provides no basis for concluding that the Act invidiously disadvantages such candidates. As noted above, the Act on its face treats all candidates equally with regard to contribution limitations. And the restriction would appear to benefit minor-party and independent candidates relative to their major-party opponents because major-party candidates receive far more money in large contributions....

In view of these considerations, we conclude that the impact of the Act's $1,000 contribution limitation on major-party challengers and on minor-party candidates does not render the provision unconstitutional on its face.

2. The $5,000 Limitation on Contributions by Political Committees

Section 608 (b)(2) of Title 18 permits certain committees, designated as "political committees," to contribute up to $5,000 to any candidate with respect to any election for federal office. In order to qualify for the higher contribution ceiling, a group must have been registered with the Commission as a political committee ... for not less than 6 months, have received contributions from more than 50 persons and, except for state political party organizations, have contributed to five or more candidates for federal office. Appellants argue that these qualifications unconstitutionally discriminate against ad hoc organizations in favor of established interest groups and impermissibly burden free association. The argument is without merit. Rather than undermining freedom of association, the basic provision enhances the opportunity of bona fide groups to participate in the election process, and the registration, contribution, and candidate conditions serve the permissible purpose of preventing individuals from evading the applicable contribution limitations by labeling themselves committees.

3. Limitations on Volunteers' Incidental Expenses

The Act excludes from the definition of contribution "the value of services provided without compensation by individuals who volunteer a portion or all of their time on behalf of a candidate or political committee." ...Certain expenses incurred by persons in providing volunteer services to a candidate are exempt from the $1,000 ceiling only to the extent that they do not exceed $500....

If, as we have held, the basic contribution limitations are constitutionally valid, then surely these provisions are a constitutionally acceptable accommodation of Congress' valid interest in encouraging citizen participation in political campaigns while continuing to guard against the corrupting potential of large financial contributions to candidates. The expenditure of resources at the candidate's direction for a fundraising event at a volunteer's residence or the provision of in-kind assistance in the form of food or beverages to be resold to raise funds or consumed by the participants in such an event provides material financial assistance to a candidate.... Treating these expenses as contributions when

made to the candidate's campaign or at the direction of the candidate or his staff forecloses an avenue of abuse without limiting actions voluntarily undertaken by citizens independently of a candidate's campaign.

4. The $25,000 Limitation on Total Contributions During any Calendar Year

In addition to the $1,000 limitation on the nonexempt contributions that an individual may make to a particular candidate for any single election, the Act contains an overall $25,000 limitation on total contributions by an individual during any calendar year.... The overall $25,000 ceiling does impose an ultimate restriction upon the number of candidates and committees with which an individual may associate himself by means of financial support. But this quite modest restraint upon protected political activity serves to prevent evasion of the $1,000 contribution limitation by a person who might otherwise contribute massive amounts of money to a particular candidate through the use of unearmarked contributions to political committees likely to contribute to that candidate, or huge contributions to the candidate's political party. The limited, additional restriction on associational freedom imposed by the overall ceiling is thus no more than a corollary of the basic individual contribution limitation that we have found to be constitutionally valid.

C. Expenditure Limitations

The Act's expenditure ceilings impose direct and substantial restraints on the quantity of political speech. The most drastic of the limitations restricts individuals and groups, including political parties that fail to place a candidate on the ballot, to an expenditure of $1,000 "relative to a clearly identified candidate during a calendar year." § 608 (e)(1) Other expenditure ceilings limit spending by candidates ... their campaigns ... and political parties in connection with election campaigns.... It is clear that a primary effect of these expenditure limitations is to restrict the quantity of campaign speech by individuals, groups, and candidates. The restrictions, while neutral as to the ideas expressed, limit political expression "at the core of our electoral process and of First Amendment freedoms...." *Williams* v. *Rhodes* ... (1968).

1. The $1,000 Limitation on Expenditures "Relative to a Clearly Identified Candidate"

...The plain effect [of this limitation] is to prohibit all individuals, who are neither candidates nor owners of institutional press facilities, and all groups, except political parties and campaign organizations, from voicing their views "relative to a clearly identified candidate" through means that entail aggregate expenditures of more than $1,000 during a calendar year. The provision, for example, would make it a federal criminal offense for a person or association to place a single one-quarter page advertisement "relative to a clearly identified candidate" in a major metropolitan newspaper.

Before examining the interests advanced in support of [this] expenditure ceiling, consideration must be given to appellants' contention that the provision is unconstitutionally vague....

...[I]n order to preserve the provision against invalidation on vagueness grounds, [this limitation] must be construed to apply only to expenditures for communications that in express terms advocate the election or defeat of a clearly identified candidate for federal office.

...We turn ... to the basic First Amendment question — whether [this limitation], even as thus narrowly and explicitly construed, impermissibly burdens the constitutional right of free expression....

...[T]he constitutionality of [this limitation] turns on whether the governmental interests advanced in its support satisfy the exacting scrutiny applicable to limitations on core First Amendment rights of political expression.

We find that the governmental interest in preventing corruption and the appearance of corruption is inadequate to justify [the] ceiling on independent expenditures. First, assuming *arguendo* that large independent expenditures pose the same dangers of actual or apparent *quid pro quo* arrangements as do large contributions, § 608 (e)(1) does not provide an answer that sufficiently relates to the elimination of those dangers. Unlike the contribution limitations' total ban on the giving of large amounts of money to candidates, § 608 (e)(1) prevents only some large expenditures. So long as persons and groups eschew expenditures that in express terms advocate the election or defeat of a clearly identified candidate, they are free to spend as much as they want to promote the candidate and his views. The exacting interpretation of the statutory language necessary to avoid unconstitutional vagueness thus undermines the limitation's effectiveness as a loophole-closing provision by facilitating circumvention by those seeking to exert improper influence upon a candidate or officeholder. It would naively underestimate the ingenuity and resourcefulness of persons and groups desiring to buy influence to believe that they would have much difficulty devising expenditures that skirted the restriction on express advocacy of election or defeat but nevertheless benefited the candidate's campaign. Yet no substantial societal interest would be served by a loophole-closing provision designed to check corruption that permitted unscrupulous persons and organizations to expend unlimited sums of money in order to obtain improper influence over candidates for elective office. . . .

Second, quite apart from the shortcomings of § 608 (e)(1) in preventing any abuses generated by large independent expenditures, the independent advocacy restricted by the provision does not presently appear to pose dangers of real or apparent corruption comparable to those identified with large campaign contributions. The parties defending § 608 (e)(1) contend that it is necessary to prevent would-be contributors from avoiding the contribution limitations by the simple expedient of paying directly for media advertisements or for other portions of the candidate's campaign activities. They argue that expenditures controlled by or coordinated with the candidate and his campaign might well have virtually the same value to the candidate as a contribution and would pose similar dangers of abuse. Yet such controlled or coordinated expenditures are treated as contributions rather than expenditures under the Act. . . . Unlike contributions, such independent expenditures may well provide little assistance to the candidate's campaign and indeed may prove counterproductive. The absence of prearrangement and coordination of an expenditure with the candidate or his agent not only undermines the value of the expenditure to the candidate, but also alleviates the danger that expenditures will be given as a *quid pro quo* for improper commitments from the candidate. Rather than preventing circumvention of the contribution limitations, § 608 (e)(1) severely restricts all independent advocacy despite its substantially diminished potential for abuse.

While the independent expenditure ceiling thus fails to serve any substantial governmental interest in stemming the reality or appearance of corruption in the electoral process, it heavily burdens core First Amendment expression. . . . Advocacy of the election or defeat of candidates for federal office is no less entitled to protection under the First Amendment than the discussion of political policy generally or advocacy of the passage or defeat of legislation.

It is argued, however, that the ancillary governmental interest in equalizing the relative ability of individuals and groups to influence the outcome of elections serves to justify the limitation on express advocacy of the election or defeat of candidates imposed by [the] expenditure ceiling. But the concept that government may restrict the speech of some elements of our society in order to enhance the relative voice of others is wholly foreign to the First Amendment. . . . The First Amendment's protection against governmental abridgement of free expression cannot properly be made to depend on a person's financial ability to engage in public discussion. . . .

. . . For the reasons stated, we conclude that [the] independent expenditure limitation is unconstitutional under the First Amendment.

2. Limitation on Expenditures by Candidates from Personal or Family Resources

The Act also sets limits on expenditures by a candidate "from his personal funds, or the personal funds of his immediate family, in connection with his campaigns during any calendar year." . . . These ceilings vary from $50,000 for Presidential or Vice Presidential candidates to $35,000 for Senate candidates, and $25,000 for most candidates for the House of Representatives.

The ceiling on personal expenditure by candidates on their own behalf, like the limitations on independent expenditures . . . imposes a substantial restraint on the ability of persons to engage in protected First Amendment expression. The candidate, no less than any other person, has a First Amendment right to engage in the discussion of public issues and vigorously and tirelessly to advocate his own election and the election of other candidates. Indeed, it is of particular importance that candidates have the unfettered opportunity to make their views known so that the electorate may intelligently evaluate the candidates' personal qualities and their positions on vital public issues before choosing among them on election day. . . . [The] ceiling on personal expenditures by a candidate in furtherance of his own candidacy thus clearly and directly interferes with constitutionally protected freedoms.

The primary governmental interest served by the Act — the prevention of actual and apparent corruption of the political process — does not support the limitation on the candidate's expenditure of his own personal funds. . . . Indeed, the use of personal funds reduces the candidate's dependence on outside contributions and thereby counteracts the coercive pressures and attendant risks of abuse to which the Act's contribution limitations are directed.

The ancillary interest in equalizing the relative financial resources of candidates competing for elective office . . . is clearly not sufficient to justify the provision's infringement of fundamental First Amendment rights. First, the limitation may fail to promote financial equality among candidates. A candidate who spends less of his personal resources on his campaign may nonetheless outspend his rival as a result of more successful fundraising efforts. . . . Second, and more fundamentally, the First Amendment simply cannot tolerate . . . [a] restriction upon the freedom of a candidate to speak without legislative limit on behalf of his own candidacy. We therefore hold that . . . [the] restrictions on a candidate's personal expenditures is [*sic*] unconstitutional.

3. Limitations on Campaign Expenditures

Section 608 (c) of the Act places limitations on overall campaign expenditures by candidates seeking nomination for election and election to federal office. Presidential candidates may spend $10,000,000 in seeking nomination for office and an additional $20,000,000 in the general election campaign. . . . The ceiling on Senate campaigns is pegged to the size of the voting age population of the State with minimum dollar amounts applicable to campaigns in States with small populations. In Senate primary elections, the limit is the greater of eight cents multiplied by the voting age population or $100,000, and in the general election the limit is increased to 12 cents multiplied by the voting age population or $150,000. . . . The Act imposes blanket $70,000 limitations on both primary campaigns and general election campaigns for the House of Representatives with the exception that the Senate ceiling applies to campaigns in States entitled to only one Representative. . . . These ceilings are to be adjusted upwards at the beginning of each calendar year by the average percentage rise in the consumer price index for the 12 preceding months. . . .

No governmental interest that has been suggested is sufficient to justify the restriction on the quantity of political expression imposed by § 608 (c)'s campaign expenditure limitations. The major evil associated with rapidly increasing campaign expenditures is the danger of candidate dependence on large contributions. The interest in alleviating the corrupting influence of large contributions is served by the Act's contribution limitations and disclosure provisions. . . . The Court of Appeal's assertion that the expenditure restrictions are necessary to reduce the incentive to circumvent direct contribution limits is not persuasive. . . .

The interest in equalizing the financial resources of candidates competing for federal office is no more convincing a justification for restricting the scope of federal election campaigns. Given the limitation on the size of outside contributions, the financial resources available to a candidate's campaign, like the number of volunteers recruited, will normally vary with the size and intensity of the candidate's support. . . .

The campaign expenditure ceilings appear to be designed primarily to serve the governmental interests in reducing the allegedly skyrocketing costs of political campaigns. . . . [T]he mere growth in the cost of federal election campaigns in and of itself provides no basis for governmental restrictions on the quantity of campaign spending and the resulting limitations on the scope of federal campaigns. The First Amendment denies government the power to determine that spending to promote one's political views is wasteful, excessive, or unwise. . . .

For these reasons we hold that § 608 (c) is constitutionally invalid.

In sum, the provisions of the Act that impose a $1,000 limitation on contributions to a single candidate, § 608 (b)(1), a $5,000 limitation on contributions by a political committee to a single candidate, § 608 (b)(2), and a $25,000 limitation on total contributions by an individual during any calendar year, § 608 (b)(3), are constitutionally valid. These limitations along with the disclosure provisions, constitute the Act's primary weapons against the reality or appearance of improper influence stemming from the dependence of candidates on large campaign contributions. The contribution ceilings thus serve the basic governmental interest in safeguarding the integrity of the electoral process without directly impinging upon the rights of individual citizens and candidates to engage in political debate and discussion. By contrast, the First Amendment requires the invalidation of the Act's independent expenditure ceiling, § 608 (e)(1), its limitation on a candidate's expenditures from his own personal funds, § 608 (c). These provisions place substantial and direct restrictions on the ability of candidates, citizens, and associations to engage in protected political expression, restrictions that the First Amendment cannot tolerate.

II. Reporting and Disclosure Requirements

Unlike the limitations on contributions and expenditures, . . . the disclosure requirements of the Act . . . are not challenged by appellants as *per se* unconstitutional restrictions on the exercise of First Amendment freedoms of speech and association. Indeed, appellants argue that "narrowly drawn disclosure requirements are the proper solution to virtually all of the evils Congress sought to remedy." The particular requirements embodied in the Act are attacked as overbroad — both in their application to minor-party and independent candidates and in their extension to contributions as small as $10 or $100. Appellants also challenge the provision for disclosure by those who make independent contributions and expenditures. . . .

. . . The Act presently under review replaced all prior disclosure laws. Its primary disclosure provisions impose reporting obligations on "political committees" and candidates. "Political committee" is defined . . . as a group of persons that receives "contributions" or makes "expenditures" of over $1,000 in a calendar year. "Contributions" and "expenditures" are defined in lengthy parallel provisions similar to those . . . discussed above. Both definitions focus on the use of money or other objects of value "for the purpose of influencing" the nomination or election of any person to federal office. . . .

Each political committee is required to register with the Commission . . . and to keep detailed records of both contributions and expenditures. . . . These records are required to include the name and address of everyone making a contribution in excess of $10, along with the date and amount of the contribution. If a person's contributions aggregate more than $100, his occupation and principal place of business are also to be included. . . . These files are subject to periodic audits and field investigations by the Commission. . . .

Each committee and each candidate also is required to file quarterly reports. . . . The reports are to contain detailed financial information, including the full name, mailing address, occupation, and principal place of business of each person who has contributed over $100 in a calendar year, as well as the amount and date of the contributions. . . . They are to be made available by the Commission "for public inspection and copying." . . . Every candidate for Federal office is required to designate a "principal campaign committee," which is to receive reports of contributions and expenditures made on the candidate's behalf from other political committees and to compile and file these reports, together with its own statements, with the Commission. . . .

Every individual or group, other than a political committee or candidate, who makes "contributions" or "expenditures" of over $100 in a calendar year "other than by contribution to a political committee or a candidate" is required to file a statement with the Commission. . . . Any violation of these record-keeping and reporting provisions is punishable by a fine of not more than $1,000 or a prison term of not more than a year, or both. . . .

A. General Principles

Unlike the overall limitations on contributions and expenditures, the disclosure requirements impose no ceiling on campaign-related activities. But we have repeatedly found that compelled disclosure, in itself, can seriously infringe on privacy of association and belief guaranteed by the First Amendment. . . .

We long have recognized that significant encroachments on First Amendment rights of the sort that compelled disclosure imposes cannot be justified by a mere showing of some legitimate governmental interest. . . . [W]e have required that the subordinating interests of the State must survive exacting scrutiny. We also have insisted that there be a "relevant correlation" or "substantial relation" between the governmental interest and the information required to be disclosed. . . .

. . . [C]ompelled disclosure has the potential for substantially infringing the exercise of First Amendment rights. But we have acknowledged that there are governmental interests sufficiently important to outweigh the possibility of infringement, particularly when the "free functioning of our national institutions" is involved. . . .

The governmental interests sought to be vindicated by the disclosure requirements are of this magnitude. They fall into three categories. First, disclosure provides the electorate with information "as to where political campaign money comes from and how it is spent by the candidate" in order to aid the voters in evaluating those who seek Federal office. . . .

Second, disclosure requirements deter actual corruption and avoid the appearance of corruption by exposing large contributions and expenditures to the light of publicity. This exposure may discourage those who would use money for improper purposes either before or after the election. . . .

Third, and not least significant, record-keeping, reporting and disclosure requirements are an essential means of gathering the data necessary to detect violations of the contribution limitations described above.

The disclosure requirements, as a general matter, directly serve substantial governmental interests. In determining whether these interests are sufficient to justify the requirements we must look to the extent of the burden that they place on individual rights.

It is undoubtedly true that public disclosure of contributions to candidates and political parties will deter some individuals who otherwise might contribute. In some instances, disclosure may even expose contributors to harassment or retaliation. These are not insignificant burdens on individual rights, and they must be weighed carefully against the interests which Congress has sought to promote by this legislation. . . . [W]e . . . agree with appellants' concession that disclosure requirements — certainly in most applications — appear to be the least restrictive means of curbing the evils of campaign ignorance and corruption that Congress found to exist. Appellants argue, however, that the balance tips against disclosure when it is required of contributors to certain parties and candidates. We turn now to this contention.

B. Application to Minor Parties and Independents

Appellants contend that the Act's requirements are overbroad insofar as they apply to contributions to minor parties and independent candidates because the governmental interest in this information is minimal and the danger of significant infringement on First Amendment rights is greatly increased.

1. Requisite Factual Showing

... It is true that the governmental interest in disclosure is diminished when the contribution in question is made to a minor party with little chance of winning an election. As minor parties usually represent definite and publicized viewpoints, there may be less need to inform the voters of the interests that specific candidates represent....

... But a minor party sometimes can play a significant role in an election. Even when a minor-party candidate has little or no chance of winning, he may be encouraged by major-party interests in order to divert votes from other major-party contenders.

We are not unmindful that the damage done by disclosure to the associational interests of the minor parties and their members and to supporters of independents could be significant.... In some instances fears of reprisal may deter contributions to the point where the movement cannot survive. The public interest also suffers if that result comes to pass, for there is a consequent reduction in the free circulation of ideas both within and without the political arena.

There could well be a case ... where the threat to the exercise of First Amendment rights is so serious and the state interest furthered by disclosure so insubstantial that the Act's requirements cannot be constitutionally applied. But no appellant in this case has tendered record evidence of [this] sort....

2. Blanket Exemption

Appellants agree that "the record here does not reflect the kind of focused and insistent harassment of contributors and members that existed in the NAACP cases." They argue, however, that a blanket exemption for minor parties is necessary lest irreparable injury be done before the required evidence can be gathered....

... We recognize that unduly strict requirements of proof could impose a heavy burden, but it does not follow that a blanket exemption for minor parties is necessary. Minor parties must be allowed sufficient flexibility in the proof of injury to assure a fair consideration of their claim. The evidence offered need show only a reasonable probability that the compelled disclosure of a party's contributors' names will subject them to threats, harassment or reprisals from either government officials or private parties....

C. Section 434 (e)

Section 434 (e) requires "[e]very person (other than a political committee or candidate) who makes contributions or expenditures" aggregating over $100 in a calendar year "other than by contribution to a political committee or candidate" to file a statement with the Commission. Unlike the other disclosure provisions, this section does not seek the contribution list of any association. Instead, it requires direct disclosure of what an individual or group contributes or spends.

In considering this provision we must apply the same strict standard of scrutiny, for the right of associational privacy developed in *Alabama* derives from the rights of the organization's members to advocate their personal points of view in the most effective way....

Appellants attack § 434 (e) as a direct intrusion on privacy of belief, in violation of *Talley* v. *California* ... (1960), and as imposing "very real, practical burdens ... certain to deter individuals from making expenditures for their independent political speech" analogous to those held to be impermissible in *Thomas* v. *Collins* ... (1945).

1. The Role of § 434 (e)

... Section 434 (e) is part of Congress' effort to achieve "total disclosure" by reaching "every kind of political activity" in order to insure that the voters are fully informed and to achieve through publicity the maximum deterrence to corruption and undue influence possible. The provision is responsive to the legitimate fear that efforts would be made, as they had been in the past, to avoid the disclosure requirements by routing financial support of candidates through avenues not explicitly covered by the general provisions of the Act.

2. Vagueness Problems

In its effort to be all-inclusive, however, the provision raises serious problems of vagueness, particularly treacherous where, as here, the violation of its terms carries criminal penalties and fear of incurring these sanctions may deter those who seek to exercise protected First Amendment rights.

Section 434 (e) applies to "[e]very person ... who makes contributions or expenditures." "Contributions" and "expenditures" are defined in parallel provisions in terms of the use of money or other valuable assets "for the purpose of ... influencing" the nomination or election of candidates for Federal office. It is the ambiguity of this phrase that poses constitutional problems....

... To insure that the reach of § 434 (e) is not impermissibly broad, we construe "expenditure" for purposes of that section in the same way we construed the terms of § 608 (e) — to reach only funds used for communications that expressly advocate the election or defeat of a clearly identified candidate. This reading is directed precisely to that spending that is unambiguously related to the campaign of a particular federal candidate.

In summary, § 434 (e) as construed imposes independent reporting requirements on individuals and groups that are not candidates or political committees only in the following circumstances: (1) when they make contributions earmarked for political purposes or authorized or requested by a candidate or his agent, to some person other than a candidate or political committee, and (2) when they make an expenditure for a communication that expressly advocates the election or defeat of a clearly identified candidate.

Unlike § 608 (e)(1), § 434 (e) as construed bears a sufficient relationship to a substantial governmental interest.... It goes beyond the general disclosure requirements to shed the light of publicity on spending that is unambiguously campaign-related but would not otherwise be reported because it takes the form of independent expenditures or of contributions to an individual or group not itself required to report the names of its contributors....

... [T]he disclosure requirement is narrowly limited to those situations where the information sought has a substantial connection with the governmental interests sought to be advanced.... The burden imposed by § 434 (e) is no prior restraint, but a reasonable and minimally restrictive method of furthering First Amendment values by opening the basic processes of our federal election system to public view.

D. Thresholds

Appellants' third contention, based on alleged overbreadth, is that the monetary thresholds in the record-keeping and reporting provisions lack a substantial nexus with the claimed governmental interests, for the amounts involved are too low even to attract the attention of the candidate, much less have a corrupting influence.

The provisions contain two thresholds. Records are to be kept by political committees of the names and addresses of those who make contributions in excess of $10 ... and these records are subject to Commission audit.... If a persons' contributions to a committee or candidate aggregate more than $100, his name and address, as well as his occupation and principal place of business, are to be included in reports filed by committees and candidates with the Commission ... and made available for public inspection....

... The $10 and $100 thresholds are indeed low.... These strict requirements may well discourage participation by some citizens in the political process, a result that Congress hardly could have intended. Indeed, there is little in the legislative history to indicate that Congress focused carefully on the appropriate level at which to require recording and disclosure. Rather, it seems merely to have adopted the thresholds existing in similar disclosure laws since 1910. But we cannot require Congress to establish that it has chosen the highest reasonable threshold. . . .

We are mindful that disclosure serves informational functions, as well as the prevention of corruption and the enforcement of the contribution limitations. Congress is not required to set a threshold that is tailored only to the latter goals. . . .

. . . [T]here is no warrant for assuming that public disclosure of contributions between $10 and $100 is authorized by the Act. Accordingly, we do not reach the question whether information concerning gifts of this size can be made available to the public without trespassing impermissibly on First Amendment rights. . . .

In summary, we find no constitutional infirmities in the record-keeping, reporting, and disclosure provisions of the act.

III. Public Financing of Presidential Election Campaigns

A series of statutes for the public financing of Presidential election campaigns produced the scheme now found in 26 U.S.C. § 6096 and Subtitle H, §§ 9001-9042, of the Internal Revenue Code of 1954. Both the District Court . . . and the Court of Appeals . . . sustained Subtitle H against a constitutional attack. Appellants renew their challenge here, contending that the legislation violates the First and Fifth Amendments. We find no merit in their claims and affirm.

A. Summary of Subtitle H

Section 9006 establishes a Presidential Election Campaign Fund, financed from general revenues in the aggregate amount designated by individual taxpayers, under § 6096, who on their income tax returns may authorize payment to the Fund of one dollar of their tax liability in the case of an individual return or two dollars in the case of a joint return. The Fund consists of three separate accounts to finance (1) party nominating conventions, . . . (2) general election campaigns, . . . and (3) primary campaigns. . . .

Chapter 95 of Title 26, which concerns financing of party nominating conventions and general election campaigns, distinguishes among "major," "minor" and "new" parties. A major party is defined as a party whose candidate for President in the most recent election received 25% or more of the popular vote. . . . A minor party is defined as a party whose candidate received at least 5% but less than 25% of the vote at the most recent election. . . . All other parties are new parties, . . . including both newly created parties and those receiving less than 5% of the vote in the last election.

Major parties are entitled to $2,000,000 to defray their national committee Presidential nominating convention expenses, must limit total expenditures to that amount . . . and they may not use any of this money to benefit a particular candidate or delegate. . . . A minor party receives a portion of the major-party entitlement determined by the ratio of the votes received by the party's candidate in the last election to the average of the votes received by the major-parties' candidates. . . . The amounts given to the parties and the expenditure limit are adjusted for inflation, using 1974 as the base year. . . . No financing is provided for new parties, nor is there any express provision for financing independent candidates or parties not holding a convention.

For expenses in the general election campaign, § 9004 (a)(1) entitles each major-party candidate to $20,000,000. This amount is also adjusted for inflation. . . . To be eligible for funds the candidate must pledge not to incur expenses in excess of the entitlement under § 9004 (a)(1) and not to accept private contributions except to the extent that the fund is insufficient to provide the full entitlement. . . . Minor-party candidates are also entitled to funding, again based on the ratio of the vote received by the party's candidate in the preceding election to the average of the major-party candidates. . . . Minor-party candidates must certify that they will not incur campaign expenses in excess of the major-party

entitlement and that they will accept private contributions only to the extent needed to make up the difference between that amount and the public funding grant. . . . New-party candidates receive no money prior to the general election, but any candidate receiving 5% or more of the popular vote in the election is entitled to post-election payments according to the formula applicable to minor-party candidates. . . . Similarly, minor-party candidates are entitled to post-election funds if they receive a greater percentage of the average major-party vote than their party's candidate did in the preceding election; the amount of such payments is the difference between the entitlement based on the preceding election and that based on the actual vote in the current election. . . . A further eligibility requirement for minor- and new-party candidates is that the candidate's name must appear on the ballot, or electors pledged to the candidate must be on the ballot, in at least 10 States. . . .

Chapter 96 establishes a third account in the Fund, the Presidential Primary Matching Payment Account. . . . This funding is intended to aid campaigns by candidates seeking Presidential nomination "by a political party," . . . in "primary elections,". . . The threshold eligibility requirement is that the candidate raise at least $5,000 in each of 20 States, counting only the first $250 from each person contributing to the candidate. . . . In addition, the candidate must agree to abide by the spending limits. . . . Funding is provided according to a matching formula: each qualified candidate is entitled to a sum equal to the total private contributions received, disregarding contributions from any person to the extent that total contributions to the candidate by that person exceed $250. . . . Payments to any candidate under Chapter 96 may not exceed 50% of the overall expenditure ceiling accepted by the candidate. . . .

B. Constitutionality of Subtitle H

Appellants argue that Subtitle H is invalid (1) as "contrary to the 'general welfare,' " Art. I, § 8, (2) because any scheme of public financing of election campaigns is inconsistent with the First Amendment, and (3) because Subtitle H invidiously discriminates against certain interests in violation of the Due Process Clause of the Fifth Amendment. We find no merit in these contentions.

Appellants' "general welfare" contention erroneously treats the General Welfare Clause as a limitation upon congressional power. It is rather a grant of power, the scope of which is quite expansive, particularly in view of the enlargement of power by the Necessary and Proper Clause. . . . Congress has power to regulate Presidential elections and primaries, . . . and public financing of Presidential elections as a means to reform the electoral process was clearly a choice within the granted power. It is for Congress to decide which expenditures will promote the general welfare. "[T]he power of Congress to authorize expenditure of public moneys for public purposes is not limited by the direct grants of legislative power found in the Constitution." *United States* v. *Butler* . . . (1936). . . . Any limitations upon the exercise of that granted power must be found elsewhere in the Constitution. In this case, Congress was legislating for the "general welfare" — to reduce the deleterious influence of large contributions on our political process, to facilitate communication by candidates with the electorate, and to free candidates from the rigors of fundraising. . . . Whether the chosen means appear "bad," "unwise," or "unworkable" to us is irrelevant; Congress has concluded that the means are "necessary and proper" to promote the general welfare, and we thus decline to find this legislation without the grant of power in Art. I, § 8.

Appellants' challenge to the dollar check-off provision (§ 6096) fails for the same reason. They maintain that Congress is required to permit taxpayers to designate particular candidates or parties as recipients of their money. But the appropriation to the Fund in § 9006 is like any other appropriation from the general revenue except that its amount is determined by reference to the aggregate of the one- and two-dollar authorization on taxpayers' income tax returns. . . .

Appellants next argue that "by analogy" to the religion clauses of the First Amendment public financing of election cam-

paigns, however meritorious, violates the First Amendment....
But the analogy is patently inapplicable to our issue here. Although "Congress shall make no law . . . abridging the freedom of speech, or of the press," Subtitle H is a congressional effort, not to abridge, restrict, or censor speech, but rather to use public money to facilitate and enlarge public discussion and participation in the electoral process, goals vital to a self-governing people.... Appellants argue, however, that as constructed public financing invidiously discriminates in violation of the Fifth Amendment. We turn therefore to that argument....

....[T]he denial of public financing to some Presidential candidates is not restrictive of voters' rights and less restrictive of candidates'. Subtitle H does not prevent any candidate from getting on the ballot or any voter from casting a vote for the candidate of his choice; the inability, if any, of minority-party candidates to wage effective campaigns will derive not from lack of public funding but from their inability to raise private contributions. Any disadvantages suffered by operation of the eligibility formulae under Subtitle H is thus limited to the claimed denial of the enhancement of opportunity to communicate with the electorate that the formula affords eligible candidates. But eligible candidates suffer a countervailing denial. As we more fully develop later, acceptance of public financing entails voluntary acceptance of an expenditure ceiling. Noneligible candidates are not subject to that limitation. Accordingly, we conclude that public financing is generally less restrictive of access to the electoral process than the ballot-access regulations dealt with in prior cases. In any event, Congress enacted Subtitle H in furtherance of sufficiently important governmental interests and has not unfairly or unnecessarily burdened the political opportunity of any party or candidate.

... [P]ublic financing as a means of eliminating the improper influence of large private contributions furthers a significant governmental interest.... In addition, ... Congress properly regarded public financing as an appropriate means of relieving major-party Presidential candidates from the rigors of soliciting private contributions.... Congress' interest in not funding hopeless candidacies with large sums of public money ... necessarily justifies the withholding of public assistance from candidates without significant public support....

1. General Election Campaign Financing

Appellants insist that Chapter 95 falls short of the constitutional requirement in that the provisions provide larger, and equal, sums to candidates of major parties, use prior vote levels as the sole criterion for pre-election funding, limit new-party candidates to post-election funds, and deny any funds to candidates of parties receiving less than 5% of the vote. These provisions, it is argued, are fatal to the validity of the scheme, because they work invidious discrimination against minor and new parties in violation of the Fifth Amendment. We disagree....

... Since the Presidential elections of 1856 and 1860, when the Whigs were replaced as a major party by the Republicans, no third party has posed a credible threat to the two major parties in Presidential elections. Third parties have been completely incapable of matching the major parties' ability to raise money and win elections. Congress was of course aware of this fact of American life, and thus was justified in providing both major parties full funding and all other parties only a percentage of the major-party entitlement. Identical treatment of all parties, on the other hand, "would not only make it easy to raid the United States Treasury, it would also artificially foster the proliferation of splinter parties."...

Furthermore, appellants have made no showing that the election funding plan disadvantages nonmajor parties by operating to reduce their strength below that attained without any public financing.... Thus, we conclude that the general election funding system does not work an invidious discrimination against candidates of nonmajor parties.

Appellants challenge reliance on the vote in past elections as the basis for determining eligibility. That challenge is foreclosed, however, by our holding in *Jenness* v. *Fortson* ... [1971] that popular vote totals in the last election are a proper measure of public support....

... Any risk of harm to minority interests is speculative due to our present lack of knowledge of the practical effects of public financing and cannot overcome the force of the governmental interests against use of public money to foster frivolous candidacies, create a system of splintered parties, and encourage unrestrained factionalism....

... Plainly campaigns can be successfully carried out by means other than public financing; they have been up to this date, and this avenue is still open to all candidates. And, after all, the important achievements of minority political groups in furthering the development of American democracy were accomplished without the help of public funds. Thus, the limited participation or nonparticipation of nonmajor parties or candidates in public funding does not unconstitutionally disadvantage them....

... Finally, appellants challenge the validity of the 5% threshold requirement for general election funding. They argue that, since most state regulations governing ballot access have threshold requirements well below 5%, and because in their view the 5% requirement here is actually stricter than that upheld in *Jenness* v. *Fortson* ... the requirement is unreasonable.... [T]he choice of the percentage requirement that best accommodates the competing interests involved was for Congress to make.... Without any doubt a range of formulations would sufficiently protect the public fisc and not foster factionalism, and also recognize the public interest in the fluidity of our political affairs. We cannot say that Congress' choice falls without the permissible range.

2. Nominating Convention Financing

The foregoing analysis and reasoning sustaining general election funding apply in large part to convention funding under Chapter 95 and suffices to support our rejection of appellants' challenge to that provision. Funding of party conventions has increasingly been derived from large private contributions ... and the governmental interest in eliminating this reliance is as vital as in the case of private contributions to individual candidates. The expenditure limitations on major parties participating in public financing enhance the ability of nonmajor parties to increase their spending relative to the major parties; further, in soliciting private contributions to finance conventions, parties are not subject to the $1,000 contribution limit pertaining to candidates. We therefore conclude that appellants' constitutional challenge to the provisions for funding nominating conventions must also be rejected.

3. Primary Election Campaign Financing

Appellants' final challenge is to the constitutionality of Chapter 96, which provides funding of primary campaigns. They contend that these provisions are constitutionally invalid (1) because they do not provide funds for candidates not running in party primaries and (2) because the eligibility formula actually increases the influence of money on the electoral process. In not providing assistance to candidates who do not enter party primaries, Congress has merely chosen to limit at this time the reach of the reforms encompassed in Chapter 96. This Congress could do without constituting the reform a constitutionally invidious discrimination....

... We also reject as without merit appellants' argument that the matching formula favors wealthy voters and candidates. The thrust of the legislation is to reduce financial barriers and to enhance the importance of smaller contributions.... In addition, one eligibility requirement for matching funds is acceptance of an expenditure ceiling, and candidates with little fundraising ability will be able to increase their spending relative to candidates capable of raising large amounts in private funds.

For the reasons stated, we reject appellants' claims that Subtitle H is facially unconstitutional.

C. Severability

The only remaining issue is whether our holdings invalidating §§ 608 (a), 608 (c), and 608 (e)(1) require the conclusion that Subtitle H is unconstitutional. There is of course a relationship between the spending limits in 18 U.S.C. § 608 (c) and the public financing provisions; the expenditure limits accepted by a candidate to be eligible for public funding are identical to the limits in §

608 (c). But we have no difficulty in concluding that Subtitle H is severable.... Our discussion ... leaves no doubt that the value of public financing is not dependent on the existence of a generally applicable expenditure limit. We therefore hold Subtitle H severable from those portions of the legislation today held constitutionally infirm.

IV. The Federal Election Commission

The 1974 Amendments to the Act created an eight-member Federal Election Commission, and vest in it primary and substantial responsibility for administering and enforcing the Act. The question that we address in this portion of the opinion is whether, in view of the manner in which a majority of its members are appointed, the Commission may under the Constitution exercise the powers conferred upon it....

Chapter 14 of Title 2 makes the Commission the principal repository of the numerous reports and statements which are required by that Chapter to be filed by those engaging in the regulated political activities. Its duties ... with respect to these reports and statements include filing and indexing, making them available for public inspection, preservation, and auditing and field investigations. It is directed to "serve as a national clearinghouse for information in respect to the administration of elections."...

Beyond these recordkeeping, disclosure, and investigative functions, however, the Commission is given extensive rulemaking and adjudicative powers....

The Commission's enforcement power is both direct and wideranging....

... The body in which this authority is reposed consists of eight members. The Secretary of the Senate and the Clerk of the House of Representatives are *ex officio* members of the Commission without the right to vote. Two members are appointed by the President *pro tempore* of the Senate "upon the recommendations of the majority leader of the Senate and the minority leader of the Senate." Two more are to be appointed by the Speaker of the House of Representatives, likewise upon the recommendations of its respective majority and minority leaders. The remaining two members are appointed by the President. Each of the six voting members of the commission must be confirmed by the majority of both Houses of Congress, and each of the three appointing authorities is forbidden to choose both of their appointees from the same political party....

A. Ripeness

... [I]n order to decide the basic question of whether the Act's provision for appointment of the members of the Commission violates the Constitution, we believe we are warranted in considering all of those aspects of the Commission's authority which have been presented by [the Court of Appeals' certified questions although many of the Commission's functions have not yet been exercised]....

B. The Merits

Appellants urge that since Congress has given the Commission wideranging rule-making and enforcement powers with respect to the substantive provisions of the Act, Congress is precluded under the principle of separation of powers from vesting in itself the authority to appoint those who will exercise such authority. Their argument is based on the language of Art. II, § 2, cl. 2, of the Constitution, which provides in pertinent part as follows:

"[The President] shall nominate, and by and with the Advice and Consent of the Senate, shall appoint ... all other Officers of the United States, whose Appointments are not herein otherwise provided for, and which shall be established by Law: but the Congress may by Law vest the Appointment of such inferior Officers, as they think proper, in the President alone, in the Courts of Law, or in the Heads of Departments."

Appellants' argument is that this provision is the exclusive method by which those charged with executing the laws of the United States may be chosen. Congress, they assert, cannot have it both ways. If the legislature wishes the Commission to exercise all of the conferred powers, then its members are in fact "Officers of the United States" and must be appointed under the Appointments Clause. But if Congress insists upon retaining the power to appoint, then the members of the Commission may not discharge those many functions of the Commission which can be performed only by "Officers of the United States," as that term must be construed within the doctrine of separation of powers.

Appellee Federal Election Commission and *amici* in support of the Commission urge that the Framers of the Constitution, while mindful of the need for checks and balances among the three branches of the National Government, had no intention of denying to the Legislative Branch authority to appoint its own officers. Congress, either under the Appointments Clause or under its grants of substantive legislative authority and the Necessary and Proper Clause in Art. I, is in their view empowered to provide for the appointment to the Commission in the manner which it did because the Commission is performing "appropriate legislative functions."...

1. Separation of Powers

... Our inquiry of necessity touches upon the fundamental principles of the Government established by the Framers of the Constitution, and all litigants and all of the courts which have addressed themselves to the matter start on common ground in the recognition of the intent of the Framers that the powers of the three great branches of the National Government be largely separate from one another.

James Madison, writing in the Federalist No. 47, defended the work of the Framers against the charge that these three governmental powers were not *entirely* separate from one another in the proposed Constitution....

Yet it is also clear from the provisions of the Constitution itself, and from the Federalist Papers, that the Constitution by no means contemplates total separation of each of these three essential branches of Government. The President is a participant in the law-making process by virtue of his authority to veto bills enacted by Congress. The Senate is a participant in the appointive process by virtue of its authority to refuse to confirm persons nominated to office by the President....

... Mr. Justice Jackson, concurring in the opinion and the judgment of the Court in *Youngstown Co.* v. *Sawyer* ... (1952), succinctly characterized this understanding:

"While the Constitution diffuses power the better to secure liberty, it also contemplates that practice will integrate the dispersed powers into a workable government. It enjoins upon its branches separateness but interdependence, autonomy but reciprocity."

The Framers regarded the checks and balances that they had built into the tripartite Federal Government as a self-executing safeguard against the encroachment or aggrandizement of one branch at the expense of the other....

2. The Appointments Clause

The principle of separation of powers was not simply an abstract generalization in the minds of the Framers: it was woven into the document that they drafted in Philadelphia in the summer of 1787. Article I declares: "All legislative Powers herein granted shall be vested in a Congress of the United States." Article II vests the executive power "in a President of the United States of America," and Art. III declares that "the judicial Power of the United States, shall be vested in one supreme Court, and in such inferior Courts as the Congress may from time to time ordain and establish." The further concern of the Framers of the Constitution with maintenance of the separation of powers is found in the so-called "Ineligibility" and "Incompatibility" Clauses contained in § 6 of Art. I:

"No Senator or Representative shall, during the Time for which he was elected, be appointed to any civil Office under the Authority of the United States, which shall have been created, or the Emoluments whereof shall have been encreased during such time; and no Person holding any Office under the United States, shall be a Member of either House during his Continuance in Office."

It is in the context of these cognate provisions of the document that we must examine the language of Art. II, § 2, cl. 2, which appellants contend provides the only authorization for appointment of those to whom substantial executive or administrative authority is given by statute.... [We] again set out the provision:

"[The President] shall nominate, and by and with the Advice and Consent of the Senate, shall appoint Ambassadors, other Public Ministers and Consuls, Judges of the supreme Court, and all other Officers of the United States, whose Appointments are not herein otherwise provided for, and which shall be established by Law, but the Congress may by Law vest the Appointment of such inferior Officers, as they think proper, in the President alone, in the Courts of Law, or in the Heads of Departments....

... We think that the term "Officers of the United States" as used in Art. II ... is a term intended to have substantive meaning. We think its fair import is that any appointee exercising significant authority pursuant to the laws of the United States is an Officer of the United States, and must, therefore, be appointed in the manner prescribed by § 2, cl. 2 of that Article.

If "all persons who can be said to hold an office under the government about to be established under the Constitution were intended to be included within one or the other of these modes of appointment," *United States* v. *Germaine,* [1878] it is difficult to see how the members of the Commission may escape inclusion....

Although two members of the Commission are initially selected by the President, his nominations are subject to confirmation not merely by the Senate, but by the House of Representatives as well. The remaining four voting members of the Commission were appointed by the President *pro tempore* of the Senate and by the Speaker of the House. While the second part of the Clause authorizes Congress to vest the appointment of the officers described in that part in "the Courts of Law, or in the Heads of Departments," neither the Speaker of the House nor the President *pro tempore* of the Senate comes within this language.

... Thus with respect to four of the six voting members of the Commission, neither the President, the head of any department, nor the judiciary has any voice in their selection.

... Appellee commission and *amici* contend somewhat obliquely that because the Framers had no intention of relegating Congress to a position below that of the coequal Judicial and Executive Branches of the National Government, the Appointments Clause must somehow be read to include Congress or its officers as among those in whom the appointment power may be vested. But ... the evolution of the draft version of the Constitution, seem[s] to us to lend considerable support to our reading of the language of the Appointments Clause itself.

An interim version of the draft Constitution had vested in the Senate the authority to appoint Ambassadors, public Ministers, and Judges of the Supreme Court, and the language of Art. II as finally adopted is a distinct change in this regard. We believe that it was a deliberate change made by the Framers with the intent to deny Congress any authority itself to appoint those who were "Officers of the United States."...

... Appellee Commission and *amici* urge that because of what they conceive to be the extraordinary authority reposed in Congress to regulate elections, this case stands on a different footing than if Congress had exercised its legislative authority in another field.... We see no reason to believe that the authority of Congress over federal election practices is of such a wholly different nature from the other grants of authority to Congress that it may be employed in such a manner as to offend well established constitutional restrictions stemming from the separation of powers.

The position that because Congress has been given explicit and plenary authority to regulate a field of activity, it must therefore have the power to appoint those who are to administer the regulatory statute is both novel and contrary to the language of the Appointments Clause. Unless their selection is elsewhere provided

for, *all* officers of the United States are to be appointed in accordance with the Clause.... No class or type of officer is excluded because of its special functions....

... We are also told by appellees and *amici* that Congress had good reason for not vesting in a Commission composed wholly of Presidential appointees the authority to administer the Act, since the administration of the Act would undoubtedly have a bearing on any incumbent President's campaign for re-election. ... [I]t would seem that those who sought to challenge incumbent Congressmen might have equally good reason to fear a Commission which was unduly responsive to Members of Congress whom they were seeking to unseat. But such fears, however rational, do not by themselves warrant a distortion of the Framers' work.

Appellee Commission and *amici* finally contend ... that whatever shortcomings the provisions of the appointment of members of the Commission might have under Art. II, Congress had ample authority under the Necessary and Proper Clause of Art. I to effectuate this result. We do not agree. The proper inquiry when considering the Necessary and Proper Clause is not the authority of Congress to create an office or a commission ... but rather its authority to provide that its own officers may appoint to such office or commission.

... [Congress may not] vest in itself, or in its officers, the authority to appoint officers of the United States when the Appointments Clause by clear implication prohibits it from doing so....

3. The Commission's Powers

Thus, on the assumption that all of the powers granted in the statute may be exercised by an agency whose members *have been* appointed in accordance with the Appointments Clause, the ultimate question in which, if any, of those powers may be exercised by the present Commissioners, none of whom *was* appointed as provided by that Clause....

Insofar as the powers confided in the Commission are essentially of an investigative and informative nature, falling in the same general category as those powers which Congress might delegate to one of its own committees, there can be no question that the Commission as presently constituted may exercise them....

But when we go beyond this type of authority to the more substantial powers exercised by the Commission, we reach a different result. The Commission's enforcement power, exemplified by its discretionary power to seek judicial relief, is authority that cannot possibly be regarded as merely in aid of the legislative function of Congress. A law suit is the ultimate remedy for a breach of the law, and it is to the President, and not to the Congress, that the Constitution entrusts the responsibility to "take Care that the Laws be faithfully executed." Art. II, § 3.

Congress may undoubtedly under the Necessary and Proper Clause create "offices" in the generic sense and provide such method of appointment to those "offices" as it chooses. But Congress' power under that Clause is inevitably bounded by the express language of Art. II, § 2, cl. 2, and unless the method it provides comports with the latter, the holders of those offices will not be "Officers of the United States." They may, therefore, properly perform duties only in aid of those functions that Congress may carry out by itself, or in an area sufficiently removed from the administration and enforcement of the public law as to permit them being performed by persons not "Officers of the United States."...

... We hold that these provisions of the Act, vesting in the Commission primary responsibility for conducting civil litigation in the courts of the United States for vindicating public rights, violate Art. II, cl 2, § 2, of the Constitution. Such functions may be discharged only by persons who are "Officers of the United States" within the language of that section.

All aspects of the Act are brought within the Commission's broad administrative powers: rule-making, advisory opinions, and determinations of eligibility for funds and even for federal elective office itself. These functions, exercised free from day-to-day supervision of either Congress or the Executive Branch, are more legislative and judicial in nature than are the Commission's enforcement powers, and are of kinds usually performed by independent regulatory agencies or by some department in the Executive Branch under the direction of an Act of Congress. Congress viewed these broad powers as essential to effective and impartial administration of the entire substantive framework of the Act. Yet each of these functions also represents the performance of a significant governmental duty exercised pursuant to a public law.... [N]one of them operates merely in aid of congressional authority to legislate or is sufficiently removed from the administration and enforcement of public law to allow it to be performed by the present Commission. These administrative functions may therefore be exercised only by persons who are "Officers of the United States."

It is also our view that the Commission's inability to exercise certain powers because of the method by which its members have been selected should not affect the validity of the Commission's administrative actions and determinations to this date, including its administration of those provisions, upheld today, authorizing the public financing of federal elections. The past acts of the Commission are therefore added *de facto* validity, just as we have recognized should be the case with respect to legislative acts performed by legislators held to have been elected in accordance with an unconstitutional apportionment plan.... We also draw on the Court's practice in the apportionment and voting rights cases and stay, for a period not to exceed 30 days, the Court's judgment insofar as it affects the authority of the Commission to exercise the duties and powers granted it under the Act. This limited stay will afford Congress an opportunity to reconstitute the Commission by law or to adopt other valid enforcement mechanisms without interrupting enforcement of the provisions the Court sustains, allowing the present Commission in the interim to function *de facto* in accordance with the substantive provisions of the Act....

Conclusion

In summary, we sustain the individual contribution limits, the disclosure and reporting provisions, and the public financing scheme. We conclude, however, that the limitations on campaign expenditures, on independent expenditures by individuals and groups, and on expenditures by a candidate from his personal funds are constitutionally infirm. Finally, we hold that most of the powers conferred by the Act upon the Federal Election Commission can be exercised only by "Officers of the United States," appointed in conformity with Art. II, § 2, cl. 2, of the Constitution, and therefore cannot be exercised by the Commission as presently constituted.

In No. 75-436, the judgment of the Court of Appeals is affirmed in part and reversed in part. The judgment of the District Court in No. 75-437 is affirmed. The mandate shall issue forthwith, except that our judgment is stayed, for a period not to exceed 30 days, insofar as it affects the authority of the Commission to exercise the duties and powers granted it under the Act.

So ordered.

MR. CHIEF JUSTICE BURGER, concurring in part and dissenting in part.

For reasons set forth more fully later, I dissent from those parts of the Court's holding sustaining the Act's provisions (a) for disclosure of small contributions, (b) for limitations on contributions, and (c) for public financing of Presidential campaigns. In my view, the Act's disclosure scheme is impermissibly broad and violative of the First Amendment liberties and suffer from the same infirmities that the Court correctly sees in the expenditure ceilings. The Act's system for public financing of Presidential campaigns is, in my judgment, an impermissible intrusion by the Government into the traditionally private political process....

Disclosure Provisions

Disclosure is, in principle, the salutary and constitutional remedy for most of the ills Congress was seeking to alleviate. I therefore agree fully with the broad proposition that public disclosure of contributions by individuals and by entities — particularly corporations and labor unions — is an effective means of revealing the type of political support that is sometimes coupled with expectations of special favors or rewards. That disclosure impinges on First Amendment rights is conceded by the Court ... but given the

objectives to which disclosure is directed, I agree that the need for disclosure outweighs individual constitutional claims....

... The Court's theory, however, goes beyond permissible limits. Under the Court's view, disclosure serves broad informational purposes, enabling the public to be fully informed on matters of acute public interest. Forced disclosure of one aspect of a citizen's political activity, under this analysis, serves the public right-to-know. This open-ended approach is the only plausible justification for the otherwise irrationally low ceilings of $10 and $100 for anonymous contributions. The burdens of these low ceilings seem to me obvious, and the court does not try to question this....

... The public right-to-know ought not be absolute when its exercise reveals private political convictions. Secrecy, like privacy, is not *per se* criminal. On the contrary, secrecy and privacy as to political preferences and convictions are fundamental in a free society....

... With respect, I suggest the Court has failed to give the traditional standing to some of the First Amendment values at stake here. Specifically, it has failed to confine the particular exercise of governmental power within limits reasonably required....

... [I]t seems to me that the threshold limits fixed at $10 and $100 for anonymous contributions are constitutionally impermissible on their face.... To argue that a 1976 contribution of $10 or $100 entails a risk of corruption or its appearance is simply too extravagant to be maintained. No public right-to-know justifies the compelled disclosure of such contributions, at the risk of discouraging them. There is, in short, no relation whatever between the means used and the legitimate goal of ventilating possible undue influence. Congress has used a shotgun to kill wrens as well as hawks....

... Finally, no legitimate public interest has been shown in forcing the disclosure of modest contributions that are the prime support of new, unpopular or unfashionable political causes. There is no realistic possibility that such modest donations will have a corrupting influence especially on parties that enjoy only "minor" status. Major parties would not notice them, minor parties need them....

I would therefore hold unconstitutional the provisions requiring reporting of contributions of $10 or more and to make a public record of the name, address, and occupation of a contributor of $100 or more.

Contribution and Expenditure Limits

I agree fully with that part of the Court's opinion that holds unconstitutional the limitations the Act puts on campaign expenditures which "place substantial and direct restrictions on the ability of candidates, citizens, and associations to engage in protected political expression, restrictions that the First Amendment cannot tolerate." ... Yet when it approves similarly stringent limitations on contributions, the Court ignores the reasons it finds so persuasive in the context of expenditures. For me contributions and expenditures are two sides of the same First Amendment coin....

... The Court's attempt to distinguish the communication inherent in political *contributions* from the speech aspects of political *expenditures* simply will not wash. We do little but engage in word games unless we recognize that people — candidates and contributors — spend money on political activity because they wish to communicate ideas, and their constitutional interest in doing so is precisely the same whether they or someone else utter the words.

The Court attempts to make the Act seem less restrictive by casting the problem as one that goes to freedom of association rather than freedom of speech. I have long thought freedom of association and freedom of expression were two peas from the same pod....

Public Financing

I dissent from Part III sustaining the constitutionality of the public financing provisions of the Act....

... I would ... fault the Court for not adequately analyzing and meeting head-on the issue whether public financial assistance to the private political activity of individual citizens and parties is a legitimate expenditure of public funds. The public monies at issue here are not being employed simply to police the integrity of the electoral process or to provide a forum for the use of all participants in the political dialog, as would, for example, be the case if free broadcast time were granted. Rather, we are confronted with the Government's actual financing, out of general revenues, a segment of the political debate itself....

...I agree with MR. JUSTICE REHNQUIST that the scheme approved by the Court today invidiously discriminates against minor parties.... The fact that there have been few drastic realignments in our basic two-party structure in 200 years is no constitutional justification for freezing the status quo of the present major parties at the expense of such future political movements....

I would also find unconstitutional the system of "matching grants" which makes a candidate's ability to amass private funds the sole criterion for eligibility for public funds. Such an arrangement can put at serious disadvantage a candidate with a potentially large, widely diffused — but poor — constituency. The ability of a candidate's supporters to help pay for his campaign cannot be equated with their willingness to cast a ballot for him....

I cannot join in the attempt to determine which parts of the Act can survive review here. The statute as it now stands is unworkable and inequitable.

I agree with the Court's holding that the Act's restrictions on expenditures made "relative to a clearly identified candidate," independent of any candidate or his committee, are unconstitutional.... Paradoxically the Court upholds the limitations on individual contributions, which embrace precisely the same sort of expenditures "relative to a clearly identified candidate" if those expenditures are "authorized or requested" by the "candidate or his agents." ... The Act as cut back by the Court thus places intolerable pressure on the distinction between "authorized" and "unauthorized" expenditures on behalf of a candidate; even those with the most sanguine hopes for the Act might well concede that the distinction cannot be maintained....

....Moreover, the Act — or so much as the Court leaves standing — creates significant inequities. A candidate with substantial personal resources is now given by the Court a clear advantage over his less affluent opponents, who are constrained by law in fundraising, because the Court holds that the "First Amendment cannot tolerate" any restrictions on spending.... Minority parties, whose situation is difficult enough under an Act that excludes them from public funding, are prevented from accepting large single-donor contributions. At the same time the Court sustains the provision aimed at broadening the base of political support by requiring candidates to seek a greater number of small contributors, it sustains the unrealistic disclosure thresholds of $10 and $100 that I believe will deter those hoped-for small contributions. Minor parties must now compete for votes against two major parties whose expenditures will be vast. Finally, the Act's distinction between contributions in money and contributions in services remains, with only the former being subject to any limits....

The Court's piecemeal approach fails to give adequate consideration to the integrated nature of this legislation. A serious question is raised, which the court does not consider, when central segments, key operative provisions, of this Act are stricken, can what remains function in anything like the way Congress intended? ...

Finally, I agree with the Court that members of the Federal Election Commission were unconstitutionally appointed. However, I disagree that we should give blanket *de facto* validation to all actions of the Commission undertaken until today....

...In my view Congress can no more ration political expression than it can ration religious expression; and limits on political or religious contributions and expenditures effectively curb expression in both areas. There are many prices we pay for the freedoms secured by the First Amendment; the risk of undue influence is one of them, confirming what we have long known: freedom is hazardous, but some restraints are worse.

MR. JUSTICE WHITE, concurring in part and dissenting in part....

[I]

...The disclosure requirements and the limitations and expenditures are challenged as invalid abridgements of the right of free speech protected by the First Amendment. I would reject these challenges. I agree with the Court's conclusion and much of its opinion with respect to sustaining the disclosure provisions. I am also in agreement with the Court's judgment upholding the limitations on contributions. I dissent, however, from the Court's view that the expenditure limitations of 18 U.S.C. §§ 608 (c) and (e) violate the First Amendment....

...Since the contribution and expenditure limitations are neutral as to the content of speech and are not motivated by fear of the consequences of the political speech of particular candidates or of political speech in general, this case depends on whether the nonspeech interests of the Federal Government in regulating the use of money in political campaigns are sufficiently urgent to justify the incidental effects that the limitations visit upon the First Amendment interests of candidates and their supporters....

...It would make little sense to me, and apparently made none to Congress, to limit the amounts an individual may give to a candidate or spend with his approval but fail to limit the amounts that could be spent on his behalf. Yet the Court permits the former while striking down the later limitation....

...Proceeding from the maxim that "money talks," the Court finds that the expenditure limitations will seriously curtail political expression by candidates and interfere substantially with their chances for election....

...[A]s it should be unnecessary to point out, money is not always equivalent to or used for speech, even in the context of political campaigns. I accept the reality that communicating with potential voters is the heart of an election campaign and that widespread communication has become very expensive. There are, however, many expensive campaign activities that are not themselves communicative or remotely related to speech. Furthermore, campaigns differ among themselves. Some seem to spend much less money than others and yet communicate as much or more than those supported by enormous bureaucracies with unlimited financing. The record before us no more supports the conclusion that the communicative efforts of congressional and Presidential candidates will be crippled by the expenditure limitations than it supports the contrary. The judgment of Congress was that reasonably effective campaigns could be conducted within the limits established by the Act and that the communicative efforts of these campaigns would not seriously suffer. In this posture of the case, there is no sound basis for invalidating the expenditure limitations, so long as the purposes they serve are legitimate and sufficiently substantial, which in my view they are....

...It is also important to restore and maintain public confidence in federal elections. It is critical to obviate or dispel the impression that federal elections are purely and simply a function of money, that federal offices are bought and sold or that political races are reserved for those who have the facility — and the stomach — for doing whatever it takes to bring together those interests, groups, and individuals that can raise or contribute large fortunes in order to prevail at the polls.

The ceiling on candidate expenditures represents the considered judgment of Congress that elections are to be decided among candidates none of whom has overpowering advantage by reason of a huge campaign war chest. At least so long as the ceiling placed upon the candidates is not plainly too low, elections are not to turn on the difference in the amounts of money that candidates have to spend. This seems an acceptable purpose and the means chosen a common sense way to achieve it. The Court nevertheless holds that a candidate has a constitutional right to spend unlimited amounts of money, mostly that of other people, in order to be elected. The holding perhaps is not that federal candidates have the constitutional right to purchase their election, but many will so interpret the Court's conclusion in this case. I cannot join the Court in this respect.

I also disagree with the Court's judgment that § 608 (a), which limits the amount of money that a candidate or his family may spend on his campaign, violates the Constitution. Although it is true that this provision does not promote any interest in preventing the corruption of candidates, the provision does, nevertheless, serve salutary purposes related to the integrity of federal campaigns....

As with the campaign expenditure limits, Congress was entitled to determine that personal wealth ought to play a less important role in political campaigns than it has in the past. Nothing in the First Amendment stands in the way of that determination....

[II]

I join the answers in Part IV of the Court's opinion ... to the questions certified by the District Court relating to the composition and powers of the Federal Election Commission (FEC)....

... It is apparent that none of the members of the FEC is selected in a manner Art. II specifies for the appointment of officers of the United States....

... The challenge to the FEC, therefore, is that its members are officers of the United States the mode of whose appointment was required to, but did not, conform to the Appointments Clause. That challenge is well taken....

... This position that Congress may itself appoint the members of a body that is to administer a wide-ranging statute will not withstand examination in light of either the purpose and history of the Appointments Clause or of prior cases in this Court....

... I thus find singularly unpersuasive the proposition that because the FEC is implementing statutory policies with respect to the conduct of elections, which policies Congress has the power to propound, its members may be appointed by Congress. One might as well argue that the exclusive and plenary power of Congress over interstate commerce authorizes Congress to appoint the members of the Interstate Commerce Commission and of many other regulatory commissions....

... Congress clearly has the power to create federal offices and to define the powers and duties of those offices ... but no case in this Court even remotely supports the power of Congress to appoint an officer of the United States aside from those officers each House is authorized by Art. I to appoint to assist in the legislative processes....

MR. JUSTICE MARSHALL, concurring in part and dissenting in part.

I join in all of the Court's opinion except Part I - C - 2, which deals with § 608 (a) of the Act. That section limits the amount a candidate can spend from his personal funds, or family funds under his control, in connection with his campaigns during any calendar year....

... One of the points on which all Members of the Court agree is that money is essential for effective communication in a political campaign. It would appear to follow that the candidate with a substantial personal fortune at his disposal is off to a significant "head start." Of course, the less wealthy candidate can potentially overcome the disparity in resources through contributions from others. But ability to generate contributions may itself depend upon a showing of a financial base for the campaign or some demonstration of pre-existing support, which in turn is facilitated by expenditures of substantial personal sums. Thus the wealthy candidate's immediate access to a substantial personal fortune may give him an initial advantage that his less wealthy opponent can never overcome. And even if the advantage can be overcome, the perception that personal wealth wins elections may not only discourage potential candidates without significant personal wealth from entering the political arena, but also undermine public confidence in the integrity of the electoral process....

... In view of § 608 (b)'s limitations on contributions, then, § 608 (a) emerges not simply as a device to reduce the natural advantage of the wealthy candidate, but as a provision providing

some symmetry to a regulatory scheme that otherwise enhances the natural advantage of the wealthy.... I therefore respectfully dissent from the Court's invalidation of § 608 (a).

MR. JUSTICE BLACKMUN, concurring in part and dissenting in part.

I am not persuaded that the Court makes, or indeed is able to make, a principled constitutional distinction between the contribution limitations, on the one hand, and the expenditure limitations, on the other, that are involved here. I therefore do not join in Part I-B of the Court's opinion or those portions of Part I-A that are consistent with Part I-B. As to those, I dissent....

MR. JUSTICE REHNQUIST, concurring in part and dissenting in part....

... I ... join in all of the Court's opinion except Subpart III-B-1, which sustains, against appellants' First and Fifth Amendment challenges, the disparities found in the congressional plan for financing general Presidential elections between the two major parties, on the one hand, and minor parties and candidacies on the other....

... Congress, of course, does have an interest in not "funding hopeless candidacies with large sums of public money," ... and many for that purpose legitimately require " 'some preliminary showing of a significant modicum of support,' *Jenness* v. *Fortson* ... as an eligibility requirement for public funds." ... But Congress in this legislation has done a good deal more than that. It has enshrined the Republican and Democratic Parties in a permanently preferred position, and has established requirements for funding minor party and independent candidates to which the two major parties are not subject. Congress would undoubtedly be justified in treating the Presidential candidates of the two major parties differently from minor party or independent Presidential candidates, in view of the long demonstrated public supports of the former. But because of the First Amendment overtones of the appellants' Fifth Amendment equal protection claim, something more than a merely rational basis for the difference in treatment must be shown, as the Court apparently recognizes. I find it impossible to subscribe to the Court's reasoning that because no third party has posed a credible threat to the two major parties in Presidential elections since 1860, Congress may by law attempt to assure that this pattern will endure forever.

I would hold that, as to general election financing, Congress has not merely treated the two major parties differently from minor parties and independents, but has discriminated in favor of the former in such a way as to run afoul of the Fifth and First Amendments to the United States Constitution.

FEDERAL ELECTION CAMPAIGN ACT OF 1971

The Federal Election Campaign Act of 1971 (FECA) was the first comprehensive revision of federal campaign legislation since the Corrupt Practices Act of 1925. The act established detailed spending limits and disclosure procedures. P.L. 92-225 contained the following major provisions, some of which have been declared unconstitutional and others superseded by later amendments or repealed:

General

- Repealed the Federal Corrupt Practices Act of 1925.
- Defined "election" to mean any general, special, primary or runoff election, nominating convention or caucus, delegate-selec-

tion primary, presidential preference primary or constitutional convention.

• Broadened the definitions of "contribution" and "expenditure" as they pertain to political campaigns, but exempted a loan of money by a national or state bank made in accordance with applicable banking laws.

• Prohibited promises of employment or other political rewards or benefits by any candidate in exchange for political support, and prohibited contracts between candidates and any federal department or agency.

• Provided that the terms "contribution" and "expenditure" did not include communications, non-partisan registration and get-out-the-vote campaigns by a corporation aimed at its stockholders or by a labor organization aimed at its members.

• Provided that the terms "contribution" and "expenditure" did not include the establishment, administration and solicitation of voluntary contributions to a separate segregated fund to be utilized for political purposes by a corporation or labor organization.

Contribution Limits

• Placed a ceiling on contributions by any candidate or his immediate family to his own campaign of $50,000 for president or vice president, $35,000 for senator and $25,000 for representative.

Spending Limits

• Limited the total amount that could be spent by federal candidates for advertising time in communications media to 10 cents per eligible voter or $50,000, whichever was greater. The limitation would apply to all candidates for president and vice president, senator and representative, and would be determined annually for the geographical area of each election by the Bureau of the Census.

• Included in the term "communications media" radio and television broadcasting stations, newspapers, magazines, billboards and automatic telephone equipment. Of the total spending limit, up to 60 percent could be used for broadcast advertising time.

• Specified that candidates for presidential nomination, during the period prior to the nominating convention, could spend no more in primary or non-primary states than the amount allowed under the 10-cent-per-voter communications spending limitation.

• Provided that broadcast and non-broadcast spending limitations be increased in proportion to annual increases in the Consumer Price Index over the base year 1970.

Disclosure and Enforcement

• Required all political committees that anticipated receipts in excess of $1,000 during the calendar year to file a statement of organization with the appropriate federal supervisory officer, and to include such information as the names of all principal officers, the scope of the committee, the names of all candidates the committee supported and other information as required by law.

• Stipulated that the appropriate federal supervisory officer to oversee election campaign practices, reporting and disclosure was the clerk of the House for House candidates, the secretary of the Senate for Senate candidates and the Comptroller General for presidential candidates.

• Required each political committee to report any individual expenditure of more than $100 and any expenditures of more than $100 in the aggregate during the calendar year.

• Required disclosure of all contributions to any committee or candidate in excess of $100, including a detailed report with the name and address of the contributor and the date the contribution was made.

• Required the supervisory officers to prepare an annual report for each committee registered with the commission and make such reports available for sale to the public.

• Required candidates and committees to file reports of contributions and expenditures on the 10th day of March, June and September every year, on the 15th and fifth days preceding the date on which an election was held and on the 31st day of January.

Any contribution of $5,000 or more was to be reported within 48 hours after its receipt.

• Required reporting of the names, addresses and occupations of any lender and endorser of any loan in excess of $100 as well as the date and amount of such loans.

• Required any person who made any contribution in excess of $100, other than through a political committee or candidate, to report such contribution to the commission.

• Prohibited any contribution to a candidate or committee by one person in the name of another person.

• Authorized the office of the Comptroller General to serve as a national clearinghouse for information on the administration of election practices.

• Required that copies of reports filed by a candidate with the appropriate supervisory officer also be filed with the secretary of state for the state in which the election was held.

Miscellaneous

• Prohibited radio and television stations from charging political candidates more than the lowest unit cost for the same advertising time available to commercial advertisers. Lowest unit rate charges would apply only during the 45 days preceding a primary election and the 60 days preceding a general election.

• Required non-broadcast media to charge candidates no more than the comparable amounts charged to commercial advertisers for the same class and amount of advertising space. The requirement would apply only during the 45 days preceding the date of a primary election and 60 days before the date of a general election.

• Provided that amounts spent by an agent of a candidate on behalf of his candidacy would be charged against the overall expenditure allocation. Fees paid to the agent for services performed also would be charged against the overall limitation.

• Stipulated that no broadcast station could make any charge for political advertising time on a station unless written consent to contract for such time had been given by the candidate, and unless the candidate certified that such charge would not exceed his spending limit.

THE REVENUE ACT OF 1971

The Revenue Act of 1971, through tax incentives and a tax checkoff plan, provided the basis for public funding of presidential election campaigns. P.L. 92-178 contained the following major provisions, some of which have been declared unconstitutional and others superseded by later amendments or repealed:

Tax Incentives and Checkoff

• Allowed a tax credit of $12.50 ($25 for a married couple) or a deduction against income of $50 ($100 for a married couple) for political contributions to candidates for local, state or federal office. [NOTE: The Revenue Act of 1978, P.L. 96-600, raised the tax credit to $50 on a single tax return, $100 on a joint return. As in the 1971 Act, the credit equaled 50 percent of the contribution, up to those limits. The 1978 law eliminated the tax deduction for political contributions while increasing the tax credit.]

• Allowed taxpayers to contribute to a general fund for all eligible presidential and vice presidential candidates by authorizing $1 of their annual income tax payment to be placed in such a fund.

Presidential Election Campaign Fund

• Authorized to be distributed to the candidates of each major party (one which obtained 25 percent of votes cast in the previous presidential election) an amount equal to 15 cents multiplied by the number of U.S. residents age 18 or over.

• Established a formula for allocating public campaign funds to candidates of minor parties whose candidates received 5 percent or more but less than 25 percent of the previous presidential election vote.

• Authorized payments after the election to reimburse the campaign expenses of a new party whose candidate received enough votes to be eligible or to a minor party whose candidate increased its vote to the qualifying level.

• Prohibited major-party candidates who chose public financing of their campaign from accepting private campaign contributions unless their share of funds contributed through the income tax checkoff procedure fell short of the amounts to which they were entitled.

• Prohibited major-party candidates who chose public financing and all campaign committees authorized by candidates from spending more than the amount to which the candidates were entitled under the contributions formula.

• Provided that if the amounts in the fund were insufficient to make the payments to which each party was entitled, payments would be allocated according to the ratio of contributions in their accounts. No party would receive from the general fund more than the smallest amount needed by a major party to reach the maximum amount of contributions to which it was entitled.

• Provided that surpluses remaining in the fund after a campaign be returned to the Treasury after all parties had been paid the amounts to which they were entitled.

Enforcement

• Provided penalties of $5,000 or one year in prison, or both, for candidates or campaign committees that spent more on a campaign than the amounts they received from the campaign fund or who accepted private contributions when sufficient public funds were available.

• Provided penalties of $10,000 or five years in prison, or both, for candidates or campaign committees who used public campaign funds for unauthorized expenses, gave or accepted kickbacks or illegal payments involving public campaign funds, or who knowingly furnished false information to the Comptroller General.

ELECTION CAMPAIGN AMENDMENTS OF 1974

The 1974 Amendments to the FECA set new contribution and spending limits, made provision for government funding of presidential pre-nomination campaigns and national nominating conventions, and created the bipartisan Federal Election Commission to administer election laws. P.L. 93-443 contained the following major provisions, some of which have been declared unconstitutional and others superseded by later amendments or repealed:

Federal Election Commission

• Created a six-member, full-time bipartisan Federal Election Commission (FEC) to be responsible for administering election laws and the public financing program.

• Provided that the president, speaker of the House and president pro tem of the Senate would appoint to the commission two members, each of different parties, all subject to confirmation by Congress. Commission members could not be officials or employees of any branch of government.

• Made the secretary of the Senate and clerk of the House ex officio, non-voting members of the FEC; provided that their offices

would serve as custodian of reports for House and Senate candidates.

• Provided that commissioners would serve six-year, staggered terms and established a rotating one-year chairmanship.

Contribution Limits

• $1,000 per individual for each primary, runoff or general election, and an aggregate contribution of $25,000 to all federal candidates annually.

• $5,000 per organization, political committee and national and state party organization for each election, but no aggregate limit on the amount organizations could contribute in a campaign nor on the amount organizations could contribute to party organizations supporting federal candidates.

• $50,000 for president or vice president, $35,000 for Senate and $25,000 for House races for candidates and their families to their own campaign.

• $1,000 for independent expenditures on behalf of a candidate.

• Barred cash contributions of over $100 and foreign contributions.

Spending Limits

• Presidential primaries — $10 million total per candidate for all primaries. In a state presidential primary, limited a candidate to spending no more than twice what a Senate candidate in that state would be allowed to spend.

• Presidential general election — $20 million per candidate.

• Presidential nominating conventions — $2 million each major political party, lesser amounts for minor parties.

• Senate primaries — $100,000 or eight cents per eligible voter, whichever was greater.

• Senate general elections — $150,000 or 12 cents per eligible voter, whichever was greater.

• House primaries — $70,000.

• House general elections — $70,000.

• National party spending — $10,000 per candidate in House general elections; $20,000 or two cents per eligible voter, whichever was greater, for each candidate in Senate general elections; and two cents per voter (approximately $2.9 million) in presidential general elections. The expenditure would be above the candidate's individual spending limit.

• Applied Senate spending limits to House candidates who represented a whole state.

• Repealed the media spending limitations in the Federal Election Campaign Act of 1971 (P.L. 92-225).

• Exempted expenditures of up to $500 for food and beverages, invitations, unreimbursed travel expenses by volunteers and spending on "slate cards" and sample ballots.

• Exempted fund-raising costs of up to 20 percent of the candidate spending limit. Thus the spending limit for House candidates would be effectively raised from $70,000 to $84,000 and for candidates in presidential primaries from $10 million to $12 million.

• Provided that spending limits be increased in proportion to annual increases in the Consumer Price Index.

Public Financing

• Presidential general elections — voluntary public financing. Major-party candidates automatically would qualify for full funding before the campaign. Minor-party and independent candidates would be eligible to receive a proportion of full funding based on past or current votes received. If a candidate opted for full public funding, no private contributions would be permitted.

• Presidential nominating conventions — optional public funding. Major parties automatically would qualify. Minor parties would be eligible for lesser amounts based on their proportion of votes received in a past election.

• Presidential primaries — matching public funds of up to $5 million per candidate after meeting fund-raising requirements of $100,000 raised in amounts of at least $5,000 in each of 20 states or more. Only the first $250 of individual private contributions would be matched. The matching funds were to be divided among the candidates as quickly as possible. In allocating the money, the order in which the candidates qualified would be taken into account. Only private gifts, raised after Jan. 1, 1975, would qualify for matching for the 1976 election. No federal payments would be made before January 1976.

● Provided that all federal money for public funding of campaigns would come from the Presidential Election Campaign Fund. Money received from the federal income tax dollar checkoff automatically would be appropriated to the fund.

Disclosure and Enforcement

● Required each candidate to establish one central campaign committee through which all contributions and expenditures on behalf of a candidate must be reported. Required designation of specific bank depositories of campaign funds.

● Required full reports of contributions and expenditures to be filed with the Federal Election Commission 10 days before and 30 days after every election, and within 10 days of the close of each quarter unless the committee received or expended less than $1,000 in that quarter. A year-end report was due in non-election years.

● Required that contributions of $1,000 or more received within the last 15 days before election be reported to the commission within 48 hours.

● Prohibited contributions in the name of another.

● Treated loans as contributions. Required a co-signer or guarantor for each $1,000 of outstanding obligation.

● Required any organization that spent any money or committed any act for the purpose of influencing any election (such as the publication of voting records) to file reports as a political committee.

● Required every person who spent or contributed more than $100, other than to or through a candidate or political committee, to report.

● Permitted government contractors, unions and corporations to maintain separate, segregated political funds.

● Provided that the commission would receive campaign reports, make rules and regulations (subject to review by Congress within 30 days), maintain a cumulative index of reports filed and not filed, make special and regular reports to Congress and the president, and serve as an election information clearinghouse.

● Gave the commission power to render advisory opinions, conduct audits and investigations, subpoena witnesses and information and go to court to seek civil injunctions.

● Provided that criminal cases would be referred by the commission to the Justice Department for prosecution.

● Increased existing fines to a maximum of $50,000.

● Provided that a candidate for federal office who failed to file reports could be prohibited from running again for the term of that office plus one year.

Miscellaneous

● Set Jan. 1, 1975, as the effective date of the act (except for immediate pre-emption of state laws).

● Removed Hatch Act restrictions on voluntary activities by state and local employees in federal campaigns, if not otherwise prohibited by state law.

● Prohibited solicitation of funds by franked mail.

● Pre-empted state election laws for federal candidates.

● Permitted use of excess campaign funds to defray expenses of holding federal office or for other lawful purposes.

ELECTION CAMPAIGN ACT AMENDMENTS OF 1976

The 1976 Amendments to the FECA revised election laws following the Supreme Court decision in Buckley v. Valeo. *The Amendments reopened the door to large contributions through "independent expenditures" and through corporate and union political action committees. P.L. 94-283 contained the following major provisions, some of which have been superseded by later amendments or repealed:*

Federal Election Commission

● Reconstituted the Federal Election Commission as a six-member panel appointed by the president and confirmed by the Senate.

● Prohibited commission members from engaging in outside business activities; gave commissioners one year after joining the body to terminate outside business interests.

● Gave Congress the power to disapprove individual sections of any regulation proposed by the commission.

Contribution Limits

● Limited an individual to giving no more than $5,000 a year to a political action committee and $20,000 to the national committee of a political party (the 1974 law set a $1,000-per-election limit on individual contributions to a candidate and an aggregate contribution limit for individuals of $25,000 a year, both provisions remaining in effect).

● Limited a multi-candidate committee to giving no more than $15,000 a year to the national committee of a political party (the 1974 law set only a limit of $5,000 per election per candidate, a provision remaining in effect).

● Limited the Democratic and Republican senatorial campaign committees to giving no more than $17,500 a year to a candidate (the 1974 law set a $5,000-per-election limit, a provision remaining in effect).

● Allowed campaign committees organized to back a single candidate to provide "occasional, isolated, and incidental support" to another candidate. (The 1974 law had limited such a committee to spending money only on behalf of the single candidate for which it was formed.)

● Restricted the proliferation of membership organization, corporate and union political action committees. All political action committees established by a company or an international union would be treated as a single committee for contribution purposes. The contributions of political action committees of a company or union would be limited to no more than $5,000 overall to the same candidate in any election.

Spending Limits

● Limited spending by presidential and vice presidential candidates to no more than $50,000 of their own, or their families', money on their campaigns, if they accepted public financing.

● Exempted from the law's spending limits payments by candidates or the national committees of political parties for legal and accounting services required to comply with the campaign law, but required that such payments be reported.

Public Financing

● Required presidential candidates who received federal matching subsidies and who withdrew from the pre-nomination election campaign to give back leftover federal matching funds.

● Cut off federal campaign subsidies to a presidential candidate who won less than 10 percent of the vote in two consecutive presidential primaries in which he ran.

● Established a procedure under which an individual who became ineligible for matching payments could have eligibility restored by a finding of the commission.

Disclosure and Enforcement

● Gave the commission exclusive authority to prosecute civil violations of the campaign finance law and shifted to the commission jurisdiction over violations formerly covered only in the criminal code, thus strengthening its power to enforce the law.

● Required an affirmative vote of four members for the commission to issue regulations and advisory opinions and initiate civil actions and investigations.

● Required labor unions, corporations and membership organizations to report expenditures of over $2,000 per election for communications to their stockholders or members advocating the election or defeat of a clearly identified candidate. The costs of communications to members or stockholders on issues would not have to be reported.

● Required that candidates and political committees keep records of contributions of $50 or more. (The 1974 law had required records of contributions of $10 or more.)

● Permitted candidates and political committees to waive the requirement for filing quarterly campaign finance reports in a non-election year if less than a total of $5,000 was raised or spent in that quarter. Annual reports would still have to be filed. (The exemption limit was $1,000 under the 1974 law.)

● Required political committees and individuals making an independent political expenditure of more than $100 that advocated the defeat or election of a candidate to file a report with the election commission. Required the committee and individual to state, under penalty of perjury, that the expenditure was not made in collusion with a candidate.

● Required that independent expenditures of $1,000 or more made within 15 days of an election be reported within 24 hours.

● Limited the commission to issuing advisory opinions only for specific fact situations. Advisory opinions could not be used to spell out commission policy. Advisory opinions were not to be considered as precedents unless an activity was "indistinguishable in all its material aspects" from an activity already covered by an advisory opinion.

● Permitted the commission to initiate investigations only after it received a properly verified complaint or had reason to believe, based on information it obtained in the normal course of its duties, that a violation had occurred or was about to occur. The commission was barred from relying on anonymous complaints to institute investigations.

● Required the commission to rely initially on conciliation to deal with alleged campaign law violations before going to court. The commission was allowed to refer alleged criminal violations to the Department of Justice for action. The attorney general was required to report back to the commission within 60 days an action taken on the apparent violation and subsequently every 30 days until the matter was disposed of.

● Provided for a one-year jail sentence and a fine of up to $25,000 or three times the amount of the contribution or expenditure involved in the violation, whichever was greater, if an individual was convicted of knowingly committing a campaign law violation that involved more than $1,000.

● Provided for civil penalties of fines of $5,000 or an amount equal to the contribution or expenditure involved in the violation, whichever was greater. For violations knowingly committed, the fine would be $10,000 or an amount equal to twice the amount involved in the violation, whichever was greater. The fines could be imposed by the courts or by the commission in conciliation agreements. (The 1974 law included penalties for civil violations of a $1,000 fine and/or a one-year prison sentence.)

Miscellaneous

● Restricted the fund-raising ability of corporate political action committees. Company committees could seek contributions only from stockholders and executive and administrative personnel and their families. Restricted union political action committees to soliciting contributions only from union members and their families. However, twice a year the law permitted union and corporate political action committees to seek campaign contributions only by mail from all employees not initially included in the restriction. Contributions would have to remain anonymous and would be received by an independent third party that would keep records but pass the money to the committees.

● Permitted trade association political action committees to solicit contributions from member companies' stockholders, executive and administrative personnel and their families.

● Permitted union political action committees to use the same method to solicit campaign contributions that the political action committee of the company uses. The union committee would have to reimburse the company at cost for the expenses the company incurred for the political fund raising.

ELECTION CAMPAIGN ACT AMENDMENTS OF 1979

The 1979 Amendments were enacted to lighten the burden the law imposed on candidates and political committees by reducing paperwork, among other changes. P.L. 96-187 contained the following major provisions:

Disclosure

● Required a federal candidate to file campaign finance reports if he or she received or expended more than $5,000. Previously any candidate, regardless of the amount raised or spent, had to file.

● Allowed local political party organizations to avoid filing reports with the FEC if expenditures for certain voluntary activities (get-out-the-vote and voter registration drives for presidential tickets and purchase of buttons, bumper stickers and other materials) were less than $5,000 a year. If other types of expenditures were more than $1,000 a year, then such a group would be required to file. Previously local political party organizations were required to file when any class of expenditure exceeded $1,000 a year.

● Permitted an individual to spend up to $1,000 in behalf of a candidate or $2,000 in behalf of a political party in voluntary expenses for providing his home, food or personal travel without its being counted as a reportable contribution.

● Eliminated the requirement that a political committee have a chairman, but continued the requirement that each have a treasurer.

● Allowed 10 days, instead of the previous five, for a person who received a contribution of more than $50 on behalf of a candidate's campaign committee to forward it to the committee's treasurer.

● Required a committee's treasurer to preserve records for three years. Previously, the FEC established the period of time that committee treasurers were required to keep records.

● Required a candidate's campaign committee to have the candidate's name in the title of the committee. Also, the title of a political action committee was required to include the name of the organization with which it was affiliated.

● Reduced to six from 11 the categories of information required on registration statements of political committees. One of the categories eliminated was one requiring political action committees to name the candidates supported. That requirement meant that PACs were forced frequently to file lists of candidates to whom they contributed when that information already was given in their contribution reports.

● Reduced to nine from 24 the maximum number of reports that a candidate would be required to file during a two-year election cycle. Those nine reports would be a pre-primary, a pre-general, a post-general, four quarterly reports during an election year and two semiannual reports during the non-election year. The pre-election reports would be due 12 days before the election; the post-general report would be due 30 days after the election; the quarterly reports would be due 15 days after the end of each quarter and the semiannual reports would be due July 31 and Jan. 31.

● Required presidential campaign committees to file monthly reports, as well as pre- and post-general reports, during an election year if they had contributions or expenditures in excess of $100,000. All other presidential campaign committees would be required to file quarterly reports, as well as pre- and post-general reports, during an election year. During a non-election year presidential campaign committees could choose whether to file monthly or quarterly reports.

● Required political committees other than those affiliated with a candidate to file either monthly reports in all years or nine reports during a two-year election cycle.

● Provided that the FEC be notified within 48 hours of contributions of $1,000 or more that were made between 20 days and 48 hours before an election. Previously the period had been between 15 days and 48 hours before an election.

● Required the names of contributors to be reported if they gave $200 or more instead of $100 or more.

● Required expenses to be itemized if they were $200 or more instead of $100 or more.

● Increased the threshold for reporting independent expenditures to $250 from $100.

Federal Election Commission

● Established a "best effort" standard for the FEC to determine compliance by candidates' committees with the law. This was intended to ease the burden on committees, particularly in the area of meeting the requirement of filing the occupations of contributors.

● Allowed any person who had an inquiry about a specific campaign transaction — not just federal officeholders, candidates, political committees and the national party committees — to request advisory opinions from the FEC.

● Required the FEC to respond to advisory opinion requests within 60 days instead of within a "reasonable time." If such a request were made within the 60-day period before an election, the FEC would be required to issue an opinion within 20 days.

● Provided that within five days of receiving a complaint that the election campaign law had been violated the FEC must notify any person alleged to have committed a violation. The accused has 15 days in which to respond to the complaint.

● Required a vote of four of the six members of the FEC to make the determination it had "reason to believe" a violation of the law had occurred. An investigation then would be required, and the accused had to be notified.

● Provided that four votes of the FEC were necessary to determine "probable cause" that a violation had occurred. The commission then would be required to attempt to correct the violation by informal methods and to enter into a conciliation agreement within 90 days. Commission action required the vote of four FEC members.

● Narrowed the scope of the FEC's national clearinghouse function from all elections to federal elections.

● Eliminated random audits of committees by the FEC and required a vote of four FEC members to conduct an audit after it had determined that a committee had not substantially complied with the election campaign law.

● Required secretaries of state in each state to keep copies of FEC reports on file for only two years compared with the previous requirement that all House candidate reports be retained for five years and all other reports for 10 years.

● Provided an expedited procedure for the Senate, as well as for the House, to disapprove a regulation proposed by the FEC.

Enforcement

● Retained the substance of the existing law providing for civil and criminal relief of election campaign law violations.

● Continued the prohibition on the use of the contents of reports filed with the FEC for the purpose of soliciting contributions or for commercial purposes, but added the exception that the names of PACs registered with the FEC may be used for solicitation of contributions.

● Permitted political committees to include 10 pseudonyms on each report to protect against illegal use of the names of contributors. A list of those names would be provided to the FEC and would not be made public.

Political Parties

● Allowed state and local party groups to buy, without limit, buttons, bumper stickers, handbills, brochures, posters and yard signs for voluntary activities.

● Authorized state and local party groups to conduct voter registration and get-out-the-vote drives on behalf of presidential tickets without financial limit.

Public Financing

● Increased the allotment of federal funds for the Democrats and Republicans to finance their nominating conventions to $3 million from $2 million.

Miscellaneous

● Permitted buttons and similar materials, but not commercial advertisements, that promoted one candidate to make a passing reference to another federal candidate without its being treated as a contribution to the second candidate.

● Permitted leftover campaign funds to be given to other political committees, as well as charities.

● Prohibited anyone, with the exception of members of Congress at the time of P.L. 96-187's enactment, to convert leftover campaign funds to personal use.

● Continued the ban on solicitation by candidates for Congress or members of Congress and by federal employees of other federal workers for campaign contributions, but dropped the prohibition on the receipt of such contributions by federal employees. An inadvertent solicitation of a federal employee would not be a violation.

● Permitted congressional employees to make voluntary contributions to members of Congress other than their immediate employers.

● Continued the ban on solicitation and receipt of contributions in a federal building. But it would not be a violation if contributions received at a federal building were forwarded within seven days to the appropriate political committee and if the contribution had not been directed initially to the federal building.

Spending in Congressional Races

The cost of campaigning for Congress continued between 1976 and 1978 to rise faster than the rate of inflation, according to figures compiled by the Federal Election Commission (FEC).

In the 1978 campaign, House candidates on the November ballot spent $88 million — a 44 percent increase above the aggregate cost of $60.9 million two years earlier.

The jump in the cost of running for the Senate was even more pronounced. In 35 Senate contests in 1978, party nominees and independent candidates spent $65.5 million, compared with $38.1 million in 1976 when 33 seats were contested. The number of candidates spending more than $1 million (21) doubled in 1978 over the previous election, when there were 10 such Senate candidates.

Inflation accounted for only part of the increase. From 1972 to 1978 spending on House campaigns had risen 34 percent over and above the increase in the Consumer Price Index for that six-year period, according to a study for the House Administration Committee by the Institute of Politics at Harvard University.

Sharp increases in the cost of public opinion polling and television advertising added substantially to candidates' financial problems. Other new burdens were added by the accounting expenses of complying with the Federal Election Campaign Act, which also limited the role of major contributors and forced candidates to canvass large numbers of voters to raise sufficient funds.

FEC Studies

Prior to the 1976 election, campaign spending data were compiled by Common Cause, the public affairs lobby. The FEC studies covered the 24 months ending on the last day of the year in which the 1976 and 1978 congressional elections were held.

The FEC's compilation of the receipts and expenditures for each congressional candidate in the general election is shown in the following tables. The figures cover all House and Senate campaign finance activity in the 1976 and 1978 election cycles except by candidates who lost in primaries. Amendments to campaign reports received by the FEC through March 16, 1979, are included.

Comparable receipt and expenditure figures for the 1980 election cycle were not available from the FEC when this book went to press.

Included in the 1976 and 1978 receipt amounts are individual and committee contributions, loans, interest and miscellaneous income. The expenditures include all campaign expenditures, as well as items such as refunds, rebates, loan repayments and returned contributions. The 1976 figures include independent expenditures made on behalf of a candidate by a political party, labor, business or trade association. The 1978 figures do not include independent expenditures made by political action committees (PACs) or individuals not affiliated with the candidate.

The primary vote percentages were taken from Congressional Quarterly *Weekly Report* articles that appeared throughout 1976 and 1978 on congressional primary results. The general election vote percentages were compiled by Congressional Quarterly from official reports of state election officials.

Explanation of Symbols

Candidates are included in the listing only if they received at least 5 percent of the total vote or spent more than $5,000.

An asterisk (*) indicates an incumbent. A double asterisk (**) denotes a candidate's percentage in a runoff primary. A dash (—) indicates candidate was unopposed in the primary. In the Senate tables, a dagger (†) designates the winner.

Abbreviations used in the House tables for minor party and independent candidates differed slightly from 1976 to 1978. Following are the abbreviations in the 1976 tables: American Party (AP), American Independent Party (AIP), Conservative Party (C), Democrat-Farmer-Labor Party (DFL), Independent (I), Independent American (IA), Independent-Republican Party of Minnesota (I-R), Independent Vermonters (I VT), Independents for Godly Government (I Godly Gov), Liberal (L), Peace and Freedom (PFP) and United States Labor Party (USLP).

Following are the abbreviations for minor and independent House candidates in the 1978 tables: American Party (AM), American Independent Party (AM I), Conservative Party (C), Communist Party (COM), Democrat-Farmer-Labor Party (DFL), Independent (I), Independent-Republican Party of Minnesota (I-R), Liberal Party (L), Libertarian Party (LIBERT), La Raza Unida (LRU), Liberty Union Party (LU), Socialist Workers Party (SOC WORK), United States Labor Party (USLP) and United Taxpayers Party (UT).

Senate Receipts, Expenditures for 1976 Races

	Percent of Primary Vote	Percent of General Election Vote	Receipts	Expenditures
ARIZONA				
Dennis DeConcini (D)†	53.4	54.0	$ 598,668	$ 597,405
Sam Steiger (R)	52.5	43.3	722,691	679,384
CALIFORNIA				
John V. Tunney (D)*	53.8	46.9	1,903,527	1,940,988
S. I. Hayakawa (R)†	38.2	50.2	1,218,485	1,184,624
CONNECTICUT				
Gloria Schaffer (D)	—	41.2	312,394	306,104
Lowell P. Weicker Jr. (R)*†	—	57.7	500,955	480,709
DELAWARE				
Thomas C. Maloney (D)	—	43.6	211,281	211,258
William V. Roth Jr. (R)*†	—	55.8	321,292	322,080
FLORIDA				
Lawton Chiles (D)*†	—	63.0	362,477	362,235
John L. Grady (R)	67.1	37.0	408,616	394,574
HAWAII				
Spark M. Matsunaga (D)†	51.0	53.7	416,775	435,130
William F. Quinn (R)	93.7	40.6	417,652	415,138
INDIANA				
Vance Hartke (D)*	52.9	40.5	662,389	654,279
Richard G. Lugar (R)†	65.4	58.8	742,736	727,720
MAINE				
Edmund S. Muskie (D)*†	—	60.2	322,964	320,427
Robert A. G. Monks (R)	83.6	39.8	602,851	598,490
MARYLAND				
Paul S. Sarbanes (D)†	55.4	56.5	892,300	891,533
J. Glenn Beall (R)*	—	38.8	578,299	572,016
MASSACHUSETTS				
Edward M. Kennedy (D)*†	73.6	69.3	975,601	896,196
Michael Robertson (R)	—	29.0	169,724	168,854
MICHIGAN				
Donald W. Riegle Jr. (D)†	43.6	52.5	849,684	795,821
Marvin L. Esch (R)	44.3	46.8	864,759	809,564
MINNESOTA				
Hubert H. Humphrey (D)*†	91.2	67.5	664,567	618,878
Gerald W. Brekke (R)	54.1	25.0	45,775	43,912
MISSISSIPPI				
John C. Stennis (D)*†	85.3	100.0	119,852	119,852
MISSOURI				
Warren E. Hearnes (D)	26.5	42.5	662,737	660,953
John C. Danforth (R)†	93.1	56.9	748,115	741,465
MONTANA				
John Melcher (D)†	88.3	64.2	321,596	311,101
Stanley C. Burger (R)	40.9	35.8	578,826	563,543
NEBRASKA				
Edward Zorinsky (D)†	48.6	52.4	240,904	237,613
John Y. McCollister (R)	78.3	47.5	391,287	391,287
NEVADA				
Howard W. Cannon (D)*†	85.7	63.0	$ 422,203	$ 405,380
David Towell (R)	67.6	31.4	58,842	58,842
NEW JERSEY				
Harrison A. Williams Jr. (D)*†	84.9	60.7	690,781	610,090
David F. Norcross (R)	68.1	38.0	74,023	73,499
NEW MEXICO				
Joseph M. Montoya (D)*	66.4	42.7	461,505	451,111
Harrison H. Schmitt (R)†	71.7	56.8	473,336	441,309
NEW YORK				
Daniel Patrick Moynihan (D)†	36.4	54.2	1,219,740	1,210,796
James L. Buckley (Cons R)*	—	44.9	2,090,126	2,101,424
NORTH DAKOTA				
Quentin N. Burdick (D)*†	—	62.1	122,605	117,514
Robert Stroup (R)	—	36.6	142,774	136,748
OHIO				
Howard M. Metzenbaum (D)†	53.2	49.5	1,097,337	1,092,053
Robert Taft Jr. (R)*	—	46.5	1,328,283	1,304,207
PENNSYLVANIA				
William J. Green (D)	68.4	46.8	1,266,375	1,269,409
H. John Heinz III (R)†	38.0	52.4	3,016,731	3,004,814
RHODE ISLAND				
Richard P. Lorber (D)	37.7	42.0	782,663	782,931
John H. Chafee (R)†	—	57.7	424,463	415,651
TENNESSEE				
James R. Sasser (D)†	43.9	52.5	841,644	839,379
Bill Brock (R)*	—	47.0	1,313,503	1,301,033
TEXAS				
Lloyd Bentsen (D)*†	62.5	56.8	1,277,364	1,237,910
Alan Steelman (R)	64.6	42.2	667.214	665,058
UTAH				
Frank E. Moss (D)*	—	44.8	365,187	343,598
Orrin G. Hatch (R)†	64.6	53.7	393,278	370,517
VERMONT				
Thomas P. Salmon (D)	52.8	45.3	170,156	169,296
Robert T. Stafford (R)*†	68.0	50.0	167,469	157,927
VIRGINIA				
Elmo R. Zumwalt Jr. (D)	—	38.3	450,229	443,107
Harry F. Byrd Jr. (Ind.)*†	—	57.2	809,346	802,928
WASHINGTON				
Henry M. Jackson (D)*†	87.2	71.8	223,322	198,375
George M. Brown (R)	28.3	24.2	10,841	10,841
WEST VIRGINIA				
Robert C. Byrd (D)*†	—	99.9	271,124	94,335
WISCONSIN				
William Proxmire (D)*†	—	72.2	25	697
Stanley York (R)	—	27.0	66,321	62,210
WYOMING				
Gale W. McGee (D)*	—	45.4	299,908	181,028
Malcolm Wallop (R)†	77.2	54.6	305,161	301,595

House Receipts, Expenditures for 1976 Races

	Per Cent of Primary Vote	Per Cent of General Election Vote	Receipts	Expenditures
ALABAMA				
1 Jack Edwards (R)*	—	62.5	$ 85,095	$ 71,310
Bill Davenport (D)	—	37.5	30,019	30,016
2 William L. Dickinson (R)*	—	57.6	81,977	51,210
J. Carole Keahey (D)	55.9**	42.4	122,816	122,265
3 Bill Nichols (D)*	91.6	99.0	15,742	16,569
4 Tom Bevill (D)*	81.0	80.4	51,375	27,484
Leonard Wilson (R)	—	19.6	8,682	8,658
5 Ronnie G. Flippo (D)	58.1**	100.0	177,580	172,689
6 John Buchanan (R)*	—	56.7	92,801	92,985
Mel Bailey (D)	—	42.7	81,246	81,246
7 Walter Flowers (D)*	70.4	100.0	60,827	27,763
ALASKA				
AL Donald E. Young (R)*	—	70.8	176,875	175,589
Eben Hopson (D)	27.8	28.9	23,780	21,184

Candidates' Personal Spending

Ten candidates for the U.S. House gave their own campaigns at least $100,000 in the form of personal contributions or loans. An asterisk (*) indicates an incumbent. The names of winners are italicized. The chart is based on information compiled by the Federal Election Commission.

	Contributions	Loans	Total
Cecil (Cec) Heftel (D Hawaii)	$ 0	$507,000	$507,000
Gary Familian (D Calif.)	214,294	276,637	490,931
Merlin E. Karlock (D Ill.)	379,675	53,191	432,866
Morgan Maxfield (D Mo.)	0	284,159	284,159
*Ken Hechler (D W.Va.)**	237,078	35,000	272,078
Nick J. Rahall (D W.Va.)	11,746	236,000	247,746
Richard A. Tonry (D La.)	52,900	125,000	177,900
Albert Gore Jr. (D Tenn.)	75,150	50,000	125,150
Jerry Huckaby (D La.)	0	111,600	111,600
Edward L. Young (R S.C.)	0	105,925	105,925

	Per Cent of Primary Vote	Per Cent of General Election Vote	Receipts	Expenditures
ARIZONA				
1 John J. Rhodes (R)*	76.9	57.3	226,698	202,086
Patricia Fullinwider (R)	—	40.7	75,227	75,528
2 Morris K. Udall (D)*	78.6	58.2	83,232	45,791
Laird Guttersen (R)	—	39.4	31,465	31,008
3 Bob Stump (D)	31.3	47.5	114,160	113,438
Fred Koory Jr. (R)	63.5	42.3	103,733	103,383
Bill McCune (Nonparty)	—	10.2	15,116	14,969
4 Eldon Rudd (R)	51.7	48.6	125,792	116,302
Tony Mason (D)	53.4	48.2	172,411	171,629
ARKANSAS				
1 Bill Alexander (D)*	—	68.9	163,069	147,088
Harlan (Bo) Holleman (R)	—	31.1	195,519	194,308
2 Jim Guy Tucker (D)	51.7	86.4	123,935	122,253
James J. Kelly (R)	62.9	13.6	2,573	2,568
3 John Paul Hammerschmidt (R)*	—	100.0	26,524	11,569
4 Ray Thornton (D)*	—	100.0	1,044	1,044
CALIFORNIA				
1 Harold T. (Bizz) Johnson (D)*	79.5	73.9	23,067	21,359

	Per Cent of Primary Vote	Per Cent of General Election Vote	Receipts	Expenditures
James E. Taylor (R)	—	26.1	8,321	7,713
2 Don H. Clausen (R)*	—	56.0	148,137	123,828
Oscar H. Klee (D)	35.1	41.0	40,576	40,576
3 John E. Moss (D)*	—	72.9	49,945	50,869
George R. Marsh Jr. (R)	—	27.1	0	1,346
4 Robert L. Leggett (D)*	—	46.7	77,436	73,047
Albert Dehr (R)	38.5	46.3	10,674	10,674
Joseph F. (Ted) Sheedy (Write-in)	—	6.9	48,097	44,977
5 John L. Burton (D)*	—	61.8	100,528	77,550
Branwell Fanning (R)	—	38.2	57,139	56,693
6 Phillip Burton (D)*	82.3	66.1	118,740	85,149
Tom Spinosa (R)	82.4	27.0	3,019	2,887
Emily Siegel (PFP)	—	5.0	0	0
7 George Miller (D)*	—	74.7	68,109	47,633
Robert L. Vickers (R)	—	23.3	23,668	23,582
8 Ronald V. Dellums (D)*	—	62.1	44,362	44,744
Philip S. Breck Jr. (R)	—	34.7	22,171	22,025
9 Fortney H. Stark Jr. (D)*	—	70.8	29,867	20,890
James K. Mills (R)	—	27.1	12,716	12,591
10 Don Edwards (D)*	—	72.0	11,847	10,788
Herb Smith (R)	—	24.5	6,825	6,625
11 Leo J. Ryan (D)*	70.8	61.1	55,851	51,864
Bob Jones (R)	—	35.4	111,178	110,328
12 Paul N. McCloskey Jr. (R)*	—	66.2	104,183	106,711
David Harris (D)	59.6	31.3	158,043	157,226
13 Norman Y. Mineta (D)*	—	66.8	188,812	187,068
Ernest L. Konnyu (R)	62.3	31.2	59,751	59,413
14 John J. McFall (D)*	82.7	72.5	102,210	91,239
Roger A. Blain (R)	—	27.5	11,927	11,909
15 B. F. Sisk (D)*	—	72.2	62,728	64,099
Carol O. Harner (R)	—	27.8	4,656	4,656
16 Leon E. Panetta (D)	52.3	53.4	185,073	181,410
Burt L. Talcott (R)*	—	46.6	206,544	217,053
17 John Krebs (D)*	—	65.7	93,650	69,800
Henry J. Andreas (R)	—	34.3	23,586	23,585
18 William M. Ketchum (R)*	—	64.2	145,554	104,003
Dean Close (D)	75.5	35.8	40,338	39,971
19 Robert J. Lagomarsino (R)*	—	64.4	103,001	81,808
Dan Sisson (D)	—	35.6	39,172	39,155
20 Barry M. Goldwater Jr. (R)*	—	67.2	140,462	109,624
Patti Lear Corman (D)	47.0	32.8	75,046	74,079
21 James C. Corman (D)*	—	66.5	170,663	142,770
Erwin G. (Ed) Hogan (R)	40.1	28.8	2,581	2,581
22 Carlos J. Moorhead (R)*	—	62.6	82,992	51,069
Robert L. Salley (D)	38.5	37.4	41,367	41,167
23 Anthony C. (Tony) Beilenson (D)	57.7	60.2	105,180	102,547
Thomas F. Bartman (R)	54.3	39.8	99,606	99,465
24 Henry A. Waxman (D)*	80.7	67.8	60,699	29,505
David I. Simmons (R)	51.8	32.2	8,508	8,310
25 Edward R. Roybal (D)*	86.1	71.9	44,319	31,141
Jim Madrid (R)	—	22.0	6,793	4,587
Marilyn Seals (PFP)	—	6.1	9	9
26 John H. Rousselot (R)*	—	65.6	105,289	86,592
Bruce Latta (D)	—	34.4	6,727	6,727
27 Robert K. Dornan (R)	31.6	54.7	407,447	403,675
Gary Familian (D)	35.0	45.3	637,800	637,080
28 Yvonne Brathwaite Burke (D)*	—	80.2	51,916	50,252
Edward S. Skinner (R)	—	19.8	604	555
29 Augustus F. Hawkins (D)*	78.7	85.4	11,335	3,873
Michael D. Germonprez (R)	—	11.2	60	60
30 George E. Danielson (D)*	—	74.4	70,043	67,893
Harry Couch (R)	59.0	25.6	10,915	10,915
31 Charles H. Wilson (D)*	62.3	100.0	70,810	56,987
32 Glenn M. Anderson (D)*	85.6	72.2	92,409	66,419
Clifford O. Young (R)	—	27.8	25,497	25,420
33 Del Clawson (R)*	—	55.1	77,268	83,115
Ted Snyder (D)	69.6	44.9	42,894	42,630
34 Mark W. Hannaford (D)*	—	50.7	172,718	167,547
Daniel E. Lungren (R)	48.5	49.3	152,705	152,109
35 Jim Lloyd (D)*	—	53.3	153,781	132,031
Louis Brutocao (R)	—	46.7	226,609	224,853
36 George E. Brown Jr. (D)*	—	61.6	49,483	38,543

	Per Cent of Primary Vote	Per Cent of General Election Vote	Receipts	Expenditures
Grant C. Carner (R)	—	33.5	36,682	36,682
William E. Pasley (AIP)	—	5.0	3,273	3,273
37 Shirley N. Pettis (R)*	—	71.1	177,691	144,153
Douglas C. Nilson Jr. (D)	—	26.1	7,671	7,635
38 Jerry M. Patterson (D)*	—	63.6	110,317	104,635
James Combs (R)	52.0	36.4	51,006	50,299
39 Charles E. Wiggins (R)*	—	58.6	66,010	51,047
William E. Farris (D)	57.5	41.4	27,511	22,676
40 Robert E. Badham (R)	31.8	59.3	137,931	124,773
Vivian Hall (D)	47.7	40.7	27,170	27,040
41 Bob Wilson (R)*	—	57.7	92,957	93,238
King Golden Jr. (D)	21.6	42.3	29,342	28,448
42 Lionel Van Deerlin (D)*	—	76.0	68,210	63,764
Wes Marden (R)	—	24.0	3,623	3,942
43 Clair W. Burgener (R)*	—	65.0	76,477	61,233
Pat Kelly (D)	64.8	35.0	5,278	5,276
COLORADO				
1 Patricia Schroeder (D)*	—	53.2	154,967	132,679
Don Friedman (R)	68.1	46.2	151,071	150,047
2 Timothy E. Wirth (D)*	—	50.5	205,792	183,708
Ed Scott (R)	69.3	49.5	148,554	147,719
3 Frank E. Evans (D)*	75.1	51.0	54,771	57,990
Melvin H. Takaki (R)	—	47.0	91,767	90,499
4 James P. Johnson (R)*	—	54.0	92,915	65,579
Dan Ogden (D)	—	34.8	46,867	46,431
Dick Davis (I)	—	9.2	58,347	58,221
5 William L. Armstrong (R)*	—	66.4	173,490	143,466
Dorothy Hores (D)	—	33.6	21,334	21,244
CONNECTICUT				
1 William R. Cotter (D)*	—	57.1	77,352	61,594
Lucien P. DiFazio Jr. (R)	—	41.8	24,097	24,023
2 Christopher J. Dodd (D)*	—	65.1	103,235	98,021
Richard M. Jackson (R)	—	34.1	19,586	19,363
3 Robert N. Giaimo (D)*	—	54.6	75,057	63,188
John G. Pucciano (R)	—	43.4	14,093	14,008
4 Stewart B. McKinney (R)*	—	61.0	109,145	113,344
Geoffrey G. Peterson (D)	53.4	37.1	49,204	49,038
5 Ronald A. Sarasin (R)*	—	66.5	136,534	122,014
Michael J. Adanti (D)	—	32.7	61,990	56,272
6 Anthony J. Moffett (D)*	—	56.6	135,247	120,987
Thomas F. Upson (R)	—	43.0	85,131	84,682
DELAWARE				
AL Thomas B. Evans Jr. (R)	—	51.5	228,756	228,349
Samuel L. Shipley (D)	—	47.7	72,352	72,225
FLORIDA				
1 Robert L. F. Sikes (D)*	73.7	100.0	28,326	25,917
2 Don Fuqua (D)*	50.2	100.0	66,212	63,434
3 Charles E. Bennett (D)*	—	100.0	2,243	2,243
4 Bill Chappell Jr. (D)*	66.4	100.0	80,022	90,018
5 Richard Kelly (R)*	—	59.0	126,175	123,135
Jo Ann Saunders (D)	58.8**	41.0	82,658	82,642
6 C. W. Bill Young (R)*	—	65.2	66,426	65,050
Gabriel Cazares (D)	—	34.8	26,736	26,516
7 Sam M. Gibbons (D)*	—	65.7	29,725	24,443
Dusty Owens (R)	—	34.3	96,887	95,383
8 Andy Ireland (D)	50.2	58.0	144,800	144,362
Robert Johnson (R)	57.1**	42.0	68,609	67,881
9 Louis Frey Jr. (R)*	—	78.1	82,130	69,349
Joseph A. Rosier (D)	69.2	21.9	16,070	16,055
10 L. A. (Skip) Bafalis (R)*	—	66.3	100,809	100,045
Bill Sikes (D)	51.3	33.7	25,177	25,177
11 Paul G. Rogers (D)*	—	91.1	30,065	24,434
Clyde Adams (AP)	—	8.9	4,320	4,320
12 J. Herbert Burke (R)*	—	53.9	71,021	69,423
Charles Friedman (D)	52.8**	46.1	83,438	83,264
13 William Lehman (D)*	71.3	78.3	133,037	126,640
Lee Arnold Spiegelman (R)	—	21.7	19,837	19,532
14 Claude Pepper (D)*	—	72.9	57,795	45,650
Evelio S. Estrella (R)	57.2	27.1	14,683	14,683
15 Dante B. Fascell (D)*	—	70.4	32,029	28,351
Paul R. Cobb (R)	—	29.6	5,242	5,242
GEORGIA				
1 Ronald B. Ginn (D)*	—	99.9	24,233	13,644
2 Dawson Mathis (D)*	—	99.8	32,706	24,900
3 Jack Brinkley (D)*	—	88.7	54,846	54,628
Steve Dugan (R)	—	11.3	10,831	10,831
4 Elliott H. Levitas (D)*	—	68.3	128,460	113,332
George Warren (R)	—	31.7	37,254	34,373
5 Andrew Young (D)*	—	66.7	122,815	116,605
Ed Gadrix (R)	57.2	33.3	23,020	21,955
6 John J. Flynt Jr. (D)*	55.7	51.7	140,810	145,793
Newt Gingrich (R)	—	48.3	135,626	134,517
7 Lawrence P. McDonald (D)*	52.8	55.1	162,591	157,651
Quincy Collins (R)	—	44.9	73,177	72,638
8 Billy Lee Evans (D)	51.7**	69.7	158,636	157,208
Billy Adams (R)	—	30.3	174,299	173,763
9 Ed Jenkins (D)	55.1**	79.0	142,981	142,431
Louise Wofford (R)	—	20.9	8,307	8,301
10 Doug Barnard (D)	51.7**	99.9	146,953	144,870
HAWAII				
1 Cecil (Cec) Heftel (D)	47.2	43.6	561,644	555,381
Fred W. Rohlfing (R)	—	39.1	238,620	229,349
Kathy Hoshijo (I Godly Gov)	—	17.3	44,675	44.672
2 Daniel K. Akaka (D)	46.8	79.5	190,558	184,697
Hank Inouye (R)	52.4	15.3	7,510	7,413
IDAHO				
1 Steven D. Symms (R)*	—	54.6	152,824	135,341
Ken Pursley (D)	—	45.4	111,934	107,732
2 George V. Hansen (R)*	65.5	50.6	123,205	122,965
Stan Kress (D)	55.8	49.4	95,955	94,487
ILLINOIS				
1 Ralph H. Metcalfe (D)*	71.8	92.3	115,734	124,236
A. A. Rayner (R)	—	7.4	939	939
2 Morgan F. Murphy (D)*	72.9	84.7	47,725	26,957
Spencer Leak (R)	—	15.3	3,005	3,468
3 Martin A. Russo (D)*	—	58.9	177,772	169,348
Ronald Buikema (R)	58.6	40.5	219,156	219,156
4 Edward J. Derwinski (R)*	—	65.8	74,700	63,307
Ronald A. Rodger (D)	—	34.2	20,564	20,563
5 John G. Fary (D)*	—	76.9	55,302	54,296
Vincent Krok (R)	—	23.1	0	0
6 Henry J. Hyde (R)*	—	60.6	149,969	110,215
Marilyn D. Clancy (D)	65.5	39.4	77,811	76,017
7 Cardiss Collins (D)*	—	84.8	33,975	19,957
Newell Ward (R)	—	15.2	0	0
8 Dan Rostenkowski (D)*	—	80.5	92,344	51,536
John F. Urbaszewski (R)	76.6	19.5	1,342	1,342
9 Sidney R. Yates (D)*	—	72.1	25,263	11,749
Thomas J. Wajerski (R)	—	27.8	1,474	1,474
10 Abner J. Mikva (D)*	—	50.0	265,435	248,551
Samuel H. Young (R)	49.7	50.0	269,905	267,255
11 Frank Annunzio (D)*	—	67.4	82,176	77,220
Daniel C. Reber (R)	43.6	32.6	6,688	6,688
12 Philip M. Crane (R)*	—	72.8	123,441	118,561
E. L. Frank (D)	—	27.2	11,527	11,418
13 Robert McClory (R)*	—	66.8	66,336	53,666
James J. Cummings (D)	55.2	30.3	6,358	6,343
14 John N. Erlenborn (R)*	83.6	74.4	65,986	62,489
Marie Agnes Fese (D)	40.6	25.6	15,522	15,286
15 Tom Corcoran (R)	39.1	53.9	172,473	171,114
Tim L. Hall (D)	—	46.1	76,594	77,722
16 John B. Anderson (R)*	—	67.9	71,293	47,459
Stephen Eytalis (D)	—	32.1	553	553
17 George M. O'Brien (R)*	—	58.2	133,113	118,888
Merlin E. Karlock (D)	—	41.8	390,266	390,266
18 Robert H. Michel (R)*	—	57.7	76,215	60,317
Matthew Ryan (D)	64.2	42.3	37,555	37,312
19 Thomas F. Railsback (R)*	—	68.5	64,584	47,499
John Craver (D)	—	31.5	10,575	10,515
20 Paul Findley (R)*	90.0	63.6	140,587	123,422
Peter F. Mack Jr. (D)	—	36.4	21,724	21,724

	Per Cent of Primary Vote	Per Cent of General Election Vote	Receipts	Expenditures
21 Edward R. Madigan (R)*	—	74.5	78,228	54,243
Anna Wall Scott (D)	—	25.5	3,433	3,433
22 George E. Shipley (D)*	—	61.4	73,296	51,571
Ralph Y. McGinnis (R)	—	38.6	3,760	5,090
23 Melvin Price (D)*	—	78.6	34,138	34,009
Sam P. Drenovac (R)	—	21.4	281	281
24 Paul Simon (D)*	—	67.4	101,935	78,873
Peter G. Prineas (R)	—	32.6	18,992	13,109

INDIANA

	Per Cent of Primary Vote	Per Cent of General Election Vote	Receipts	Expenditures
1 Adam Benjamin Jr. (D)	56.0	71.3	111,447	111,391
Robert J. Billings (R)	73.8	28.7	79,468	78,366
2 Floyd Fithian (D)*	—	54.8	191,261	179,309
William W. Erwin (R)	53.8	44.5	190,413	188,118
3 John Brademas (D)*	76.8	56.9	183,134	165,905
Thomas L. Thorson (R)	59.7	43.1	45,384	45,214
4 Dan Quayle (R)	63.2	54.4	123,908	114,888
J. Edward Roush (D)*	86.7	44.6	63,614	63,399
5 Elwood H. Hillis (R)*	—	61.7	60,235	61,368
William C. Stout (D)	43.9	38.3	6,461	6,432
6 David W. Evans (D)*	90.3	54.9	102,381	99,024
David G. Crane (R)	54.5	45.1	193,016	179,863
7 John T. Myers (R)*	87.7	62.7	88,006	55,723
John Elden Tipton (D)	47.6	37.3	1,300	1,300
8 David L. Cornwell (D)	47.7	50.5	89,087	87,163
Belden Bell (R)	49.7	49.5	141,151	134,178
9 Lee H. Hamilton (D)*	—	100.0	68,768	46,537
10 Philip R. Sharp (D)*	88.5	59.8	90,305	85,620
William G. Frazier (R)	46.7	40.2	110,599	108,653
11 Andrew Jacobs Jr. (D)*	89.6	60.4	25,237	26,895
Lawrence L. Buell (R)	71.9	39.0	66,531	66,198

IOWA

	Per Cent of Primary Vote	Per Cent of General Election Vote	Receipts	Expenditures
1 James A. S. Leach (R)	—	51.9	202,237	199,590
Edward Mezvinsky (D)*	—	47.8	189,379	187,122
2 Michael T. Blouin (D)*	85.8	50.3	163,039	151,389
Tom Riley (R)	—	49.1	148,668	150,458
3 Charles E. Grassley (R)*	—	56.5	177,658	131,492
Stephen J. Rapp (D)	—	43.5	98,664	95,133
4 Neal Smith (D)*	—	69.1	38,682	34,416
Charles E. Minor (R)	—	30.9	19,313	19,190
5 Tom Harkin (D)*	—	64.9	169,930	146,642
Kenneth R. Fulk (R)	56.8	34.1	146,806	144,958
6 Berkley Bedell (D)*	—	67.4	87,933	88,715
Joanne D. Soper (R)	—	31.5	59,110	58,214

KANSAS

	Per Cent of Primary Vote	Per Cent of General Election Vote	Receipts	Expenditures
1 Keith G. Sebelius (R)*	—	73.1	84,383	72,217
Randy D. Yowell (D)	62.4	26.9	3,966	3,966
2 Martha E. Keys (D)*	—	50.7	126,730	119,277
Ross R. Freeman (R)	45.1	47.4	190,552	189,181
3 Larry Winn Jr. (R)*	—	68.7	85,001	45,437
Philip S. Rhoads (D)	—	29.0	2,543	2,637
4 Dan Glickman (D)	62.1	50.3	105,140	104,924
Garner E. Shriver (R)*	—	48.5	151,168	135,283
5 Joe Skubitz (R)*	82.2	60.7	80,963	57,142
Virgil L. Olson (D)	34.7	36.2	9,226	9,226

KENTUCKY

	Per Cent of Primary Vote	Per Cent of General Election Vote	Receipts	Expenditures
1 Carroll Hubbard Jr. (D)*	—	82.0	97,837	81,641
Bob Bersky (R)	56.4	18.0	2,460	2,460
2 William H. Natcher (D)*	—	60.4	8,162	8,162
Walter A. Baker (R)	—	39.6	51,917	51,856
3 Romano L. Mazzoli (D)*	55.8	57.2	94,345	95,344
Denzil J. Ramsey (R)	64.5	41.2	53,416	53,274
4 M. G. (Gene) Snyder (R)*	—	55.9	133,023	110,160
Edward J. Winterberg (D)	53.7	44.1	47,083	45,590
5 Tim Lee Carter (R)*	89.2	66.6	58,822	56,999
Charles C. Smith (D)	45.9	32.6	19,983	19,644
6 John Breckinridge (D)*	88.2	94.0	9,285	12,455
Anthony A. McCord (AP)	—	6.0	0	0
7 Carl D. Perkins (D)*	89.6	73.2	2,032	2,032
Granville Thomas (R)	—	26.8	0	0

LOUISIANA

	Per Cent of Primary Vote	Per Cent of General Election Vote	Receipts	Expenditures
1 Richard A. Tonry (D)	50.2**	47.2	224,914	220,495
Bob Livingston (R)	—	43.4	157,699	154,388
John R. Rarick (I)	—	9.4	36,451	36,451
2 Corinne (Lindy) Boggs (D)*	83.1	92.6	47,813	66,850
Jules W. Hillery (I)	—	7.4	163	163
3 David C. Treen (R)*	—	73.3	97,088	66,270
David H. Scheuermann Sr. (D)	66.5	26.7	10,655	10,615
4 Joe D. Waggonner Jr. (D)*	81.9	100.0	92,034	41,638
5 Jerry Huckaby (D)	52.7	52.5	224,048	217,031
Frank Spooner (R)	—	47.5	168,851	168,762
6 W. Henson Moore III (R)*	—	65.2	194,042	157,165
J. D. DeBlieux (D)	71.2	34.8	23,116	23,000
7 John B. Breaux (D)*	—	83.3	97,642	56,433
Charles F. Huff (R)	—	16.7	4,749	4,749
8 Gillis W. Long (D)*	—	94.2	146,433	62,188
Kent Courtney (I)	—	5.8	3,548	4,876

MAINE

	Per Cent of Primary Vote	Per Cent of General Election Vote	Receipts	Expenditures
1 David F. Emery (R)*	—	57.4	156,941	155,139
Frederick D. Barton (D)	23.5	42.6	124,293	124,236
2 William S. Cohen (R)*	—	77.1	98,350	81,342
Leighton Cooney (D)	—	19.7	16,779	16,641

MARYLAND

	Per Cent of Primary Vote	Per Cent of General Election Vote	Receipts	Expenditures
1 Robert E. Bauman (R)*	—	54.1	194,858	192,719
Roy Dyson (D)	62.1	45.9	58,504	58,023
2 Clarence D. Long (D)*	—	70.9	74,614	77,457
John M. Seney (R)	49.3	18.0	5,436	5,436
Ronald A. Meroney (I)	—	11.1	18,076	17,616
3 Barbara Mikulski (D)	43.8	74.6	79,000	72,418
Samuel A. Culotta (R)	36.5	25.4	8,701	8,632
4 Marjorie S. Holt (R)*	—	57.7	111,228	110,684
Werner Fornos (D)	29.6	42.3	40,460	39,989
5 Gladys N. Spellman (D)*	72.6	57.7	148,015	148,103
John B. Burcham Jr. (R)	70.6	42.3	103,513	98,149
6 Goodloe E. Byron (D)*	55.3	70.8	90,544	71,015
Arthur T. Bond (R)	—	29.2	13,390	13,165
7 Parren J. Mitchell (D)*	—	94.4	54,808	46,771
William Salisbury (I)	—	5.6	0	0
8 Newton Steers (R)	42.6	46.8	120,203	119,707
Lanny Davis (D)	27.2	42.2	190,389	188,555
Robin Ficker (I)	—	11.0	24,505	24,505

MASSACHUSETTS

	Per Cent of Primary Vote	Per Cent of General Election Vote	Receipts	Expenditures
1 Silvio O. Conte (R)*	—	63.8	86,272	74,486
Edward A. McColgan (D)	50.0	36.2	47,015	46,498
2 Edward P. Boland (D)*	—	72.4	47	47
Thomas P. Swank (R)	—	22.4	1,729	1,729
John D. McCarthy (USLP)	—	5.3	164	154
3 Joseph D. Early (D)*	—	100.0	52,690	42,300
4 Robert F. Drinan (D)*	—	52.1	222,769	219,297
Arthur D. Mason (R)	—	47.9	186,614	186,262
5 Paul E. Tsongas (D)*	—	67.3	132,392	101,228
Roger P. Durkin (R)	—	32.7	29,210	29,124
6 Michael J. Harrington (D)*	—	54.8	99,117	100,673
William E. Bronson (R)	60.0	41.3	45,184	44,084
7 Edward J. Markey (D)	21.4	76.9	111,411	114,583
Richard W. Daly (R)	—	17.6	3,632	3,612
8 Thomas P. O'Neill Jr. (D)*	71.9	74.4	99,556	88,045
William A. Barnstead (R)	—	18.7	6,057	6,057
9 John Joseph Moakley (D)*	67.4	69.6	133,950	118,268
Robert G. Cunningham (R)	—	23.1	132	132
Joseph M. O'Loughlin (I)	—	5.3	0	0
10 Margaret M. Heckler (R)*	—	100.0	43,948	26,867
11 James A. Burke (D)*	57.3	69.0	1,270	1,270
Danielle DeBenedictis (I)	—	31.0	27,640	27,160
12 Gerry E. Studds (D)*	84.3	100.0	104,963	80,458

MICHIGAN

	Per Cent of Primary Vote	Per Cent of General Election Vote	Receipts	Expenditures
1 John Conyers Jr. (D)*	85.9	92.4	20,827	21,757
Isaac Hood (R)	50.6	6.5	0	0

	Per Cent of Primary Vote	Per Cent of General Election Vote	Receipts	Expenditures
2 Carl D. Pursell (R)	57.4	49.8	104,653	98,778
Edward C. Pierce (D)	52.3	49.6	99,176	99,176
3 Garry Brown (R)*	64.2	50.6	90,737	81,363
Howard Wolpe (D)	60.6	48.6	116,228	116,654
4 David Stockman (R)	60.5	60.0	163,087	163,733
Richard E. Daugherty (D)	—	38.8	19,950	23,769
5 Harold S. Sawyer (R)	60.7	53.3	213,840	213,718
Richard F. Vander Veen (D)*	73.5	46.2	161,829	161,523
6 Bob Carr (D)*	—	52.7	159,867	142,935
Clifford W. Taylor (R)	—	46.5	195,731	190,476
7 Dale E. Kildee (D)	76.5	70.0	48,763	48,595
Robin Widgery (R)	—	28.3	44,438	44,300
8 Bob Traxler (D)*	—	59.0	158,930	140,502
E. Brady Denton (R)	58.0	40.4	128,366	127,238
9 Guy A. Vander Jagt (R)*	—	70.0	141,422	122,513
Stephen Fawley (D)	—	29.4	7,197	6,840
10 Elford A. Cederberg (R)*	—	56.5	116,459	121,518
Donald J. Albosta (D)	49.6	42.8	80,524	78,586
11 Philip E. Ruppe (R)*	82.2	54.8	167,677	163,887
Francis D. Brouillette (D)	—	44.8	95,062	94,859
12 David E. Bonior (D)	37.4	52.4	96,352	95,986
David M. Serotkin (R)	50.5	47.2	108,451	108,593
13 Charles C. Diggs Jr. (D)*	—	89.0	8,070	8,667
Richard A. Golden (R)	75.0	9.6	1	1
14 Lucien N. Nedzi (D)*	85.9	66.5	25,021	18,374
John Edward Getz (R)	—	32.8	2,240	2,159
15 William D. Ford (D)*	—	74.0	55,758	39,702
James D. Walaskay (R)	—	24.7	0	0
16 John D. Dingell Jr. (D)*	82.1	75.9	69,513	70,503
William E. Rostron (R)	—	22.7	0	0
17 William M. Brodhead (D)*	90.6	64.3	67,598	67,260
James W. Burdick (R)	—	34.5	122,898	122,562
18 James J. Blanchard (D)*	—	66.1	106,725	98,539
John E. Olsen (R)	57.7	32.8	11,452	11,315
19 William S. Broomfield (R)*	—	66.7	51,985	26,078
Dorothea Becker (D)	52.6	32.6	17,994	17,994

MINNESOTA

	Per Cent of Primary Vote	Per Cent of General Election Vote	Receipts	Expenditures
1 Albert H. Quie (I-R)*	—	68.2	54,426	40,063
Robert C. Olson Jr. (DFL)	54.3	30.5	1,307	1,330
2 Tom Hagedorn (I-R)*	—	60.3	159,761	121,010
Gloria Griffin (DFL)	—	39.7	74,423	74,283
3 Bill Frenzel (I-R)*	—	66.1	146,620	57,244
Jerome W. Coughlin (DFL)	61.0	32.0	8,915	8,303
4 Bruce F. Vento (DFL)	52.4	66.4	108,263	107,510
Andrew Engebretson (I-R)	55.9	29.8	21,356	20,634
5 Donald M. Fraser (DFL)*	93.3	70.7	82,376	71,128
Richard M. Erdall (I-R)	—	26.0	12,185	11,630
6 Richard M. Nolan (DFL)*	—	59.8	191,444	189,558
James Anderson (I-R)	—	40.2	112,098	110,895
7 Bob Bergland (DFL)*	—	72.0	95,352	92,793
Bob Leiseth (I-R)	—	26.6	16,746	14,075
8 James L. Oberstar (DFL)*	—	100.0	57,786	33,795

MISSISSIPPI

	Per Cent of Primary Vote	Per Cent of General Election Vote	Receipts	Expenditures
1 Jamie L. Whitten (D)*	—	100.0	1,525	1,525
2 David R. Bowen (D)*	—	63.0	46,861	35,349
Roland Byrd (R)	—	35.7	72,321	70,888
3 G. V. (Sonny) Montgomery (D)*	—	93.9	48,072	9,941
Dorothy Colby Cleveland (R)	—	6.1	0	0
4 Thad Cochran (R)*	—	76.0	60,936	42,053
Sterling P. Davis (D)	—	21.6	3,380	1,459
5 Trent Lott (R)*	—	68.2	180,629	182,585
Gerald Blessey (D)	—	31.8	102,193	101,144

MISSOURI

	Per Cent of Primary Vote	Per Cent of General Election Vote	Receipts	Expenditures
1 William Clay (D)*	54.7	65.5	40,511	32,576
Robert L. Witherspoon (R)	49.2	34.4	1,404	1,404
2 Robert A. Young (D)	48.1	51.1	135,412	124,793
Robert O. Snyder (R)	38.5	48.9	193,385	165,800
3 Richard A. Gephardt (D)	55.5	63.7	168,708	168,146
Joseph L. Badaracco (R)	66.5	36.3	65,319	61,862
4 Ike Skelton (D)	38.8	55.9	207,238	206,115
Richard A. King (R)	55.4	44.1	139,491	139,279
5 Richard Bolling (D)*	71.7	68.0	45,811	44,645

	Per Cent of Primary Vote	Per Cent of General Election Vote	Receipts	Expenditures
Joanne M. Collins (R)	50.7	28.1	16,968	16,925
6 E. Thomas Coleman (R)	—	58.5	101,776	97,294
Morgan Maxfield (D)	43.9	40.5	384,233	383,277
7 Gene Taylor (R)*	—	62.0	149,277	72,750
Dolan G. Hawkins (D)	—	38.0	2,374	2,374
8 Richard Ichord (D)*	—	67.3	71,472	40,472
Charles R. Leick (R)	—	30.6	12,690	12,690
9 Harold L. Volkmer (D)	34.3	55.9	109,468	109,405
J. H. Frappier (R)	66.9	44.1	89,461	85,829
10 Bill D. Burlison (D)*	69.6	72.1	46,862	31,616
Joe Carron (R)	75.8	27.9	3,914	3,914

MONTANA

	Per Cent of Primary Vote	Per Cent of General Election Vote	Receipts	Expenditures
1 Max S. Baucus (D)*	—	66.4	119,011	102,148
W. D. (Bill) Diehl (R)	—	33.6	86,625	86,387
2 Ron Marlenee (R)	39.2	55.0	205,435	205,216
Thomas E. Towe (D)	32.3	45.0	106,560	106,254

NEBRASKA

	Per Cent of Primary Vote	Per Cent of General Election Vote	Receipts	Expenditures
1 Charles Thone (R)*	—	73.2	148,411	102,990
Pauline F. Anderson (D)	—	26.8	24,196	24,196
2 John J. Cavanaugh (D)	—	54.6	133,942	133,888
Lee Terry (R)	44.1	45.4	116,810	115,666
3 Virginia Smith (R)*	74.0	72.9	76,497	74,642
James T. Hansen (D)	56.2	24.7	9,321	9,321

NEVADA

	Per Cent of Primary Vote	Per Cent of General Election Vote	Receipts	Expenditures
AL James Santini (D)*	—	77.1	173,627	158,510
Walden Charles Earhart (R)	29.3	12.1	209	209
Janine M. Hansen (IA)	—	6.0	4,637	4,545

NEW HAMPSHIRE

	Per Cent of Primary Vote	Per Cent of General Election Vote	Receipts	Expenditures
1 Norman E. D'Amours (D)*	—	68.1	94,102	80,126
John Adams (R)	39.3	30.4	0	0
2 James C. Cleveland (R)*	—	60.5	75,596	74,914
J. Joseph Grandmaison (D)	79.1	39.5	84,160	83,971

NEW JERSEY

	Per Cent of Primary Vote	Per Cent of General Election Vote	Receipts	Expenditures
1 James J. Florio (D)*	—	70.1	140,389	126,455
Joseph I. McCullough Jr. (R)	—	28.9	47,044	46,002
2 William J. Hughes (D)*	89.5	61.7	121,037	116,671
James R. Hurley (R)	86.2	38.3	63,977	62,703
3 James J. Howard (D)*	—	62.1	77,692	57,627
Ralph A. Siciliano (R)	76.6	37.1	19,339	19,339
4 Frank Thompson Jr. (D)*	—	66.3	51,780	48,181
Joseph S. Indyk (R)	—	32.1	19,114	19,114
5 Millicent Fenwick (R)*	—	66.9	61,338	59,082
Frank R. Nero (D)	—	31.3	38,309	37,339
6 Edwin B. Forsythe (R)*	—	58.8	74,055	63,541
Catherine A. Costa (D)	—	39.7	25,775	25,775
7 Andrew Maguire (D)*	—	56.5	188,198	163,715
James J. Sheehan (R)	48.3	43.5	114,154	113,359
8 Robert A. Roe (D)*	88.6	70.6	95,534	69,485
Bessie Doty (R)	—	29.0	6,623	6,623
9 Harold C. Hollenbeck (R)	—	53.1	54,286	53,608
Henry Helstoski (D)*	46.9	44.3	72,814	69,636
10 Peter W. Rodino Jr. (D)*	—	82.6	34,762	26,840
Tony Grandison (R)	—	16.0	105	53
11 Joseph G. Minish (D)*	—	67.6	101,023	62,853
Charles A. Poekel Jr. (R)	—	31.1	9,608	7,870
12 Matthew J. Rinaldo (R)*	—	73.1	195,831	156,693
Richard A. Buggelli (D)	66.6	26.3	17,394	17,669
13 Helen S. Meyner (D)*	80.9	50.4	128,178	114,862
William E. Schluter (R)	69.7	47.9	103,012	99,787
14 Joseph A. LeFante (D)	—	49.9	33,563	28,030
Anthony L. Campenni (R)	—	45.2	11,515	11,515
15 Edward J. Patten (D)*	—	59.0	29,086	24,950
Charles W. Wiley (R)	—	30.3	11,059	9,272
Dennis Adams Sr. (I)	—	8.1	25,046	24,725

	Per Cent of Primary Vote	Per Cent of General Election Vote	Receipts	Expenditures
NEW MEXICO				
1 Manuel Lujan Jr. (R)*	—	72.1	89,651	77,533
Raymond Garcia (D)	67.9	27.4	8,830	8,825
2 Harold Runnels (D)*	—	70.3	92,425	75,526
Donald W. Trubey (R)	—	29.7	19,171	18,839
NEW YORK				
1 Otis G. Pike (D,L)*	—	65.3	38,575	37,066
Salvatore Nicosia (R)	—	29.7	19,006	19,006
2 Thomas J. Downey (D,I)*	87.9	57.1	151,333	148,913
Peter Cohalan (R,C)	—	42.4	139,139	137,859
3 Jerome A. Ambro Jr. (D)*	—	52.0	60,949	60,230
Howard T. Hogan Jr. (R,C)	—	46.8	93,770	92,224
4 Norman F. Lent (R,C)*	—	55.8	83,642	83,008
Gerald P. Halpern (D,L)	—	44.2	47,614	45,761
5 John W. Wydler (R,C)*	—	55.7	97,282	90,568
Allard K. Lowenstein (D,L)	—	44.3	94,400	93,195
6 Lester L. Wolff (D,L)*	—	61.8	55,977	58,599
Vincent R. Balletta Jr. (R)	—	33.3	50,070	49,371
7 Joseph P. Addabbo (D,R,L)*	—	94.7	29,610	23,342
8 Benjamin S. Rosenthal (D,L)*	—	77.8	23,847	21,788
Albert Lemishow (R,C)	—	21.9	1,875	1,875
9 James J. Delaney (D,R,C)*	—	95.1	55,935	41,121
10 Mario Biaggi (D,R)*	—	91.6	71,758	66,271
Joanne S. Fuchs (C)	—	5.1	0	0
11 James H. Scheuer (D)*	71.3	74.1	39,222	37,141
Arthur Cuccia (R)	—	16.8	0	0
Bryan F. Levinson (C)	—	5.5	9,761	9,761
12 Shirley Chisholm (D,L)*	53.7	87.0	61,841	56,503
Horace Morancie (R)	—	10.8	5,723	5,723
13 Stephen J. Solarz (D,L)*	—	83.7	42,928	23,201
Jack N. Dobosh (R,C)	—	16.3	895	914
14 Frederick W. Richmond (D,L)*	79.3	85.0	47,240	36,991
Frank X. Gargiulo (R,C)	—	13.7	500	500
15 Leo C. Zeferetti (D,C)*	47.6	63.2	104,859	107,217
Ronald J. D'Angelo (R)	—	30.7	9,758	9,758
Arthur J. Paone (L)	—	6.0	14,492	14,350
16 Elizabeth Holtzman (D,L)*	—	82.9	22,556	24,679
Gladys Pemberton (R,C)	—	17.1	3,250	3,115
17 John M. Murphy (D)*	59.8	65.6	105,987	102,580
Kenneth J. Grossberger (R)	—	20.4	15,579	15,509
John M. Peters (C)	—	7.7	13,550	13,432
Ned Schneir (L)	—	6.4	3,940	3,921
18 Edward I. Koch (D,L)*	—	75.1	85,521	41,262
Sonia Landau (R)	—	19.9	9,923	9,923
19 Charles B. Rangel (D,R,L)*	—	97.0	53,521	48,970
20 Theodore S. Weiss (D,L)	—	83.2	24,663	24,170
Denise Weiseman (R)	—	12.8	0	0
21 Herman Badillo (D,R,L)*	73.5	98.6	63,437	63,759
22 Jonathan B. Bingham (D,L)*	86.0	86.4	10,422	12,788
Paul Slotkin (R)	—	10.4	2,589	2,589
23 Bruce F. Caputo (R,C)	—	53.6	197,612	192,520
J. Edward Meyer (D,L)	46.5	46.4	177,219	177,219
24 Richard L. Ottinger (D)*	—	54.5	61,744	61,406
David V. Hicks (R,C)	—	44.3	58,882	56,070
25 Hamilton Fish Jr. (R,C)*	89.5	70.6	62,548	57,088
Minna Post Peyser (D)	—	29.5	37,375	37,375
26 Benjamin A. Gilman (R)*	—	65.3	77,649	42,496
John R. Maloney (D)	36.6	32.9	9,017	8,361
27 Matthew F. McHugh (D,L)*	—	66.6	165,299	161,775
William H. Harter (R,C)	77.4	33.4	100,423	99,970
28 Samuel S. Stratton (D)*	—	79.0	7,300	12,089
Mary A. Bradt (R,C)	—	20.5	190	190
29 Edward W. Pattison (D,L)*	—	47.0	86,549	80,441
Joseph A. Martino (R)	55.1	45.0	59,839	61,547
James E. DeYoung (C)	—	7.2	31,937	31,661
30 Robert C. McEwen (R,C)*	—	55.7	42,794	43,303
Norma A. Bartle (D)	—	44.3	52,116	52,106
31 Donald J. Mitchell (R,C)*	—	66.5	81,701	59,607
Anita Maxwell (D)	—	33.5	15,052	14,855
32 James M. Hanley (D)*	—	54.8	91,373	95,671
George C. Wortley (R,C)	—	44.1	89,445	89,265
33 William F. Walsh (R)*	—	68.5	73,649	69,555
Charles R. Welch (D)	—	26.7	11,580	11,339
34 Frank J. Horton (R)*	—	65.9	50,305	51,532
William C. Larsen (D)	—	30.3	47,998	47,998
35 Barber B. Conable Jr. (R)*	—	64.3	39,474	32,575
Michael Macaluso (D,C)	—	35.7	16,213	16,183
36 John J. LaFalce (D,L)*	—	66.6	113,769	90,322
Ralph J. Argen (R,C)	—	33.4	150,970	157,047
37 Henry J. Nowak (D,L)*	75.8	78.2	35,003	27,644
Calvin Kimbrough (R)	—	18.5	2,443	2,443
38 Jack F. Kemp (R,C)*	—	78.2	84,448	73,243
Peter J. Geraci (D,L)	—	21.8	6,510	5,726
39 Stanley N. Lundine (D)*	—	61.8	170,506	158,091
Richard A. Snowden (R,C)	—	38.2	65,629	65,622
NORTH CAROLINA				
1 Walter B. Jones (D)*	65.7	75.9	34,295	27,780
Joseph M. Ward (R)	52.7	22.5	30,606	29,692
2 L. H. Fountain (D)*	51.6	99.8	89,597	88,696
3 Charlie Whitley (D)	53.6**	68.7	92,681	90,336
Willard J. Blanchard (R)	—	31.3	86,437	86,324
4 Ike F. Andrews (D)*	—	60.6	60,991	56,607
Johnnie L. Gallemore Jr. (R)	58.2	39.4	20,621	20,111
5 Stephen L. Neal (D)*	88.3	54.2	167,469	161,937
Wilmer D. Mizell (R)	—	45.6	166,270	161,338
6 Richardson Preyer (D)*	—	96.3	21,935	5,685
7 Charles Rose (D)*	—	81.3	35,578	31,333
M. H. (Mike) Vaughan (R)	—	18.7	9,107	7,332
8 W. G. (Bill) Hefner (D)*	—	65.7	55,473	51,985
Carl Eagle (R)	55.3	32.5	6,764	6,764
9 James G. Martin (R)*	—	53.5	151,788	145,751
Arthur Goodman Jr. (D)	75.6	46.1	29,033	28,818
10 James T. Broyhill (R)*	—	59.8	132,645	114,298
John J. Hunt (D)	62.3	40.2	53,419	53,357
11 Lamar Gudger (D)	51.9**	50.9	104,173	103,648
Bruce B. Briggs (R)	59.5	48.1	108,280	107,792
NORTH DAKOTA				
AL Mark Andrews (R)*	—	62.4	99,938	103,803
Lloyd Omdahl (D)	86.2	36.0	29,686	26,541
OHIO				
1 Willis D. Gradison Jr. (R)*	75.9	64.8	122,414	111,945
William F. Bowen (D)	—	33.6	37,053	37,053
2 Thomas A. Luken (D)	58.9	51.4	89,284	91,047
Donald D. Clancy (R)*	—	48.6	126,047	141,991
3 Charles W. Whalen Jr. (R)*	52.6	69.4	32,493	32,422
Leonard Stubbs (D)	—	23.3	1,683	1,606
4 Tennyson Guyer (R)*	—	70.1	36,575	22,789
Clinton G. Dorsey (D)	—	29.9	1,324	1,256
5 Delbert L. Latta (R)*	—	67.4	43,153	25,134
Bruce Edwards (D)	—	32.6	2,871	2,802
6 William H. Harsha (R)*	—	61.5	51,898	31,029
Ted Strickland (D)	43.2	38.5	21,174	20,692
7 Clarence J. Brown Jr. (R)*	—	64.9	82,356	50,512
Dorothy Franke (D)	—	35.1	2,605	2,428
8 Thomas N. Kindness (R)*	86.8	68.7	59,261	54,451
John W. Griffin (D)	—	28.8	2,257	2,257
9 Thomas L. Ashley (D)*	70.4	54.2	155,434	150,693
C. S. Finkbeiner (R)	—	44.0	140,400	141,314
10 Clarence E. Miller (R)*	—	68.8	21,795	19,920
James A. Plummer (D)	56.1	31.2	4,120	4,080
11 J. William Stanton (R)*	—	71.7	21,877	15,010
Thomas R. West Jr. (D)	43.0	28.3	7,435	7,417
12 Samuel L. Devine (R)*	—	46.5	131,517	134,680
Fran Ryan (D)	79.0	45.7	114,665	112,903
William R. Moss (I)	—	7.9	2,306	2,232
13 Don J. Pease (D)	67.4	66.0	68,469	57,758
Woodrow W. Mathna (R)	58.7	30.4	13,238	13,211
14 John F. Seiberling Jr. (D)*	86.2	74.1	20,924	21,635
James E. Houston (D)	—	24.3	12,405	12,391
15 Chalmers P. Wylie (R)*	—	65.5	71,568	69,601
Mike McGee (D)	50.2	34.5	12,008	11,776
16 Ralph S. Regula (R)*	—	66.8	87,566	59,954
John G. Freedom (D)	65.6	32.0	9,595	8,716
17 John M. Ashbrook (R)*	82.9	56.8	174,340	173,078
John C. McDonald (D)	—	43.2	92,880	96,406

	Per Cent of Primary Vote	Per Cent of General Election Vote	Receipts	Expenditures
18 Douglas Applegate (D)	—	62.9	40,879	27,394
Ralph R. McCoy (R)	—	24.6	12,219	12,219
William Crabbe (I)	—	11.6	7,335	7,335
19 Charles J. Carney (D)*	58.2	50.2	106,143	85,906
Jack C. Hunter (R)	93.1	47.9	75,796	76,044
20 Mary Rose Oakar (D)	23.9	81.0	103,142	101,949
Raymond J. Grabow (I)	—	16.9	64,063	64,063
21 Louis Stokes (D)*	77.5	83.8	45,766	45,452
Barbara Sparks (R)	—	11.3	1,063	1,063
22 Charles A. Vanik (D)*	93.9	72.7	65	65
Harry A. Hanna (R)	46.5	24.2	8,845	7,189
23 Ronald M. Mottl (D)*	92.9	73.2	36,637	17,238
Michael T. Scanlon (R)	76.6	26.8	23,161	22,836
OKLAHOMA				
1 James R. Jones (D)*	79.7	54.0	163,912	184,250
James M. Inhofe (R)	66.6	45.1	147,109	145,572
2 Theodore Risenhoover (D)*	51.4	54.0	154,401	123,109
E. L. (Bud) Stewart (R)	60.1	46.0	102,918	102,736
3 Wes Watkins (D)	63.2**	82.0	143,202	138,124
Gerald L. Beasley Jr. (R)	50.2	17.2	23,681	23,677
4 Tom Steed (D)*	—	74.9	22,970	20,273
M. C. Stanley (R)	54.0	22.0	7,134	7,134
5 M. H. Edwards (R)	50.2	49.9	346,907	330,064
Tom Dunlap (D)	52.9**	47.4	190,977	190,271
6 Glenn English (D)*	—	71.1	130,765	102,235
Carol McCurley (R)	57.5**	28.9	36,006	36,006
OREGON				
1 Les AuCoin (D)*	—	58.7	152,747	132,330
Philip N. Bladine (R)	—	41.3	94,750	94,547
2 Al Ullman (D)*	—	72.0	75,108	79,023
Thomas H. Mercer (R)	44.3	28.0	25,601	25,235
3 Robert Duncan (D)*	—	83.9	29,683	23,435
Martin Simon (I)	—	16.0	150	150
4 James Weaver (D)*	67.8	50.0	74,542	73,589
Jerry Lausmann (R)	70.8	35.1	114,460	112,483
Jim Howard (I)	—	9.0	14,562	14,399
Theodora Nathan (I)	—	5.8	10,077	9,968
PENNSYLVANIA				
1 Michael (Ozzie) Myers (D)	—	73.5	21,500	21,500
Samuel N. Fanelli (R)	55.9	25.2	2,990	2,990
2 Robert N. C. Nix (D)*	48.0	73.5	27,425	24,620
Jesse W. Woods Jr. (R)	—	25.4	4,075	4,072
3 Raymond F. Lederer (D)	57.0	73.2	46,508	45,430
Terrence J. Schade (R)	—	26.3	10,545	10,571
4 Joshua Eilberg (D)*	—	67.5	40,256	38,439
James E. Mugford (R)	—	32.5	5,489	5,489
5 Richard T. Schulze (R)*	—	59.5	74,207	73,960
Anthony Campolo (D)	63.4	40.5	26,071	25,850
6 Gus Yatron (D)*	—	73.8	59,871	53,124
Stephen Postupack (R)	63.5	25.5	8,214	8,222
7 Robert W. Edgar (D)*	—	54.1	130,708	129,172
John N. Kenney (R)	76.8	45.9	170,739	170,508
8 Peter H. Kostmayer (D)	36.3	49.5	58,697	58,481
John S. Renninger (R)	34.0	48.8	80,612	80,612
9 E. B. Shuster (R,D)	—	100.0	104,386	88,297
10 Joseph M. McDade (R)*	—	62.6	64,406	61,225
Edward Mitchell (D)	71.3	37.4	87,652	87,635
11 Daniel J. Flood (D)*	—	70.8	44,804	41,276
Howard G. Williams (R)	—	29.2	0	0
12 John P. Murtha (D)*	—	67.7	43,190	36,961
Ted Humes (R)	—	32.3	49,562	49,562
13 R. Lawrence Coughlin (R)*	—	63.4	75,691	69,920
Gertrude Strick (D)	66.5	36.6	42,881	35,565
14 William S. Moorhead (D)*	—	71.7	41,486	46,635
John F. Bradley (R)	—	27.1	779	779
15 Fred B. Rooney (D)*	—	65.2	78,724	44,605
Alice Sivulich (R)	—	34.5	3,260	3,149
16 Robert S. Walker (R)	19.5	62.3	32,483	29,241
Michael J. Minney (D)	—	37.0	13,430	13,409
17 Allen E. Ertel (D)	40.1	50.7	105,735	105,394
H. Joseph Hepford (R)	51.3	48.5	87,603	87,162
18 Douglas Walgren (D)	44.5	59.5	92,964	87,335
Robert J. Casey (R)	25.8	40.5	147,057	145,708
19 William F. Goodling (R)*	—	70.6	51,042	48,997
Richard P. Noll (D)	70.0	29.4	15,455	14,725
20 Joseph M. Gaydos (D)*	80.6	75.0	78,084	73,549
John P. Kostelac (R)	—	24.7	3,314	3,306
21 John H. Dent (D)*	62.7	59.4	115,153	82,277
Robert H. Miller (R)	—	40.6	34,064	33,704
22 Austin J. Murphy (D)	28.6	55.3	114,674	111,297
Roger Fischer (R)	—	43.9	32,476	31,220
23 Joseph S. Ammerman (D)	68.7	56.5	97,267	95,118
Albert W. Johnson (R)*	52.0	43.5	132,293	123,488
24 Marc L. Marks (R)	57.0	55.4	141,931	141,915
Joseph P. Vigorito (D)*	51.5	43.8	57,795	61,021
25 Gary A. Myers (R)*	—	56.8	41,594	42,658
Eugene V. Atkinson (D)	44.8	43.2	85,365	77,516
RHODE ISLAND				
1 Fernand J. St Germain (D)*	81.2	62.4	103,908	85,248
John J. Slocum Jr. (R)	—	36.4	106,284	106,114
2 Edward P. Beard (D)*	70.2	76.5	78,111	61,619
Thomas V. Iannitti (R)	—	22.5	43,037	42,336
SOUTH CAROLINA				
1 Mendel J. Davis (D)*	83.9	68.9	53,464	59,442
Lonnie Rowell (R)	—	31.1	1,800	1,751
2 Floyd D. Spence (R)*	—	57.5	87,583	59,672
Clyde B. Livingston (D)	—	41.8	0	0
3 Butler C. Derrick (D)*	—	99.9	31,901	21,504
4 James R. Mann (D)*	—	73.5	41,355	46,071
Robert L. Watkins (R)	64.5	26.4	3,798	3,798
5 Kenneth L. Holland (D)*	—	51.4	141,069	129,560
Bobby Richardson (R)	—	48.3	178,098	177,384
6 John W. Jenrette Jr. (D)*	57.5	55.5	274,847	278,457
Edward L. Young (R)	—	44.0	300,707	291,153
SOUTH DAKOTA				
1 Larry Pressler (R)*	—	79.8	112,626	106,680
James V. Guffey (D)	—	19.4	42,329	40,021
2 James Abdnor (R)*	—	69.9	122,653	108,896
Grace Mickelson (D)	—	30.1	48,513	48,481
TENNESSEE				
1 James H. (Jimmy) Quillen (R)*	89.1	57.9	60,750	55,915
Lloyd Blevins (D)	—	41.2	74,446	74,582
2 John J. Duncan (R)*	72.7	62.8	196,107	155,990
Mike Rowland (D)	65.6	37.2	90,825	90,798
3 Marilyn Lloyd (D)*	—	67.5	120,719	100,187
LaMar Baker (R)	90.3	31.1	70,752	69,715
4 Albert Gore Jr. (D)	32.0	94.0	197,363	188,560
William H. McGlamery (I)	—	6.0	0	0
5 Clifford R. Allen (D)*	87.8	92.4	105,942	96,684
Roger E. Bissell (I)	—	7.6	0	0
6 Robin L. Beard (R)*	—	64.5	222,884	222,656
Ross Bass (D)	62.0	35.5	84,220	83,368
7 Ed Jones (D)*	61.0	100.0	163,625	164,859
8 Harold E. Ford (D)*	—	60.7	177,932	147,288
A. D. Alissandratos (R)	90.4	38.5	126,375	126,154
TEXAS				
1 Sam B. Hall Jr. (D)*	52.6**	83.7	219,582	216,184
James Hogan (R)	68.6	16.3	12,881	12,881
2 Charles Wilson (D)*	65.8	95.0	116,776	106,983
James William Doyle III (AP)	—	5.0	2,110	2,110
3 James M. Collins (R)*	70.4	74.0	251,506	137,306
Les E. Shackelford Jr. (D)	70.4	26.0	8,736	8,736
4 Ray Roberts (D)*	85.0	62.7	63,870	76,102
Frank S. Glenn (R)	—	37.3	87,784	87,578
5 Jim Mattox (D)	60.9	54.0	261,212	257,744
Nancy Judy (R)	—	44.6	148,954	145,764
6 Olin E. Teague (D)*	54.3	65.9	238,321	250,330
Wes Mowery (R)	84.6	33.4	45,280	44,547
7 Bill Archer (R)*	—	100.0	19,451	10,751
8 Bob Eckhardt (D)*	81.5	60.7	115,333	125,587
Nick Gearhart (R)	—	39.2	303,158	302,587

	Per Cent of Primary Vote	Per Cent of General Election Vote	Receipts	Expenditures
9 Jack Brooks (D)*	—	99.9	78,331	32,689
10 J. J. (Jake) Pickle (D)*	82.3	76.8	77,744	45,721
Paul McClure (R)	56.6	23.2	13,882	13,882
11 W. R. Poage (D)*	73.2	57.4	33,900	42,967
Jack Burgess (R)	—	42.6	69,643	69,547
12 Jim Wright (D)*	—	75.8	146,351	49,004
W. R. Durham (R)	—	23.8	2,165	2,159
13 Jack Hightower (D)*	—	59.3	116,962	112,418
Bob Price (R)	—	40.4	99,465	85,364
14 John Young (D)*	—	61.4	40,715	16,835
L. Dean Holford (R)	—	38.6	44,891	44,612
15 Eligio de la Garza (D)*	74.4	74.4	73,751	70,626
R. L. (Lendy) McDonald (R)	—	25.6	14,118	14,118
16 Richard C. White (D)*	56.6	57.8	161,380	161,473
Vic Shackelford (R)	—	42.2	84,832	80,872
17 Omar Burleson (D)*	—	99.9	24,080	10,131
18 Barbara C. Jordan (D)*	—	85.5	74,677	36,585
Sam H. Wright (R)	—	14.0	4,459	4,459
19 George Mahon (D)*	—	54.6	131,071	124,855
Jim Reese (R)	—	45.4	165,446	164,794
20 Henry B. Gonzalez (D)*	—	100.0	18,288	18,214
21 Robert Krueger (D)*	85.9	71.0	127,175	104,175
Bobby A. Locke (R)	55.2	26.7	2,577	2,577
22 Bob Gammage (D)	64.6	50.1	253,572	249,956
Ron Paul (R)*	93.5	49.9	557,535	554,358
23 Abraham Kazen Jr. (D)*	—	100.0	34,433	5,968
24 Dale Milford (D)*	69.7	63.4	90,608	76,031
Leo Berman (R)	53.9	36.1	62,216	55,677
UTAH				
1 K. Gunn McKay (D)*	—	58.2	52,364	52,142
Joe H. Ferguson (R)	54.9	39.8	29,904	28,197
2 Dan Marriott (R)	68.7	52.4	120,440	119,349
Allan T. Howe (D)*	—	40.1	64,696	64,696
D. J. McCarty (Write-in)	—	7.4	27,990	27,918
VERMONT				
AL James M. Jeffords (R)*	—	67.4	80,359	62,770
John A. Burgess (D,IVT)	77.3	32.6	46,575	46,574
2				
VIRGINIA				
1 Paul S. Trible Jr. (R)	—	48.6	129,278	125,626
Robert E. Quinn (D)	49.4	47.5	176,782	175,843
2 G. William Whitehurst (R)*	—	65.7	112,037	104,659
Robert E. Washington (D)	69.6	34.3	58,400	54,341
3 David E. Satterfield III (D)*	—	87.9	4,604	1,599
A. R. Ogden (I)	—	11.9	75	75
4 Robert W. Daniel Jr. (R)*	—	53.0	97,698	93,836
J. W. (Billy) O'Brien (D)	56.5	47.0	94,386	93,734
5 W. C. (Dan) Daniel (D)*	—	100.0	4,210	1,373
6 M. Caldwell Butler (R)*	—	62.2	69,493	59,453
Warren D. Saunders (I)	—	37.8	53,940	53,833
7 J. Kenneth Robinson (R)*	—	81.6	54,019	42,724
James B. Hutt Jr. (I)	—	18.2	9,040	9,040
8 Herbert E. Harris (D)*	—	51.6	87,047	86,339
James R. Tate (R)	39.2	42.6	129,884	127,105

	Per Cent of Primary Vote	Per Cent of General Election Vote	Receipts	Expenditures
Michael D. Cannon (I)	—	5.8	617	513
9 William C. Wampler (R)*	—	57.3	127,359	126,354
Charles J. Horne (D)	—	42.6	86,186	86,045
10 Joseph L. Fisher (D)*	—	54.7	137,472	130,126
Vincent F. Callahan Jr. (R)	45.4	38.8	128,895	128,752
E. Stanley Rittenhouse (I)	—	6.4	1,595	1,552
WASHINGTON				
1 Joel Pritchard (R)*	—	71.9	66,619	70,204
Dave Wood (D)	66.4	25.8	13,725	13,725
2 Lloyd Meeds (D)*	76.9	49.3	167,273	157,259
John Nance Garner (R)	—	49.0	111,805	111,013
3 Don Bonker (D)*	—	70.8	52,322	36,125
Chuck Elhart (R)	70.7	28.0	8,691	8,680
4 Mike McCormack (D)*	—	57.8	116,609	103,123
Dick Granger (R)	44.8	41.0	102,632	100,015
5 Thomas S. Foley (D)*	—	58.0	77,287	46,418
Duane Alton (R)	—	40.6	12,614	12,582
6 Norman D. Dicks (D)	35.0	73.5	145,792	140,816
Robert M. Reynolds (R)	45.5	25.3	5,395	5,301
7 Brock Adams (D)*	92.3	73.0	52,708	81,874
Raymond Pritchard (R)	65.1	25.4	2,269	2,269
WEST VIRGINIA				
1 Robert H. Mollohan (D)*	—	58.0	37,648	36,188
John F. McCuskey (R)	67.7	42.0	52,144	56,623
2 Harley O. Staggers (D)*	—	73.2	10,346	10,346
Jim Sloan (R)	—	26.8	6,657	6,656
3 John M. Slack (D)*	88.0	99.7	48,065	16,641
4 Nick J. Rahall (D)	34.8	45.6	345,082	336,301
Ken Hechler (Write-in)*	—	36.6	276,710	273,487
E. S. (Steve) Goodman (R)	—	17.8	13,694	13,518
WISCONSIN				
1 Les Aspin (D)*	—	64.9	36,824	33,280
William W. Petrie (R)	—	34.0	19,908	20,004
2 Robert W. Kastenmeier (D)*	—	65.6	22,873	25,762
Elizabeth T. Miller (R)	—	34.4	14,271	13,779
3 Alvin J. Baldus (D)*	—	58.1	131,432	131,399
Adolf L. Gundersen (R)	89.8	41.9	202,489	200,882
4 Clement J. Zablocki (D)*	87.8	100.0	11,177	6,153
5 Henry S. Reuss (D)*	63.5	77.8	68,679	55,442
Robert L. Hicks (R)	—	21.0	2,463	2,463
6 William A. Steiger (R)*	—	63.3	86,587	79,659
Joseph C. Smith (D)	—	36.6	27,620	27,620
7 David R. Obey (D)*	—	73.3	52,717	46,038
Frank A. Savino (R)	—	26.1	20,778	20,689
8 Robert J. Cornell (D)*	71.9	50.9	87,061	75,024
Harold V. Froehlich (R)	61.1	46.9	94,685	99,732
9 Robert W. Kasten Jr. (R)*	—	65.9	121,406	97,591
Lynn M. McDonald (D)	—	34.1	17,701	17,446
WYOMING				
AL Teno Roncalio (D)*	85.9	56.4	103,042	116,024
Larry Joe Hart (R)	—	43.6	33,143	31,824

Senate Receipts, Expenditures for 1978 Races

	Percent of Primary Vote	Percent of General Election Vote	Receipts	Expenditures
ALABAMA				
(Six-year term)				
Howell Heflin (D)†	64.9**	94.0	$1,107,015	$1,059,113
Jerome B. Couch (P)	—	6.0	NA	NA
(Two-year term)				
Donald Stewart (D)†	57.2**	54.9	823,619	816,456
James D. Martin (R)	—	43.2	539,267	552,504

	Percent of Primary Vote	Percent of General Election Vote	Receipts	Expenditures
ALASKA				
Donald W. Hobbs (D)	55.0	24.1	15,527	21,234
Ted Stevens (R)†*	—	75.6	366,895	346,837
ARKANSAS				
David Pryor (D)†	54.9**	76.5	802,861	774,824
Thomas Kelly Jr. (R)	—	16.3	16,210	16,208
John G. Black (I)	—	7.2	32,863	32,863

	Percent of Primary Vote	Percent of General Election Vote	Receipts	Expenditures
COLORADO				
Floyd K. Haskell (D)*	—	40.3	658,657	664,249
William L. Armstrong (R)†	73.4	58.7	1,163,790	1,081,944
DELAWARE				
Joseph R. Biden Jr. (D)†*	—	58.0	487,637	487,504
James H. Baxter (R)	53.7	41.0	207,637	206,250
GEORGIA				
Sam Nunn (D)†*	80.0	83.1	708,417	548,814
John W. Stokes (R)	58.5	16.9	7,291	6,640
IDAHO				
Dwight Jensen (D)	—	31.6	55,163	55,163
James A. McClure (R)†*	—	68.4	378,084	385,536
ILLINOIS				
Alex R. Seith (D)	69.5	45.5	1,370,457	1,371,185
Charles H. Percy (R)†*	84.3	53.3	2,185,153	2,163,555
IOWA				
Dick Clark (D)*	80.5	47.9	862,635	860,774
Roger Jepsen (R)†	57.3	51.1	738,581	728,268
KANSAS				
Bill Roy (D)	76.7	42.4	824,537	813,754
Nancy Landon Kassebaum (R)†	30.6	53.9	864,288	856,644
KENTUCKY				
Walter (Dee) Huddleston (D)†*	75.6	61.0	395,557	456,432
Louie R. Guenthner (R)	47.2	36.9	77,012	76,445
LOUISIANA				
J. Bennett Johnston Jr. (D)†*	59.4	100.0	983,343	857,860
MAINE				
William D. Hathaway (D)*	—	33.9	423,499	423,027
William S. Cohen (R)†	—	56.6	658,254	648,739
Hayes E. Gahagan (I)	—	7.4	115,903	115,901
MASSACHUSETTS				
Paul E. Tsongas (D)†	32.9	55.1	772,513	768,383
Edward W. Brooke (R)*	51.9	44.8	957,252	1,284,855
MICHIGAN				
Carl Levin (D)†	38.9	52.1	994,439	971,775
Robert P. Griffin (R)*	78.3	47.9	1,691,534	1,681,550
MINNESOTA (Six-year term)				
Wendell R. Anderson (D)*	56.9	40.4	1,155,562	1,154,351
Rudy Boschwitz (R)†	86.8	56.6	1,902,861	1,870,163
(Four-year term)				
Robert E. Short (D)	48.0	34.6	$1,982,442	$1,972,060
David Durenberger (R)†	67.3	61.5	1,073,135	1,062,271
MISSISSIPPI				
Maurice Dantin (D)	65.3**	31.8	874,590	873,518
Thad Cochran (R)†	69.0	45.1	1,201,259	1,052,303
Charles Evers (I)	—	22.9	142,684	135,119
MONTANA				
Max Baucus (D)†	65.3	55.7	668,189	653,756
Larry Williams (R)	61.7	44.3	352,848	346,721
NEBRASKA				
J.J. Exon (D)†	—	67.7	262,404	234,862
Donald E. Shasteen (R)	78.5	32.3	222,190	218,148
NEW HAMPSHIRE				
Thomas J. McIntyre (D)*	80.7	48.5	298,608	289,628
Gordon Humphrey (R)†	50.4	50.7	366,632	357,107
NEW JERSEY				
Bill Bradley (D)†	58.9	55.3	1,689,975	1,688,499
Jeffrey Bell (R)	50.7	43.1	1,432,924	1,418,931
NEW MEXICO				
Toney Anaya (D)	—	46.6	175,659	175,633
Pete V. Domenici (R)†*	—	53.4	925,622	914,634
NORTH CAROLINA				
John R. Ingram (D)	54.2**	45.5	261,982	264,088
Jesse Helms (R)†*	—	54.5	7,463,282	7,460,966
OKLAHOMA				
David L. Boren (D)†	60.5	65.5	779,544	751,286
Robert Kamm (R)	—	32.9	444,734	443,712
OREGON				
Vern Cook (D)	58.7	38.3	38,977	38,976
Mark O. Hatfield (R)†*	65.7	61.6	277,059	223,874
RHODE ISLAND				
Claiborne Pell (D)†*	87.0	75.1	398,898	373,077
James G. Reynolds (R)	—	24.9	85,615	85,614
SOUTH CAROLINA				
Charles D. (Pug) Ravenel (D)	55.9	44.4	1,145,542	1,134,168
Strom Thurmond (R)†*	—	55.6	1,753,628	2,013,431
SOUTH DAKOTA				
Don Barnett (D)	55.1	33.2	152,665	152,006
Larry Pressler (R)†	73.9	66.8	489,983	449,541
TENNESSEE				
Jane Eskind (D)	34.5	40.3	1,906,603	1,903,532
Howard H. Baker Jr. (R)†*	83.4	55.5	1,946,071	1,922,573
TEXAS				
Robert (Bob) Krueger (D)	54.9	49.3	2,431,204	2,428,666
John G. Tower (R)†*	—	49.8	4,264,015	4,324,601
VIRGINIA				
Andrew P. Miller (D)	—	49.8	850,313	832,773
John W. Warner (R)†	—	50.2	2,907,073	2,897,237
WEST VIRGINIA				
Jennings Randolph (D)†*	80.5	50.5	732,484	684,605
Arch A. Moore Jr. (R)	90.6	49.5	474,218	458,823
WYOMING				
Raymond B. Whitaker (D)	47.6	37.8	143,051	142,749
Alan K. Simpson (R)†	54.7	62.2	442,484	439,805

House Receipts, Expenditures for 1978 Races

	Percent of Primary Vote	Percent of General Election Vote	Receipts	Expenditures
ALABAMA				
1 L. W. (Red) Noonan (D)	61.4	36.1	85,775	85,773
Jack Edwards (R)*	—	63.9	158,770	166,456
2 Wendell Mitchell (D)	58.3	46.0	115,823	115,372
William L. Dickinson (R)*	—	54.0	137,003	139,313
3 Bill Nichols (D)*	—	100.0	17,162	13,112

	Percent of Primary Vote	Percent of General Election Vote	Receipts	Expenditures
4 Tom Bevill (D)*	93.5	100.0	18,480	8,413
5 Ronnie G. Flippo (D)*	91.7	96.8	72,037	41,660
6 Don Hawkins (D)	50.6	38.3	20,238	20,238
John Buchanan (R)*	57.5	61.7	124,079	123,808
7 Richard C. Shelby (D)	61.3**	95.9	181,573	181,405
ALASKA				
AL Patrick Rodey (D)	—	44.4	150,279	149,211
Don Young (R)*	—	55.4	259,897	270,359
ARIZONA				
1 Ken Graves (D)	56.3	29.0	6,411	6,306
John J. Rhodes (R)*	—	71.0	200,661	201,177
2 Morris K. Udall (D)*	—	52.5	295,268	294,849
Tom Richey (R)	72.6	45.4	139,491	134,130
3 Bob Stump (D)*	70.7	85.0	200,305	198,085
Kathleen Cooke (LIBERT)	—	15.0	0	0
4 Michael L. McCormick (D)	34.6	33.8	23,548	23,548
Eldon Rudd (R)*	84.0	63.1	227,908	178,134
ARKANSAS				
1 Bill Alexander (D)*	—	100.0	50,015	37,844
2 Doug Brandon (D)	52.1**	48.8	338,387	329,590
Ed Bethune (R)	—	51.2	255,176	255,098
3 William C. Mears (D)	—	25.5	4,235	3,981
John Paul Hammerschmidt (R)*	—	74.5	64,368	47,521
4 Beryl F. Anthony Jr. (D)	52.0**	100.0	374,165	372,652
CALIFORNIA				
1 Harold T. Johnson (D)*	72.7	59.4	27,329	26,260
James E. Taylor (R)	59.6	40.6	10,012	10,617
2 Norma Bork (D)	41.9	45.3	81,745	80,437
Don H. Clausen (R)*	—	52.0	213,598	200,924
3 Robert T. Matsui (D)	36.0	53.4	468,263	468,028
Sandy Smoley (R)	62.9	46.6	328,049	329,408
4 Vic Fazio (D)	57.1	55.4	235,605	235,600
Rex Hime (R)	36.8	44.6	138,479	138,085
5 John L. Burton (D)*	—	66.8	128,772	88,923
Dolores Skore (R)	—	33.2	3,307	3,306
6 Phillip Burton (D)*	—	68.3	96,039	96,933
Tom Spinosa (R)	—	28.0	3,246	2,756
7 George Miller (D)*	—	63.4	70,435	65,404
Paula Gordon (R)	64.5	33.7	57,805	57,786
8 Ronald V. Dellums (D)*	—	57.4	76,577	75,945
Charles V. Hughes (R)	—	42.6	7,185	7,933
9 Fortney H. (Pete) Stark (D)*	78.4	65.4	45,194	24,697
Robert S. Allen (R)	—	30.5	7,236	7,234
10 Don Edwards (D)*	—	67.1	33,531	31,740
Rudy Hansen (R)	54.8	32.9	25,128	25,124
11 Leo J. Ryan (D)*	74.7	60.5	41,705	40,588
David Welch (R)	69.2	35.6	27,710	26,229
12 Kirsten Olsen (D)	57.4	21.5	54,572	54,203
Paul N. McCloskey Jr. (R)*	76.1	73.1	85,663	56,144
13 Norman Y. Mineta (D)*	—	57.5	195,359	176,628
Dan O'Keefe (R)	—	39.5	54,946	54,741
14 John J. McFall (D)*	69.4	42.6	215,428	240,114
Norman D. Shumway (R)	37.5	53.4	272,282	251,948
15 Tony Coelho (D)	79.0	60.1	304,513	266,094
Chris Patterakis (R)	49.2	39.9	105,707	104,164
16 Leon E. Panetta (D)*	—	61.4	227,374	219,357
Eric Seastrand (R)	—	38.6	184,543	184,169
17 John Krebs (D)*	—	45.5	142,865	156,932
Charles (Chip) Pashayan Jr. (R)	64.9	54.5	268,247	260,412
18 Bob Sogge (D)	—	40.7	143,998	142,280
William Thomas (R)	—	59.3	186,836	166,534
19 Jerome Zamos (D)	—	24.3	14,196	14,042
Robert J. Lagomarsino (R)*	—	71.7	126,841	95,044
20 Pat Lear (D)	63.9	33.6	236,643	229,306
Barry M. Goldwater Jr. (R)*	—	66.4	151,582	122,120
21 James C. Corman (D)*	—	59.5	239,004	241,423
G. (Rod) Walsh (R)	43.1	35.9	25,801	25,429
22 Robert S. Henry (D)	—	35.4	13,714	13,386
Carlos J. Moorhead (R)*	80.7	64.6	72,403	56,371
23 Anthony C. (Tony) Beilenson (D)*	80.5	65.6	68,700	47,776
Joseph Barbara (R)	—	34.4	9,172	9,170
24 Henry A. Waxman (D)*	80.5	62.7	18,472	26,019
Howard G. Schaefer (R)	68.3	32.6	46,138	48,400
25 Edward R. Roybal (D)*	—	67.4	76,920	41,232
Robert K. Watson (R)	—	32.6	575	575
26 John H. Rousselot (R)*	—	100.0	115,864	54,386
27 Carey Peck (D)	66.1	49.0	308,573	308,017
Robert K. Dornan (R)*	—	51.0	292,615	291,762
28 Julian C. Dixon (D)	48.0	100.0	233,910	231,444
29 Augustus F. Hawkins (D)*	—	85.0	20,925	13,887
Uriah J. Fields (R)	—	15.0	6,609	6,602
30 George E. Danielson (D)*	—	71.4	82,516	98,834
Henry Ares (R)	—	28.6	50,820	50,823
31 Charles H. Wilson (D)*	39.8	67.8	134,041	139,728
Dan Grimshaw (R)	63.3	32.2	3,047	2,928
32 Glenn M. Anderson (D)*	—	71.4	91,260	109,228
Sonya (Sonny) Mathison (R)	—	22.4	2,313	2,185
Ida Bader (AM I)	—	6.1	4,400	3,898
33 Dennis S. Kazarian (D)	22.3	44.0	124,901	109,248
Wayne Grisham (R)	24.2	56.0	162,707	162,423
34 Mark W. Hannaford (D)*	69.1	43.7	326,710	329,904
Daniel E. Lungren (R)	69.7	53.7	270,917	268,604
35 Jim Lloyd (D)*	—	54.0	147,742	147,556
David Dreier (R)	41.5	46.0	152,748	152,315
36 George E. Brown Jr. (D)*	—	62.9	40,562	39,914
Dana Warren Carmody (R)	—	37.1	11,183	11,179
37 Dan Corcoran (D)	58.3	34.8	50,035	50,005
Jerry Lewis (R)	54.8	61.4	159,553	159,433
38 Jerry M. Patterson (D)*	—	58.6	136,668	134,557
Don Goedeke (R)	30.0	41.4	61,769	61,319
39 William E. Farris (D)	54.6	36.3	49,760	47,172
William E. Dannemeyer (R)	—	63.7	161,204	161,151
40 Jim McGuy (D)	—	34.1	5,147	5,182
Robert E. Badham (R)*	—	65.9	95,770	51,719
41 King Golden Jr. (D)	44.4	41.9	26,330	26,331
Bob Wilson (R)*	—	58.1	142,048	118,820
42 Lionel Van Deerlin (D)*	81.8	73.7	84,871	72,903
Lawrence C. Mattera (R)	—	26.3	17,064	16,833
43 Ruben B. Brooks (D)	38.6	31.3	8,720	8,511
Clair W. Burgener (R)*	75.3	68.7	93,368	90,072
COLORADO				
1 Patricia Schroeder (D)*	—	61.5	145,556	119,930
Gene Hutcheson (R)	55.0	37.0	154,739	146,210
2 Timothy E. Wirth (D)*	—	52.9	416,585	396,798
Ed Scott (R)	—	47.1	560,325	554,538
3 Ray Kogovsek (D)	66.4	49.3	121,678	121,323
Harold L. McCormick (R)	44.8	49.0	86,277	81,500
4 Morgan Smith (D)	—	38.8	163,026	160,520
James P. (Jim) Johnson (R)*	63.7	61.2	84,336	92,842
5 Gerry Frank (D)	—	34.4	63,462	63,325
Ken Kramer (R)	53.5	59.8	162,156	161,413
L. W. Dan Bridges (I)	—	5.8	43,979	43,978
CONNECTICUT				
1 William R. Cotter (D)*	—	59.5	114,320	96,791
Ben F. Andrews Jr. (R)	—	39.3	55,340	54,733
2 Christopher J. Dodd (D)*	—	69.9	134,263	125,326
Thomas H. Connell (R)	—	30.1	18,622	17,714
3 Robert N. Giaimo (D)*	—	58.1	140,198	157,304
John G. Pucciano (R)	—	40.0	100,845	102,667
Joelle R. Fishman (COM)	—	1.8	13,539	12,548
4 Michael G. Morgan (D)	—	41.6	50,784	51,744
Stewart B. McKinney (R)*	—	58.4	125,012	123,628
5 William R. Ratchford (D)	—	52.3	139,970	139,778
George C. Guidera (R)	—	47.7	245,653	245,933
6 Toby Moffett (D)*	—	64.2	168,174	162,006
Daniel F. MacKinnon (R)	—	35.8	86,011	83,896
DELAWARE				
AL Gary E. Hindes (D)	—	41.2	57,329	57,252
Thomas B. Evans Jr. (R)*	—	58.2	242,546	241,410

	Percent of Primary Vote	Percent of General Election Vote	Receipts	Expenditures
FLORIDA				
1 Earl D. Hutto (D)	61.6**	63.3	119,866	118,847
Warren Briggs (R)	—	36.7	192,916	186,711
2 Don Fuqua (D)*	85.5	81.7	101,759	88,381
Peter L. W. Brathwaite (R)	—	18.3	20,081	19,379
3 Charles E. Bennett (D)*	—	100.0	2,890	2,890
4 Bill Chappell Jr. (D)*	—	73.1	112,243	87,346
Tom Boney (R)	—	26.9	9,520	9,118
5 David R. Best (D)	56.8**	48.9	149,414	149,383
Richard Kelly (R)*	—	51.1	187,390	182,597
6 James A. Christison (D)	—	21.2	128,579	128,579
C. W. Bill Young (R)*	—	78.8	65,801	57,482
7 Sam Gibbons (D)*	69.0	100.0	89,415	65,558
8 Andy Ireland (D)*	—	100.0	115,297	102,265
9 Bill Nelson (D)	85.9	61.5	320,591	313,325
Edward J. Gurney (R)	70.3	38.5	215,090	212,679
10 L. A. (Skip) Bafalis (R)*	—	100.0	44,550	22,007
11 Dan Mica (D)	51.0	55.3	159,002	158,573
Bill James (R)	—	44.7	251,610	228,969
12 Edward J. Stack (D)	53.2**	61.6	134,163	133,351
J. Herbert Burke (R)*	58.3	38.4	63,463	74,967
13 William Lehman (D)*	—	100.0	109,179	70,087
14 Claude Pepper (D)*	81.0	63.1	242,260	239,864
Al Cardenas (R)	79.9	36.9	243,568	242,131
15 Dante B. Fascell (D)*	—	74.2	48,499	47,724
Herbert J. Hoodwin (R)	—	25.8	70,066	69,590
GEORGIA				
1 Bo Ginn (D)*	—	100.0	99,233	58,340
2 Dawson Mathis (D)*	76.7	100.0	92,906	100,914
3 Jack Brinkley (D)*	—	100.0	45,843	14,531
4 Elliott H. Levitas (D)*	84.4	80.9	95,240	94,745
Homer Cheung (R)	—	19.1	0	0
5 Wyche Fowler Jr. (D)*	79.5	75.5	165,267	142,684
Thomas P. Bowles Jr. (R)	67.8	24.5	30,283	27,374
6 Virginia Shapard (D)	52.0**	45.6	318,035	313,056
Newt Gingrich (R)	74.7	54.4	225,863	219,336
7 Larry P. McDonald (D)*	51.5**	66.5	344,150	331,925
Ernie Norsworthy (R)	63.1	33.5	8,788	9,767
8 Billy Lee Evans (D)*	—	100.0	194,037	186,027
9 Ed Jenkins (D)*	62.2	76.9	128,237	127,124
David G. Ashworth (R)	—	23.1	16,182	16,163
10 Doug Barnard (D)*	71.9	100.0	65,186	41,709
HAWAII				
1 Cecil (Cec) Heftel (D)*	87.3	73.3	175,083	174,306
William D. Spillane (R)	63.5	21.2	2,860	18,694
Peter D. Larsen (LIBERT)	—	3.7	7,698	5,756
2 Daniel K. Akaka (D)*	—	85.7	210,574	208,958
Charles Isaak (R)	—	11.4	8,317	7,016
IDAHO				
1 Roy Truby (D)	—	40.1	113,351	112,361
Steven D. Symms (R)*	—	59.9	266,037	278,503
2 Stan Kress (D)	61.7	42.7	149,817	150,956
George Hansen (R)*	56.6	57.3	284,650	282,203
ILLINOIS				
1 Bennett Stewart (D)	—	58.5	20,621	18,471
A. A. Rayner (R)	—	41.3	15,460	13,622
2 Morgan F. Murphy (D)*	—	86.0	56,719	43,328
James Wognum (R)	—	11.8	NA	NA
3 Marty Russo (D)*	—	65.2	217,245	219,377
Robert L. Dunne (R)	—	34.8	115,881	113,083
4 Andrew D. Thomas (D)	54.5	33.1	74,316	73,437
Edward J. Derwinski (R)*	—	66.9	90,635	72,941
5 John G. Fary (D)*	—	84.0	42,745	37,315
Joseph A. Barracca (R)	—	16.0	715	1,096
6 Jeanne P. Quinn (D)	70.4	33.8	5,882	6,834
Henry J. Hyde (R)*	—	66.2	154,079	153,066
7 Cardiss Collins (D)*	71.8	86.3	18,925	34,857
James C. Holt (R)	—	13.7	15,474	13,610
8 Dan Rostenkowski (D)*	—	86.0	185,773	150,266
Carl C. LoDico (R)	—	14.0	4,460	4,444

	Percent of Primary Vote	Percent of General Election Vote	Receipts	Expenditures
9 Sidney R. Yates (D)*	87.2	75.3	1,400	14,870
John M. Collins (R)	—	24.7	1,530	2,126
10 Abner J. Mikva (D)*	—	50.2	408,016	385,007
John E. Porter (R)	50.4	49.8	547,198	536,515
11 Frank Annunzio (D)*	87.3	73.7	89,372	82,201
John Hoeger (R)	72.0	26.3	6,680	6,164
12 Gilbert Bogen (D)	—	20.5	4,100	4,100
Philip M. Crane (R)*	—	79.5	209,722	191,075
13 Frederick J. Steffen (D)	58.7	38.8	84,186	82,216
Robert McClory (R)*	59.2	61.2	93,672	111,477
14 James A. Romanyak (D)	—	24.9	4,290	4,098
John N. Erlenborn (R)*	—	75.1	81,821	52,212
15 Tim L. Hall (D)	88.2	37.6	21,073	21,368
Tom Corcoran (R)	—	62.4	180,387	180,076
16 Ernest W. Dahlin (D)	—	34.5	17,257	17,257
John B. Anderson (R)*	57.9	65.4	226,834	232,379
17 Clifford J. Sinclair (D)	—	29.4	15,984	14,808
George M. O'Brien (R)*	—	70.6	118,350	112,346
18 Virgil R. Grunkemeyer (D)	—	34.1	509	498
Robert H. Michel (R)*	—	65.9	72,330	57,439
19 Tom Railsback (R)*	—	100.0	38,529	28,647
20 Victor W. Roberts (D)	54.0	30.4	7,320	7,318
Paul Findley (R)*	—	69.6	126,180	117,721
21 Kenneth E. Baughman (D)	—	21.7	1,955	1,955
Edward R. Madigan (R)*	—	78.3	89,033	78,219
22 Terry L. Bruce (D)	47.8	46.0	109,465	107,281
Daniel B. Crane (R)	46.1	54.0	439,305	438,764
23 Melvin Price (D)*	88.1	74.2	29,955	42,416
Daniel J. Stack (R)	71.4	25.8	12,578	12,298
24 Paul Simon (D)*	—	65.6	92,362	99,017
John T. Anderson (R)	75.0	34.4	14,022	13,998
INDIANA				
1 Adam Benjamin Jr. (D)*	90.9	80.3	90,186	77,483
Owen W. Crumpacker (R)	51.4	19.3	30,378	26,459
2 Floyd Fithian (D)*	—	56.5	206,213	196,945
J. Philip Oppenheim (R)	—	36.2	138,223	136,475
William Costas (I)	—	6.4	51,794	47,312
3 John Brademas (D)*	—	55.5	262,665	251,394
Thomas L. Thorson (R)	71.3	43.3	103,295	102,766
4 John D. Walda (D)	54.6	33.8	68,205	59,155
Dan Quayle (R)*	—	64.4	155,504	142,446
Terry Hively (AM)	—	1.9	5,177	4,461
5 Max E. Heiss (D)	47.8	32.4	2,490	2,504
Elwood Hillis (R)*	—	67.6	102,574	72,873
6 David W. Evans (D)*	—	52.2	213,048	180,870
David G. Crane (R)	68.5	47.6	422,812	431,943
7 Charlotte Zietlow (D)	45.8	43.7	162,265	161,992
John T. Myers (R)*	90.4	56.3	152,664	136,796
8 David L. Cornwell (D)*	—	48.0	112,065	112,985
H. Joel Deckard (R)	49.0	52.0	232,433	231,632
9 Lee H. Hamilton Jr. (D)*	—	65.6	120,178	111,793
Frank I. Hamilton Jr. (R)	—	34.4	48,786	48,720
10 Phil Sharp (D)*	89.6	56.1	111,761	107,372
William G. Frazier (R)	58.6	42.8	127,876	129,665
11 Andy Jacobs Jr. (D.)*	94.5	57.2	20,767	18,394
Charles F. Bosma (R)	72.0	42.6	56,187	55,971
IOWA				
1 Dick Myers (D)	—	35.8	123,965	123,626
Jim Leach (R)*	—	63.5	242,314	241,356
2 Michael T. Blouin (D)*	47.1	47.7	129,765	141,533
Tom Tauke (R)	—	52.3	250,995	250,432
3 John Knudson (D)	—	25.2	12,593	11,581
Charles E. Grassley (R)*	—	74.8	160,051	160,100
4 Neal Smith (D)*	—	64.7	47,606	43,447
Charles E. Minor (R)	—	35.3	10,285	9,615
5 Tom Harkin (D)*	—	58.9	140,399	144,160
Julian B. Garrett (R)	53.4	41.1	65,948	64,680
6 Berkley Bedell (D)*	—	66.3	98,854	93,188
Willis E. Junker (R)	—	33.7	14,517	14,477
KANSAS				
1 Keith G. Sebelius (R)*	—	100.0	52,928	52,986
2 Martha Keys (D)*	—	48.0	146,822	145,473
Jim Jeffries (R)	59.2	52.0	333,902	332,482

	Percent of Primary Vote	Percent of General Election Vote	Receipts	Expenditures
3 Larry Winn Jr. (R)*	—	100.0	13,195	17,691
4 Dan Glickman (D)*	—	69.5	133,128	90,827
James P. Litsey (R)	—	30.5	73,275	73,264
5 Donald L. Allegrucci (D)	34.5	41.4	118,256	114,247
Robert Whittaker (R)	38.6	57.0	262,337	259,120
KENTUCKY				
1 Carroll Hubbard Jr. (D)*	—	100.0	120,811	79,097
2 William H. Natcher (D)*	—	100.0	20	20
3 Romano L. Mazzoli (D)*	78.9	65.7	119,606	110,638
Norbert D. Leveronne (R)	36.0	31.3	3,930	3,929
4 George C. Martin (D)	37.2	34.2	30,384	30,231
Gene Snyder (R)*	—	65.8	146,055	122,834
5 Jesse M. Ramey (D)	51.8	20.8	953	952
Tim Lee Carter (R)*	92.9	79.2	48,878	44,631
6 Tom Easterly (D)	50.1	46.1	137,123	134,770
Larry J. Hopkins (R)	—	50.6	294,354	291,920
7 Carl D. Perkins (D)*	85.4	76.5	3,711	3,710
Granville Thomas (R)	—	23.5	0	0
LOUISIANA				
1 Robert L. Livingston (R)*	86.3	100.0	370,366	347,844
2 Lindy Boggs (D)*	86.9	100.0	75,738	60,404
3 David C. Treen (R)*	—	100.0	100,642	48,855
4 Claude (Buddy) Leach (D)	27.1	50.1	775,562	771,303
Jimmy Wilson (R)	27.1	49.9	405,921	402,713
5 Jerry Huckaby (D)*	52.4	100.0	382,825	384,207
6 W. Henson Moore (R)*	91.0	100.0	126,905	78,686
7 John B. Breaux (D)*	60.4	100.0	143,515	183,424
8 Gillis W. Long (D)*	79.5	100.0	222,703	189,507
MAINE				
1 John Quinn (D)	31.9	35.8	78,424	73,755
David F. Emery (R)*	—	61.5	200,514	200,480
2 Markham L. Gartley (D)	63.5	40.8	132,743	132,156
Olympia J. Snowe (R)	—	50.8	221,594	220,981
Frederick W. Whittaker (I)	—	4.6	13,746	13,745
MARYLAND				
1 Joseph D. Quinn (D)	—	36.5	88,841	88,759
Robert E. Bauman (R)*	—	63.5	222,172	220,076
2 Clarence D. Long (D)*	86.1	66.4	53,331	61,863
Malcolm M. McKnight (R)	71.5	33.6	31,442	30,777
3 Barbara A. Mikulski (D)*	90.0	100.0	40,084	38,333
4 Sue F. Ward (D)	48.9	38.0	39,015	37,478
Marjorie S. Holt (R)*	—	62.0	115,743	107,607
5 Gladys Noon Spellman (D)*	84.4	77.2	114,816	72,520
Saul J. Harris (R)	41.8	22.8	25,781	32,209
6 Beverly Byron (D)	—	89.7	11,920	1,542
Melvin Perkins (R)	—	10.3	NA	NA
7 Parren J. Mitchell (D)*	—	88.7	90,831	93,693
Debra Hanania Freeman (I)	—	11.3	7,001	7,052
8 Michael D. Barnes (D)	71.4	51.3	136,244	134,588
Newton I. Steers Jr. (R)*	—	48.7	165,669	162,980
MASSACHUSETTS				
1 Silvio O. Conte (R)*	—	99.9	21,261	5,771
2 Edward P. Boland (D)*	—	72.8	42	42
Thomas P. Swank (R)	—	27.2	NA	NA
3 Joseph D. Early (D)*	—	75.2	66,451	50,609
Charles Kevin MacLeod (R)	54.1	24.7	8,648	8,645
4 Robert F. Drinan (D)*	65.3	99.9	160,973	149,345
5 James M. Shannon (D)	27.3	52.2	180,732	180,667
John J. Buckley (R)	54.1	28.2	109,036	97,637
James J. Gaffney III (I)	—	19.6	17,804	17,740
6 Nicholas Mavroules (D)	44.0	53.8	296,672	290,331
William E. Bronson (R)	—	46.2	192,022	185,029
7 Edward J. Markey (D)*	—	84.8	61,508	60,542
James J. Murphy (I)	—	15.2	215	196
8 Thomas P. O'Neill Jr. (D)*	—	74.6	30,922	16,274
William A. Barnstead (R)	—	20.9	2,280	1,459
9 Joe Moakley (D)*	—	91.8	83,098	46,217
Brenda Lee Franklin (SOC WORK)	—	5.8	25	8
10 John J. Marino (D)	51.1	38.9	79,292	78,848
Margaret M. Heckler (R)*	—	61.1	200,883	210,730

	Percent of Primary Vote	Percent of General Election Vote	Receipts	Expenditures
11 Brian J. Donnelly (D)	42.8	91.7	190,946	184,204
H. Graham Lowry (USLP)	—	8.3	1,785	1,785
12 Gerry E. Studds (D)*	—	99.9	25,993	20,899
MICHIGAN				
1 John Conyers Jr. (D)*	—	92.9	17,267	23,759
Robert S. Arnold (R)	—	7.1	235	234
2 Earl Greene (D)	—	31.6	27,348	27,212
Carl D. Pursell (R)*	—	67.6	111,159	94,764
3 Howard Wolpe (D)	—	51.3	221,161	219,397
Garry Brown (R)*	—	48.7	226,170	242,768
4 Morgan L. Hager Jr. (D)	—	28.3	4,075	4,095
Dave Stockman (R)*	—	70.6	70,127	62,211
5 Dale R. Sprik (D)	—	48.7	69,710	69,641
Harold S. Sawyer (R)*	—	49.4	139,056	134,454
6 Bob Carr (D)*	—	56.7	173,535	174,104
Mike Conlin (R)	—	43.3	143,497	145,074
7 Dale E. Kildee (D)*	—	76.6	50,826	46,558
Gale M. Cronk (R)	—	21.8	23,504	23,487
8 Bob Traxler (D)*	—	66.6	107,097	97,020
Norman R. Hughes (R)	—	33.4	46,022	40,795
9 Howard M. Leroux (D)	—	30.4	39,483	38,498
Guy Vander Jagt (R)*	—	69.6	204,418	197,290
10 Donald J. Albosta (D)	58.8	51.5	261,407	258,244
Elford A. Cederberg (R)*	—	48.5	148,426	146,993
11 Keith McLeod (D)	25.5	45.1	132,777	131,304
Robert W. Davis (R)	57.6	54.9	163,423	158,755
12 David E. Bonior (D)*	—	54.9	121,106	119,682
Kirby Holmes (R)	79.6	45.1	69,531	69,251
13 Charles C. Diggs Jr. (D)*	62.1	79.2	8,523	6,700
Dovie T. Pickett (R)	—	20.8	8,541	7,959
14 Lucien N. Nedzi (D)*	78.3	67.4	22,641	23,898
John Edward Getz (R)	—	32.6	6,146	6,225
15 William D. Ford (D)*	—	79.6	56,137	61,157
Edgar Nieten (R)	—	19.4	30	33
16 John D. Dingell (D)*	—	76.5	90,071	61,246
Melvin E. Hever (R)	—	22.0	0	0
17 William M. Brodhead (D)*	—	95.2	25,028	12,158
18 James J. Blanchard (D)*	—	74.5	95,215	89,842
Robert J. Salloum (R)	—	24.3	100	13
19 Betty F. Collier (D)	50.5	28.7	1,256	1,323
William S. Broomfield (R)*	—	71.3	58,234	41,916
MINNESOTA				
1 Gerry Sikorski (DFL)	68.2	42.5	151,893	149,089
Arlen Erdahl (I-R)	74.2	56.2	199,142	194,363
2 John F. Considine (DFL)	—	29.6	22,085	22,086
Tom Hagedorn (I-R)*	—	70.4	177,974	172,482
3 Michael O. Freeman (DFL)	—	34.3	154,840	154,738
Bill Frenzel (I-R)*	—	65.7	188,387	179,807
4 Bruce F. Vento (DFL)*	—	58.0	92,083	80,225
John R. Berg (R)	—	42.0	77,689	76,705
5 Martin Olav Sabo (DFL)	81.3	62.3	87,906	84,652
Michael Till (I-R)	—	37.7	129,740	129,487
6 Richard Nolan (DFL)*	—	55.3	207,679	212,542
Russ Bjorhus (I-R)	—	44.7	139,682	138,982
7 Gene R. Wenstrom (DFL)	73.1	45.1	114,729	112,549
Arlan Stangeland (I-R)*	—	51.7	212,291	192,034
8 James L. Oberstar (DFL)*	—	87.2	56,698	64,117
John W. Hull (AM)	—	12.7	2,600	2,599
MISSISSIPPI				
1 Jamie L. Whitten (D)*	59.4	66.6	100,902	87,331
T. K. Moffett (R)	—	31.0	72,164	71,620
2 David R. Bowen (D)*	74.5	61.7	78,174	90,850
Roland Byrd (R)	—	38.3	90,455	91,580
3 G. V. (Sonny) Montgomery (D)*	90.5	92.4	69,297	45,478
Dorothy Cleveland (R)	—	7.6	0	0
4 John Hampton Stennis (D)	57.8**	26.4	312,192	311,474
Jon C. Hinson (R)	69.4	51.6	249,068	249,548
Evan Doss (I)	—	19.0	20,784	20,564
5 Trent Lott (R)*	—	100.0	43,900	32,708
MISSOURI				
1 William (Bill) Clay (D)*	60.5	66.6	96,983	91,254
William E. White (R)	65.7	31.3	40,671	40,834

	Percent of Primary Vote	Percent of General Election Vote	Receipts	Expenditures
2 Robert A. Young (D)*	85.1	56.4	178,220	158,326
Robert C. Chase (R)	72.7	43.6	150,323	148,440
3 Richard A. Gephardt (D)*	91.1	81.9	116,605	113,977
Lee Buchschacher (R)	51.8	18.1	3,093	3,085
4 Ike Skelton (D)*	86.8	72.8	158,789	149,080
William D. Baker (R)	—	27.2	3,424	3,422
5 Richard Bolling (D)*	77.6	72.0	88,193	66,241
Steven L. Walter (R)	60.2	26.6	9,110	9,096
6 Phil Snowden (D)	31.8	44.1	282,713	280,118
E. Thomas Coleman (R)*	—	55.9	286,807	274,804
7 Jim Thomas (D)	63.7	38.8	26,104	25,037
Gene Taylor (R)*	—	61.2	113,273	104,612
8 Richard H. Ichord (D)*	—	60.5	140,758	120,482
Donald D. Meyer (R)	—	39.5	79,607	78,847
9 Harold L. Volkmer (D)*	—	74.7	107,190	101,375
Jerry A. Dent (R)	61.3	25.3	1,048	1,048
10 Bill D. Burlison (D)*	63.5	65.3	72,293	51,165
James A. Weir (R)	41.9	34.7	3,296	2,565
MONTANA				
1 Pat Williams (D)	40.9	57.3	177,712	177,536
Jim Waltermire (R)	30.0	42.7	244,129	241,888
2 Thomas G. Monahan (D)	70.0	43.1	27,020	27,019
Ron Marlenee (R)*	—	56.9	298,774	286,863
NEBRASKA				
1 Hess Dyas (D)	60.9	41.9	164,452	164,227
Douglas K. Bereuter (R)	52.1	58.1	172,896	167,688
2 John J. Cavanaugh (D)*	88.3	52.3	147,190	144,071
Harold J. Daub Jr. (R)	82.5	47.7	238,268	237,741
3 Marilyn Fowler (D)	—	20.0	41,554	40,313
Virginia Smith (R)*	—	80.0	66,731	66,795
NEVADA				
AL Jim Santini (D)*	80.2	69.5	251,040	204,389
Bill O'Mara (R)	31.7	23.3	34,543	34,543
NEW HAMPSHIRE				
1 Norman E. D'Amours (D)*	—	61.7	78,828	92,791
Daniel M. Hughes (R)	49.9	36.5	49,520	48,897
2 Edgar J. Helms (D)	—	31.9	22,460	22,207
James C. Cleveland (R)*	—	68.1	66,875	65,961
NEW JERSEY				
1 James J. Florio (D)*	—	79.4	88,384	76,026
Robert M. Deitch (R)	—	20.1	500	1,120
2 William J. Hughes (D)*	—	66.4	128,501	108,704
James H. Biggs (R)	—	33.6	4,598	4,180
3 James J. Howard (D)*	—	56.0	150,559	123,220
Bruce G. Coe (R)	—	43.5	145,179	145,048
4 Frank Thompson Jr. (D)*	—	61.1	72,263	66,828
Christopher H. Smith (R)	—	36.9	15,872	15,717
5 James T. Fahy (D)	—	27.4	43,555	43,509
Millicent Fenwick (R)*	—	72.6	62,252	61,777
6 W. Thomas McGann (D)	52.9	38.4	60,546	60,647
Edwin B. Forsythe (R)*	84.3	60.4	82,170	87,804
7 Andrew Maguire (D)*	—	52.5	184,459	202,210
Margaret S. Roukema (R)	39.3	46.6	143,026	142,266
8 Robert A. Roe (D)*	—	74.5	67,907	66,635
Thomas Melani (R)	—	25.5	5,801	5,800
9 Nicholas S. Mastorelli (D)	49.8	37.9	119,367	121,447
Harold C. Hollenbeck (R)*	81.8	48.9	75,618	84,548
Henry Helstoski (I)	—	12.7	25,776	25,622
10 Peter W. Rodino Jr. (D)*	—	86.4	34,644	46,110
John L. Pelt (R)	—	12.6	656	496
11 Joseph G. Minish (D)*	91.8	70.5	102,932	71,900
Julius George Feld (R)	—	28.5	1,265	1,173
12 Richard McCormack (D)	—	26.6	14,336	13,556
Matthew J. Rinaldo (R)*	—	73.4	245,934	192,778
13 Helen Meyner (D)*	—	48.2	173,850	194,641
James A. Courter (R)	38.4	51.8	332,037	330,688
14 Frank J. Guarini (D)	81.9	63.6	88,727	83,325
Henry J. Hill (R)	—	20.3	5,806	7,566
Thomas E. McDonough (I)	—	14.3	17,271	17,271

	Percent of Primary Vote	Percent of General Election Vote	Receipts	Expenditures
15 Edward J. Patten (D)*	58.9	48.3	53,882	50,407
Charles W. Wiley (R)	—	45.8	46,156	46,314
NEW MEXICO				
1 Robert Hawk (D)	59.7	37.5	49,829	49,707
Manuel Lujan Jr. (R)*	—	62.5	111,322	121,421
2 Harold Runnels (D)*	—	100.0	71,515	69,953
NEW YORK				
1 John F. Randolph (D)	39.3	41.9	82,843	76,810
William Carney (R, C)	30.7	56.3	130,764	130,642
2 Thomas J. Downey (D)*	—	54.9	154,680	149,400
Harold J. Withers Jr. (R, C)	—	45.1	33,763	33,119
3 Jerome A. Ambro (D)*	—	50.9	79,249	80,256
Gregory W. Carman (R, C)	—	47.9	318,956	311,390
4 Everett A. Rosenblum (D)	—	32.5	12,667	11,774
Norman F. Lent (R, C)*	—	66.1	116,543	83,658
5 John W. Matthews (D, L)	—	41.6	34,572	34,334
John W. Wydler (R, C)*	—	58.4	92,401	84,425
6 Lester L. Wolff (D, L)*	—	60.0	48,952	39,886
Stuart L. Ain (R)	—	32.9	87,005	77,565
Howard Horowitz (C)	—	7.1	0	0
7 Joseph P. Addabbo (D, R, L)*	—	94.9	63,700	41,049
Mark Elliott Scott (C)	—	5.1	453	453
8 Benjamin S. Rosenthal (D, L)*	—	78.6	40,729	30,220
Albert Lemishow (R)	—	15.9	1,441	1,441
Paul C. Ruebenacker (C)	—	5.4	5	0
9 Geraldine A. Ferraro (D)	52.7	54.2	382,119	382,074
Alfred A. DelliBovi (R, C)	—	44.4	119,823	110,679
10 Mario Biaggi (D, R, L)*	—	95.0	78,236	71,493
Carmen Ricciardi (C)	—	5.0	NA	NA
11 James H. Scheuer (D, L)*	—	78.5	42,410	24,861
Kenneth Huhn (R, C)	—	21.5	0	0
12 Shirley Chisholm (D, L)*	—	87.8	14,797	14,498
Charles Gibbs (R)	—	12.2	0	581
13 Stephen J. Solarz (D, L)*	—	81.1	101,872	21,565
Max Carasso (R, C)	—	18.9	914	914
14 Frederick Richmond (D, L)*	51.3	76.9	437,949	419,663
Arthur Bramwell (R)	—	18.4	1,630	1,399
15 Leo C. Zeferetti (D, C)*	73.9	68.1	86,367	67,960
Robert P. Whelan (R)	67.6	28.4	16,803	15,028
16 Elizabeth Holtzman (D, L)*	—	81.9	61,056	44,428
Larry Penner (R, UT)	—	12.9	NA	NA
John H. Fox (C)	—	5.2	509	510
17 John M. Murphy (D)*	46.3	54.2	206,179	190,048
John Michael Peters (R, C)	—	33.1	46,360	45,525
Thomas H. Stokes (L)	—	12.7	60,682	60,197
18 Carter Burden (D, L)	44.8	46.7	1,139,188	1,136,112
S. William Green (R)*	—	53.3	572,814	580,463
19 Charles B. Rangel (D, R, L)*	—	96.4	52,601	43,246
20 Ted Weiss (D, L)*	—	84.6	43,467	37,859
Harry Torczyner (R)	—	15.4	21,463	21,463
21 Robert Garcia (D, R, L)*	—	98.0	39,748	45,068
22 Jonathan B. Bingham (D, L)*	—	84.1	6,040	6,040
Anthony J. Geidel Jr. (R, C)	—	15.9	4,060	4,059
23 Peter A. Peyser (D)	58.1	51.6	106,160	105,552
Angelo A. Martinelli (R, C)	—	46.2	143,519	141,229
24 Richard L. Ottinger (D)*	—	56.1	85,833	85,769
Michael R. Edelman (R, C)	—	42.7	63,668	64,314
25 Gunars M. Ozols (D)	—	21.3	1,231	1,379
Hamilton Fish Jr. (R)*	—	78.2	93,226	82,983
26 Charles E. Holbrook (D, L)	43.7	30.0	12,588	12,588
Benjamin A. Gilman (R)*	—	62.3	109,727	92,014
William R. Schaeffer Jr. (C)	—	7.7	1,270	1,269
27 Matthew F. McHugh (D)*	—	55.8	197,615	199,786
Neil Tyler Wallace (R, C)	—	44.2	139,107	139,043
28 Samuel S. Stratton (D)*	81.0	76.3	29,133	28,057
Paul H. Tocker (R, C)	—	19.7	1,687	1,665
Richard A. Hind (L)	—	4.0	10,043	10,040
29 Edward W. Pattison (D, L)*	—	46.0	164,874	155,525
Gerald B. Solomon (R, C)	—	54.0	168,169	167,723
30 Norma A. Bartle (D, L)	—	39.5	50,416	50,692
Robert C. McEwen (R, C)*	—	60.5	53,858	56,731
31 Donald J. Mitchell (R, C)*	—	100.0	75,064	44,635
32 James M. Hanley (D)*	—	52.4	122,833	113,595
Peter J. Del Giorno (R, C)	—	46.1	75,396	71,961

	Percent of Primary Vote	Percent of General Election Vote	Receipts	Expenditures
33 Roy A. Bernardi (D)	68.5	39.5	69,715	69,614
Gary A. Lee (R)	88.9	56.0	165,916	162,725
Robert J. Byrne (C)	—	3.4	6,364	6,359
34 Frank Horton (R, D)*	—	87.1	24,157	8,262
Leo J. Kesselring (C)	—	12.9	3,055	1,888
35 Francis C. Repicci (D)	—	26.3	31,009	30,837
Barber B. Conable Jr. (R)*	—	69.4	52,607	59,204
36 John J. LaFalce (D, L)*	—	74.1	114,208	44,407
Francina J. Cartonia (R)	—	23.5	9,478	9,476
37 Henry J. Nowak (D, L)*	—	78.6	52,235	37,521
Charles Poth III (R)	—	19.5	3,275	3,162
38 Jack F. Kemp (R, C)*	—	94.8	76,771	64,251
James A. Peck (L)	—	5.2	5,050	6,418
39 Stanley N. Lundine (D)*	—	58.5	99,960	92,454
Crispin M. Maguire (R, C)	61.2	41.5	63,815	65,508

NORTH CAROLINA

	Percent of Primary Vote	Percent of General Election Vote	Receipts	Expenditures
1 Walter B. Jones (D)*	82.3	80.1	46,357	24,067
James Newcomb (R)	—	19.9	4,535	4,534
2 L. H. Fountain (D)*	75.0	78.2	32,964	21,984
Barry L. Gardner (R)	—	20.2	7,409	7,335
3 Charlie Whitley (D)*	83.1	71.1	56,598	44,971
Willard J. Blanchard (R)	—	28.9	14,240	13,583
4 Ike F. Andrews (D)*	82.2	94.4	36,474	27,970
Naudeen Beek (LIBERT)	—	5.6	388	329
5 Stephen L. Neal (D)*	—	54.2	164,332	166,643
Hamilton C. Horton Jr. (R)	—	45.8	122,721	118,484
6 Richardson Preyer (D)*	—	68.4	41,491	18,274
George Bemus (R)	—	31.6	10,432	10,386
7 Charlie Rose (D)*	—	69.9	59,503	57,723
Raymond C. Schrump (R)	—	30.1	51,468	47,933
8 W. G. (Bill) Hefner (D)*	—	59.0	81,773	74,546
Roger Austin (R)	53.2	41.0	23,405	22,949
9 Charles Maxwell (D)	—	30.7	38,795	37,657
James G. Martin (R)*	—	68.3	255,542	252,126
10 James T. Broyhill (R)*	—	100.0	29,076	32,586
11 Lamar Gudger (D)*	50.7	53.4	158,017	156,790
R. Curtis Ratcliff (R)	—	46.6	62,580	62,579

NORTH DAKOTA

	Percent of Primary Vote	Percent of General Election Vote	Receipts	Expenditures
AL Bruce Hagen (D)	—	30.9	17,015	17,014
Mark Andrews (R)*	—	67.1	118,445	83,120

OHIO

	Percent of Primary Vote	Percent of General Election Vote	Receipts	Expenditures
1 Timothy M. Burke (D)	—	33.9	13,075	12,710
Bill Gradison (R)*	—	64.5	105,081	84,745
2 Thomas A. Luken (D)*	—	52.4	231,471	230,690
Stanley J. Aronoff (R)	57.2	47.6	275,692	275,400
3 Tony P. Hall (D)	80.0	53.8	216,675	216,117
Dudley P. Kircher (R)	63.5	44.4	349,374	346,193
4 John W. Griffin (D)	57.6	31.5	609	609
Tennyson Guyer (R)*	—	68.5	37,254	23,696
5 James R. Sherck (D)	—	37.4	40,988	40,249
Delbert L. Latta (R)*	—	62.6	59,968	45,705
6 Ted Strickland (D)	76.7	35.1	33,401	32,950
William H. Harsha (R)*	84.5	64.9	86,776	107,252
7 Clarence J. Brown (R)*	—	100.0	58,541	33,877
8 Lou Schroeder (D)	64.4	28.6	15,898	15,430
Thomas N. Kindness (R)*	—	71.4	66,728	64,077
9 Thomas L. Ashley (D)*	—	63.4	117,228	100,223
John C. Hoyt (R)	—	30.3	37,320	37,320
10 James A. Plummer (D)	—	26.1	905	884
Clarence E. Miller (R)*	—	73.9	26,647	22,957
11 Patrick J. Donlin (D)	46.2	28.3	11,880	11,671
J. William Stanton (R)*	—	68.1	28,039	24,816
12 James L. Baumann (D)	58.2	28.4	162,190	162,162
Samuel L. Devine (R)*	—	56.9	158,338	132,634
13 Don J. Pease (D)*	78.1	65.1	46,798	44,919
Mark W. Whitfield (R)	72.4	34.9	82,433	81,502
14 John F. Seiberling (D)*	—	72.5	19,325	20,438
Walter J. Vogel (R)	—	27.5	12,379	12,352
15 Henry W. Eckhart (D)	—	28.9	774	771
Chalmers P. Wylie (R)*	—	71.1	95,113	87,741
16 Owen S. Hand Jr. (D)	—	22.0	5,375	5,309
Ralph S. Regula (R)*	—	78.0	75,720	55,300
17 Kenneth R. Grier (D)	—	32.6	1,367	892
John M. Ashbrook (R)*	—	67.4	180,957	158,543

	Percent of Primary Vote	Percent of General Election Vote	Receipts	Expenditures
18 Douglas Applegate (D)*	82.0	59.5	74,214	75,802
Bill Ress (R)	65.6	40.5	69,294	69,217
19 Charles J. Carney (D)*	34.5	49.3	142,355	168,257
Lyle Williams (R)	53.6	50.7	107,948	101,551
20 Mary Rose Oakar (D)*	81.3	100.0	77,334	77,081
21 Louis Stokes (D)*	—	86.1	64,989	47,176
Bill Mack (R)	—	13.9	0	0
22 Charles A. Vanik (D)*	—	66.0	68	68
Richard W. Sander (R)	54.4	23.3	27,250	26,715
James F. Sexton (I)	—	5.4	6,254	6,451
23 Ronald M. Mottl (D)*	83.9	74.8	59,103	40,630
Homer S. Taft (R)	—	25.2	11,208	11,197

OKLAHOMA

	Percent of Primary Vote	Percent of General Election Vote	Receipts	Expenditures
1 James R. Jones (D)*	—	59.9	235,647	210,179
Paula Unruh (R)	79.6	40.1	237,379	236,437
2 Mike Synar (D)	53.6	54.8	192,142	190,050
Gary L. Richardson (R)	—	45.2	131,771	130,530
3 Wes Watkins (D)*	—	100.0	93,415	23,999
4 Tom Steed (D)*	64.3	60.3	55,223	55,854
Scotty Robb (R)	—	39.7	153,946	150,420
5 Jesse Dennis Knipp (D)	55.3	20.1	4,505	5,637
Mickey Edwards (R)*	—	79.9	252,562	247,380
6 Glenn English (D)*	—	74.2	116,866	109,668
Harold Hunter (R)	—	25.8	65,532	65,053

OREGON

	Percent of Primary Vote	Percent of General Election Vote	Receipts	Expenditures
1 Les AuCoin (D)*	—	62.9	252,847	236,313
Nick Bunick (R)	61.1	37.1	302,735	297,719
2 Al Ullman (D)*	—	69.1	79,749	55,401
Terry L. Hicks (R)	52.2	30.7	2,568	2,568
3 Robert Duncan (D)*	—	84.6	47,009	38,318
Martin Simon (USLP)	—	15.1	943	942
4 James Weaver (D)*	59.6	56.3	177,703	178,950
Jerry L. Lausmann (R)	57.7	43.7	205,643	206,613

PENNSYLVANIA

	Percent of Primary Vote	Percent of General Election Vote	Receipts	Expenditures
1 Michael (Ozzie) Myers (D)*	49.8	71.9	51,850	50,069
Samuel N. Fanelli (R)	—	26.1	0	0
2 William H. Gray III (D)	57.6	82.0	227,070	225,887
Roland J. Atkins (R)	62.6	15.9	34,362	24,877
3 Raymond F. Lederer (D)*	—	71.8	119,178	106,284
Raymond S. Kauffman (R)	—	28.2	7,412	6,850
4 Joshua Eilberg (D)*	57.2	44.2	150,501	159,904
Charles F. Dougherty (R)	—	55.8	131,650	130,837
5 Murray P. Zealor (D)	—	24.9	5,695	5,354
Richard T. Schulze (R)*	92.3	75.1	185,691	124,390
6 Gus Yatron (D)*	—	73.8	58,715	55,589
Stephen Mazur (R)	55.1	26.2	0	0
7 Robert W. Edgar (D)*	84.8	50.3	143,188	142,238
Eugene D. Kane (R)	78.1	49.4	216,547	216,347
8 Peter H. Kostmayer (D)*	82.7	61.1	133,513	131,010
G. Roger Bowers (R)	34.3	38.9	53,325	52,584
9 Blaine L. Havice Jr. (D)	—	25.1	26,694	16,809
Bud Shuster (R)*	—	74.9	139,050	146,318
10 Gene Basalyga (D)	—	23.5	3,293	3,293
Joseph M. McDade (R)*	—	76.5	65,276	66,769
11 Daniel J. Flood (D)*	74.9	57.5	23,609	25,794
Robert P. Hudock (R)	48.5	42.5	19,204	19,149
12 John P. Murtha (D)*	—	68.7	49,865	33,377
Luther V. Elkins (R)	—	31.3	15,176	15,175
13 Alan B. Rubenstein (D)	51.8	29.5	32,282	32,279
Lawrence Coughlin (R)*	89.4	70.5	118,032	105,534
14 William S. Moorhead (D)*	75.9	57.0	117,448	114,623
Stan Thomas (R)	—	41.9	124,671	119,799
15 Fred B. Rooney (D)*	—	46.8	121,796	131,005
Donald L. Ritter (R)	46.3	53.2	63,361	63,205
16 Charles W. Boohar (D)	—	23.0	4,046	4,048
Robert S. Walker (R)*	76.1	77.0	39,463	40,289
17 Allen E. Ertel (D)*	—	59.6	157,027	149,236
Thomas R. Rippon (R)	—	40.4	141,955	138,223
18 Doug Walgren (D)*	77.2	57.1	176,599	171,756
Ted Jacob (R)	—	42.1	188,250	187,926
19 Rajeshwar Kumar (D)	—	21.3	3,656	4,138
Bill Goodling (R)*	—	78.7	41,652	37,067
20 Joseph M. Gaydos (D)*	84.5	72.1	72,385	67,339
Kathleen M. Meyer (R)	—	27.9	2,577	2,040

	Percent of Primary Vote	Percent of General Election Vote	Receipts	Expenditures
21 Don Bailey (D)	22.6	52.9	125,800	125,146
Robert H. Miller (R)	38.7	47.1	114,097	113,186
22 Austin J. Murphy (D)*	69.4	71.6	170,621	144,228
Marilyn C. Ecoff (R)	—	28.4	668	363
23 Joseph S. Ammerman (D)*	—	45.7	172,493	174,587
William F. Clinger Jr. (R)	64.5	54.3	251,718	250,697
24 Joseph P. Vigorito (D)	—	36.0	33,695	35,220
Marc L. Marks (R)*	82.5	64.0	179,277	171,653
25 Eugene V. Atkinson (D)	24.9	46.5	103,432	106,521
Tim Shaffer (R)	38.9	42.3	91,432	91,294
John W. Cook (I)	—	4.0	8,734	8,699
Robert Morris (I)	—	7.2	159,896	159,728

RHODE ISLAND

1 Fernand J. St Germain (D)*	67.7	61.2	135,357	125,013
John J. Slocum Jr. (R)	54.9	38.8	98,944	98,082
2 Edward P. Beard (D)*	79.6	52.6	75,068	84,688
Claudine Schneider (R)	—	47.4	56,002	53,879

SOUTH CAROLINA

1 Mendel J. Davis (D)*	86.8	60.6	139,050	124,943
C. C. Wannamaker (R)	—	39.4	49,559	49,079
2 Jack Bass (D)	57.7	42.7	129,479	136,959
Floyd Spence (R)*	—	57.3	164,067	182,995
3 Butler Derrick (D)*	—	82.0	90,494	84,641
Anthony Panuccio (R)	—	18.0	0	0
4 Max M. Heller (D)	53.2	46.2	240,432	240,150
Carroll A. Campbell Jr. (R)	88.4	52.1	184,933	182,461
Don Sprouse (I)	—	1.7	18,175	18,174
5 Ken Holland (D)*	65.9	82.7	133,535	91,690
Harold Hough (I)	—	17.3	NA	NA
6 John W. Jenrette Jr. (D)*	75.4	100.0	108,239	100,829

SOUTH DAKOTA

1 Thomas A. Daschle (D)	59.4	50.1	225,402	223,221
Leo K. Thorsness (R)	64.6	49.9	270,367	270,366
2 Bob Samuelson (D)	52.5	44.0	331,356	329,425
James Abdnor (R)*	—	56.0	153,193	160,804

TENNESSEE

1 Gordon Ball (D)	—	35.5	48,987	46,199
James H. (Jimmy) Quillen (R)*	—	64.5	207,868	218,151
2 Margaret Francis (D)	51.2	18.2	3,347	3,347
John J. Duncan (R)*	—	81.8	171,066	139,956
3 Marilyn Lloyd (D)*	—	88.9	88,385	75,923
Dan East (I)	—	11.1	2,082	2,042
4 Albert Gore Jr. (D)*	—	100.0	99,866	47,097
5 Bill Boner (D)	54.0	51.4	194,894	192,960
Bill Goodwin (R)	88.3	35.4	40,492	40,494
Henry Haile (I)	—	13.2	6,231	5,838
6 Ron Arline (D)	—	25.4	15,474	10,175
Robin L. Beard Jr. (R)*	—	74.6	192,312	156,405
7 Ed Jones (D)*	—	72.9	134,369	124,445
Ross Cook (R)	66.9	27.1	51,489	49,769
8 Harold E. Ford (D)*	80.6	69.7	198,969	179,244
Duncan Ragsdale (R)	83.9	29.1	12,913	12,372

TEXAS

1 Sam B. Hall Jr. (D)*	—	78.1	84,941	44,229
Fred Hudson (R)	—	21.9	76,519	76,520
2 Charles Wilson (D)*	—	70.1	234,356	218,901
Jim (Matt) Dillon (R)	—	29.9	8,569	7,091
3 James M. Collins (R)*	—	100.0	225,965	80,442
4 Ray Roberts (D)*	67.3	61.5	137,245	125,814
Frank S. Glenn (R)	—	38.5	80,401	80,606
5 Jim Mattox (D)*	—	50.3	282,547	269,015
Tom Pauken (R)	—	49.1	252,000	252,047
6 Phil Gramm (D)	52.9**	65.1	552,534	480,778
Wesley H. Mowrey (R)	87.0	34.9	116,411	116,386
7 Robert L. Hutchings (D)	—	14.9	2,500	2,459
Bill Archer (R)*	—	85.1	222,613	120,720
8 Bob Eckhardt (D)*	53.1	61.5	286,129	285,214
Nick Gearhart (R)	70.1	38.5	139,564	139,102
9 Jack Brooks (D)*	70.6	63.3	100,163	80,171
Randy Evans (R)	52.3	36.7	2,954	3,003
10 J. J. Pickle (D)*	—	76.3	80,966	46,726
Emmett L. Hudspeth (R)	62.9	23.7	19,266	19,263

	Percent of Primary Vote	Percent of General Election Vote	Receipts	Expenditures
11 J. Marvin Leath (D)	54.9**	51.6	590,482	588,492
Jack Burgess (R)	—	48.4	322,083	320,084
12 Jim Wright (D)*	—	68.5	272,026	283,125
Claude K. Brown (R)	—	31.5	12,620	12,571
13 Jack Hightower (D)*	—	74.9	61,825	44,551
Clifford A. Jones (R)	52.1	25.1	30,409	30,086
14 Joe Wyatt (D)	56.4**	72.4	311,491	310,890
Joy Yates (R)	—	27.6	10,768	10,766
15 E. (Kika) de la Garza (D)*	—	66.2	101,453	85,184
Robert L. McDonald (R)	—	33.8	31,847	30,535
16 Richard C. White (D)*	79.5	70.0	106,839	107,976
Michael Giere (R)	—	30.0	34,952	34,881
17 Charles W. Stenholm (D)	67.1**	68.1	332,844	331,516
Billy Lee Fisher (R)	—	31.9	149,962	149,705
18 Mickey Leland (D)	56.7**	96.8	258,367	258,366
19 Kent Hance (D)	64.2	53.2	334,299	314,110
George W. Bush (R)	55.9	46.8	441,518	434,909
20 Henry B. Gonzalez (D)*	—	100.0	28,397	28,703
21 Nelson W. Wolff (D)	50.5	43.0	440,255	438,013
Tom Loeffler (R)	59.4	57.0	406,300	402,299
22 Bob Gammage (D)*	56.7	49.4	478,044	476,852
Ron Paul (R)	—	50.6	323,482	322,156
23 Abraham Kazen Jr. (D)*	82.4	89.7	42,294	55,734
Augustin Mata (LRU)	—	10.3	3,543	5,337
24 Martin Frost (D)	55.1	54.1	348,611	347,177
Leo Berman (R)	84.8	45.9	227,465	228,740

UTAH

1 Gunn McKay (D)*	—	51.0	138,180	149,143
Jed J. Richardson (R)	—	46.2	148,356	147,556
Robert T. Owens (AM)	—	2.3	7,272	6,960
2 Edwin B. Firmage (D)	50.5	35.3	233,347	230,760
Dan Marriott (R)*	—	62.3	344,918	353,520

VERMONT

AL S. Marie Dietz (D)	51.6	19.3	8,767	8,768
James M. Jeffords (R)*	—	75.3	79,064	66,589
Peter Diamondstone (LU)	—	5.4	1,180	150

VIRGINIA

1 Lew Puller (D)	—	27.9	134,313	134,051
Paul S. Trible Jr. (R)*	—	72.1	254,099	257,257
2 G. William Whitehurst (R)*	—	100.0	30,600	37,796
3 David E. Satterfield III (D)*	—	87.7	15,020	5,626
Alan R. Ogden (I)	—	12.1	805	675
4 Robert W. Daniel Jr. (R)*	—	99.9	51,628	31,644
5 Dan Daniel (D)*	—	99.9	16,850	4,991
6 M. Caldwell Butler (R)*	—	99.8	24,159	16,307
7 Lewis Fickett (D)	—	35.7	58,506	58,493
J. Kenneth Robinson (R)*	—	64.3	98,348	87,087
8 Herbert E. Harris II (D)*	—	50.5	165,637	164,352
John F. Herrity (R)	52.4	47.1	226,368	223,973
9 Champ Clark (D)	—	38.1	62,182	56,121
William C. Wampler (R)*	—	61.9	115,773	112,016
10 Joseph L. Fisher (D)*	—	53.3	148,625	147,340
Frank Wolf (R)	—	46.6	233,962	232,286

WASHINGTON

1 Janice Niemi (D)	86.5	33.7	60,396	60,121
Joel Pritchard (R)*	—	64.0	115,362	125,399
2 Al Swift (D)	44.1	51.4	150,818	150,435
John Nance Garner (R)	72.3	48.6	328,383	324,456
3 Don Bonker (D)*	—	58.6	54,951	43,324
Rick Bennett (R)	51.4	41.4	52,497	51,753
4 Mike McCormack (D)*	86.4	61.1	136,129	132,190
Susan Roylance (R)	—	38.9	68,271	65,371
5 Thomas S. Foley (D)*	90.3	48.0	307,028	347,573
Duane Alton (R)	52.1	42.7	178,544	174,978
Mel Tonasket (I)	—	9.3	18,155	18,141
6 Norman D. Dicks (D)*	84.0	60.9	166,968	166,731
James E. Beaver (R)	—	37.4	19,445	19,308
7 Mike Lowry (D)	74.2	53.3	215,806	214,609
John E. Cunningham (R)*	—	46.7	516,053	523,905

	Percent of Primary Vote	Percent of General Election Vote	Receipts	Expenditures
WEST VIRGINIA				
1 Robert H. Mollohan (D)*	—	63.4	56,375	37,680
Gene A. Haynes (R)	—	36.6	14,177	14,129
2 Harley O. Staggers (D)*	—	55.3	40,985	37,481
Cleveland K. Benedict (R)	—	44.7	168,883	168,782
3 John M. Stack (D)*	—	59.2	71,592	34,433
David M. Staton (R)	—	40.8	14,961	14,878
4 Nick J. Rahall (D)*	55.5	100.0	243,339	242,298
WISCONSIN				
1 Les Aspin (D)*	—	54.5	76,825	73,570
William W. Petrie (R)	—	45.5	101,733	102,205
2 Robert W. Kastenmeier (D)*	—	57.7	39,025	43,643
James A. Wright (R)	—	41.3	86,174	86,041
Dick G. Fields (I)	—	1.0	8,941	8,940
3 Alvin Baldus (D)*	—	62.8	75,935	75,983
Michael S. Ellis (R)	70.5	37.2	4,661	5,414

	Percent of Primary Vote	Percent of General Election Vote	Receipts	Expenditures
4 Clement J. Zablocki (D)*	—	66.1	12,165	10,398
Elroy G. Honadel (R)	—	33.9	15,154	14,665
5 Henry S. Reuss (D)*	—	73.1	77,597	68,092
James R. Medina (R)	—	25.9	7,411	4,952
6 Robert J. Steffes (D)	—	29.6	2,465	2,302
William A. Steiger (R)*	—	69.6	93,058	67,664
7 David R. Obey (D)*	—	62.2	60,248	53,463
Vinton A. Vesta (R)	58.3	36.9	13,477	13,403
8 Robert J. Cornell (D)*	—	42.1	59,612	72,202
Tobias A. Roth (R)	68.2	57.9	203,921	202,021
9 Matthew J. Flynn (D)	51.3	38.8	41,853	41,028
F. James Sensenbrenner Jr. (R)	43.2	61.1	190,687	197,749
WYOMING				
AL Bill Bagley (D)	53.0	41.4	175,300	175,297
Richard Cheney (R)	43.1	58.6	220,865	209,064

Selected Bibliography

Books

Adamany, David. *Campaign Finance In America*. North Scituate, Mass.: Duxbury Press, 1972.

——, and Agree, George E. *Political Money: A Strategy for Campaign Financing In America*. Baltimore: Johns Hopkins University Press, 1975.

Alexander, Herbert E. *Financing Politics: Money, Elections and Political Reform*. Washington, D.C. Congressional Quarterly Press, 1976; 2nd ed., 1980.

——. *Financing the 1960 Election*. Princeton, N.J.: Citizens' Research Foundation, 1962.

——. *Financing the 1964 Election*. Princeton, N.J.: Citizens' Research Foundation, 1966.

——. *Financing the 1968 Election*. Lexington, Mass.: Lexington Books, 1971.

——. *Financing the 1972 Election*. Lexington, Mass.: Lexington Books, 1976.

——. *Financing the 1976 Election*. Washington, D.C.: Congressional Quarterly Press, 1979.

——. *Money In Politics*. Washington, D.C.: Public Affairs Press, 1972.

——, ed. *Political Finance*. Beverly Hills, Calif.: Sage Publications, 1979.

An Analysis of the Impact of the Federal Election Campaign Act, 1972-1978. Report by the Campaign Finance Study Group to the Committee on House Administration, of the U.S. House of Representatives. Cambridge, Mass.: Institute of Politics, John Fitzgerald Kennedy School of Government, Harvard University, 1979.

Belmont, Perry. *Return to Secret Party Funds*. New York, N.Y.: Arno Press, 1974.

Caddy, Doughlas. *The Hundred Million Dollar Payoff*. New Rochelle, N.Y.: Arlington House, 1974.

Committee for Economic Development. *Financing a Better Election System. A Statement on National Policy by the Research and Policy Committee*. New York: 1968.

Demaris, Ovid. *Dirty Business: The Corporate - Political Money - Power Game*. New York: Harper's Magazine Press, 1974.

Congressional Quarterly Inc. *Dollar Politics: The Issue of Campaign Spending*. Washington, D.C.: vol. 1, 1971; vol. 2, 1974.

Domhoff, G. William. *Fat Cats and Democrats: The Role of the Big Rich In the Party of the Common Man*. Englewood Cliffs, N.J.: Prentice-Hall, 1972.

Dunn, Delmer. *Financing Presidential Campaigns*. Washington, D.C.: Brookings Institution, 1972.

Electing Congress. Washington, D.C.: Congressional Quarterly Inc., 1978.

Electing Congress: The Financial Dilemma. Report of the Twentieth Century Fund Task Force on Financing Congressional Campaigns. New York: Twentieth Century Fund, 1970.

Epstein, Edwin M. *The Corporation In American Politics*. Englewood Cliffs, N.J.: Prentice-Hall, 1969.

Heard, Alexander. *The Costs of Democracy*. Chapel Hill, N.C.: University of North Carolina Press, 1960.

Heidenheimer, Arnold J., ed. *Comparative Political Finance: The Financing of Party Organizations and Election Campaigns*. Lexington, Mass.: Lexington Books, 1970.

Hess, Stephen. *The Presidential Campaign: The Leadership Selection Process After Watergate*. Washington, D.C.: Brookings Institution, 1974.

Hinckley, Barbara. *Congressional Elections*. Washington, D.C.: Congressional Quarterly Press, 1981.

How Money Talks In Congress, a Common Cause Study of the Impact of Money on Congressional Decision-Making. Washington, D.C.: Common Cause, 1979.

Jacobson, Gary C. *Money In Congressional Elections*. New Haven, Conn.: Yale University Press, 1980.

Kennedy, Tom and Simon, Charles E. *An Examination of Questionable Payments and Practices*. New York: Praeger, 1978.

Leonard, Dick. *Paying for Party Politics: The Case for Public Subsidies*. London: PEP, 1975.

McCarthy, Eugene and others. *Regulation of Political Campaigns: How Successful*. Washington, D.C.: American Enterprise Institute for Public Policy Research, 1976.

McCarthy, Max. *Elections for Sale*. Boston: Houghton-Mifflin, 1972.

Malbin, Michael J., ed. *Parties, Interest Groups, and Campaign Finance Laws*. Washington, D.C.: American Enterprise Institute for Public Policy Research, 1980.

McGinniss, Joe. *The Selling of the President, 1968*. New York: Trident Press, 1969.

Moore, Jonathan, and Fraser, Janet, eds. *Campaign for President*. Cambridge, Mass.: Ballinger, 1977.

Nichols, David. *Financing Elections: The Politics of An American Ruling Class*. New York: Franklin Watts, 1974.

1972 Congressional Campaign Finances. Prepared by the Campaign Finance Monitoring Project, 3 vols. Washington, D.C.: Common Cause, 1974.

1974 Congressional Campaign Finances. Prepared by Campaign Monitoring Project, 5 vols. Washington, D.C.: Common Cause, 1976.

1976 Federal Campaign Finances. Prepared by the Campaign Monitoring Project, 3 vols. Washington, D.C.: Common Cause, 1977.

1972 Federal Campaign Finances: Interest Groups and Political Parties. Prepared by the Campaign Monitoring Project, 10 vols. Washington, D.C.: Common Cause, 1974.

Ornstein, Norman J. and Elder, Shirley. *Interest Groups, Lobbying, and Policymaking*. Washington, D.C.: Congressional Quarterly Press, 1978.

Overacker, Louise. *Money In Elections*. New York: Macmillan, 1932.

——. *Presidential Campaign Funds.* New York: AMS Press, 1977.

Peabody, Robert L. and others. *To Enact a Law: Congress and Campaign Financing.* New York: Praeger, 1972.

Penniman, Howard R. and Winter, Ralph K., Jr. *Campaign Finances: Two Views of the Political and Constitutional Implications.* Washington, D.C.: American Enterprise Institute for Public Policy Research, 1971.

Pollock, James K., Jr. *Party Campaign Funds.* New York: Alfred A. Knopf, 1962.

Ries, John C., ed. *Public Financing of Political Campaigns: Reform or Rip-off?* Los Angeles: Institute of Government and Public Affairs, 1974.

Rosenthal, Albert J. *Federal Regulation of Campaign Finance: Some Constitutional Questions.* Princeton, N.J.: Citizens' Research Foundation, 1972.

Schwarz, Thomas J. *Public Financing of Elections: A Constitutional Division of the Wealth.* Chicago: American Bar Association, Special Committee on Election Reform, 1975.

Shannon, Jasper B. *Money and Politics.* New York: Random House, 1959.

Thayer, George. *Who Shakes the Money Tree?: American Campaign Financing from 1789 to the Present.* New York: Simon & Schuster, 1973.

Voter's Time. Report of the Twentieth Century Fund Commission on Campaign Costs in the Electronic Era. New York: Twentieth Century Fund, 1969.

White, Theodore H. *The Making of the President, 1960.* New York: Atheneum, 1961.

——. *The Making of the President, 1964.* New York: Atheneum, 1965.

——. *The Making of the President, 1968.* New York: Atheneum, 1969.

——. *The Making of the President, 1972.* New York: Atheneum, 1973.

Winter, Ralph K., Jr. *Watergate and the Law: Political Campaigns and Presidential Power.* Washington, D.C.: American Enterprise Institute for Public Policy Research, 1974.

——, and Bolton, John R. *Campaign Financing and Political Freedom.* Washington, D.C.: American Enterprise Institute for Public Policy Research, 1973.

Articles

Adamany, David and Agree, George. "Election Campaign Financing: The 1974 Reforms." *Political Science Quarterly,* Summer 1975, pp. 201-220.

——. "Public Financing: A Cure for the Curse of the Slush Funds." *Progressive,* October 1973, pp. 38-42.

Alexander, Herbert E. "Financing American Politics." *Political Quarterly,* October/December 1974, pp. 439-448.

——. "The Folklore of Buying Elections." *Business and Society,* Summer 1972, pp. 48-53.

——. "Political Finance: Reform and Reality." *Annals of the American Academy of Political and Social Science,* May 1976, pp. 1-149.

Barrow, Roscoe L. "Regulation of Campaign Funding and Spending for Federal Office." *Journal of Law Reform,* Winter 1972, pp. 159-192.

Berry, Jeffrey M. and Goldman, Jerry. "Congress and Public Policy: A Study of the Federal Election Campaign Act of 1971." *Harvard Journal on Legislation,* no. 2, 1973, p. 361.

Biden, Joseph R. "Public Financing of Elections: Legislative Proposals and Constitutional Questions." *Northwestern University Law Review,* February 1975, pp. 1-70.

"Campaign Contributions and Federal Bribery Law." *Harvard Law Review,* December 1978, pp. 451-469.

"Campaign Fund Fog: Question of Transfer of Funds from the Carter Peanut Warehouse Into the 1976 Campaign." *Nation,* July 7, 1979, p. 1.

"Campaign Funding: Still a Problem." *Christian Century,* June 6, 1973, pp. 644-648.

"Campaign Spending Controls Under the Federal Election Campaign Act of 1971." *Journal of Law and Social Problems,* Spring 1972, pp. 285-320.

Cohen, Richard E. "Corporate Bribery, Something's Wrong, But What Can Be Done About It?" *National Journal,* May 15, 1976, pp. 658-663.

——. "Pecking at PAC Power." *National Journal,* July 28, 1979, p. 1257.

——. "Public Financing for House Races: Will It Make a Difference?" *National Journal,* May 12, 1979, pp. 783-787.

"Controversy Over Campaign Financing of House Elections: Pro and Con." *Congressional Digest,* December 1979, pp. 289-314.

"Curbing Political Action Committees." *Commonweal,* October 12, 1979, pp. 547-548.

Danilenko, V. "The Money Bag Behind the Election." *International Affairs,* October 1980, pp. 55-62.

David, Paul T. "The Federal Election Commission: Origins and Early Activities." *National Civil Review,* June 1976, pp. 278-833.

Davies, David G. "Political Campaigns: Public vs. Private Financing." *Governmental Finance,* August 1974, pp. 7-10.

Epstein, Edwin M. 'Corporate and Labor Unions In Electoral Politics." *Annals of American Academy of Political and Social Science,* May 1976, pp. 33-58.

——. "An Irony of Electoral Reform: The Business PAC Phenomenon." *Regulation,* May/June 1979, pp. 35-41.

"FEC Left Dangling as Congress Adjourns." *Campaign Practices Reports,* December 21, 1981, pp. 1-2.

"The Federal Election Campaign Act of 1971: Reform of the Political Process?" *Georgetown Law Journal,* vol. 60, 1972, pp. 249-269.

"The Federal Election Commission, the First Amendment, and Due Process." *Yale Law Journal,* May 1980, pp. 1199-1224.

Ferman, Irving. "Congressional Controls on Campaign Financing: An Expansion or Contradiction of the First Amendment?" *American University Law Review,* Fall 1972, pp. 337-374.

Fingerhut, Vic. "A Limit on Campaign Spending: Who Will Benefit?" *Public Interest,* Fall 1971, pp. 3-13.

Fleishman, Joel L. "Public Financing of Election Campaigns: Constitutional Constraints or Steps Toward Equality of Political Influence of Citizens." *North Carolina Law Review,* December 1973, pp. 349-416.

Fletcher, Stephen H. "Corporate Political Contributions." *Business Lawyer,* July 1974, pp. 1071-1100.

Frank, Reuven. "Beating the High Prices of Politics." *New Leader,* August 5, 1974, pp. 8-10.

Glantz, Stanton A. and others. "Election Outcomes: Who's Money Matters?" *Journal of Politics,* November 1976, pp. 1033-1038.

Glass, Andrew J. "Campaign and the Money Game." *New Leader,* October 6, 1980, pp. 4-5.

Glen, Maxwell. "Conservatives, Liberals Challenge Election Laws." *National Journal,* December 22, 1979, p. 2165.

——. "How to Get Around the Campaign Spending Limits." *National Journal,* June 23, 1979, pp. 1044-1046.

——. "The PACs Are Back, Richer and Wiser, to Finance the 1980 Elections." *National Journal,* November 24, 1979, pp. 1982-1984.

Goldstein, Joel H. "The Influence of Money on the Pre-nomination Stage of the Presidential Selection Process: The Case of the 1976 Election." *Presidential Studies Quarterly,* Spring 1978, pp. 164-179.

Greene, Wade. "Who Should Pay for Political Campaigns?" *Columbia Journalism Review,* January/February 1974, pp. 24-31.

Harris, Thomas E. "Implementing the Federal Campaign Finance Laws." *National Civic Review,* May 1978, pp. 217-222.

Hellebust, Lynn. "The Limitations of Campaign Finance Disclosure." *National Civic Review,* May 1978, pp. 223-227.

Kazman, Sam and Reynolds, Alan. "The Economics of Campaign Reform: Will the New Election Laws Put an End to Influence-Peddling or Merely Change Its Form?" *Alternative,* May 1977, pp. 14-15.

Kirschten, Dick. "Corporate PACs: The GOP's Ace In the Hole?" *National Journal*, November 25, 1978, pp. 1899-1902.

Kozyakov, V. "Where the Dollar Votes." *New Times*, March 1972, pp. 22-23.

Lanouette, William J. "Complex Financing Laws Shape Presidential Campaign Strategies." *National Journal*, August 4, 1979, pp. 1252-1286.

Levantrosser, William F. "Financing Presidential Campaigns: The Impact of Reform Campaign Finance Laws on the Democratic Presidential Nomination of 1976." *Presidential Studies Quarterly*, Spring 1981, pp. 280-288.

Leventhal, Harold. "Courts and Political Thickets." *Columbia Law Review*, April 1977, pp. 345-387.

"Liberal Independent PAC Copies Conservatives' Strategy." *Campaign Practices Reports*, December 7, 1981, p. 5.

Lindsay, David S. "The Political Money Machine." *Midwest Quarterly*, Autumn 1970, pp. 41-55.

Louviere, Vernon. "Every Candidate Needs a Landslide of Dollars." *Nation's Business*, October 1979, pp. 41-44.

——. "How Special Interest Groups Use Their Power." *Nation's Business*, June 1980, pp. 38-41.

Malbin, Michael J. "Campaign Financing and the 'Special Interest.'" *Public Interest*, Summer 1979, pp. 21-42.

——. "After Surviving Its First Election Year, FEC Is Wary of the Future." *National Journal*, March 26, 1977, pp. 469-473.

"Mathias Sees Little Support for Killing Election Commission," *Campaign Practices Reports*, December 7, 1981, pp. 1-2.

McDonald, Kimberly. "The Impact of Political Action Committees," *Economic Forum*, Summer 1981, pp. 94-103.

McKenzie, Richard B. and Yandle, Bruce. "The Logic of 'Irrational' Politics: Nixon's Reelection Committee." *Public Finance Quarterly*, January 1980, pp. 39-55.

"Money for Politics; Public Subsidies Seen as Most Effective Means to Ensure Adequate Financial Resources for Parties." *National Civic Review*, April 1970, pp. 191-197.

Nicholson, Marlene A. "Buckley v. Valeo," The Constitutionality of the Federal Election Campaign Act Amendments of 1974." *Wisconsin Law Review*, no. 2, 1977, pp. 323-374.

——. "Campaign Financing and Equal Protection." *Stanford Law Review*, April 1974, pp. 815-854.

——. "The Constitutionality of the Federal Restrictions on Corporate and Union Campaign Contributions and Expenditures." *Cornell Law Review*, August 1980, pp. 945-1010.

Osborne, John. "Campaign Money." *New Republic*, July 26, 1980, pp. 6-7.

Pincus, Walter. "Raising the Money to Run." *New Republic*, September 29, 1973, p. 16.

Plattner, Marc F. "Campaign Financing: The Dilemma of Reform." *Public Interest*, Fall 1974, pp. 112-230.

Polk, James R. "The New Rules of Money In Politics." *Working Papers for a New Society*, Fall 1975, pp. 1961-1965.

Polk, J. R. "Piracy and Politics: That $200,000 Secret Contribution." *New Republic*, March 17, 1973, pp. 18-21.

Prior, James T. "PAC's: The Quiet Revolution." *New Jersey Business*, June 1976, pp. 14-17.

"The Question of Financing of National Election Campaigns: Pro and Con." *Congressional Digest*, February 1974, pp. 33-64.

Quinn, Tony. "Political Action Committees, the New Campaign Bankrollers." *California Journal*, March 1979, pp. 96-98.

Redish, Martin H. "Campaign Spending Laws and the First Amendment." *New York University Law Review*, November 1971, pp. 900-934.

Staats, Elmer B. "Impact of the Federal Election Campaign Act of 1971." *Annals of the American Academy of Political and Social Science*, May 1976, pp. 98-113.

Sterling, Carleton W. "Control of Campaign Spending: The Reformer's Paradox." *American Bar Association Journal*, October 1973, pp. 1148-1153.

Thayer, George. "Return of Campaign Financing." *Current History*, August 1974, pp. 70-74.

Tiernan, Robert O. "The Presidential Campaign: Public Financing Accepted." *National Civic Review*, March 1980, pp. 133-140.

Walters, Robert. "Campaign Spending Reform Loopholes." *National Journal*, January 11, 1975, p. 67.

"Washing Dirty Dollars: Undisclosed Contributions to Republican Campaigns." *New Republic*, May 19, 1973, pp. 20-21.

Webster, George D. "How Federal Election Amendments Affect Political Action Committees." *Association Management*, September 1976, p. 20.

Wheeler, Tim. "Who's Paying the Piper In the '80 Elections?" *Political Affairs*, March 1980, pp. 23-28.

Wright, J. Skelly. "Politics and the Constitution: Is Money Speech?" *Yale Law Journal*, July 1976, pp. 1001-1021.

Documents

Federal Election Commission. *Annual Report*. Washington, D.C.: 1974-.

Federal Election Commission. *FEC Disclosure Series*. Washington, D.C.: 1975-.

Federal Election Commission. *FEC Reports on Financial Activities*. Washington, D.C.: 1975-.

Financing Presidential Campaigns. Report of the President's Commission on Campaign Costs. Washington, D.C.: Government Printing Office, 1962.

U.S. Congress. House. Commission on Administrative Review. *Financial Ethics*. House Report, 95-73. 95th Cong., 1st sess. Washington, D.C.: Government Printing Office, 1977.

U.S. Congress. House. Committee on House Administration. *Federal Election Campaign Act of 1971*. Conference Report, December 14, 1971. 92nd Cong., 1st sess. Washington, D.C.: Government Printing Office, 1971.

U.S. Congress. House. Committee on House Administration. *Federal Election Reform*. 92nd Cong., 1st sess. Washington, D.C.: Government Printing Office, 1971.

U.S. Congress. House. Committee on House Administration. *Public Financing of Congressional Elections: Hearings May 18, 19; June 21, 23, 28; July 12, 1977*. 95th Cong., 1st sess. Washington, D.C.: Government Printing Office, 1978.

U.S. Congress. House. Committee on Standards of Official Conduct. *Campaign Finances: Hearings December 1, 8, 9, 15, 1970*. 91st Cong., 2nd sess. Washington, D.C.: Government Printing Office, 1971.

U.S. Congress. Joint Committee on Congressional Operations. *Decision of the U.S. Supreme Court: Buckley v. Valeo, January 30, 1976*. 94th Cong., 2nd sess. Washington, D.C.: Government Printing Office, 1976.

U.S. Congress. Senate. Committee on Rules and Administration. *Public Financing of Federal Elections: Hearings September 18-21, 1973*. 93rd Cong., 1st sess. Washington, D.C.: Government Printing Office, 1973.

U.S. Congress. Senate. Committee on Rules and Administration. Subcommittee on Privilege and Elections. *Federal Election Campaign Act of 1971: Hearings May 24, 25, 1971*. 92nd Cong., 1st sess. Washington, D.C.: Government Printing Office, 1971.

U.S. Congress. Senate. Committee on Rules and Administration. Subcommittee on Privileges and Elections. *Federal Election Campaign Act Amendments, 1976: Hearing February 18, 1976*. 94th Cong., 2nd sess. Washington, D.C.: Government Printing Office, 1976.

U.S. Congress. Senate. Committee on Rules and Administration. Subcommittee on Privileges and Elections. *Federal Election Campaign Act Amendments, 1979: Hearing July 13, 1979*. 96th Cong., 2nd sess. Washington, D.C.: Government Printing Office, 1980.

U.S. Congress. Senate. Committee on Rules and Administration. Subcommittee on Privileges and Elections. *Public Financing of Federal Elections: Hearings September 18-21, 1973*. 93rd Cong., 1st sess. Washington, D.C.: Government Printing Office, 1973.

U.S. Congress. Senate. Select Committee on Presidential Campaign Activities. *Final Report,* Senate Report 93-981, February 7, 1973. 93rd Cong., 2nd sess. Washington, D.C.: Government Printing Office, 1974.

U.S. Congress. Senate. Select Committee on Presidential Activities. *Watergate and Related Activities, Phase III: Campaign Financing, Book 13.* 93rd Cong., 2nd sess. Washington, D.C.: Government Printing Office, 1974.

Index